STATIONERY DESIGN NOW!

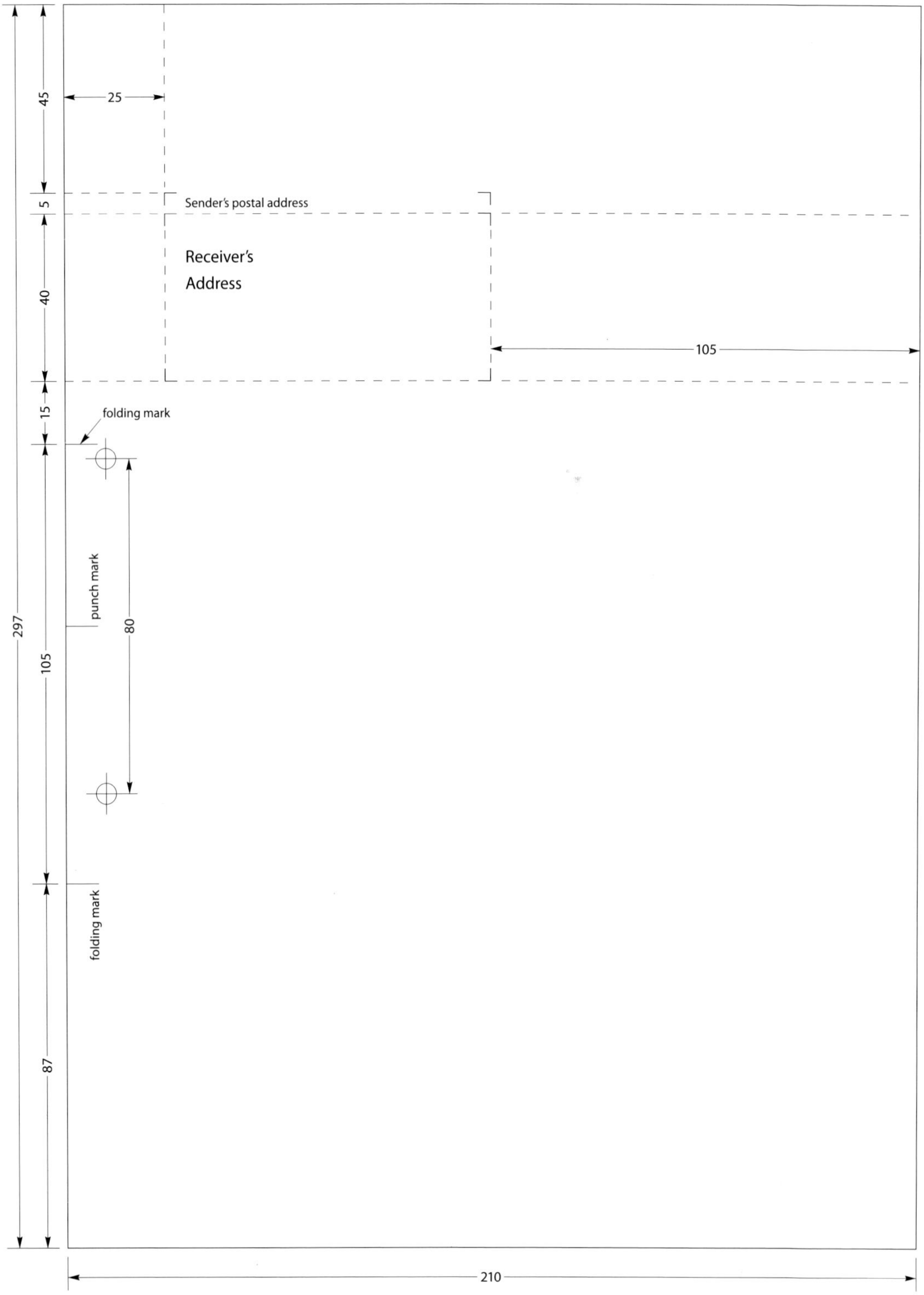

45
25
5
Sender's postal address
Receiver's
Address
40
105
15
folding mark
punch mark
80
297
105
folding mark
87
210

Ed. Julius Wiedemann

STATIONERY DESIGN NOW!

TASCHEN

THOMAS GRELL
PREPRESS PRODUCER

T.GRELL@TASCHEN.CO...
HENZOLLERNRING 53, D-50...
TEL +49 221

STIAN BÖHNING
PRODUCTION MANAGER

HOHEN...

TASCHEN

TASCHEN

PETRA FRANZ
ASSISTANT TO BENEDIKT TASCHEN

/W.TASCHEN.COM
TASCHEN PER

ANNE SAUVADET
LEKTORIN/EDITOR

TASCHEN

TASCHEN

JENNY ROYEC...
MANAGING EDITOR & ASSISTANT TO

J.ROYECK@TASCHEN...
...NG 53, D-50672 KÖ...
...0 192 SKYPE

TASCHEN

BENEDIKT TASCHEN
PUBLISHER

TASCHEN

VERONICA WELLER
DIRECTOR OF CORPORATE COMMUNICATIONS

RIMOND
...ECTOR

AS...

QUES
DIRECT

TASCHEN

ANDY DISL
ART DIRECTOR

NZOLLER...
A.DIS...

TASCHEN

JULIUS WIEDEMANN
DIRECTOR DIGITAL PUBLICATIONS

J.WIEDEMANN...
...LOSE MILTON ROAD CAMBR...
...44 7789 887 970

SCHEN.COM
...72 KÖLN WWW.TASCHEN.COM
2-656 30 64 SKYPE TASCHEN

TASCHEN

TASCHEN

DANIEL SICILIANO BRÊTAS
EDITOR

HEN.C
2 KÖL
KYPE

IE PAAS
CT MANA

TASCHEN

UTE KIESEYER
EDITOR

U.KIESEYER@TAS...
ENZOLLERNRING 53, D-50672
TEL +49 221

TASCHEN

JUTTA HENDRICKS
LEKTORIN/EDITOR

...ICILIANOBRETAS@TASCHEN.COM
...50672 KÖLN WWW.TASCHEN.COM
TASCHEN_DSB

...S-SCH
...G EDITOR

TASCHE...

LOU MOLLGAARD
PUBLIC RELATIONS MAN...

L.MOLLGAARD@TASCH...
MAZARINE, F-75006 PARIS
1 73 08 CEL +33 6 80 90 15

TASCHEN

加藤　久美
セールス　リプレゼンタティブ

K.KATOU@TAS...
〒107-0062 東京都港...
TEL 03 3499 4479

TASCHEN

MAHROS ALLAMEZADE
EDITOR

E@TASCHE
2 KÖLN W
-937 50 77

TASCHEN

TASCHEN

ANNICK VOLK
INTERNATIONAL EDITIONS MANAGER

DR. CHRISTINE WAIBLING...
...C RELATIONS MANAGER
... ÖFFENTLICHKE...

TASCHEN

NADIA NAJM
PRODUCTION MANAGER

...K@TASCHEN.COM
...72 KÖLN WWW.TASCHEN.COM
...98 SKYPE TASCHEN_AVO

TASCHEN

UTE WAC...

Contents

Page 2
Business letter guidelines
DIN 676 and DIN 5008 standards
(2005), A4 format (210 x 297 mm)

Foreword

by Julius Wiedemann

If you write a letter to someone today, you would be very unlikely to use a typewriter. Instead, you would type it on your computer, print it with an ink-jet or laser printer, and then post it (if that is what you want) in a printed envelope. However, if you were to send out today a hand-written letter on your personal letterhead, I am sure that you would receive much more attention, even with the same letter contents. We used to take the stationery we used for granted, because it was the only thing we had. The tactility, the textures, the spot colours, and the varnish were just a way of approaching such essential accessories in every single office.

All this has changed, and many design studios are getting fewer commissions for the three most important parts of the stationery set: the letterhead, the envelope, and the business card. The latter is still in some use currently, while the other two are going through a steady decline. However, none of the three are completely finished, in fact quite the opposite, with designers rethinking how to create fresh value for the perfect office trio. One approach designers can take advantage of is to make particular use of the medium, in this case with printing, for example, looking at special colours, embossing, hot-stamping, and all sorts of new and emerging forms to create a novel and unique experience.

For this book, we have set out to collect some great examples of this and similar stationery, from big to small companies and institutions, high and low budget, from luxurious to simple solutions. Still, all are tailored to attract the attention of various people, customers, friends, and prospective partners, in a way that is no longer taken for granted because of the digital age. We certainly need and want to use emails, social networking sites, let alone mobile phones, but we can certainly impress people with a real personal touch, which is the idea behind all good stationery. We hope too that this book will motivate its readers to bring this same experience to many around them in the years and decades to come.

Left
Specimen Printing Department
Composing Room
From the book "1796–1896, One Hundred Years", MacKellar, Smiths and Jordan Foundry, Philadelphia

Vorwort

von Julius Wiedemann

Wenn Sie heutzutage jemandem einen Brief schreiben, nehmen Sie dafür höchstwahrscheinlich keine Schreibmaschine mehr. Stattdessen tippen Sie die Worte in den Computer, drucken den Brief mit einem Tintenstrahl- oder Laserdrucker aus, stecken ihn in einen gedruckten Umschlag und bringen ihn gegebenenfalls zur Post. Allerdings bin ich ganz sicher, dass Ihr Brief heute deutlich mehr Aufmerksamkeit bekommt, wenn er handschriftlich auf Ihrem ganz persönlichen Briefpapier geschrieben und dann versendet wird. Für uns war Briefpapier eine Selbstverständlichkeit, weil es das war, was wir kannten. Das Taktile, die Papierbeschaffenheit, Schmuckfarben und Oberflächenversiegelung waren die Art, wie ein solch wesentliches Zubehör in jedem einzelnen Büro umgesetzt wurde.

All das hat sich geändert, und viele Designstudios erhalten für die drei wichtigsten Bestandteile des Briefpapiersets – Briefkopf, Umschlag und Visitenkarte – immer weniger Aufträge. Letztere wird momentan immer noch eingesetzt, während die beiden anderen langsam, aber sicher im Rückzug begriffen sind. Jedoch kann man auch nicht behaupten, dass eins dieser drei Elemente nun vollständig erledigt ist: Tatsächlich ist genau das Gegenteil der Fall, und Designer überdenken gerade, wie man dem perfekten Bürotrio mehr Bedeutung verschaffen kann. Ein solcher Ansatz wäre für die Designer, das Medium auf bestimmte Art anders einzusetzen, in diesem Fall z.B. im Druck, indem auf besondere Farben, Prägedruck oder Heißprägung geachtet wird, und alle Arten neuer und neu entstehender Formen genutzt werden, um ein originelles und einzigartiges Erlebnisobjekt zu schaffen.

Für dieses Buch haben wir uns auf den Weg gemacht, eine Reihe ausgezeichneter Beispiele zu sammeln. Dabei haben wir uns in kleinen wie großen Firmen und Institutionen umgeschaut, die mit einem bescheidenen oder auch umfangreichen Budget jeweils ganz einfache oder sehr luxuriöse Lösungen gefunden haben. Doch alle sind genau darauf zugeschnitten, von unterschiedlichsten Personen, Kunden, Freunden und potenziellen Geschäftspartnern beachtet zu werden, und das auf eine Weise, die im digitalen Zeitalter absolut nicht mehr selbstverständlich ist. Wir werden mit Sicherheit weiter mit E-Mails und den Sites der sozialen Netzwerke arbeiten, ganz zu schweigen von der Handynutzung, aber wir können andere gewiss mit unserem ganz persönlichen Touch beeindrucken – und das ist ja die einem guten Briefpapier zugrunde liegende Idee! Wir hoffen außerdem, dass dieses Buch seine Leserinnen und Leser dazu anregt, in den folgenden Jahren und Jahrzehnten die gleiche Erfahrung auch in ihrer eigenen Umgebung umzusetzen.

Préface

de Julius Wiedemann

Pour écrire une lettre aujourd'hui, vous n'utilisez certainement pas une machine à écrire : vous la faites sur votre ordinateur, l'imprimer avec une imprimante à jet d'encre et la poster (le cas échéant) dans une enveloppe imprimée. Si vous deviez en revanche envoyer une lettre manuscrite sur votre papier à lettres, le destinataire prêterait à coup sûr plus attention, même à un contenu identique. Nous avions peu d'égards pour notre papier à lettres, auparavant seul support disponible. Le toucher, les textures, les couleurs d'accompagnement et le verni n'étaient qu'une façon d'aborder des accessoires si importants dans un bureau.

La réalité est maintenant autre et nombreux sont les studios de design dont les commandes baissent pour les trois principaux éléments d'un jeu de courrier : le papier à lettres, l'enveloppe et la carte de visite. Cette dernière trouve encore un usage, les deux autres étant pour leur part en déclin. Aucun des trois n'est cependant totalement condamné, bien au contraire, car les designers repensent comment relancer ce parfait trio. L'une des solutions est d'utiliser le support (via l'impression dans ce cas) de façon particulière, par exemple avec des couleurs spéciales, du gaufrage, de l'estampage à chaud et d'autres nouvelles formes émergentes permettant une expérience unique et inédite.

Nous avons pour cet ouvrage rassemblé de beaux exemples de papiers à lettres, appartenant à des entreprises et institutions de toutes tailles, d'un budget élevé ou bas, pour des solutions luxueuses ou simples. Toutes ces créations visent à attirer l'attention de personnes diverses, clients, amis ou partenaires potentiels, d'une façon qui n'est plus la norme à l'ère du numérique. Certes, nous devons et voulons recourir aux e-mails, aux sites de réseaux sociaux, sans parler des téléphones portables ; nous pouvons néanmoins faire sensation grâce à une touche personnelle, l'objectif de tout bon papier à lettres. Nous espérons aussi que ce livre motivera ses lecteurs à partager cette expérience avec leur entourage au cours des années et décennies qui viennent.

Death of the Letterhead?

Jay Rutherford
Chair, Visual Communications
Faculty of Art and Design
Bauhaus University Weimar
www.uni-weimar.de

All over the world, postal letter traffic is falling away drastically. America's postal service, for example, saw a drop in postal mail volume of almost 14% in the year to September 2009. Analysts have predicted that European postal traffic will drop by half over the next ten years. So isn't email easier and cheaper, more convenient, more current anyway? While email certainly won't go away soon, most of us will admit to a small thrill when we get a real letter in the post, especially if it was written by hand. After organising a conference recently, I received quite a number of congratulatory emails. One piece of communication made a big difference though: one of our speakers sent me a letter on his own beautifully designed letterhead, with a hand-written note stating merely, "Great conference – thanks for inviting me to speak!" This small gesture meant a lot. I still cherish a letter I received in 1992 from a teacher of design at the Hochschule für Grafik und Buchkunst in Leipzig, thanking me for supervising two of her students in a workshop on type design. She used her school letterhead sideways and wrote in her inimitable scratchy style with something like a bamboo stick. Wonderful! Good handwriting is, by the way, a skill which every literate person should possess; it is unfortunately a rarity these days.

The invention of paper

It is generally agreed that the Chinese invented paper roughly two thousand years ago. It took a few hundred years for their invention to reach Europe, but the use of paper from wood pulp did not become widespread until the 15th Century with the advent of the printing press. Before this time, parchment or pulped rag paper was used for letter writing.

The spread of literacy

There wasn't that much letter writing back then anyway: only a very small percentage of the population could read and write at all. Verbal messages were sent by courier – trust was paramount, and not always respected. It was not until well into the 19th Century with the advent of the industrial revolution that paper and books became financially affordable to most members of industrialised societies. As late as 1841, one third of all men and almost half of all women in England, for example, signed their marriage certificates with an "x". France was somewhat more advanced in this area: in the early 1700s, about a third of the French population could read and write; by the late 1800s, however, almost everyone there could. Governments in some countries, even today – albeit largely in less-industrialised societies – tightly manage access to education (including reading) in order to keep control over their populations. It is, however, not only governments who control this. In much of Africa literacy is associated with colonialism, whereas orality is associated with native traditions.

The term literacy has itself evolved over time. Being able to sign your name

Right
Specimen Printing Department
Composing Room
From the book "1796–1896, One Hundred Years", MacKellar, Smiths and Jordan Foundry, Philadelphia

was once considered adequate. At one time, memorising specific passages from the Bible put you in the category of "literate" for the purpose of deciding under which legal system you might be judged. This was often a matter of life and death. There have also been periods in history where literacy was a trade secret of professional scribes. Since the 1990s, being able to use a computer, a Web browser, word-processing software, and sending an SMS are considered important aspects of literacy. Now we even have *(multi-)media literacy*, *art literacy*, *information literacy* and *visual literacy*, just to keep us on our toes. But there are those who believe that an over-reliance on literacy is a kind of tyranny, a means to control, rather than to illuminate populations. This discussion will not end soon.

Origins of the word "letterhead"

The term "letterhead" was first used in late 19th-Century America. It originally meant merely the name and address of the sender, usually appearing at the top or "head" of a sheet of letter-sized paper. The term has now more generally come to be used to refer to the whole sheet of paper. *The Oxford Pocket Dictionary of Current English* defines a letterhead as: "a printed heading on stationery stating a person's or organisation's name and address" or "a sheet of paper with such a heading." Stationery, according to *Webster's Dictionary*, is "paper cut to an appropriate size for writing letters, usually with matching envelopes." The word "stationery" (with an "e") comes from its cousin "stationary", which was originally used to describe pedlars who sold goods from a fixed location, as opposed to those who travelled the countryside to sell their wares. In the Middle Ages, these "stationary" sellers were often bookshops licensed by universities. The Company of Stationers was founded in 1556 and the term stationery was coined in approximately 1727.

The graphic designer's job

Contemporary letterhead design usually entails the layout of the entire sheet area, from name and address of the sender, through positioning of logos or other corporate design elements, sometimes bank account information, down to the position of written content. Ink colours are specified based on corporate design standards; choice of paper sort is often seen as crucial: thickness and/or weight, colour, surface texture, grain direction, watermark, etc. Paper merchants go all out to convince designers and printers to use higher quality (and more expensive) paper for their printed pieces. Their promotions are often extravagant objects, with die-cutting, foil stamping, embossing, and other refinements. The quality of the paper itself is of course paramount. Rag paper, for example, is used when a more robust and longer-lasting product is wished for. It is, however, considerably more expensive to produce than that made only from wood pulp. "Bible paper" is

very thin, but opaque and long lasting. It is generally made from about 25 % cotton and linen rags or flax in combination with chemical wood pulp. Despite its thinness and lightness, Bible paper's opacity allows it to be used for fine letterheads.

A letterhead or business card can be quite a personal object. Letters often land in accounting departments or other administrative units, but will sometimes reach a person to whom their tactile qualities will make an important impression. Different versions of a letterhead, printed on more or less valuable paper, may therefore be designed for different intended audiences, depending on how much the receiver is likely to be influenced by such things. A business card is another matter: it is almost always handed directly from one person to another and remains, for at least a short time, in a pocket or bag. It may be handled several times before being filed or, for that matter, thrown away. One might have several different business cards and hand them out based on who is standing or sitting opposite at the time. My university cards, for example, are part of the corporate identity of our school – everyone here has a similar-looking card. For personal use, I designed my own cards and had them printed letterpress by a friend in the United States. They always create a positive impression.

The "stationery suite"

As part of a corporate identity assignment, graphic designers are usually asked to create a stationery suite, which will include a letterhead (perhaps several versions), business cards, envelopes of various sizes, perhaps mailing labels, note pads, and presentation folders. The pre-printed personal letterhead is quite a rarity these days, but for most designers working with print, corporate identity, and the like, business letterheads are a staple of the assignment universe.

Watermarks

Watermarks on letterheads, where they exist at all, are usually provided by paper manufacturers and differ according to paper sort within certain ranges. They usually sit horizontally in the centre, somewhere in the top third of the sheet, but are sometimes placed in a more random fashion, the location depending on untrimmed paper sizes and how they are cut. Designers might choose a paper sort for a client based on the design of the watermark as much as other criteria. It is indeed possible to design a special watermark for a specific client, but comparatively large quantities must be ordered before such an undertaking can be carried out. Paper manufacturers differ, but quantities in the 100,000 area are usual. Smaller quantities can be ordered, but then of course costs can climb dramatically.
Once the paper has been manufactured, delivered, and trimmed, one must be sure that it is printed "right way up". I have on more than one occasion had to send letterheads back because they had been printed upside down, or back to front.

Left
The Foundry Stock Room
From the book "1796–1896, One Hundred Years", MacKellar, Smiths and Jordan Foundry, Philadelphia

Standardisation, DIN, ISO, etc.
Georg Christoph Lichtenberg wrote as early as 1786 to Johann Beckmann about the benefits of paper cut to the ratio of $1{:}\sqrt{2}$ (e.g. folding a sheet in half produces a sheet with exactly the same proportions as the original). In 1798 the French government published a law on stamps and postage (*"Loi sur le timbre"*) in which several standard paper sizes were mentioned, some of which correspond with modern DIN or ISO standards. This standard series never became widely known and seems unfortunately to have been forgotten soon thereafter. The introduction of the typewriter in the 19th Century encouraged some standardisation of letter-paper sizes, but it wasn't until around 1900 that a certain Dr. Walter Porstmann independently reinvented the aforementioned French paper formats in Germany. They were adopted as the German standard DIN 476 in 1922 as a replacement for the vast variety of other paper formats that had been used before. This was in order to make paper stocking and document reproduction cheaper and more efficient. By the way, DIN stands for "Deutsches Institut für Normung", formerly "Deutsche Industrie Norm".

Porstmann's concept from the early 20th Century was convincing and was introduced as a national standard in many other countries over the following decades – for example, Belgium (1924), Japan (1951), and Australia (1974). It finally became both an international standard (ISO 216) as well as the official United Nations document format in 1975. It is used today in almost all countries on this planet, leaving North America and parts of Mexico as the only remaining exceptions. American and Canadian letter-size paper, at 8 ½" × 11" (approx. 215 × 280 mm), is different from the A4 (210 × 297 mm) used in most of the rest of the world. Just to keep things interesting, "monarch size" paper, at 7 ¼" × 10 ½" (184 × 267 mm), is often used for "executive" letterheads in Canada and the United States. They also have "legal size" paper, at 8 ½" × 14" (approx. 215 × 355 mm), although, in spite of its name, it has nothing to do with the law.

The DIN 676 and DIN 5008 standards (2005) specify in precise detail not only the size of the paper, but how letterheads should be laid out, including positioning of addressee texts for window envelopes, the return address, the "information block", and where the letter text should be positioned, including where it should end. Many designers will follow some of these standards, choosing to ignore others, for aesthetic or other reasons. One needn't be a slave to every detail as though it were law. Aside from standard envelope window sizes and positions, one is pretty much free to design a letterhead following common sense and good typographic guidelines: 1. leave space for hole-punching and consider filing standards; 2. use corporate typefaces as appropriate, but when letters in editable format (e.g. MS Word files) are to be sent as email

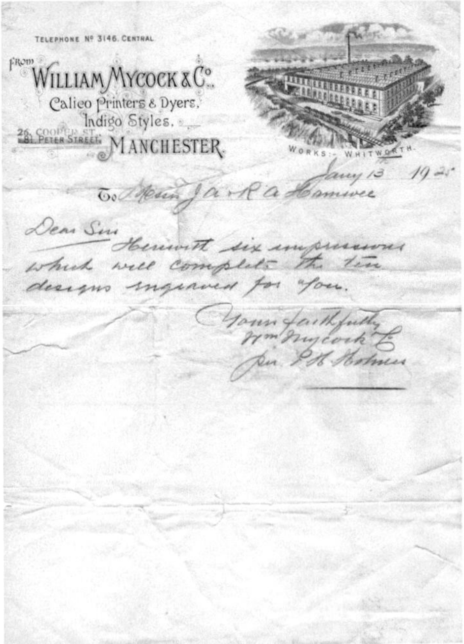
TELEPHONE Nº 3146, CENTRAL

FROM WILLIAM MYCOCK & Co.
Calico Printers & Dyers,
Indigo Styles,
26, COOPER ST.
81, PETER STREET,
MANCHESTER.

WORKS:- WHITWORTH.

Jany 13 1925

Dear Sir
Herewith six impressions which will complete the ten designs engraved for you.

Yours faithfully
Wm Mycock & Co

Left
Letterhead
1925, William Mycock & Co.
Calico Printers & Dyers, Indigo Styles, Manchester

Right
Letterhead detail
1925, Sulman Nathan, Basrah

attachments, using a system font (Calibri, Georgia, Times, etc.) for the text body will help avoid surprises at the receiving end. Logos and taglines can be created as images to ensure their typographic integrity; 3. set column widths for 55-65 characters per line; 4. use a (minimal!) visual hierarchy to represent the content hierarchy. Summarising subheads can be written and placed in the margins (if there is space), using a complementary typeface or cut; 5. leave adequate white space for comfortable reading and handling.

Note: It was proposed for an early draft of ISO 216 (ISO is the International Organization for Standardization) to recommend the special size of 210 × 280 mm (a format sometimes called PA4) as an interim measure for countries that use 215 × 280 mm (approximately 8½" × 11") paper and have not yet adopted the ISO A series. Some magazines and other products that have to be printed economically on both A4 and U.S. letter-size presses use the PA4 format today. Incidentally, this PA4 format has a ratio of 3:4, the same (when used horizontally) as traditional TV screens and most computer monitors, data projectors, and video modes.

A lot of people are under the impression that ISO or DIN standards are some sort of law. Indeed they are not. They are suggestions for standardisation from an organisation composed of government agencies and commercial interests. As a designer, one is quite free to create a letterhead in pretty much any shape and/or size one pleases. There are limits, of course. A 50 cm (20 in.) round letterhead would certainly create an impression, but one would have to balance the value of such an impression with the expense of printing and die-cutting such a thing, the inconvenience for secretaries and other users, and the bother for recipients in filing and storage. Once a letter is placed in an envelope, standardisation plays a more important role. Post offices often return non-standard items to the sender, resulting in delays and extra costs. You might design a non-standard envelope – an irregular size, for example, or printed items in areas which should be left clear. The client might get away with using it for a short while, but the post office just might suddenly decide to be strict and your "creativity" will cost your client money and time. This is seldom a smart idea.

So, what about email?

As stated at the beginning, postal mail has dropped off considerably since email has become ubiquitous in industrialised countries. Sending a PDF, for example, of a letter created on company letterhead as an email attachment allows the receiver to print out a reasonable facsimile of a "traditional" corporate letter, perhaps even with a signature in blue ink for extra "authenticity". Rather than go to this effort, many people customise their email "signatures", creating a kind of electronic letterhead, including logos, wordmarks in specific typefaces, corporate colours, etc. The body of the email, however, must

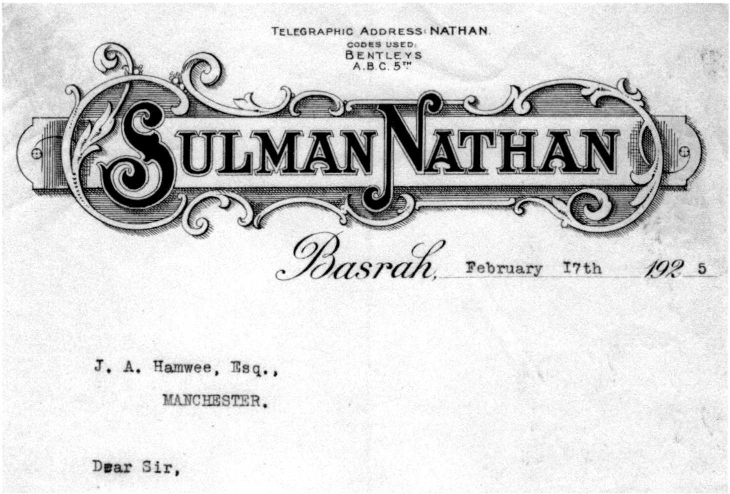
TELEGRAPHIC ADDRESS: NATHAN.
CODES USED:
BENTLEYS
A.B.C. 5TH

SULMAN NATHAN

Basrah, February 17th 1925

J. A. Hamwee, Esq.,
MANCHESTER.

Dear Sir,

usually be set in one of the standardised system fonts (Times, Georgia, Verdana, etc.), otherwise it will be converted at the recipient's end into something you might not expect. Those who use mail in a Web browser may rely on "@fontface" capabilities or other Web font standards, such as EOT (Embedded OpenType) or WOFF (Web Open Font Format), to specify certain typefaces for email correspondence. When this becomes more widespread, it will strengthen corporate identity for companies, as well as allowing individuals to standardise their communications, should they wish. What has long been taken for granted in the print world will soon be common in the Web as well (what's the hurry, it's only been about fifteen years).

One might be reminded that the earliest books had no page numbers or tables of contents – what we take for granted today took about 200 years to become common practice in book production. With regard to the letterhead, as well as pretty much all other print products, we have been more or less in a state of transition for about 25 years, since the advent of so-called Desktop Publishing. This state of transition appears likely to continue for at least a while longer.

Das Ende des Briefpapiers?

Jay Rutherford

Professur Visuelle Kommunikation
Fakultät Gestaltung
Bauhaus-Universität Weimar
www.uni-weimar.de

Weltweit werden immer weniger Briefe auf postalischem Weg zugestellt. So schrumpfte beispielsweise 2009 das Aufkommen postalisch zugestellter Briefe bei der amerikanischen Post allein bis September um fast 14 %. Analysen sagen voraus, dass der europäische Briefverkehr im Laufe der nächsten zehn Jahre auf die Hälfte zurückgehen wird. Ist der Briefkontakt per E-Mail nicht sowieso unkomplizierter, preiswerter, praktischer und viel moderner? Wir werden sicherlich noch sehr lange mit E-Mails zu tun haben, doch die meisten von uns werden zugeben, meist recht gespannt zu sein, wenn wir einmal einen „echten" Brief mit der Post bekommen – vor allem, wenn er von Hand geschrieben wurde. Nachdem ich vor Kurzem eine Konferenz organisiert hatte, erhielt ich eine ganze Reihe E-Mails mit Dankesworten. Ein Schreiben stach allerdings besonders hervor: Einer unserer Vortragsredner schickte mir einen Brief auf seinem eigenen, ansprechend gestalteten Briefpapier mit der schlichten handschriftlichen Notiz: „Großartige Konferenz – danke, dass ich dort meinen Vortrag halten durfte!" Diese kleine Geste war sehr bedeutsam. Ich halte immer noch einen Brief in Ehren, den ich 1992 von einer Lehrerin für Gestaltung an der Leipziger Hochschule für Grafik und Buchkunst erhielt. Darin dankte sie mir, dass ich zwei ihrer Studierenden in einem Schriftgestaltungsworkshop betreut hatte. Der Brief war auf dem Briefbogen ihrer Schule verfasst, den sie um 90 Grad gedreht und mit einer Art Bambusfeder in ihrer unnachahmlichen Kritzelschrift beschrieben hatte. Wundervoll! Eine gute Handschrift ist übrigens eine Fertigkeit, die jede gebildete Person besitzen sollte – leider heutzutage eine Seltenheit!

Die Erfindung des Papiers

Es ist eine allgemein bekannte Tatsache, dass die Chinesen das Papier vor etwa zweitausend Jahren erfanden. Es dauerte einige Jahrhunderte, bis ihre Erfindung auch Europa erreichte, aber erst mit dem Aufkommen der Druckerpresse im 15. Jahrhundert setzte sich die Verwendung von Papier durch, das aus zerkleinerten Holzfasern geschöpft wurde. Zuvor hatte man Pergament oder aus Stofffasern produziertes Papier verwendet, um Briefe zu schreiben.

Die Ausbreitung der Lese- und Schreibfähigkeit

Damals gab es ohnehin kaum Menschen, die Briefe hätten schreiben können: Nur ein Bruchteil der Bevölkerung war überhaupt in der Lage zu lesen und zu schreiben. Nachrichten wurden mündlich per Kurier übermittelt, wobei dem Grundsatz von Treu und Glauben zwar oberste Priorität eingeräumt, er aber nicht immer respektiert wurde. Es dauerte bis weit ins 19. Jahrhundert hinein, bis im Zuge der industriellen Revolution Papier und Bücher für die meisten Mitglieder der industrialisierten Gesellschaften finanziell erschwinglich waren. Noch 1841 unterschrieben in England beispielsweise ein Drittel aller Männer und fast die Hälfte aller Frauen

Right
Watermark effect detail
NewState Entertainment Ltd,
designed by David Bowden,
2009, Zip Design

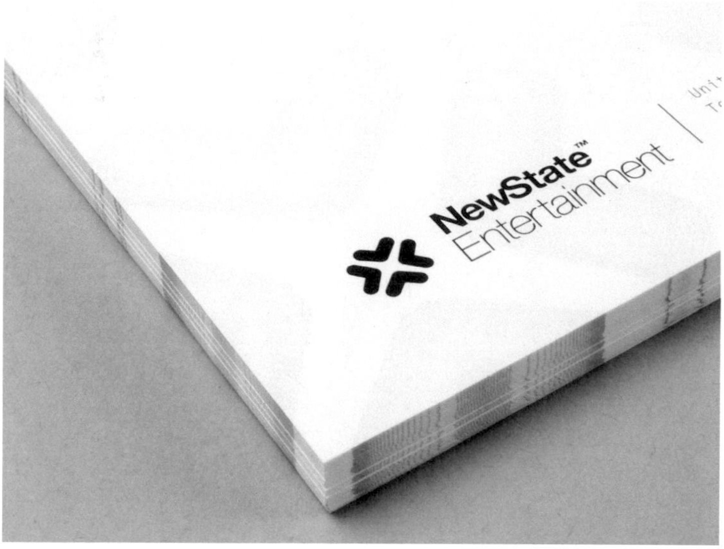

ihre Heiratsurkunden nur mit einem Kreuz. Frankreich war in gewisser Hinsicht in diesem Bereich fortschrittlicher: Anfang des 17. Jahrhunderts konnte nur ein Drittel des französischen Volkes lesen und schreiben – zum Ende des 18. Jahrhunderts hingegen praktisch jeder Franzose. Die Regierungen mancher Länder kontrollieren auch heute noch sehr streng den Zugang zur Bildung, einschließlich der Lesefähigkeit, um ihre Bevölkerung besser kontrollieren zu können – allerdings vor allem in weniger industrialisierten Nationen. Es sind auch nicht immer Regierungen, die Kontrolle ausüben: In weiten Teilen Afrikas verknüpft man Lesen und Schreiben negativ mit Kolonialismus, wohingegen die mündliche Weitergabe von Wissen positiv mit einheimischen Traditionen in Verbindung gebracht wird.

Der Begriff der Lese- und Schreibfähigkeit hat sich im Laufe der Zeit weiterentwickelt. Den eigenen Namen schreiben zu können, betrachtete man früher als ausreichend. Einstmals galt schon als „belesen", wer Teile der Bibel auswendig konnte. Diese Zuordnung war entscheidend, um festzulegen, auf welcher Rechtsgrundlage jemand verurteilt wurde – vielfach eine Frage von Leben und Tod. Es gab in der Geschichte auch Zeiten, in denen das Wissen um Lesen und Schreiben als Berufsgeheimnis professioneller Schriftgelehrter galt. Seit den 90er-Jahren des vorigen Jahrhunderts betrachtet man es außerdem als wichtigen Bestandteil der Lese- und Schreibfähigkeit, einen Computer, einen Webbrowser und Textverarbeitungssoftware bedienen sowie SMS versenden zu können. Heutzutage müssen wir, nur um mithalten zu können, auch noch in *(Multi-)Media*, *Kunst* und *Informationsbeschaffung* bewandert sein und Informationen auch visuell aufnehmen, also quasi Bilder „lesen" können. Doch es gibt auch Menschen, die in dem übermäßigen Vertrauen, das in die Lese- und Schreibfähigkeit als Bildungsinstrument gelegt wird, eher eine Form von Tyrannei sehen, ein Mittel, das vielmehr der Kontrolle als der Aufklärung der Bevölkerung dient.

Der Ursprung des „Briefkopfs"

Der Begriff „Briefkopf" (engl. *letterhead*) wurde zuerst im Amerika des späten 19. Jahrhunderts verwendet. Er bezeichnete ursprünglich nur den Namen und die Anschrift des Absenders, die meist oben, also in den „Kopf" eines Briefbogens gesetzt wurden. Der Begriff bezieht sich heutzutage allgemeiner auf den ganzen Briefbogen. Der *Oxford Pocket Dictionary of Current English* definiert einen Briefkopf als „gedruckte Überschrift in einem Brief, die den Namen einer Person oder Organisation und eine Adresse enthält" oder als „ein Blatt Papier mit einer solchen Überschrift". Briefpapier (engl. *stationery*) ist dem *Webster's Dictionary* zufolge ein „Papier, das auf eine zum Briefschreiben geeignete Größe zugeschnitten ist, meist zusammen mit passenden Umschlägen". Das Wort *stationery* (mit „e") ist verwandt mit *stationary* (engl. etwa *stationär* bzw. *parkend*). So bezeichnete man ursprünglich Straßenhändler, die ihre Waren von einem festen Standort aus verkauften, um sich

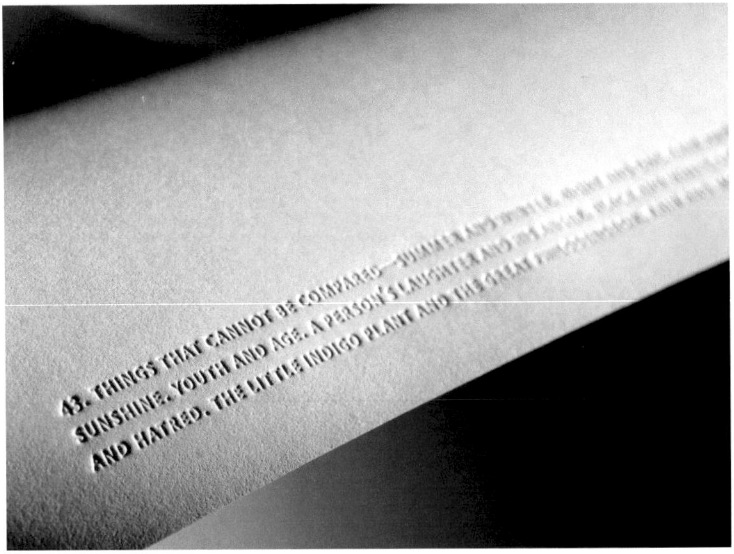
43. THINGS THAT CANNOT BE COMPARED—
SUNSHINE. YOUTH AND AGE. A PERSON'S LAUGHTER
AND HATRED. THE LITTLE INDIGO PLANT AND THE

von fliegenden Händlern zu unterscheiden. Im Mittelalter handelte es sich bei diesen „stationären" Verkaufsstellen häufig um von Universitäten lizenzierte Buchläden. Die „Company of Stationers" wurde 1556 gegründet, und der Begriff *stationery* wurde etwa 1727 geprägt.

Die Aufgaben des Grafikdesigners

Heutzutage gehört zur Gestaltung des Briefkopfs normalerweise auch das Layout für den gesamten Briefbogen: vom Namen und der Adresse des Absenders über die Positionierung von Logos oder anderen Gestaltungselementen des Corporate Designs bis hin zur Bankverbindung und schließlich der Positionierung der schriftlichen Inhalte. Die Druckfarben richten sich nach den Gestaltungsvorgaben der Firma, und die Wahl der richtigen Papiersorte wird oft als ganz wesentlich betrachtet, wozu Papierstärke und/oder -gewicht, die Farbe, Oberflächenbeschaffenheit, Faserausrichtung, Wasserzeichen etc. gehören. Papierhändler treiben es bis zum Äußersten, indem sie Designer und Drucker davon zu überzeugen suchen, für ihre Druckwerke qualitativ bessere (und kostspieligere) Papiersorten zu verwenden. Dafür werben sie oft mit extravagant gestalteten Objekten mit Stanzungen, Folienprägung, Hoch- und Tiefprägungen und anderen Raffinessen. Die Qualität des Papiers selbst ist natürlich von allergrößter Wichtigkeit. Hadernpapier wird beispielsweise dann verwendet, wenn ein robustes und langlebiges Produkt gewünscht wird. Es ist allerdings auch beträchtlich teurer als das Papier, das nur aus Holzfasern produziert wird. „Bibel"- oder „Dünndruckpapier" ist sehr dünn, aber undurchsichtig und lange haltbar. Es wird meist aus etwa 25% Baumwoll- und Leinenfasern oder Flachs in Kombination mit chemisch behandelten Holzfasern hergestellt. Obwohl es so dünn und leicht ist, kann das undurchsichtige „Bibelpapier" auch für Briefbögen verwendet werden.

Ein Briefkopf oder eine Visitenkarte kann einen sehr persönlichen Charakter haben. Briefe landen oft in der Buchhaltung oder in anderen Verwaltungsbereichen, doch hin und wieder werden sie auch von einer Person in die Hand genommen, die ihre taktilen Qualitäten zu würdigen weiß und bei der sie einen besonderen Eindruck hinterlassen. Verschiedene Versionen eines Briefkopfs, der auf mehr oder weniger wertvolles Papier gedruckt wurde, können somit für unterschiedliche Adressaten gestaltet werden – abhängig davon, wie sehr sich der Empfänger von solchen Dingen wahrscheinlich beeinflussen lässt. Mit einer Visitenkarte geht man anders um: Sie wird fast immer einem Gegenüber direkt überreicht und verbleibt – zumindest für kurze Zeit – in einer Jackentasche oder Mappe. Man nimmt sie öfter in die Hand, bevor sie abgeheftet oder vielleicht auch weggeworfen wird. Man könnte also mehrere unterschiedlich gestaltete Visitenkarten bereithalten und, je nachdem mit wem man es zu tun hat, die jeweils passende Ausführung überreichen. Die Visitenkarten

Left
Blind debossing detail
Design is Play business card,
designed by Angie Wang, Mark Fox,
2008, Design is Play

Right
Letterhead die-cutting detail
Ralf Obergfell Photography
designed by Magpie Studio, 2007

meiner Universität sind beispielsweise der Corporate Identity unserer Bildungseinrichtung entsprechend gestaltet: Alle Karten sehen gleich aus. Für den persönlichen Gebrauch entwerfe ich meine eigenen Karten und lasse sie von einem Freund in den USA speziell mit Bleilettern drucken. Sie hinterlassen stets einen positiven Eindruck.

Briefpapier als Kollektion

Grafikdesigner, die mit der Gestaltung einer Corporate Identity beauftragt werden, werden oft damit betraut, Briefbögen als Teil einer Kollektion zu entwerfen, zu der der Briefkopf (vielleicht in verschiedenen Versionen), Visitenkarten, Umschläge in unterschiedlichen Größen, eventuell auch Briefaufkleber, Notizzettel und Präsentationsmappen gehören. Der aufgedruckte persönliche Briefkopf ist heutzutage eine echte Rarität, doch für die meisten Designer, die im Bereich Print oder Corporate Identity tätig sind, bilden Firmenbriefköpfe die Klammer ihres Auftrags.

Wasserzeichen

Für die Wasserzeichen im Briefpapier – sofern es überhaupt welche gibt – sorgen normalerweise die Papierhersteller. Wasserzeichen unterscheiden sich innerhalb bestimmter Grenzen bei den verschiedenen Papiersorten. Sie befinden sich normalerweise horizontal in der Mitte, etwa im oberen Drittel des Blattes, aber manchmal werden sie auch eher zufällig platziert, was von der Größe des unbeschnittenen Papiers abhängt und davon, wie das Papier letztlich geschnitten wird. Die Designer können die Papiersorte für einen Kunden z. B. abhängig vom Design des Wasserzeichens wählen, aber auch andere Kriterien berücksichtigen. Es ist tatsächlich möglich, ein spezielles Wasserzeichen für den Kunden zu designen, doch zu einem solchen Unterfangen gehört normalerweise die Bestellung von vergleichsweise großen Papiermengen. Das regeln die Papierhersteller unterschiedlich, doch üblich sind Mengen in der Größenordnung von 100.000 Blatt. Natürlich können auch kleinere Mengen geordert werden, aber das lässt dann die Kosten dramatisch steigen. Sobald das Papier produziert, geliefert und zugeschnitten wurde, gilt es unbedingt darauf zu achten, dass es auf der richtigen Seite bedruckt wird. Ich habe bei mehr als einer Gelegenheit Briefpapier zurückgehen lassen, weil es auf der Rückseite bedruckt worden war oder das Wasserzeichen auf dem Kopf stand.

Standardisierung, DIN, ISO usw.

Georg Christoph Lichtenberg beschrieb Johann Beckmann bereits im Jahre 1786 die Vorzüge von Papier, das im Verhältnis von 1:√2 beschnitten wurde (d. h., egal wie oft man ein Blatt Papier in der Mitte faltet, jedes Format, das sich daraus ergibt, behält exakt die Proportionen des Originals bei). 1798 erließ die französische Regierung ein Gesetz, das die Handhabung von Briefmarken und Porto regelte (*„Loi sur le timbre"*) und in dem verschiedene Standardpapiergrößen erwähnt wurden; einige davon korrespondieren mit heutigen

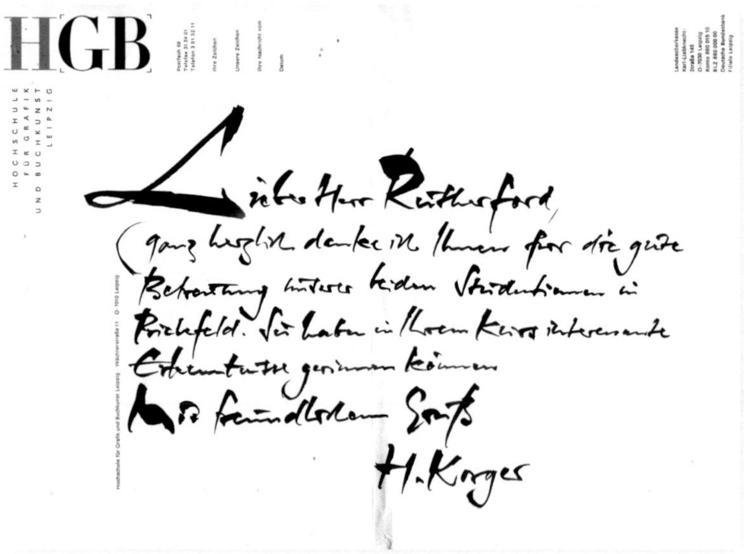
HGB

HOCHSCHULE FÜR GRAFIK UND BUCHKUNST LEIPZIG

Lieber Herr Rutherford,
ganz herzlich danke ich Ihnen für die gute Betreuung unserer beiden Studentinnen in [illegible]. Sie haben in Ihrem Kurs interessante Erkenntnisse gewinnen können.
Mit freundlichem Gruß
H. Korger

Left
Letterhead paper of the Hochschule für Grafik und Buchkunst Leipzig
A letter from Hildegard Korger to Jay Rutherford, 1992

Right
Portfolio set and website
Truth Marketing, designed by Nigel Bates, 2009, Socio Design

DIN- oder ISO-Standards. Diese Standardgrößen konnten sich damals nicht durchsetzen und scheinen leider bereits kurz darauf wieder in Vergessenheit geraten zu sein. Die Einführung der Schreibmaschine im 19. Jahrhundert begünstigte einige Standardisierungsbestrebungen von Briefpapierformaten, doch erst nach 1900 erfand ein gewisser Dr. Walter Porstmann die erwähnten französischen Papierformate in Deutschland neu. Sie wurden im Jahre 1922 als deutscher Standard DIN 476 übernommen, um die übergroße Vielfalt anderer Papierformate zu ersetzen, die bis dato verwendet worden waren. Damit sollte die Papiervorratshaltung und Dokumentenreproduktion billiger und effizienter gestaltet werden. DIN steht übrigens für „Deutsches Institut für Normung", früher auch für „Deutsche Industrienorm".

Porstmanns Konzept von Anfang des 20. Jahrhunderts war überzeugend und wurde im Laufe der nächsten Jahrzehnte auch in vielen anderen Ländern als nationaler Standard übernommen, z. B. Belgien (1924), Japan (1951) und Australien (1974). Es wurde als ISO 216 sowohl zum internationalen Standard als auch im Jahre 1975 das offizielle Dokumentformat der Vereinten Nationen. Es wird heutzutage in fast allen Ländern dieser Erde verwendet, wobei Nordamerika und Teile von Mexiko die einzigen verbleibenden Ausnahmen darstellen. Amerikanische und kanadische Briefpapiergrößen mit 8 ½" × 11" (etwa 215 × 280 mm) unterscheiden sich vom Format A4 (210 × 297 mm), das fast in der ganzen restlichen Welt verwendet wird. Nur um die Sache interessant zu halten: Für „Manager"-Briefköpfe in Kanada und den USA gibt es noch die Größe „Monarch" (7 ¼" × 10 ½", also 184 × 267 mm). Es gibt auch noch das Format „legal size" (wörtlich etwa „gesetzliche Größe") mit 8 ½" × 14", also etwa 215 × 355 mm, das trotz seines Namens gar nichts mit der Jurisprudenz zu tun hat.

Die Standards DIN 676 und DIN 5008 (2005) legen detailliert und präzise nicht nur das Papierformat fest, sondern auch, wie die Elemente des Briefkopfs auf dem Papier verteilt sein sollen – inklusive Positionierung der Empfängeradresse für Fensterbriefumschläge, der Rücksendeadresse, des „Informationsblocks" und des eigentlichen Brieftextes sowie des Textendes. Viele Designer befolgen bestimmte Standards und ignorieren andere – das kann ästhetische aber auch anderweitige Gründe haben. Dabei muss nicht jedes Detail sklavisch befolgt werden, als wäre es in Stein gemeißelt. Abgesehen von den Standardgrößen und -positionen für Fensterumschläge hat man freie Hand, mit gesundem Menschenverstand und unter Einhaltung typografischer Richtlinien einen Briefkopf zu designen: 1. Es sollte Platz für Lochungen des Blattes vorhanden sein und Standards der Aktenablage berücksichtigt werden. 2. Soweit erforderlich oder gewünscht, sollte mit Firmenschriften gearbeitet werden, aber wenn Briefe als E-Mail-Anhang bearbeitbar gesendet werden (z. B. als Microsoft Word-Dateien), erspart man dem Empfänger böse Überraschungen,

The
Whole

Truth is
Strat-
egic
Insight

Truth consulting isn't about mountains of facts or reams of research. It's about distilling this raw material into compelling and profitable advantage.

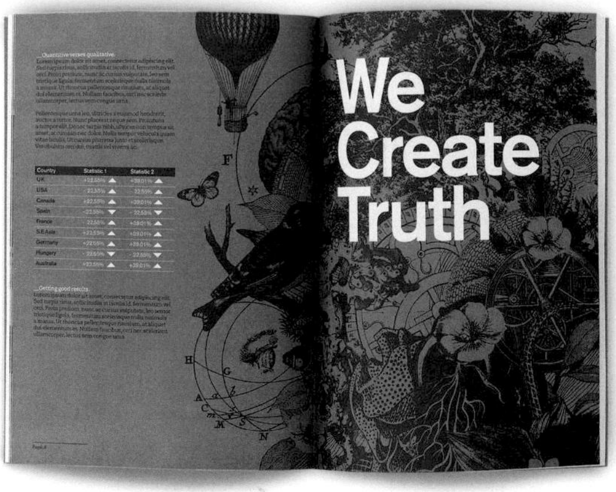
We
Create
Truth

File Edit View History Bookmarks Window Help
Who we are
About Us
Quick facts
People
What we do
Map of our world
Four Pillars
What we think
Postcards
Point of View
Philosophy
What we have done
News & Events
Achievements & Awards
Who we work with
Case studies
Suppliers
Clients
Contact us
Address & Contact
Location Map
The
Whole
Truth
Blaise Pascal
Truth is more important
than just facts.
MacBook Pro

Left
Card made of 0.8 mm thick plywood
Rubber stamped in green
ADP Joinery & Carpentry,
design by Andrew Lodge, 2008

Right
Hot stamping foil and dye-cutting detail
Celia Keyworth's Food, design by
Pentagram London, 2007

wenn man mit Systemfonts wie Calibri, Georgia, Times etc. arbeitet. Logos und Werbeslogans können als Bild umgesetzt werden, um die typografische Integrität zu bewahren. 3. Spalten sollten auf 55 bis 65 Zeichen pro Zeile gesetzt werden. 4. Mit einer (minimalen!) Hierarchie kann man eine inhaltliche Hierarchie und Abfolge im Text repräsentieren. Zusammenfassende Zwischenüberschriften können mit entsprechend abgestimmter Schriftart oder Schriftschnitt in den Seitenrand eingefügt werden (wenn dort Platz ist). 5. Um die Lesbarkeit des Textes und den Umgang damit zu erleichtern, arbeitet man im Briefkopf mit adäquatem Weißraum.

Anmerkung: Als früher Entwurf von ISO 216 (International Organization for Standardization) wurde vorgeschlagen, das Sonderformat 210 × 280 mm (diese Größe wird manchmal auch PA4 genannt) als Interimsmaße für Länder zu empfehlen, die mit Papier der Größe 215 × 280 mm arbeiten (etwa 8½" × 11") und die ISO-A-Serien noch nicht umgesetzt haben. Manche Magazine und andere Produkte, die aus ökonomischen Gründen sowohl auf A4 als auch im US-Letter-Format gedruckt werden müssen, verwenden heutzutage das PA4-Format. Übrigens weist dieses besagte Format PA4, wenn es horizontal eingesetzt wird, zufällig das Seitenverhältnis 3:4 auf – genau wie traditionelle Fernsehbildschirme und die meisten Computermonitore, Beamer und Videomodi.

Sehr viele Menschen haben den Eindruck, dass es sich bei ISO- oder DIN-Standards irgendwie um ein Gesetz handelt. Tatsächlich sind diese Standards kein Gesetz. Vielmehr handelt es sich um die Standardisierungsvorschläge einer Organisation, die sich aus staatlichen Stellen und kommerziellen Interessenvertretern zusammensetzt. Als Designer steht es jedem frei, Briefformate in beliebiger Form und/oder Größe bzw. Seitenverhältnis zu entwerfen. Natürlich hat das auch seine Grenzen: Ein runder Bogen Briefpapier mit einem Durchmesser von 50 cm wirkt sicherlich beeindruckend, doch man sollte diesen Eindruck in Relation zu den Ausgaben für Druck und Zuschnitt eines solchen Formats, zu der umständlichen Handhabung durch Sekretärinnen und andere Nutzer setzen und dazu, wie unpraktisch es für den Empfänger wäre, dieses Format in den Akten abzulegen und aufzubewahren. Sobald ein Brief in einem Umschlag landen soll, spielt die Standardisierung eine wichtigere Rolle: Postfirmen lassen nicht standardkonforme Briefsendungen oft zurückgehen oder verlangen mehr Porto, was zu Verzögerungen und zusätzlichen Kosten führt. Natürlich können Sie auch einen nicht standardkonformen Umschlag gestalten, z. B. in unregelmäßiger Größe oder mit gedruckten Elementen in Bereichen, die eigentlich frei bleiben sollten. Ihr Kunde könnte damit eine Zeit lang zurechtkommen, aber sollten die Postdienstleister es irgendwann einmal strenger sehen, wird diese „Kreativität" Ihre Kunden Zeit und Geld kosten. So etwas ist selten eine kluge Idee.

Was ist nun mit den E-Mails?
Wie schon zu Anfang erwähnt, sind postalische Briefzustellungen beträchtlich zurückgegangen, seitdem E-Mails in industrialisierten Ländern allgegenwärtig sind. Wenn z. B. das PDF eines Briefes, der mit dem Briefkopf der Firma gestaltet wurde, als E-Mail-Anhang gesendet wird, kann der Empfänger eine akzeptable originalgetreue Kopie des „traditionellen" Firmenbriefs ausdrucken, vielleicht sogar mit einer Unterschrift in blauer Farbe für die besondere „Authentizität". Anstatt sich diese Mühe zu machen, passen viele Menschen ihre E-Mail-Signaturen entsprechend an und schaffen so eine Art elektronischen Briefkopf mit Logo, Wortmarken in besonderen Schriftarten, Unternehmensfarben etc. Der Text der E-Mail muss normalerweise in einer der standardisierten Systemschriften erscheinen (Times, Georgia, Verdana etc.), ansonsten könnte er beim Empfänger konvertiert werden, und das kann möglicherweise zu ungewollten Ergebnissen führen. Wer E-Mails in einem Browser nutzt, kann auch das „@font-face"-Feature oder andere Standards für Webschriften einsetzen, z. B. EOT (Embedded OpenType) oder WOFF (Web Open Font Format), um für die E-Mail-Korrespondenz bestimmte Schriftarten festzulegen. Wenn sich das weiter verbreitet, wird es die Corporate Identity für Unternehmen stärken und auch anderen Personen erlauben, ihre Kommunikation auf Wunsch zu standardisieren. Was in der Welt der Druckmedien schon lange gang und gäbe ist, wird auch bald im Web allgemein üblich sein (Warum hektisch werden? Wir haben das World Wide Web doch erst seit 15 Jahren …).

Man sollte sich daran erinnern, dass die ersten Bücher keine Seitenzahlen oder Inhaltsverzeichnisse hatten. Was für uns heute selbstverständlich ist, brauchte fast 200 Jahre, um in der Buchherstellung allgemeine Praxis zu werden. Was das Briefpapier angeht, aber auch alle anderen Print-Produkte, befinden wir uns seit dem Aufkommen des sogenannten Desktop-Publishings vor ungefähr 25 Jahren mehr oder weniger in einer Übergangsphase. Diese Übergangszeit wird offenbar zumindest noch eine ganze Weile länger andauern.

La mort du papier à en-tête ?

Jay Rutherford

Professeur à la faculté de communication visuelle dans l'art et le design, université du Bauhaus de Weimar
www.uni-weimar.de

Dans le monde entier, le trafic postal est en chute libre. Aux États-Unis par exemple, les services postaux ont connu une baisse de volume de près de 14 % du courrier au cours des 3 premiers trimestres de 2009. Les analystes prévoient que le trafic postal en Europe diminuera de moitié au fil des dix prochaines années. Envoyer un e-mail n'est-il en effet pas plus simple, plus économique, plus pratique et plus courant ? L'e-mail n'est pas prêt de disparaître, mais la plupart d'entre nous avouera l'émotion ressentie en recevant une lettre par la poste, d'autant plus si elle est manuscrite. Après avoir organisé récemment une conférence, j'ai reçu un certain nombre d'e-mails de félicitations. L'une des communications reçues s'est toutefois clairement démarquée : l'un des quatre intervenants m'a envoyé une lettre sur un papier à en-tête élégant, avec une note manuscrite qui disait simplement : « Remarquable conférence, merci de m'avoir invité pour y parler ! » Ce petit geste a signifié beaucoup. Je conserve encore une lettre reçue en 1992 d'une professeur de design de l'école Hochschule für Grafik und Buchkunst à Leipzig, me remerciant d'avoir dirigé deux de ses élèves lors d'un atelier de typographie. Elle a pour cela pris le papier à en-tête de l'école et écrit de ses inimitables pattes de mouches avec une sorte de tige de bambou. Une merveille ! De fait, toute personne instruite devrait posséder le don de l'écriture, chose malheureusement devenue rare ces derniers temps.

L'invention du papier

Il est reconnu que les Chinois ont inventé le papier il y a deux mille ans environ. L'invention n'est arrivée en Europe que quelques siècles plus tard, mais l'emploi du papier à base de pâte de bois ne s'est répandu qu'à partir du XVe siècle, avec l'avènement de la machine à imprimer. Avant cela, les lettres étaient rédigées sur des parchemins ou du papier chiffon.

L'étendue de l'alphabétisation

La rédaction de lettres n'était dans tous les cas guère répandue : seul un faible pourcentage de la population savait en effet lire et écrire. Les messages verbaux étaient transmis par messager : la confiance était suprême, mais pas toujours respectée. C'est seulement au XIXe siècle bien entamé, avec l'avènement de la révolution industrielle, que le papier et les livres sont devenus abordables pour la plupart des membres des sociétés industrialisées. Encore en 1841 en Angleterre, un tiers des hommes et près de la moitié des femmes signaient leur acte de mariage d'une croix. La France était un peu plus en avance dans ce domaine : au début des années 1700, environ un tiers de sa population savait lire et écrire ; à la fin des années 1800 toutefois, la grande majorité était alphabétisée. Dans certains pays, les gouvernements gèrent rigoureusement l'accès à l'éducation (y compris la lecture) afin de garder la population sous contrôle. C'est encore vrai à l'heure actuelle, mais surtout dans des sociétés moins industrialisées. Les gouvernements ne sont néanmoins pas les seuls responsables. L'alphabétisation

Right
Stationery set
MICA, Maryland Institute College of Art,
design by Pentagram, 2007

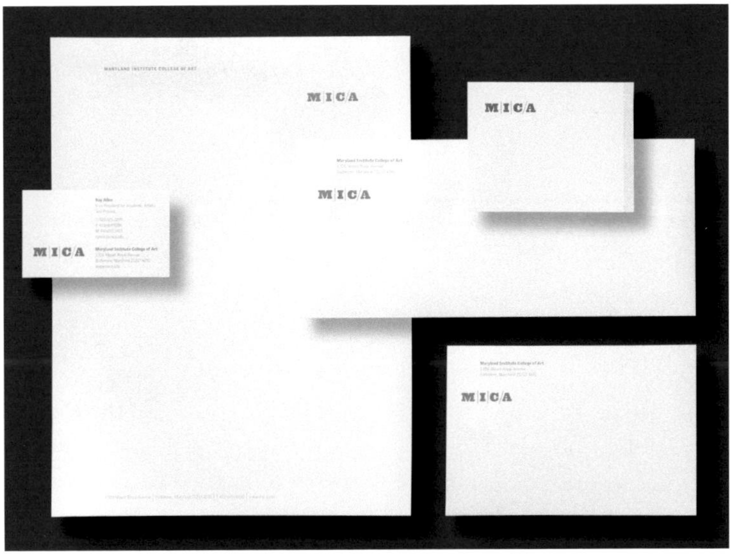

en Afrique est en grande partie associée au colonialisme, alors que la communication orale est liée aux traditions.

Le terme même d'alphabétisation a évolué avec le temps. Pendant un temps, il suffisait de savoir signer son nom. À une autre époque, le fait de mémoriser des passages concrets de la Bible vous plaçait dans la catégorie « instruit », car vous pouviez décider selon quel système juridique vous pouviez être jugé. Il s'agissait souvent d'une question de vie ou de mort. L'histoire a également connu des périodes où l'alphabétisation était un secret gardé des scribes professionnels. Depuis les années 90, savoir se servir d'un ordinateur, d'un navigateur Web, d'un logiciel de traitement de texte et envoyer un SMS sont autant d'aspects clés d'alphabétisation. Pour compliquer les choses, il est maintenant même question d'*alphabétisation (multi)média, alphabétisation artistique, alphabétisation de l'information* et *alphabétisation visuelle*. Il y a aussi ceux convaincus qu'une dépendance excessive envers l'alphabétisation est une sorte de tyrannie, un moyen de contrôle, plutôt qu'un outil pour illuminer les foules. Le débat est ouvert, et pour longtemps encore.

Origines du terme « papier à en-tête »

Le terme « papier à en-tête » est employé pour la première fois aux États-Unis, à la fin du XIXe siècle. Au départ, il désignait simplement le nom et l'adresse de l'expéditeur et figurait normalement en haut (à la « tête ») d'une feuille de papier à lettres. Aujourd'hui, il fait référence à l'ensemble de la feuille. *The Oxford Pocket Dictionary of Current English* définit ainsi un papier à en-tête : « en-tête imprimé sur du papier à lettres et indiquant le nom et l'adresse d'une personne ou d'une organisation » ou « feuille de papier assortie de ce type d'en-tête ». Selon le *Webster's Dictionary*, le papier à lettres est un « papier de la taille appropriée pour écrire des lettres et venant normalement avec des enveloppes assorties ». Le terme anglais équivalent « stationery » (avec un « e ») vient de son cousin « stationary », qui désignait à l'origine les camelots qui vendaient des marchandises à un endroit fixe, contrairement aux vendeurs ambulants qui traversaient les campagnes pour vendre leurs biens. Au Moyen-Âge, ces marchands « stationnaires » correspondaient souvent à des librairies autorisées par des universités. La *Company of Stationers* (corporation des libraires) a été fondée en 1556 et le terme « stationery » inventé autour de 1727.

Le travail du designer graphique

Le design actuel d'en-têtes porte normalement sur la composition de la page entière : nom et adresse de l'expéditeur, emplacement de logos ou d'autres éléments de design institutionnels, données bancaires éventuelles, place du contenu écrit. Les couleurs obéissent aux normes de design d'identité visuelle, et le choix du type de papier est souvent considéré déterminant (épaisseur et/ou grammage, couleur, texture de la surface, sens du grain, filigrane, etc.). Les

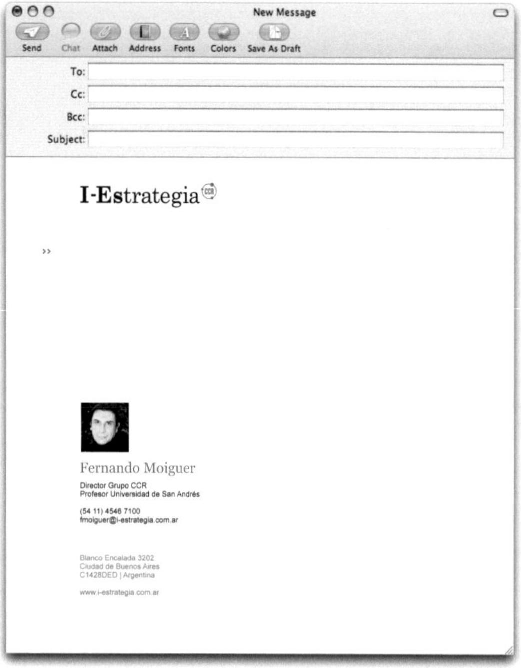

Left
Email letterhead
I-Estrategia, design by Lucas D'Amore, 2007

Right
Business card set
Maud, design by Hampus Jageland, David Park, 2009

vendeurs de papier s'attachent à convaincre les designers et les imprimeurs d'utiliser du papier de qualité élevée (et donc plus coûteux) pour les documents imprimés. Leurs publicités sont souvent des objets extravagants, exhibant emporte-pièce, dorure à la feuille, gaufrage et autres raffinements. La qualité du papier à proprement parler est évidemment cruciale. Par exemple, le papier chiffon est employé pour obtenir un produit plus résistant et durable. Il est toutefois nettement plus cher à fabriquer que le papier à base de pâte de bois. Le papier Bible est très fin, mais opaque et résistant. Il se compose normalement d'environ 25 % de fibres de coton et de lin associées à une pâte de bois chimique. Malgré sa finesse et sa légèreté, le papier Bible a une opacité lui permettant d'offrir des papiers à en-tête raffinés.

Un papier à en-tête ou une carte de visite sont des objets plutôt personnels. Les lettres atterrissent souvent dans des services de comptabilité ou autres entités administratives ; parfois pourtant, elles parviennent à une personne sensible à leurs qualités au toucher. Différentes versions d'un en-tête, imprimé sur un papier de plus ou moins grande qualité, peuvent donc être pensées en fonction du public visé, selon la tendance du destinataire à se laisser influencer par ce genre de choses. La carte de visite est une autre histoire : elle est presque toujours remise en mains propres et est rangée, au moins à court terme, dans une poche ou un sac. Elle peut être manipulée plusieurs fois avant d'être conservée ou jetée. Une personne peut posséder diverses cartes de visite et les distribuer en fonction de l'interlocuteur du moment. Par exemple, mes cartes de l'université appartiennent à l'identité visuelle de notre école, et tout le monde en possède une similaire. Pour un usage personnel, j'ai conçu mes propres cartes et ai demandé à un ami aux États-Unis d'en faire une impression sur presse typographique. Elles créent toujours une sensation positive.

Le «set de courrier»

Dans le cadre d'un projet d'identité visuelle, les designers graphiques doivent normalement créer un set de courrier, comprenant papier à en-tête (plusieurs versions possibles), cartes de visite, enveloppes de différentes tailles, éventuellement étiquettes d'adresse, blocs-notes et dossiers de présentation. Le papier à en-tête personnel préimprimé est plutôt rare actuellement ; pour la plupart des designers travaillant sur des projets d'impression, d'identité visuelle et autres, les en-têtes professionnels font le gros des commandes qu'ils reçoivent.

Filigranes

Les filigranes présents sur du papier à en-tête sont généralement fournis par les fabricants de papier et varient dans une certaine mesure en fonction du type de papier. En principe, ils sont horizontaux, centrés, et occupent le tiers supérieur de la feuille ; leur emplacement peut aussi parfois être plus aléatoire, selon la taille du papier non rogné et de la façon dont il est

coupé. Les designers peuvent opter pour un type de papier en fonction du design du filigrane ou de tout autre critère. De fait, il est possible de concevoir un filigrane spécial pour un client déterminé, à condition de commander d'importantes quantités pour justifier cette demande. Le volume est variable entre fabricants de papier, mais il tourne en théorie autour de 100 000 unités. En cas de quantités inférieures, les coûts grimpent évidemment de façon radicale. Une fois le papier fabriqué, livré et découpé, il faut veiller à ce qu'il soit imprimé avec « la bonne face en haut ». À plusieurs occasions, j'ai dû renvoyer des papiers à en-tête car ils avaient été imprimés à l'envers ou du mauvais côté.

Standardisation, DIN, ISO, etc.

Dès 1786, Georg Christoph Lichtenberg écrivait à Johann Beckmann pour vanter les avantages du papier découpé dans une proportion de 1:√2 (par exemple, le fait de plier en deux une feuille en donne une autre de proportions identiques à l'original). En 1798, le gouvernement français publiait la Loi sur le timbre, qui stipulait plusieurs tailles de papier standards, dont certaines correspondent aux standards DIN ou ISO actuels. Cette série ne s'est jamais vraiment imposée et semble malheureusement avoir été oubliée peu de temps après. L'introduction de la machine à écrire au XIXe siècle a encouragé la standardisation des tailles de papier à lettres, mais ce n'est qu'autour de 1900 qu'un certain Dr. Walter Porstmann a réinventé en Allemagne les formats de papier français mentionnés plus haut. Ils ont été adoptés comme standard allemand DIN 476 en 1922, en remplacement de la large gamme de formats utilisés jusqu'alors. L'objectif était de réduire le coût et de faciliter le stockage du papier et la reproduction de documents. Au passage, DIN est l'acronyme de « Deutsches Institut für Normung », anciennement « Deutsche Industrie Norm ».

Au début du XXe siècle, l'approche de Porstmann a convaincu et a été appliquée comme standard national dans de nombreux pays au cours des décennies suivantes : par exemple, la Belgique (1924), le Japon (1951) et l'Australie (1974). Il s'est finalement imposé comme standard international (ISO 216) et comme format de document officiel des Nations Unies en 1975. Il s'emploie aujourd'hui dans la quasi-totalité des pays, à l'exception de l'Amérique du Nord et de certaines régions du Mexique. Le papier à lettres américain et canadien, d'environ 215 x 280 mm est différent du format A4 (210 × 297 mm) utilisé dans le reste du monde en majorité. Pour compliquer un peu les choses, le papier au format « monarch » de 184 x 267 mm est souvent utilisé pour les papiers à en-tête de « direction » au Canada et aux États-Unis. Il existe aussi un papier au format dit « legal » d'environ 251 x 355 mm même si, malgré son nom, il n'a rien à voir avec la loi.

Les standards DIN 676 et DIN 5008 (2005) expliquent en détail la taille du papier, mais aussi comment y ajouter

Right
DVD, CD, and envelope set
Firsteight, design by Falko Ohlmer, 2008

Page 30
Label on package
Finish, design by SViDesign, 2008

des en-têtes, y compris l'emplacement du texte d'adresse pour les enveloppes à fenêtre, l'adresse de l'expéditeur, le « bloc d'informations », la position du corps de la lettre et où il doit se finir. De nombreux designers suivent certains de ces standards et en ignorent délibérément d'autres pour des raisons esthétiques ou autres. Ces standards ne font pas loi, inutile donc de les appliquer à la lettre. En dehors de la taille et de l'emplacement standard de la fenêtre d'une enveloppe, le design d'un papier à en-tête peut parfaitement être le fruit du bon sens et de bonnes règles typographiques : 1. Laisser un espace pour les perforations et prendre en compte les normes d'archivage ; 2. Employer des polices institutionnelles, sauf quand une lettre dont le format est éditable (comme les fichiers MS Word) doit être envoyée en pièce jointe d'un e-mail : dans ce cas, utiliser une police système (Calibri, Georgia, Times, etc.) pour le corps du texte afin d'éviter une surprise du côté du destinataire. Les logos et les signatures peuvent être créés en tant qu'images pour assurer leur intégrité typographique ; 3. Définir la largeur de colonne à 55–65 caractères par ligne ; 4. Utiliser une hiérarchie visuelle (minimale) pour illustrer la hiérarchie du contenu. Les intertitres récapitulatifs peuvent être écrits et placés dans la marge (si l'espace est suffisant) à l'aide d'une police ou d'une coupe complémentaires ; 5. Laisser assez d'espace pour rendre la lecture et la manipulation confortables.

Remarque : il a été proposé pour un premier brouillon de la norme ISO (acronyme de « International Organization for Standardization ») 216 de recommander la taille spéciale de 210 × 280 mm (format parfois appelé PA4) comme mesure provisoire dans les pays utilisant le format 215 × 280 mm et n'a pas encore adopté la série ISO A. Certains magazines et d'autres produits dont l'impression doit être économique sur des presses à la fois A4 et de format américain se servent actuellement du format PA4. Entre parenthèses, le format PA4 a une proportion de 3:4, la même (à l'horizontale) que les traditionnels écrans télé et la plupart des moniteurs d'ordinateur, projecteurs et modes vidéo.

Nombre de personnes ont l'impression que les standards ISO ou DIN ont effet de loi, mais il n'en est rien. Ce sont de simples suggestions de standardisation d'une organisation composée d'agences gouvernementales et alimentée d'intérêts commerciaux. En tant que designer, chacun est libre de créer un papier à en-tête de n'importe quelle forme et/ou taille. Il existe bien sûr des limites. Un papier à en-tête rond de 50 cm créerait sans doute un grand impact ; il faudrait toutefois se demander si le coût de l'impression et de la découpe se justifie, tout comme la complication pour les secrétaires et autre utilisateurs pour le manipuler et celle pour les destinataires pour le ranger. Une fois la lettre insérée dans une enveloppe, la standardisation joue un rôle plus important. Les services postaux retournent souvent les plis non

firsteight
HELLO,
I'M
YOUR
PERSONAL
DISC.
HELLO, I'M YOUR PERSONAL COMPACT DISC.
HELLO, I'M YOUR PERSONAL DIGITAL VERSATILE DISC.

standards à l'expéditeur, d'où des retards et des frais supplémentaires. Vous pouvez concevoir une enveloppe non standard (de taille irrégulière par exemple, ou avec des éléments imprimés là où il ne devrait pas y en avoir. Le client l'utilisera peut-être pendant un temps, mais la poste peut tout à coup décider d'être stricte et votre « créativité » coûtera de l'argent et du temps à votre client. Ce n'est donc guère une bonne idée.

Qu'en est-il de l'e-mail?

Comme expliqué au début, le courrier postal a connu une chute considérable depuis l'expansion de l'e-mail dans les pays industrialisés. Par exemple, l'envoi en pièce jointe du PDF d'une lettre sur un papier à en-tête de l'entreprise permet au destinataire d'imprimer un fac-similé acceptable d'une lettre professionnelle « traditionnelle », y compris avec éventuellement une signature à l'encre bleue pour une « authenticité » supplémentaire. Pour se simplifier la vie, de nombreuses personnes personnalisent leur « signatures » d'e-mail, ce qui donne une sorte d'en-tête électronique, avec éventuellement des logos, des lettres de marque dans une typographie concrète, des couleurs institutionnelles etc. Le corps de l'e-mail doit cependant être écrit dans l'une des polices système standardisées (Times, Georgia, Verdana, etc.), afin qu'il conserve la même apparence à l'écran du destinataire. Les utilisateurs qui rédigent des e-mails dans un navigateur Web peuvent employer les fonctions « @fontface » ou autres standards de polices Web comme EOT (Embedded OpenType) ou WOFF (Web Open Font Format), afin de choisir des polices déterminées pour leur correspondance. Quand tout cela sera plus répandu, l'identité visuelle des entreprises s'en trouvera renforcée, et les individus pourront standardiser leurs communications s'ils le souhaitent. Ce qui a longtemps été considéré naturel dans le monde de l'impression le sera aussi bientôt sur le Web (pas d'urgence, on ne parle que d'une quinzaine d'années).

Pour rappel, les tous premiers livres n'avaient pas de numéros de pages et de table des matières : ce qui semble normal aujourd'hui a pris 200 ans pour devenir coutume dans la production de livres. Concernant le papier à en-tête, comme presque tous les autres produits imprimés, nous sommes plus ou moins restés dans un état de transition pendant 25 ans, depuis l'avènement de la fameuse PAO. Cette transition a l'air de vouloir durer encore un certain temps.

Finish:
Finish: Creative Services Ltd
37-42 Compton Street
London EC1V 0AP
Tel: +44 (0)20 7251 2122
Fax: +44 (0)20 7251 3221
ISDN: +44 (0)20 7250 0629
enquires@finish-creative.com
www.finish-creative.com
SVI DESIGN
Unit 124
Westbourne Studios
242 Acklam Rd
London W10 5JJ
Attn: Sasha Vidakovic

PROJECTS

Client 1/1 DESIGN
Year 2009
Design Base Design

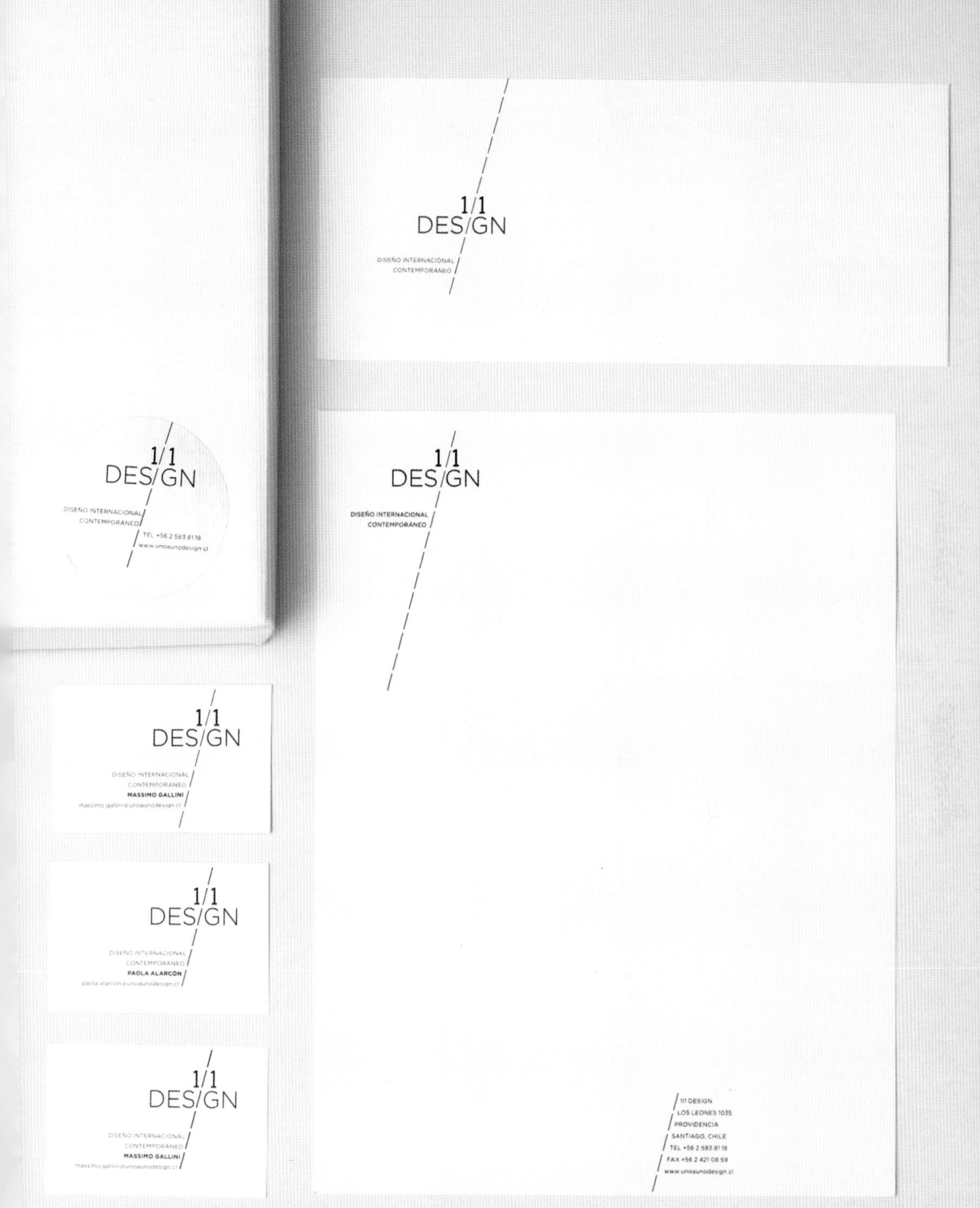
1/1 DESIGN
DISEÑO INTERNACIONAL
CONTEMPORÁNEO
TEL +56 2 583 81 18
www.unoaunodesign.cl
MASSIMO GALLINI
PAOLA ALARCÓN
1/1 DESIGN
LOS LEONES 1035
PROVIDENCIA
SANTIAGO, CHILE
FAX +56 2 421 08 59

Client 9MYLES
Year 2004
Design 9MYLES

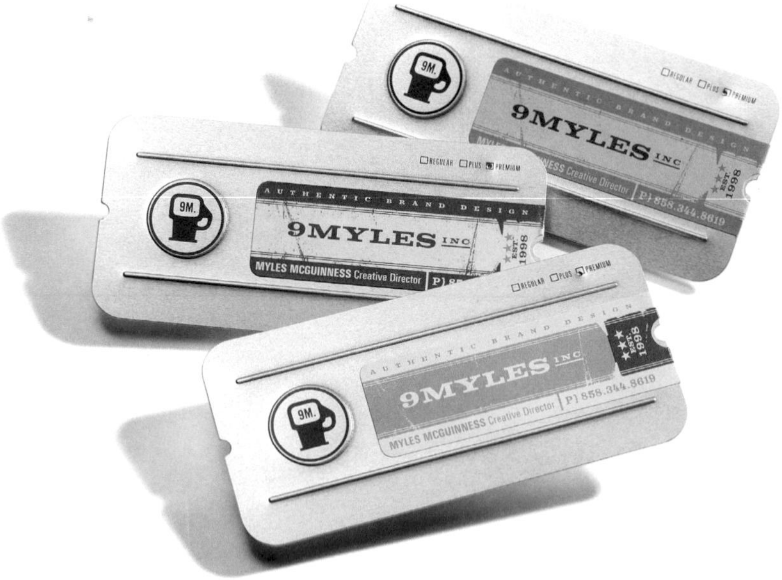

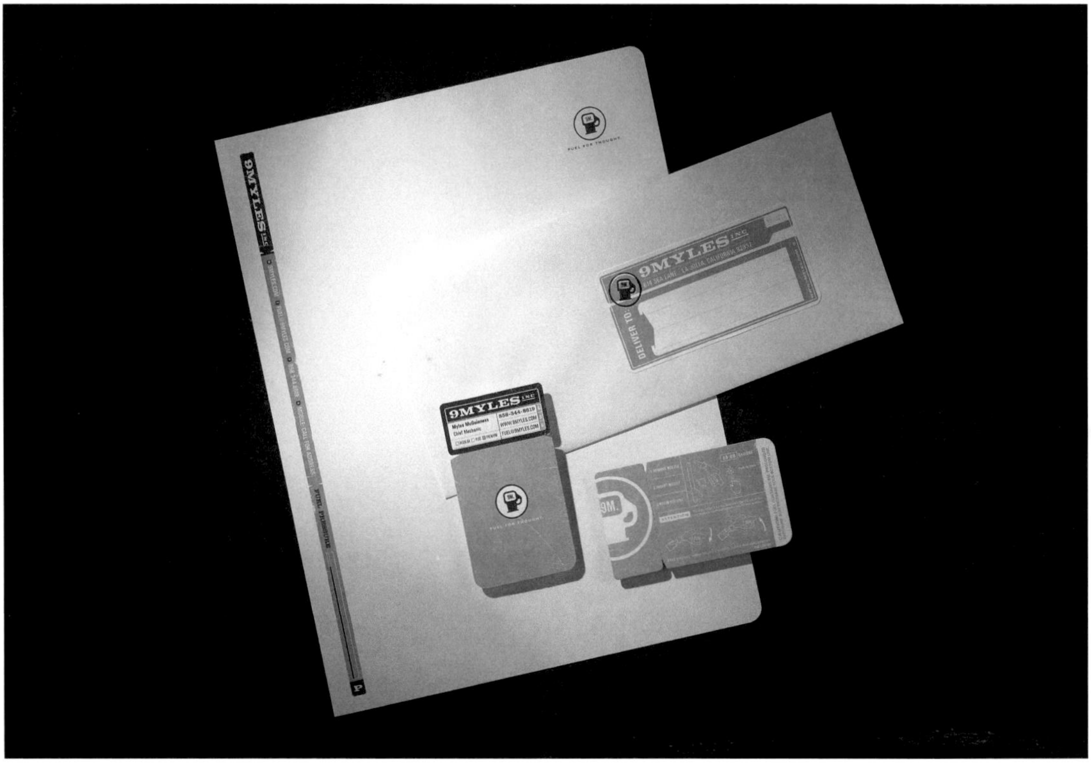

Client 3 Beat Records
Year 2008
Design huvi

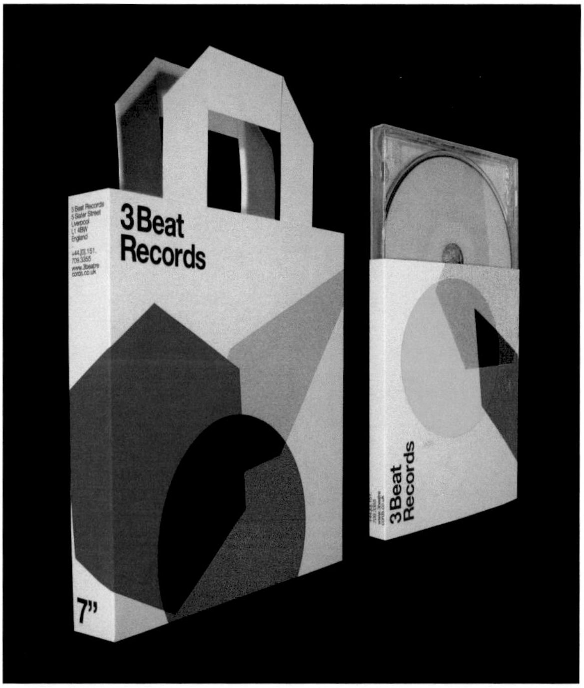

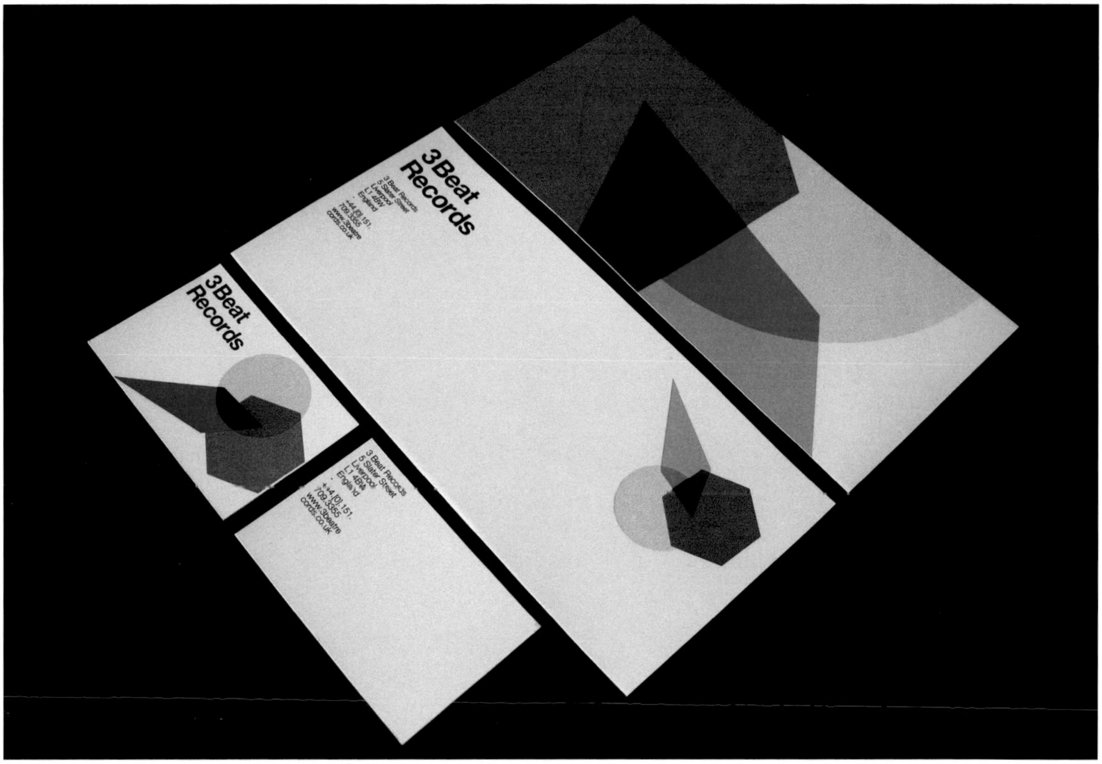

19
19 ENTERTAINMENT LTD
33 Ransomes Dock
35—37 Parkgate Road
London
SW11 4NP
www.19.co.uk

19 ENTERTAINMENT
www.19.co.uk
LONDON
33 Ransomes Dock
35—37 Parkgate Road
SW11 4NP
T +44 (0)20 7801 1919
F +44 (0)20 7801 1920
GMT 0
LOS ANGELES
8560 West Sunset Blvd
CA 90069
T +1 310 7771940
F +1 310 7771949
GMT -8
NEW YORK
595 Madison Avenue
8th Floor, NY 1002
T +1 212 201 0019
F +1 (646) 506 9505
GMT -5
NASHVILLE
GMT -5

Client 19 Entertainment Ltd
Year 2009
Design Zip Design
Team David Bowden

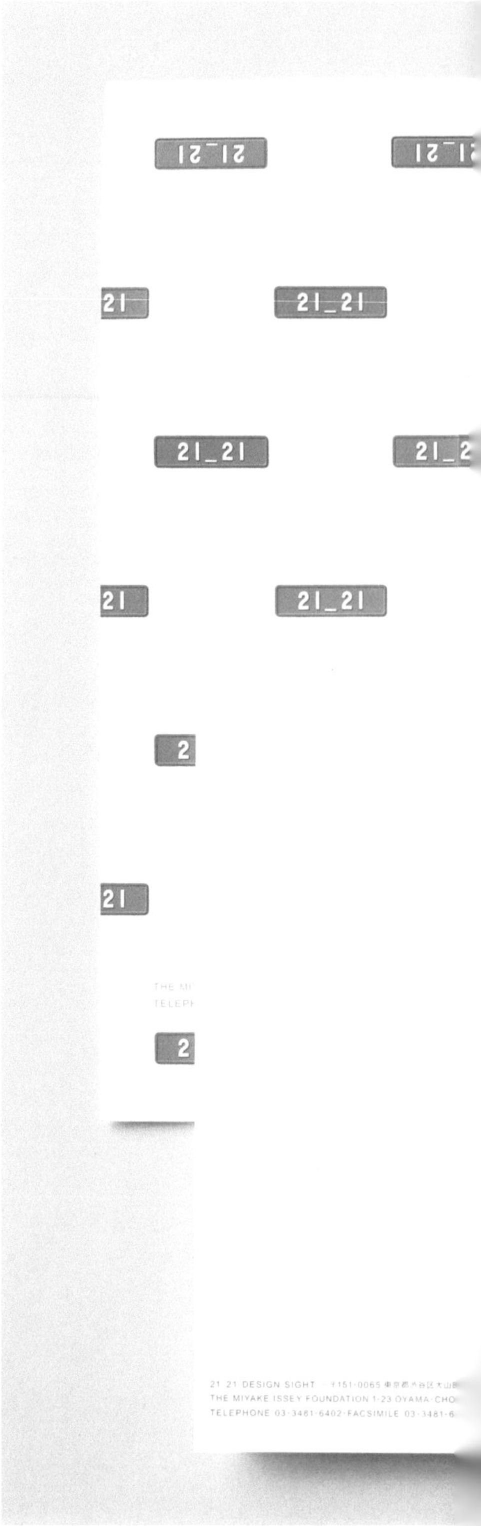

Client 21_21 Design Sight Inc.
Year 2007
Design Taku Satoh

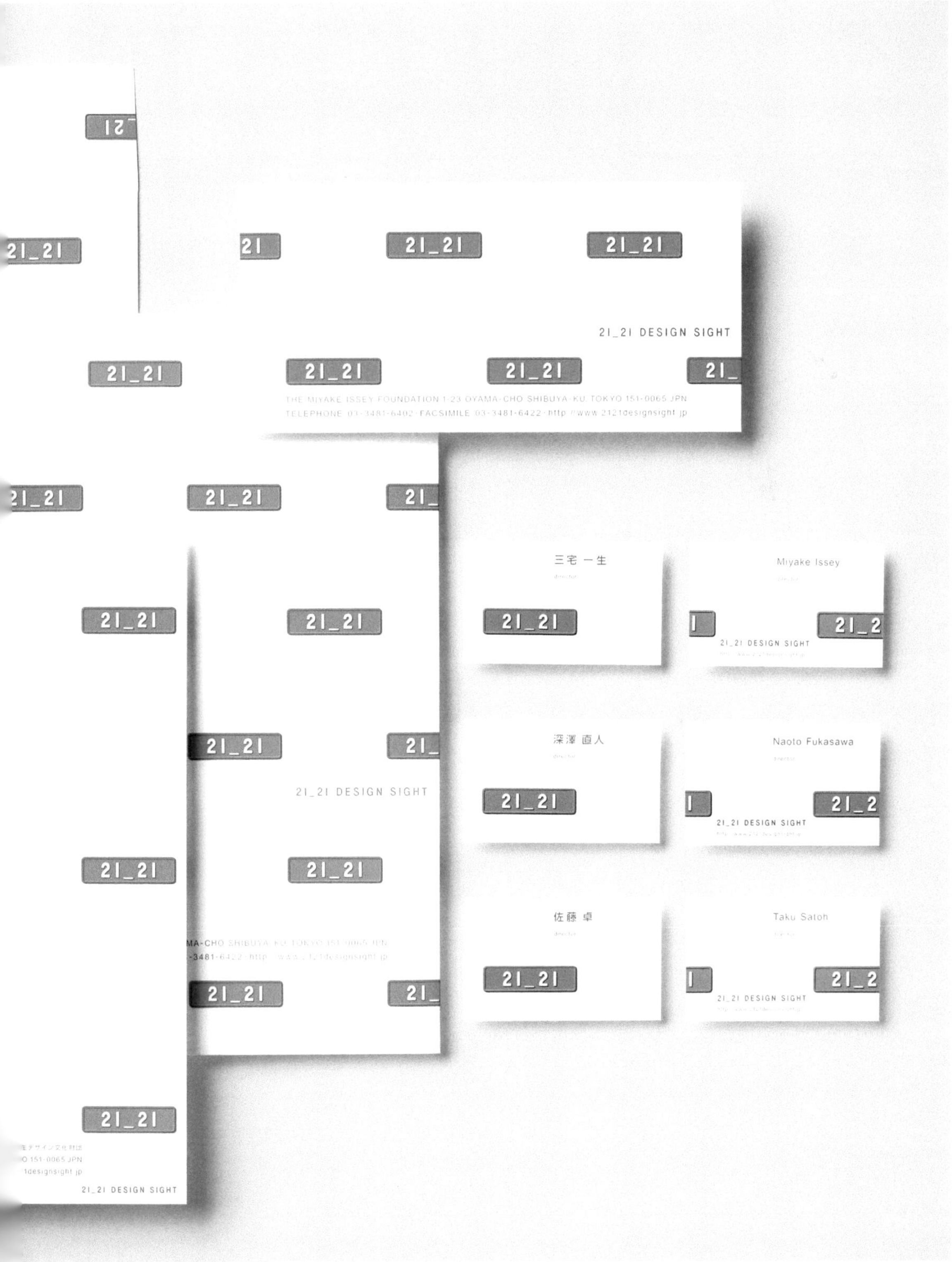
21_21 DESIGN SIGHT
THE MIYAKE ISSEY FOUNDATION 1-23 OYAMA-CHO SHIBUYA-KU TOKYO 151-0065 JPN
TELEPHONE 03-3481-6402 FACSIMILE 03-3481-6422 http://www.2121designsight.jp
三宅 一生
Miyake Issey
深澤 直人
Naoto Fukasawa
佐藤 卓
Taku Satoh

Client	21st Century Museum of Contemporary Art, Kanazawa
Year	2004
Design	Taku Satoh

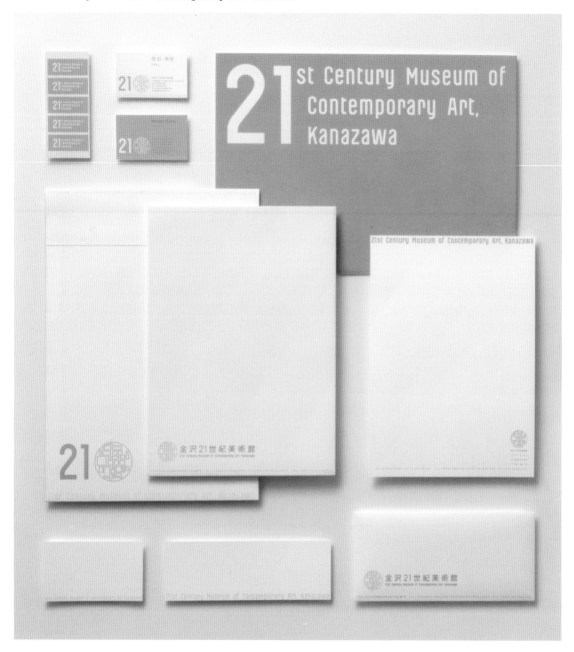

21 st Century Museum of Contemporary Art, Kanazawa
21

Client 52 NORD
Year 2002
Design Superieur Graphique
Team Sven Stüber, Markus Wente, Christina Fiedler

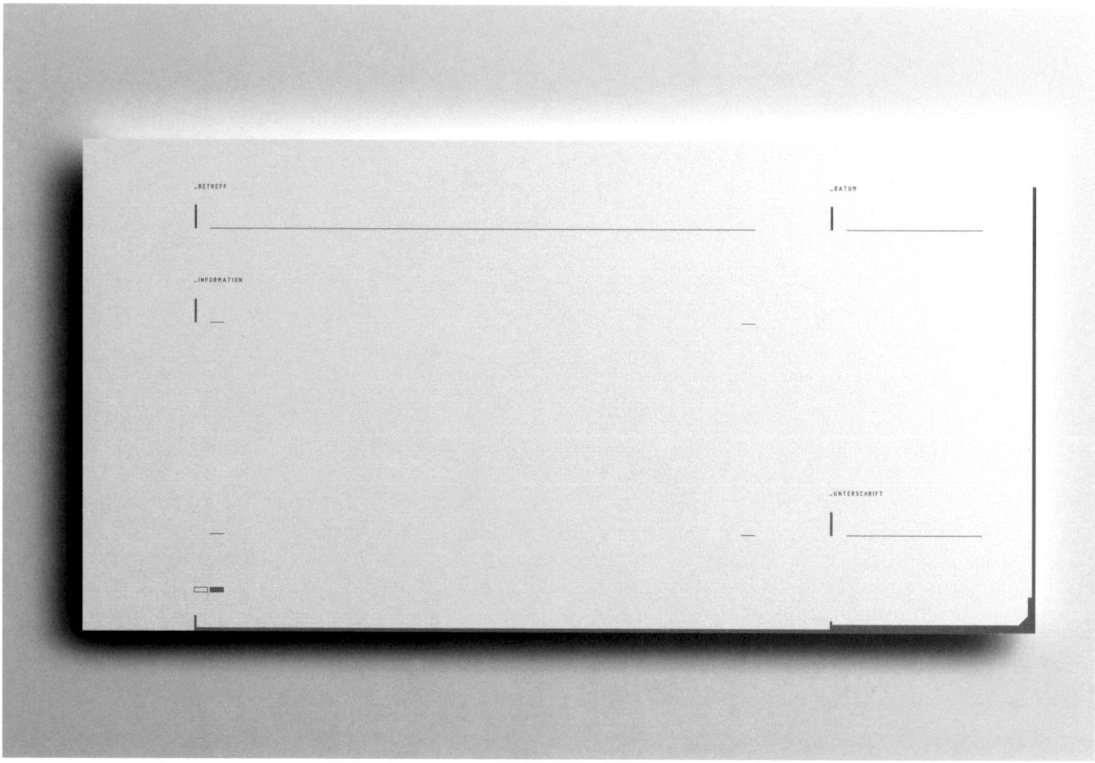

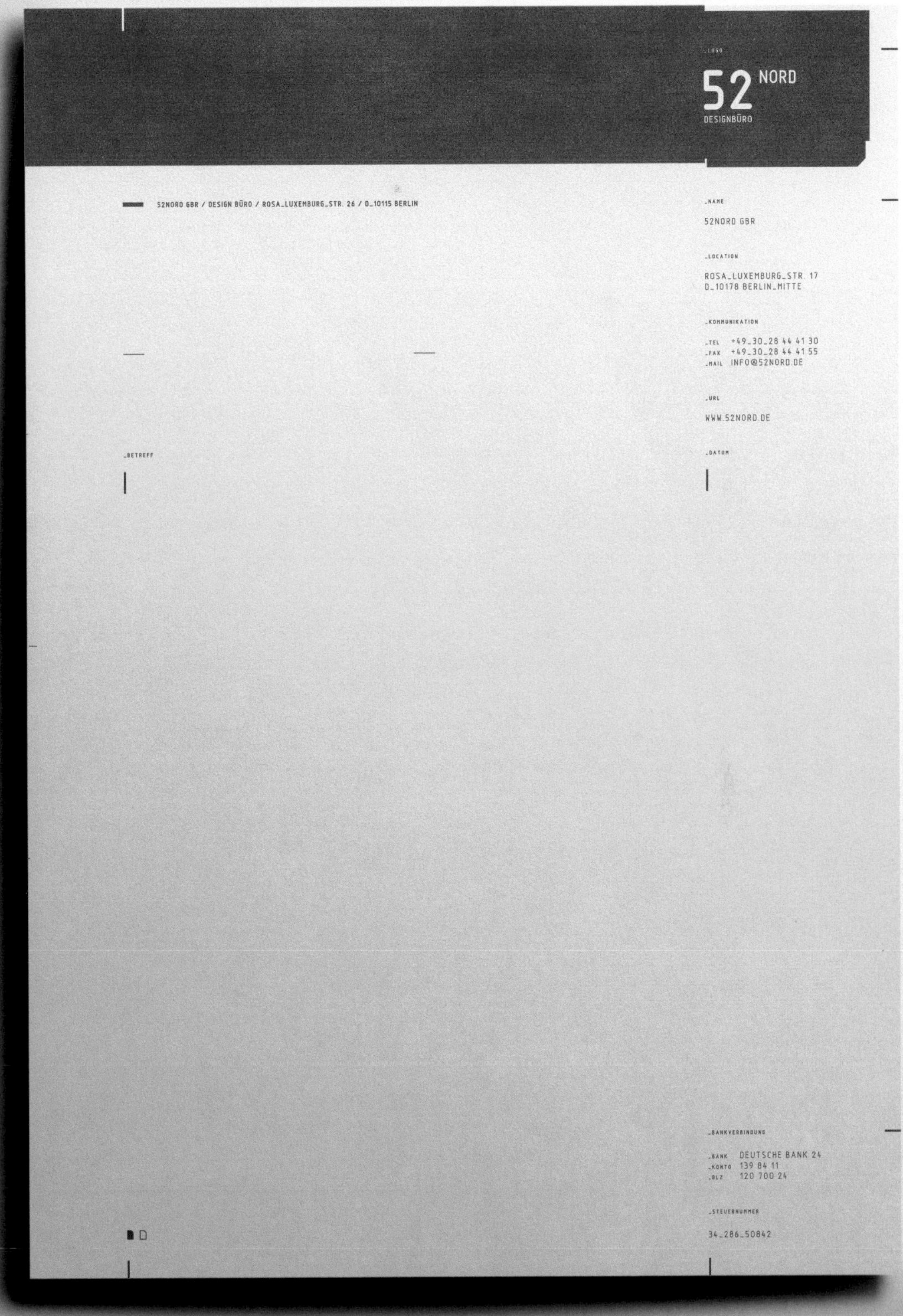
_LOGO
52 NORD
DESIGNBÜRO
52NORD GBR / DESIGN BÜRO / ROSA_LUXEMBURG_STR. 26 / D_10115 BERLIN
_NAME
52NORD GBR
_LOCATION
ROSA_LUXEMBURG_STR. 17
D_10178 BERLIN_MITTE
_KOMMUNIKATION
_TEL +49_30_28 44 41 30
_FAX +49_30_28 44 41 55
_MAIL INFO@52NORD.DE
_URL
WWW.52NORD.DE
_BETREFF
_DATUM
_BANKVERBINDUNG
_BANK DEUTSCHE BANK 24
_KONTO 139 84 11
_BLZ 120 700 24
_STEUERNUMMER
34_286_50842

Client	59 Poincaré
Year	2001
Design	Philippe David

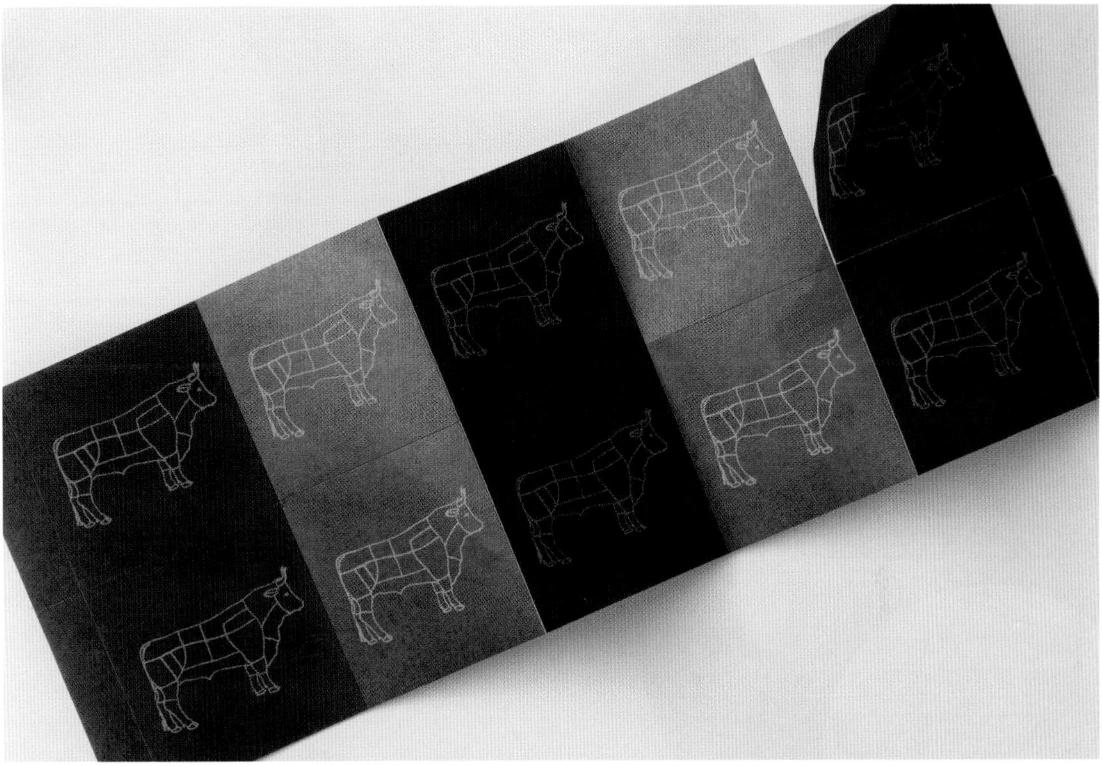

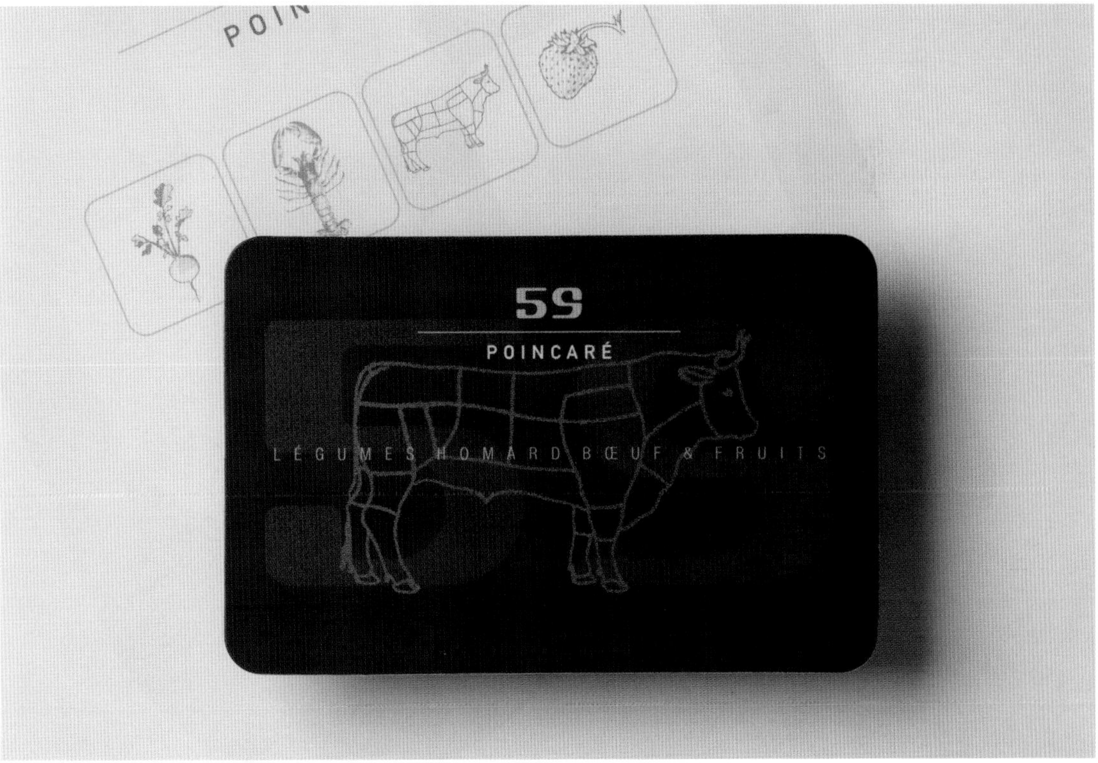
POI
59
POINCARÉ
LÉGUMES HOMARD BŒUF & FRUITS

Achleitner
Achleitner
Achleitner
Achleitner
Achleitner
Achleitner

Client Dr. Achleitner
Steuerberatungsges. m.b.H
Year 2007
Design Transporter Visuelle Logistik

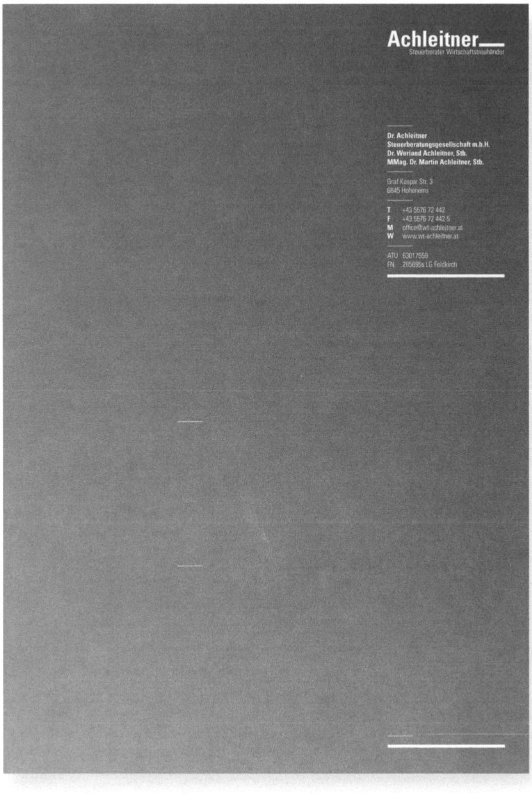

ACHT FRANKFURT
digital solutions
CD
DVD

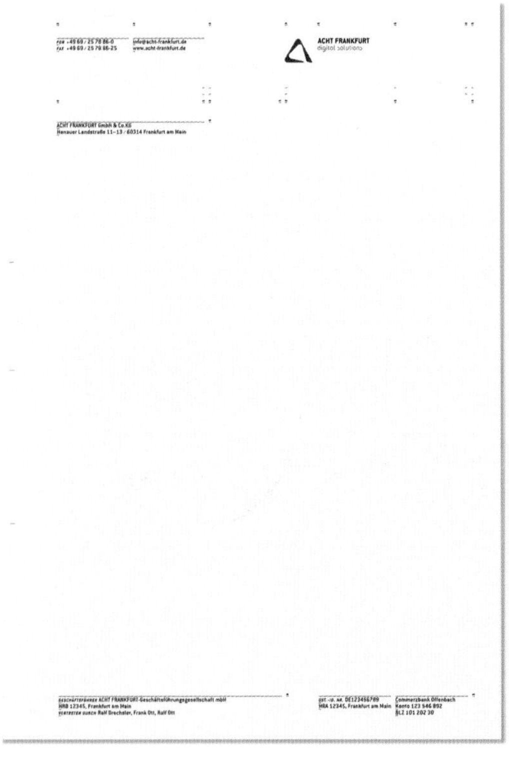
ACHT FRANKFURT
digital solutions

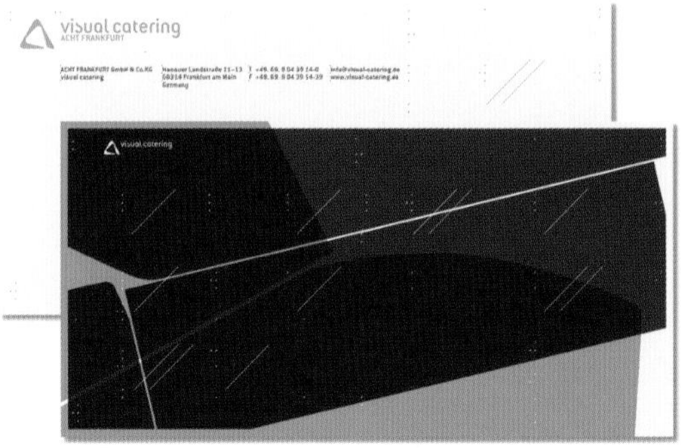
visual catering
ACHT FRANKFURT

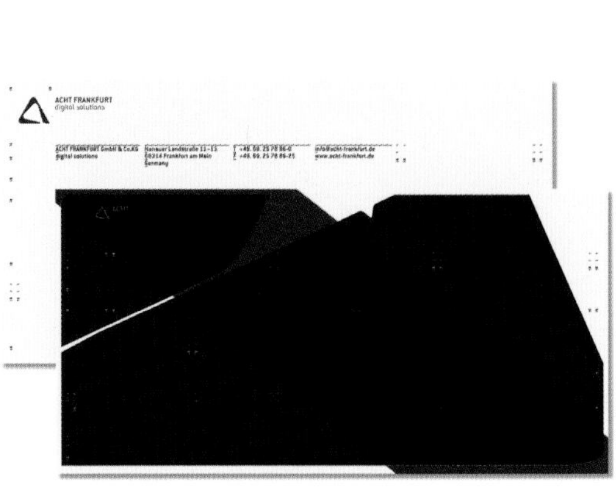
ACHT FRANKFURT
digital solutions

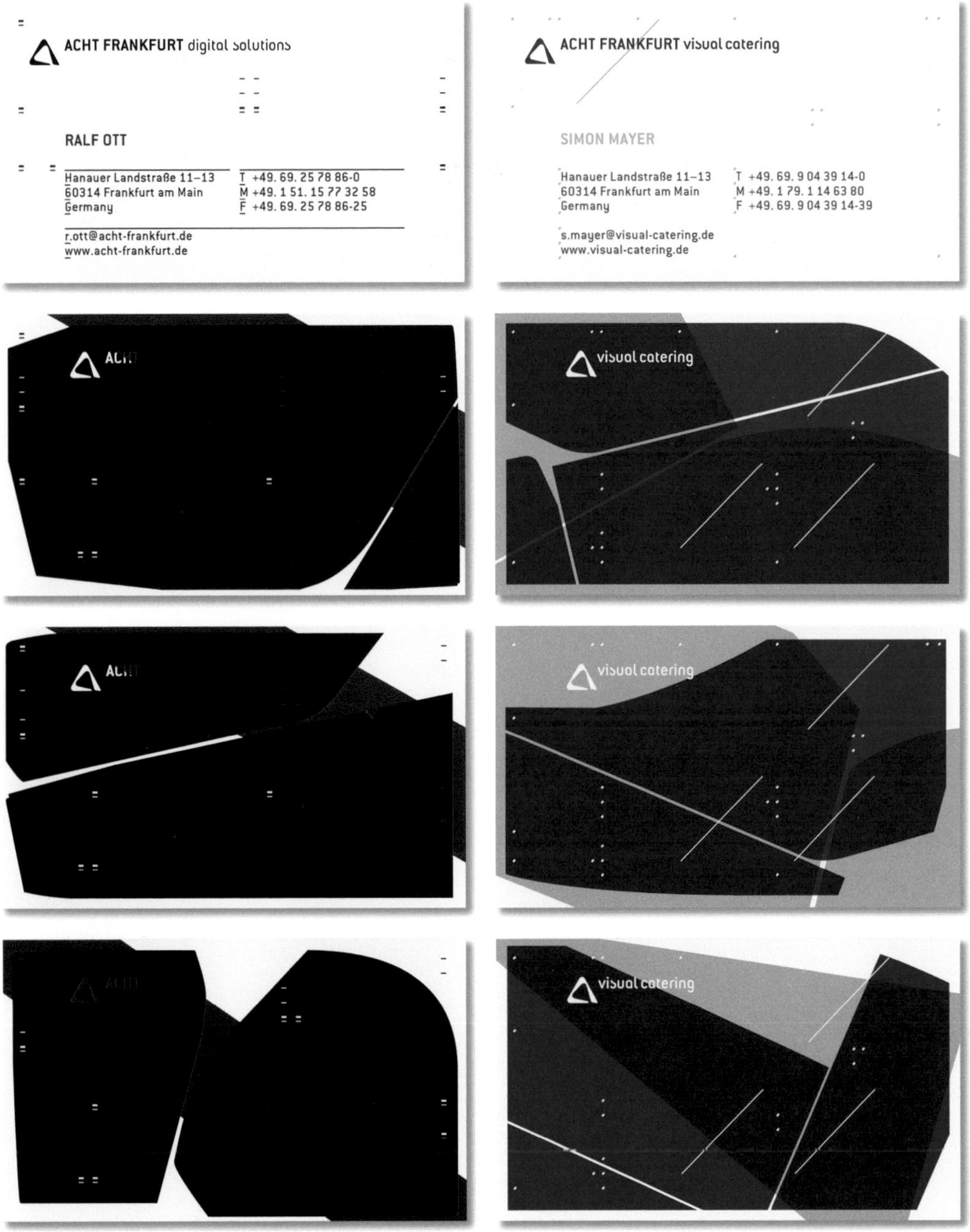

Client Acht Frankfurt
Year 2008
Design Falko Ohlmer

adape
Asociación de Autónomos Administradores
de Pequeñas y Medianas Empresas
adape
Enrique Gallego Navarrete
Cargo en la Empresa
adape
adape
Asociación de Autónomos Administradores de Pequeñas y Medianas Empresas
www.adape.es
adape

Client Adape
Year 2009
Design Ártico Estudio

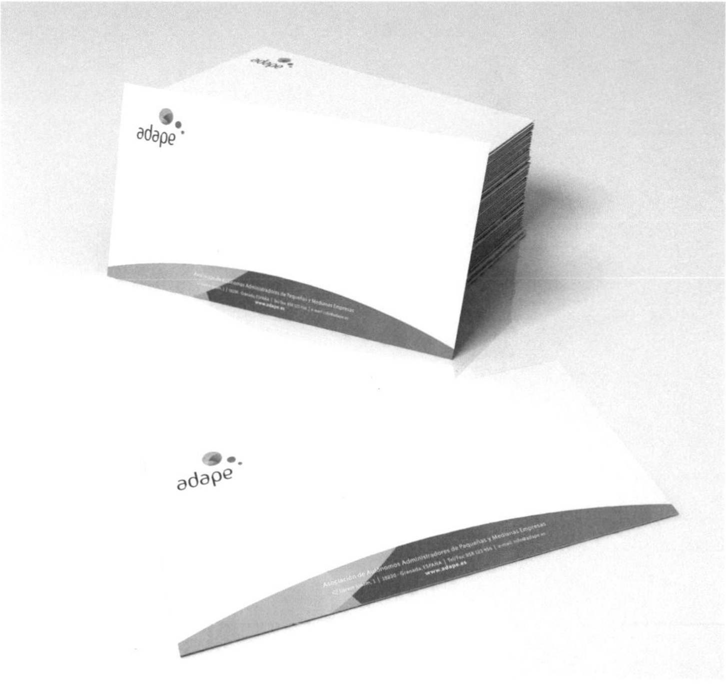

Client	Adoreum Partner
Year	2010
Design	four23

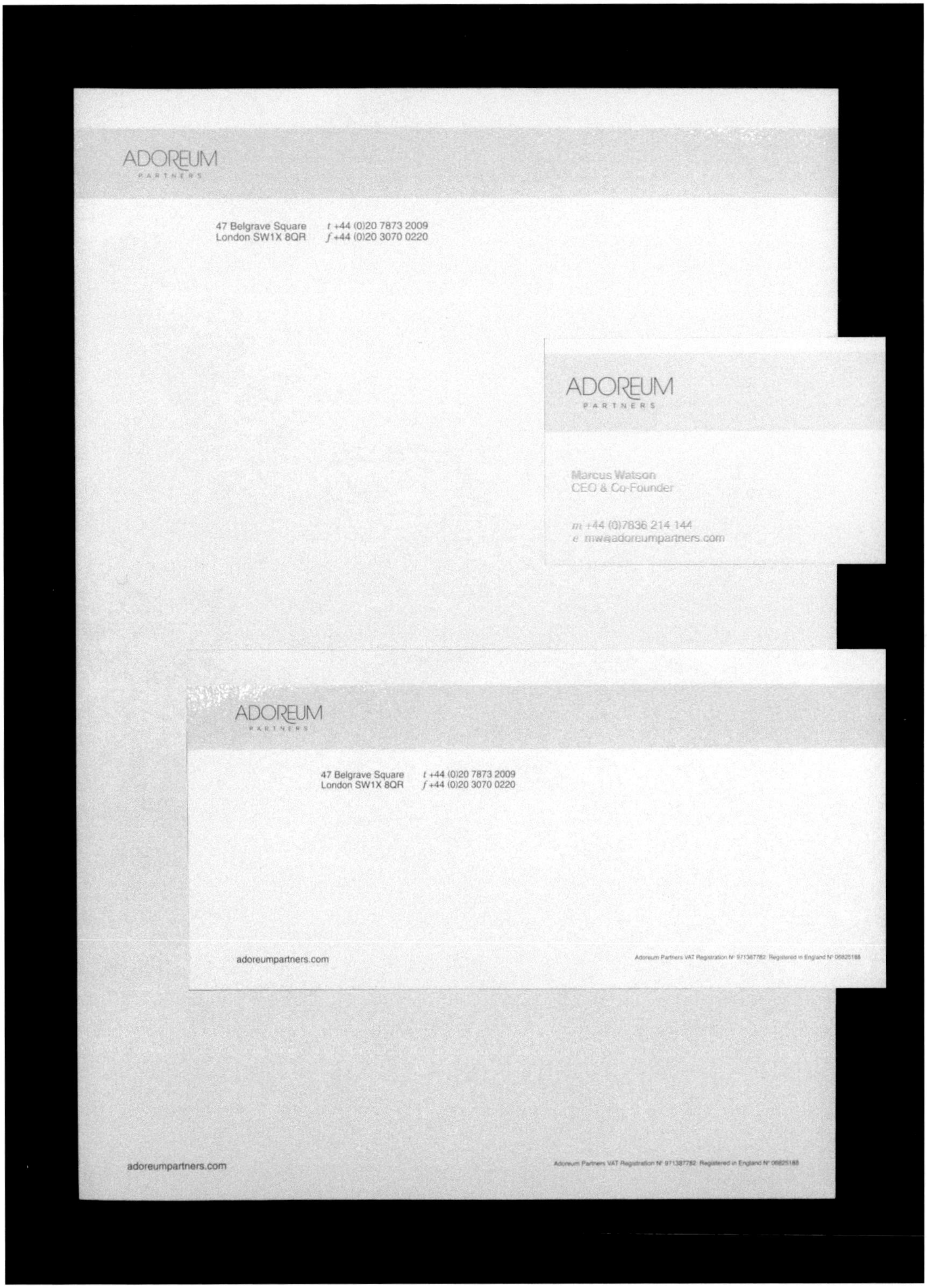
ADOREUM
PARTNERS
47 Belgrave Square
London SW1X 8QR
t +44 (0)20 7873 2009
f +44 (0)20 3070 0220
adoreumpartners.com
Adoreum Partners VAT Registration Nº 971387782 Registered in England Nº 06825188
ADOREUM
PARTNERS
Marcus Watson
CEO & Co-Founder
m +44 (0)7836 214 144
e mw@adoreumpartners.com
ADOREUM
PARTNERS
47 Belgrave Square
London SW1X 8QR
t +44 (0)20 7873 2009
f +44 (0)20 3070 0220
adoreumpartners.com
Adoreum Partners VAT Registration Nº 971387782 Registered in England Nº 06825188

ADP Joinery & Carpentry/Andrew Lodge

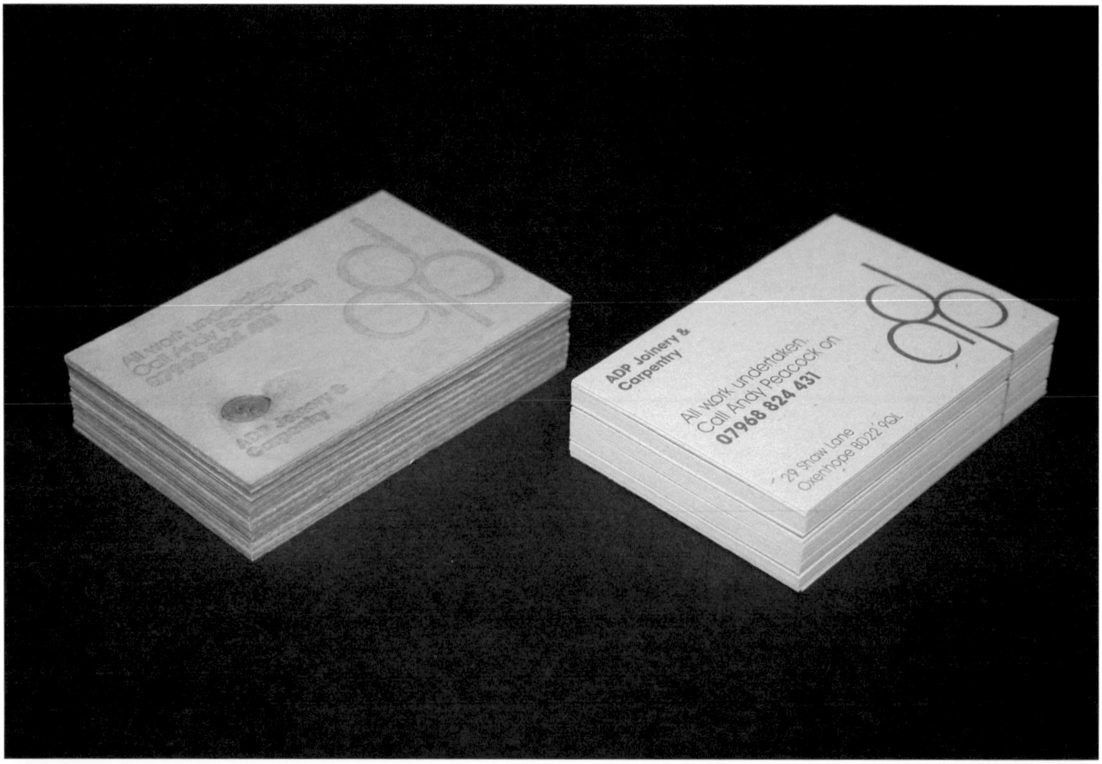

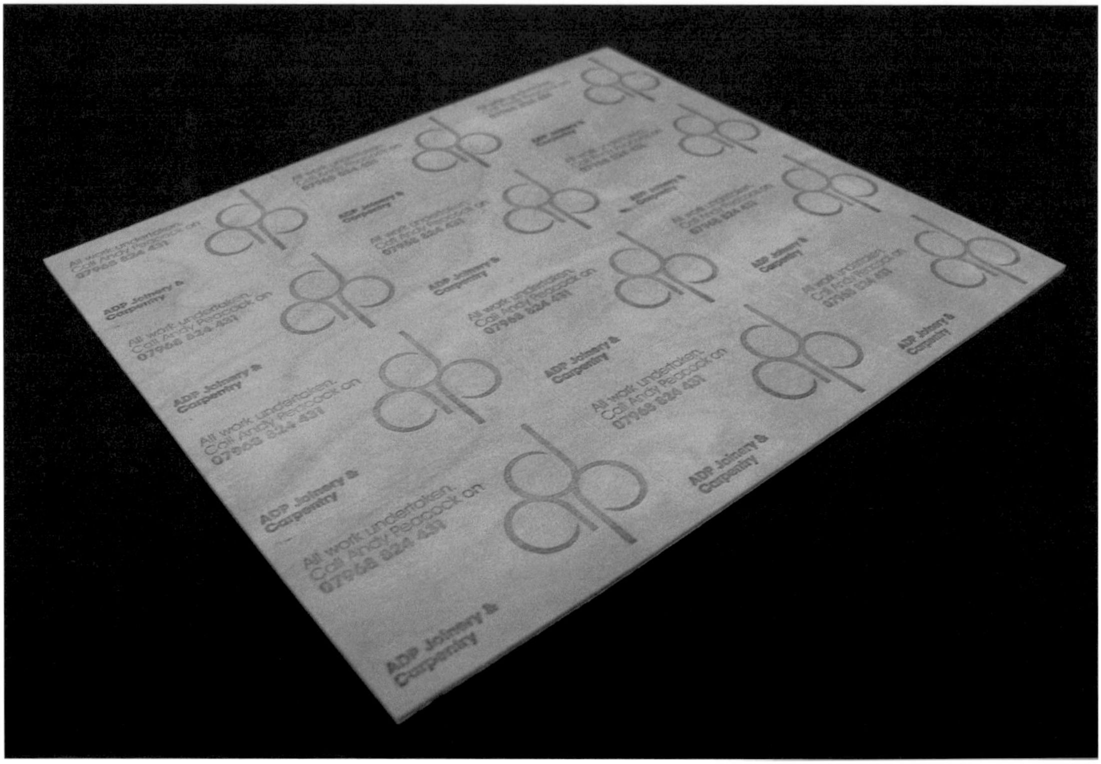

Client ADP Joinery & Carpentry
Year 2008
Design Andrew Lodge

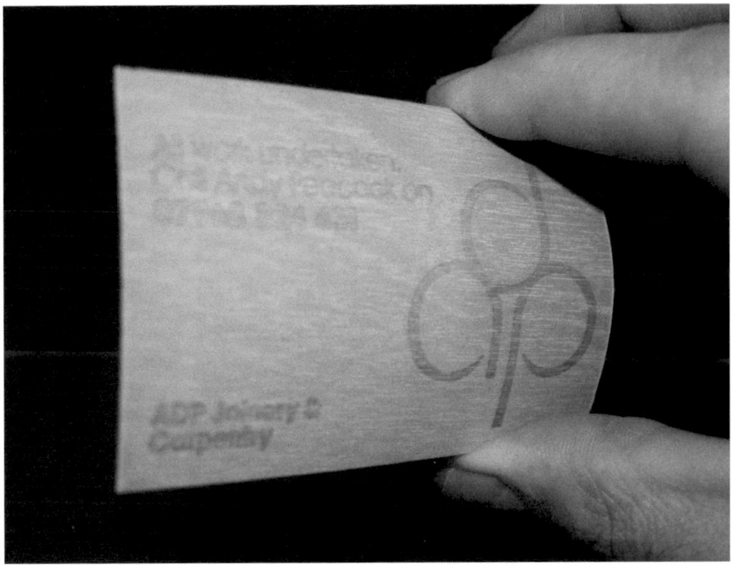

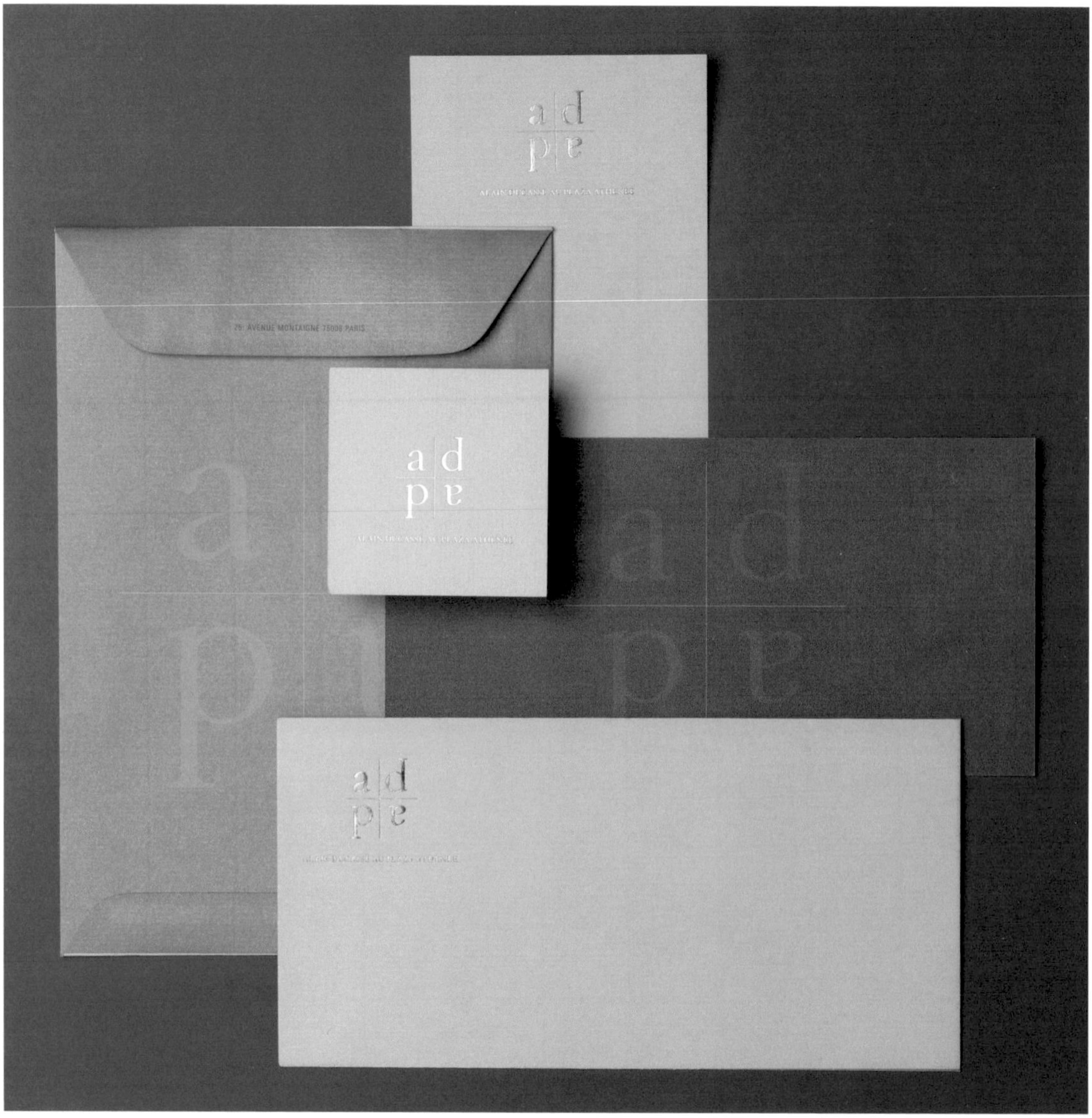

Client adpa
Year 2000
Design Philippe David

25, AVENUE MONTAIGNE 75008 PARIS
a d
p e
ALAIN DUCASSE AU PLAZA ATHÉNÉE

AEROPLANO
DIRECCION
ANDRES FERREYRA 3121
LOCALIDAD
LA LUCILA (B1637AOA)
CIUDAD
BUENOS AIRES
PAIS
ARGENTINA
TELEFONO
54 11 4790 8331
MAIL
EZEQUIEL@AEROPLANOCINE.COM
WEB
WWW.AEROPLANOCINE.COM
CELULAR
54 911 4997 2544
ASISTENTE DE PRODUCCION
EZEQUIEL ROSSI
AEROPLANO

AEROPLANO
DIRECCION
ANDRES FERREYRA 3121
LOCALIDAD
LA LUCILA (B1637AOA)
CIUDAD
BUENOS AIRES
PAIS
ARGENTINA
TELEFONO
54 11 4790 8331
MAIL
EZEQUIEL@AEROPLANOCINE.COM
WEB
WWW.AEROPLANOCINE.COM
BUENOS AIRES
CELULAR
54 911 4997 2544
ASISTENTE DE PRODUCCION
EZEQUIEL ROSSI
AEROPLANO

Client Aeroplano
Year 2006
Design NNSS Visual Universes

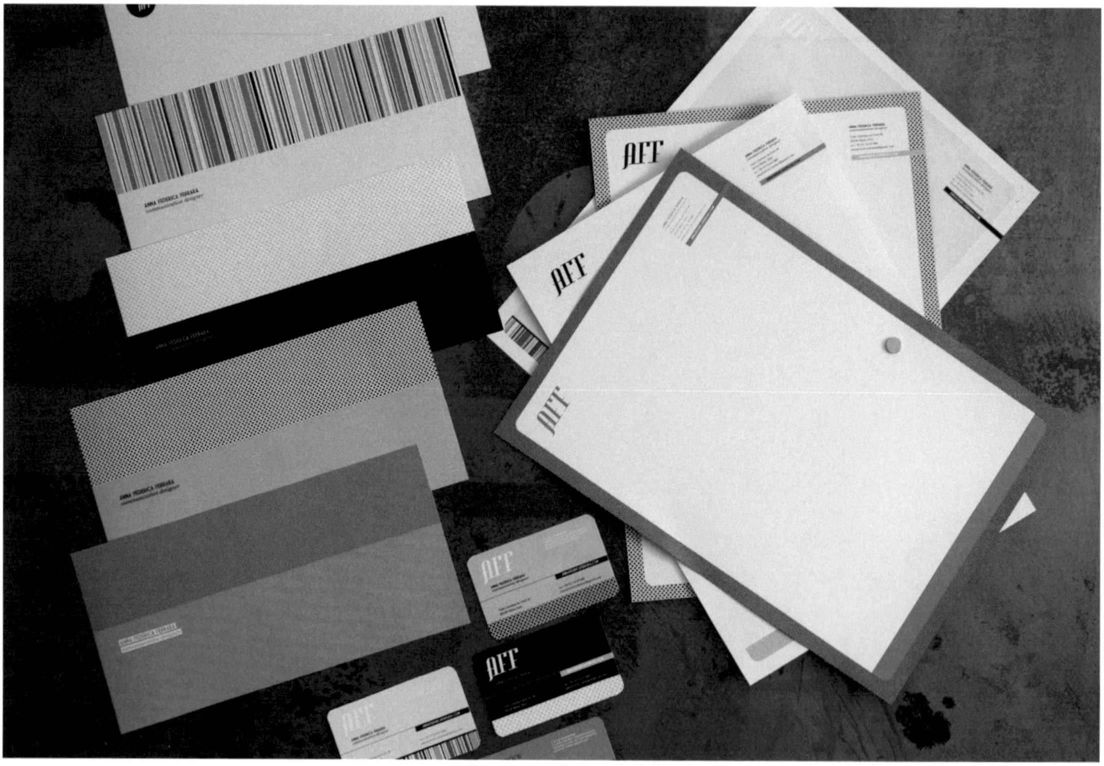

Client AFF Communication Design
Year 2009
Design AFF Communication Design

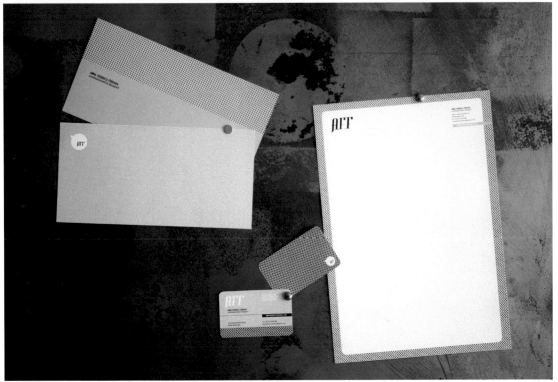

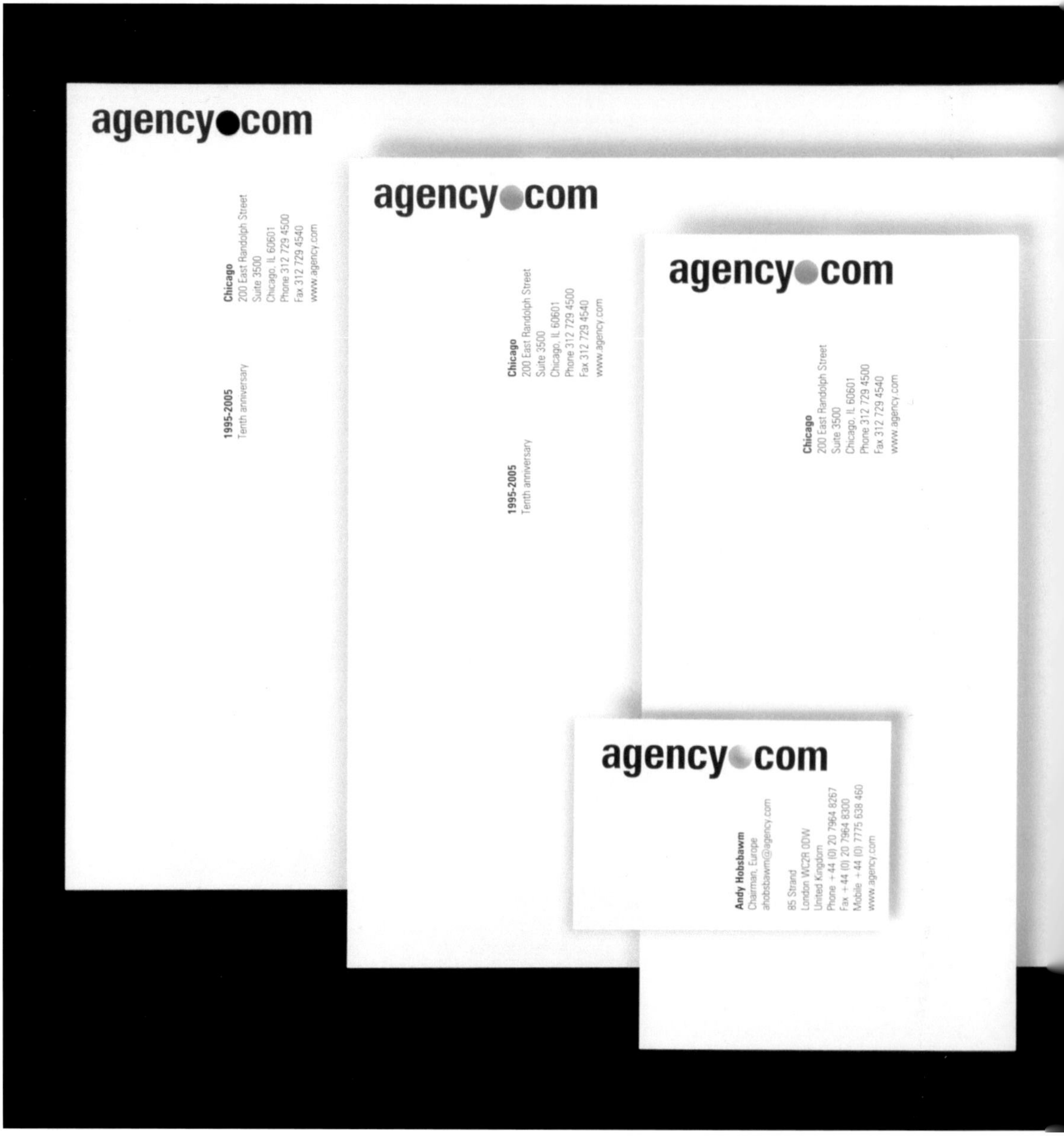
agency.com
Chicago
200 East Randolph Street
Suite 3500
Chicago, IL 60601
Phone 312 729 4500
Fax 312 729 4540
www.agency.com
1995-2005
Tenth anniversary
agency.com
Chicago
200 East Randolph Street
Suite 3500
Chicago, IL 60601
Phone 312 729 4500
Fax 312 729 4540
www.agency.com
1995-2005
Tenth anniversary
agency.com
Chicago
200 East Randolph Street
Suite 3500
Chicago, IL 60601
Phone 312 729 4500
Fax 312 729 4540
www.agency.com
agency.com
Andy Hobsbawm
Chairman, Europe
ahobsbawm@agency.com
85 Strand
London WC2R 0DW
United Kingdom
Phone +44 (0) 20 7964 8267
Fax +44 (0) 20 7964 8300
Mobile +44 (0) 7775 638 460
www.agency.com

Client Agency.com
Year 2007
Design Pentagram
Team Pentagram Design London

Client Altafilms
Year 2007
Design Barfutura

Client amb/ar
Year 2010
Design COPO Design
Team Diego Orta Zamora

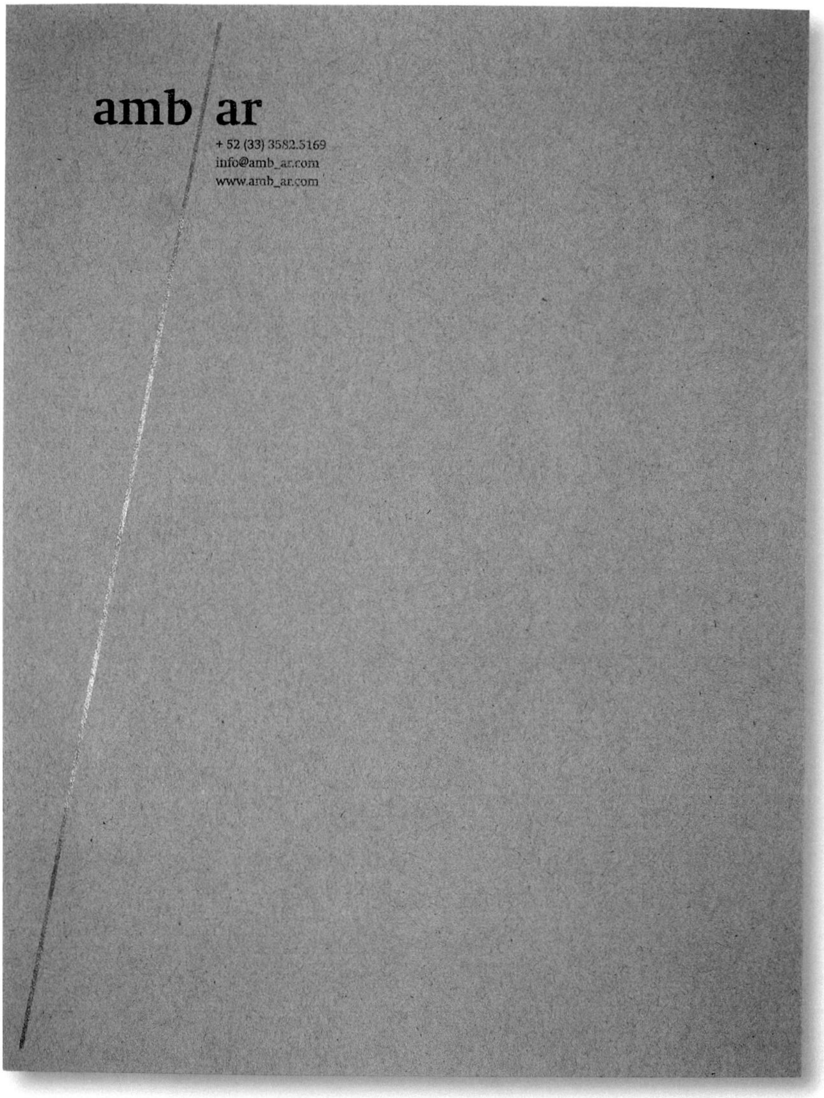

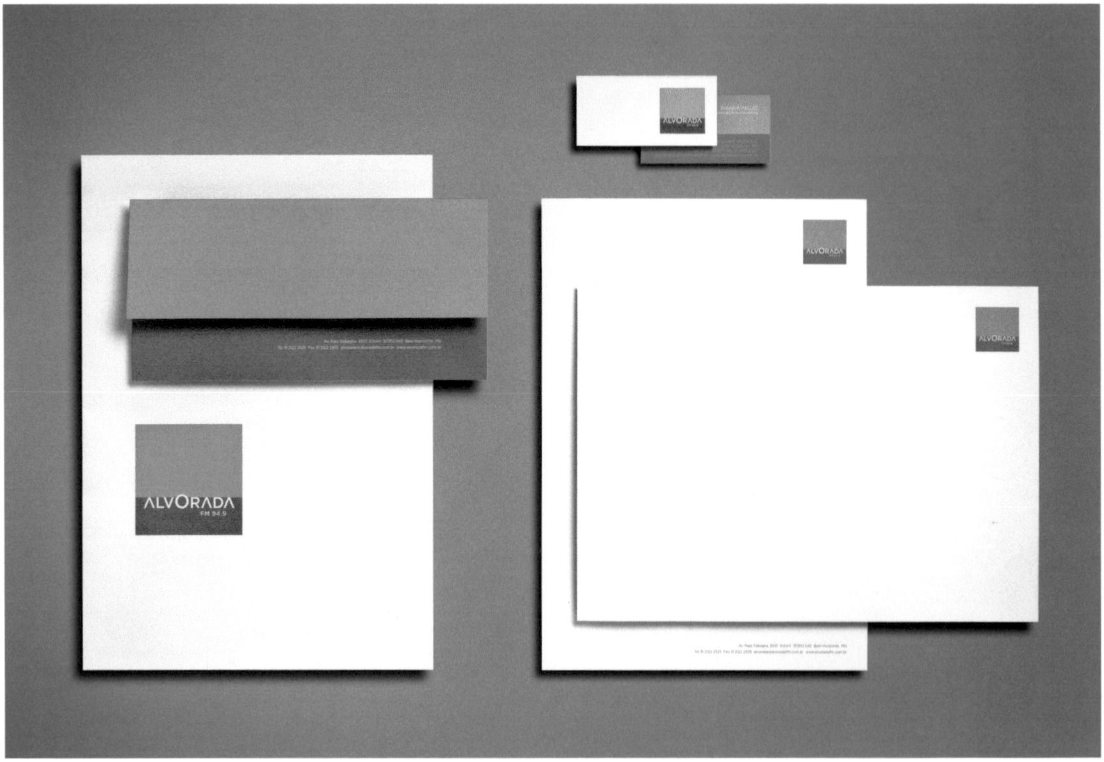
ALVORADA
FM 94.9

Av. Raja Gabaglia, 3100 Estoril 30350.540 Belo Horizonte MG
Tel 31 2122 2525 Fax 31 2122 2555 alvorada@alvoradafm.com.br www.alvoradafm.com.br

ALVORADA

Client Alvorada
Year 2008
Design Hardy Design

Client Amodesign
Year 2004
Design Amodesign
Team Bruno Galrito

amodesign.net
amodesign
amodesign
amodesign

Amped

Client Amped
Year 2008
Design huvi

Amped
7"

Amped
24 Lanton Street
Stockport, Cheshire
SK3 7JK
0161 578 3833
www.amped.co.uk

Amped
24 Lanton Street
Stockport, Cheshire
SK3 7JK
0161 578 3833
www.amped.co.uk

Anthill/Kollor Design Agency

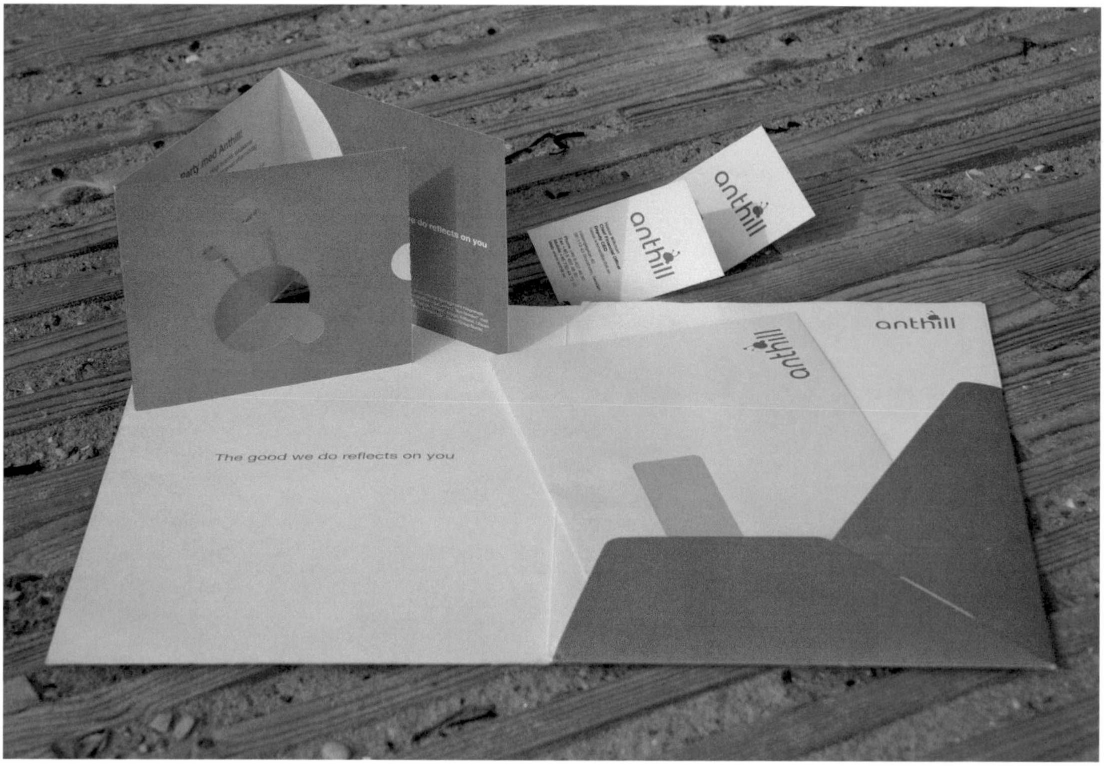
anthill
The good we do reflects on you

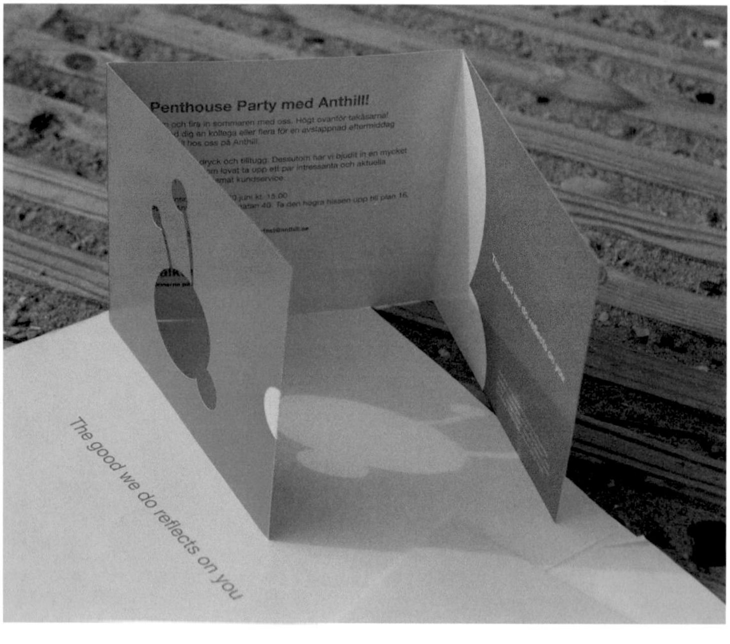
Penthouse Party med Anthill!
The good we do reflects on you

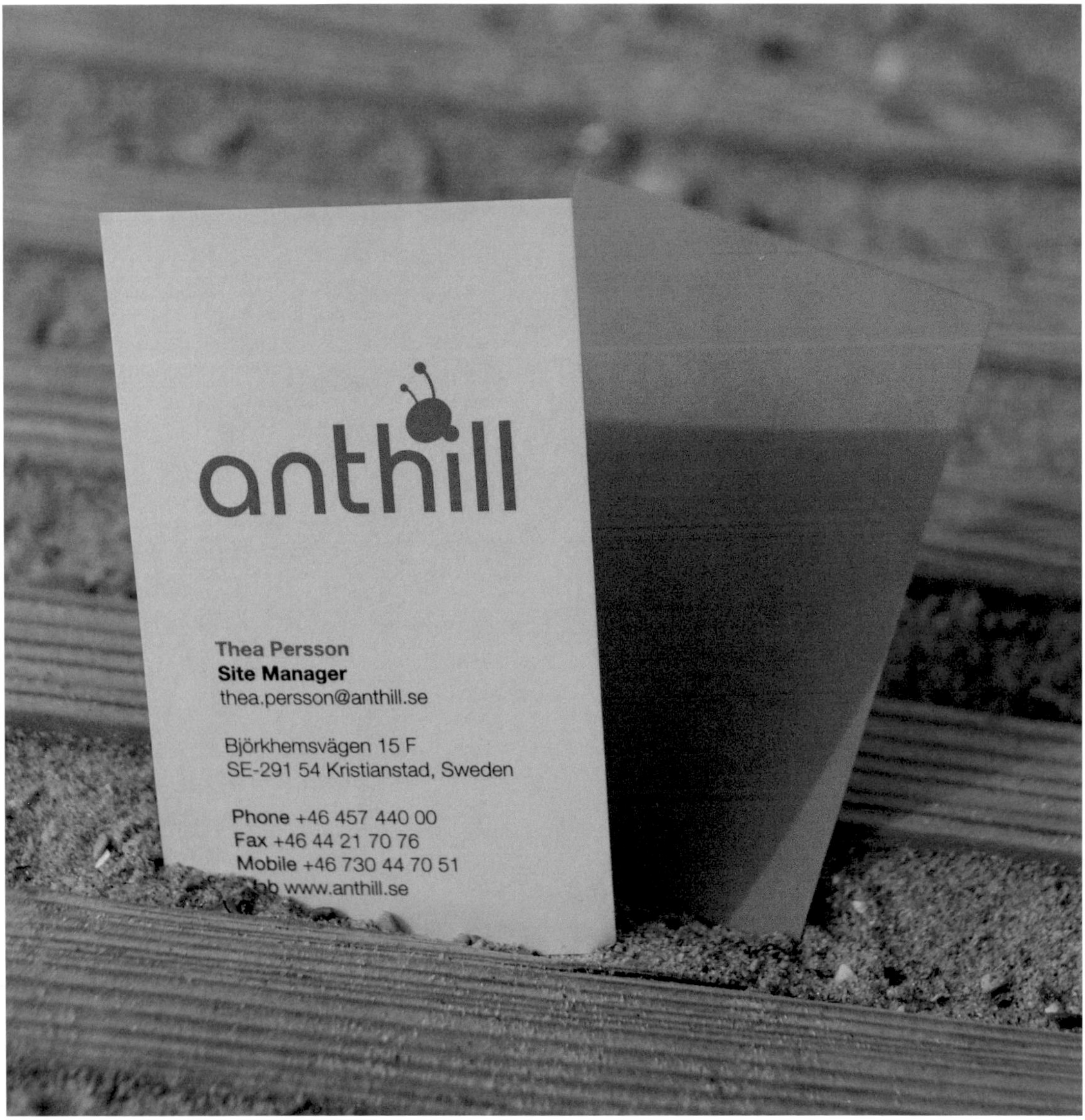

Client Anthill
Year 2007
Design Kollor Design Agency

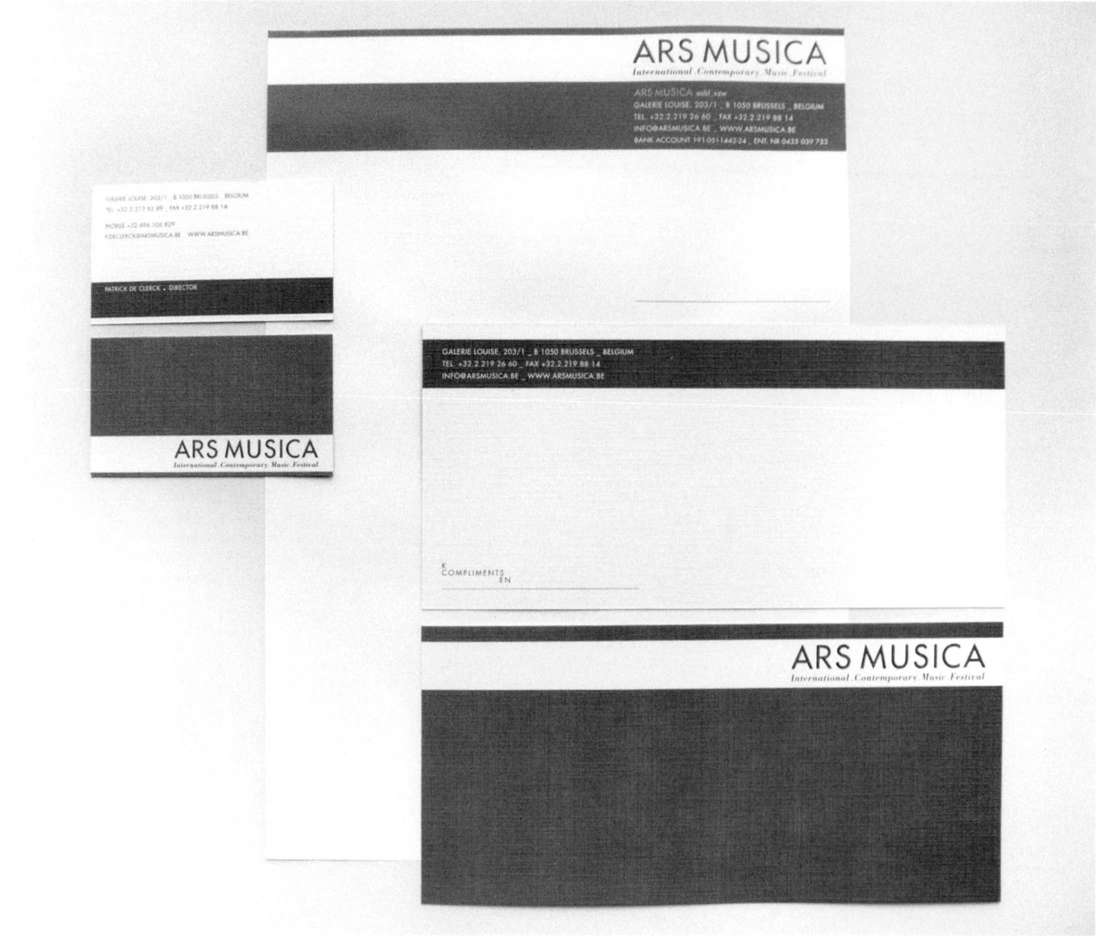

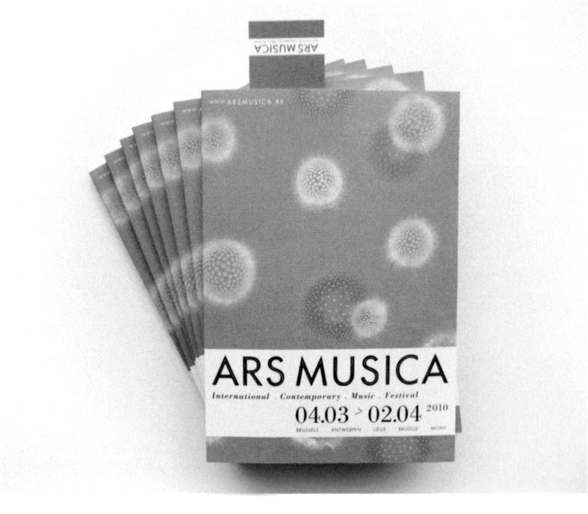

Client ArsMusica
Year 2010
Design Sign*
Team Franck Sarfati, Cédric Aubrion

ARS MUSICA

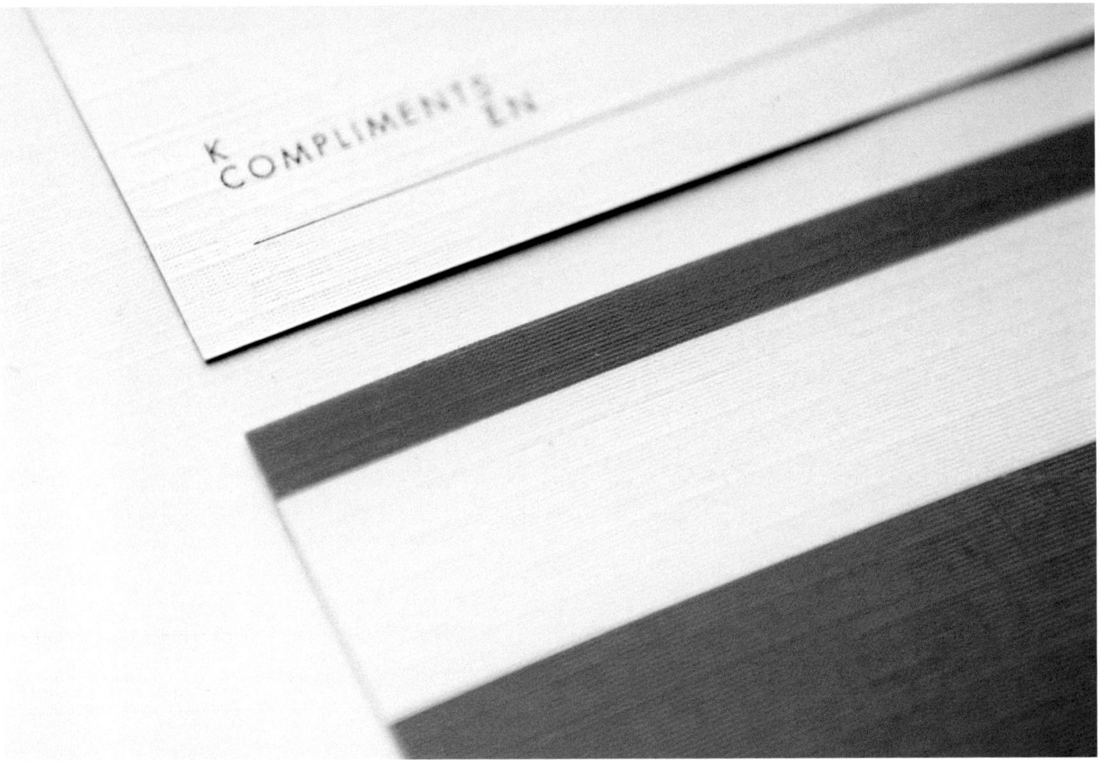
COMPLIMENTS

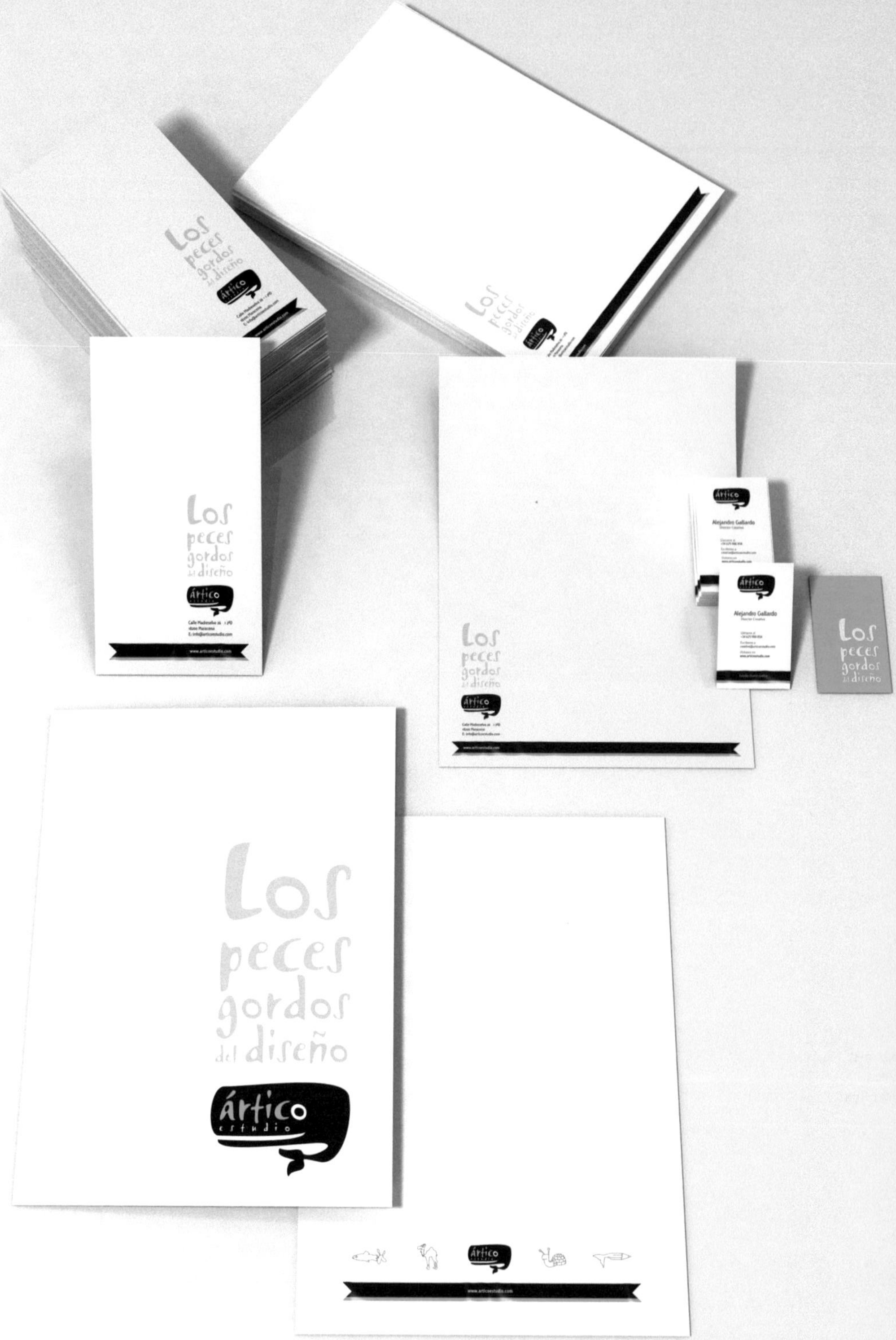
Los peces gordos del diseño
ártico estudio

Client Ártico Estudio
Year 2009
Design Ártico Estudio

Client Assistair
Year 2008
Design Jose Palma Visual Works

ASSISTAIRGROUP
ASSISTAIR
FLIGHT SUPPORT
ASSISTAIR
BUSINESS AVIATION HANDLING SINCE 1988
Catherine Gaisenband
CEO
HEAD OFFICE
Edificio Naves Blancas
Vial 4, Oficinas 55-56
07610 Palma de Mallorca · Spain
T +34 971 720 591
F +34 971 425 100
www.assistair.net
Sita PMIDCCR
Nice to meet you.
Luc Marchenay
QUALITY CONTROL & COMMERCIAL DEPARTMENT
HEAD OFFICE
Edificio Naves Blancas
Vial 4, Oficinas 55-56
07610 Palma de Mallorca · Spain
T +34 971 720 591
F +34 971 425 100
www.assistair.net
Sita PMIDCCR
Nice to meet you.
David Vallve
FBO DIRECTOR / STATION MANAGER BARCELONA
dvallve@assistair.net
BARCELONA AIRPORT
General Aviation Terminal
Aeropuerto del Prat · 08820
Barcelona · Spain
T +34 932983337
F +34 932983317
www.assistair.net
Sita BCNACCR
Vhf: 130,65 Mhz
Nice to meet you.
Aeropuerto de Manises
46940 Valencia · Spain
T +34 961598392 F+ 34 961598393
vlcairport@assistair.net
Sita: VLCACCR · Vhf: 131,85 Mhz
07610 Palma de Mallorca · Spain
T +34 971789423 F +34 971789427
pmiairport@assistair.net
Sita: PMIACCR · Vhf: 131,85 Mhz
T +34 932983337 F +34 932983317
bcnairport@assistair.net
Sita: BCNACCR · Vhf: 130,65 Mhz

Atomium/Sign*

Client Atomium
Year 2008
Design Sign*
Team Franck Sarfati

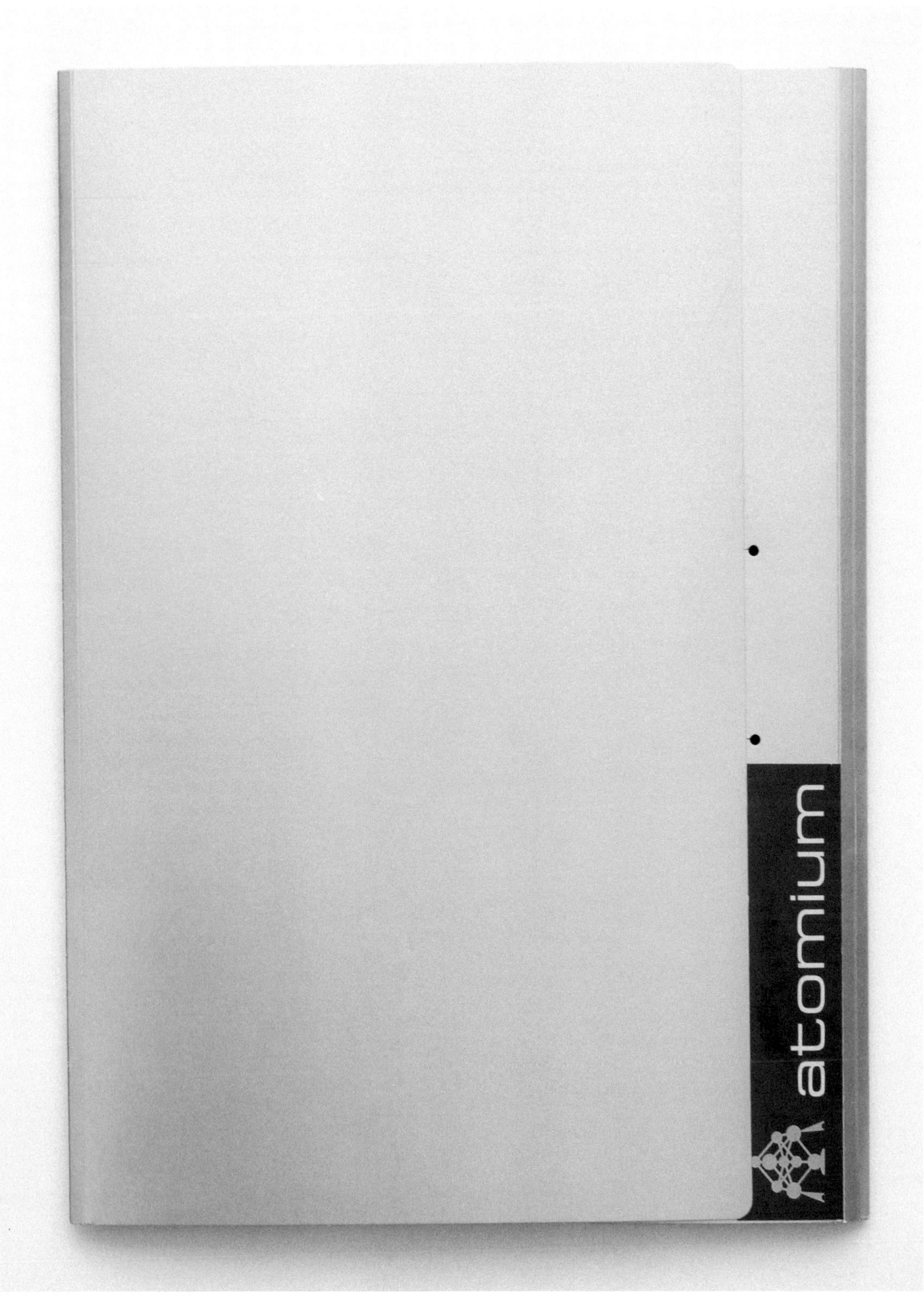
atomium

awards.cine.
Villanueva 1175. C1426 BME.
Bs As. Argentina.
Tel. (5411) 4778-3700.
www.awardscine.com

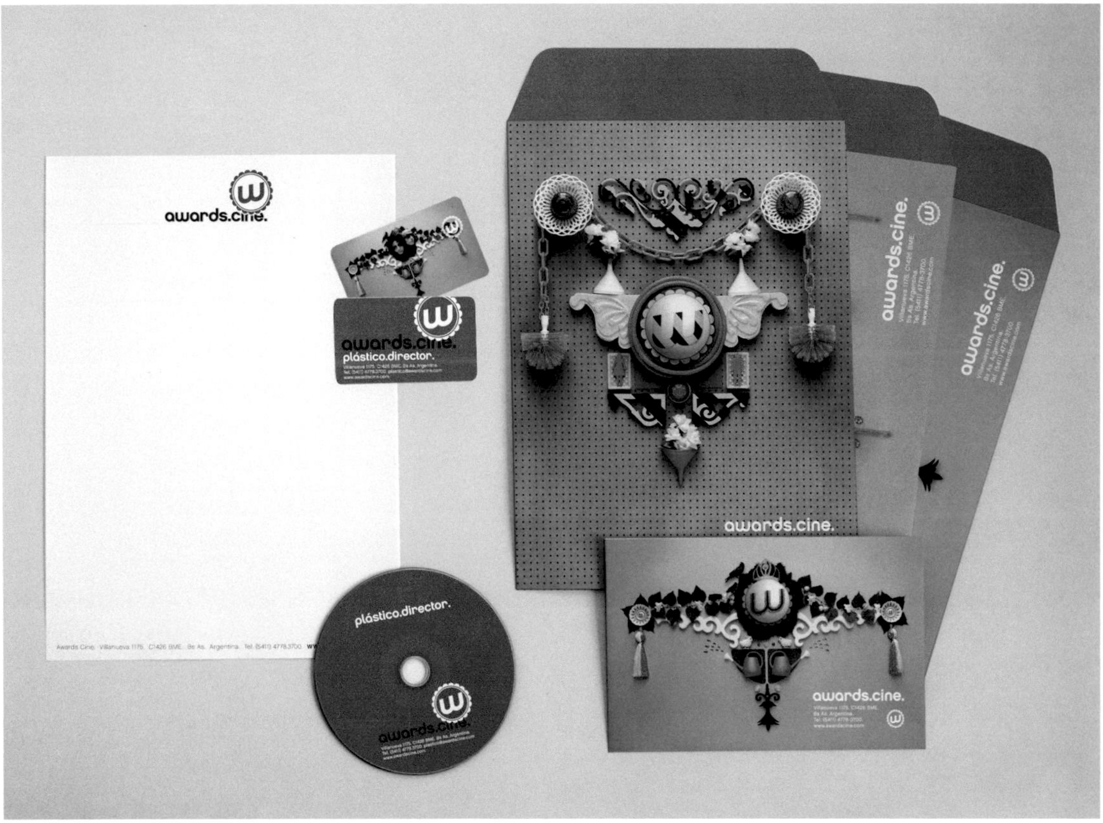

Client Awards Cine
Year 2008
Design CINCO

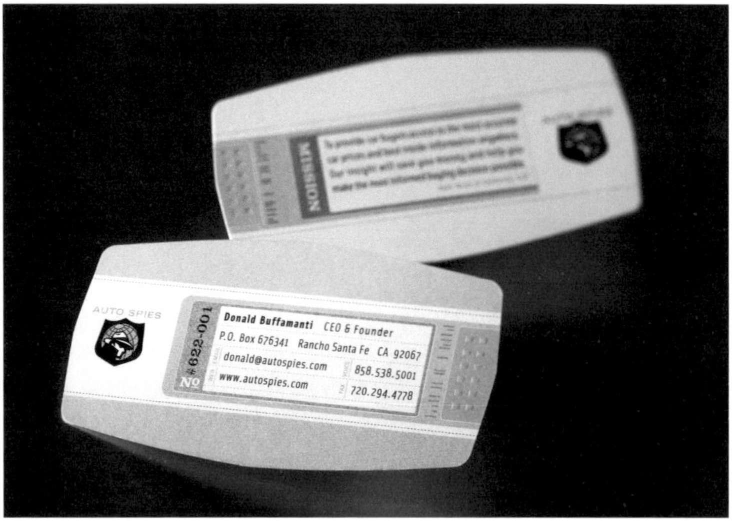

Client	Auto Spies
Year	2005
Design	9MYLES

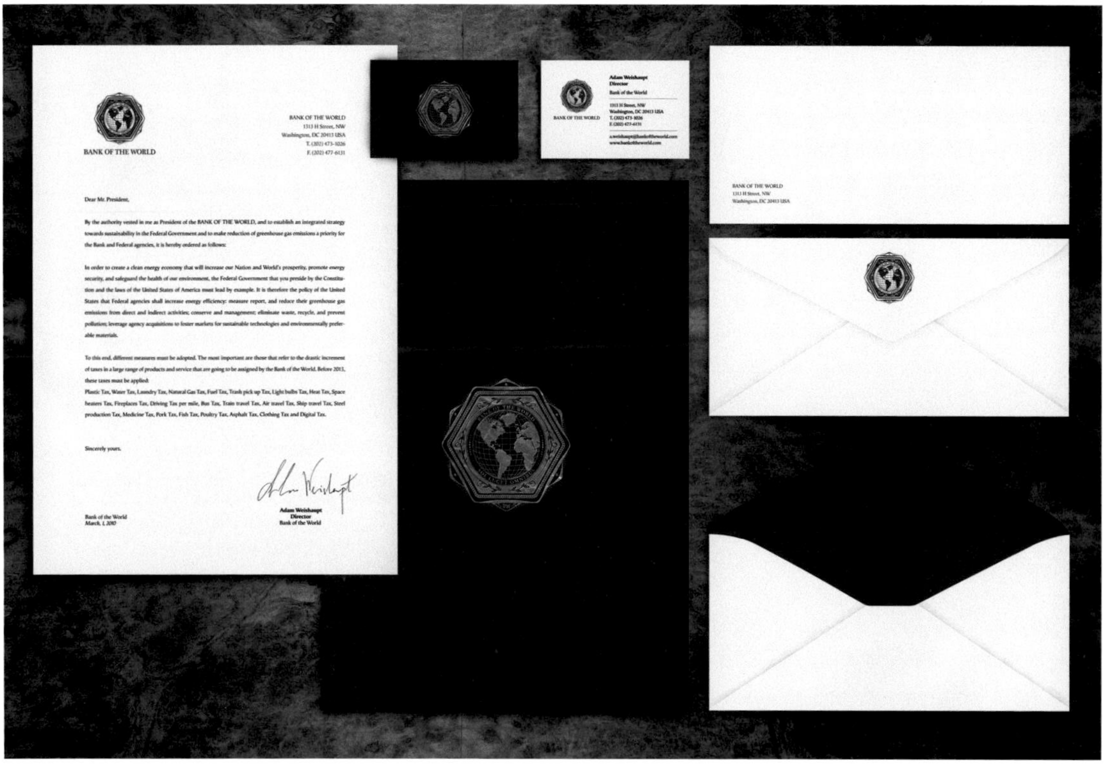
BANK OF THE WORLD
BANK OF THE WORLD
1313 H Street, NW
Washington, DC 20413 USA
T. (202) 473-1026
F. (202) 477-6131
Dear Mr. President,
By the authority vested in me as President of the BANK OF THE WORLD, and to establish an integrated strategy towards sustainability in the Federal Government and to make reduction of greenhouse gas emissions a priority for the Bank and Federal agencies, it is hereby ordered as follows:
In order to create a clean energy economy that will increase our Nation and World's prosperity, promote energy security, and safeguard the health of our environment, the Federal Government that you preside by the Constitution and the laws of the United States of America must lead by example. It is therefore the policy of the United States that Federal agencies shall increase energy efficiency: measure report, and reduce their greenhouse gas emissions from direct and indirect activities; conserve and management; eliminate waste, recycle, and prevent pollution; leverage agency acquisitions to foster markets for sustainable technologies and environmentally preferable materials.
To this end, different measures must be adopted. The most important are those that refer to the drastic increment of taxes in a large range of products and service that are going to be assigned by the Bank of the World. Before 2013, these taxes must be applied:
Plastic Tax, Water Tax, Laundry Tax, Natural Gas Tax, Fuel Tax, Trash pick up Tax, Light bulbs Tax, Heat Tax, Space heaters Tax, Fireplaces Tax, Driving Tax per mile, Bus Tax, Train travel Tax, Air travel Tax, Ship travel Tax, Steel production Tax, Medicine Tax, Pork Tax, Fish Tax, Poultry Tax, Asphalt Tax, Clothing Tax and Digital Tax.
Sincerely yours,
Bank of the World
March, 1, 2010
Adam Weishaupt
Director
Bank of the World
Adam Weishaupt
Director
Bank of the World
1313 H Street, NW
Washington, DC 20413 USA
BANK OF THE WORLD
1313 H Street, NW
Washington, DC 20413 USA

Client Bank of the World
Year 2010
Design Nomade

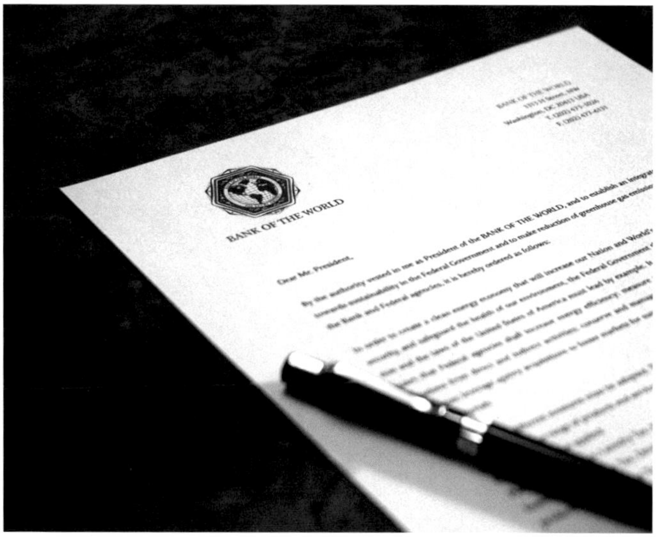
BANK OF THE WORLD
Dear Mr. President,

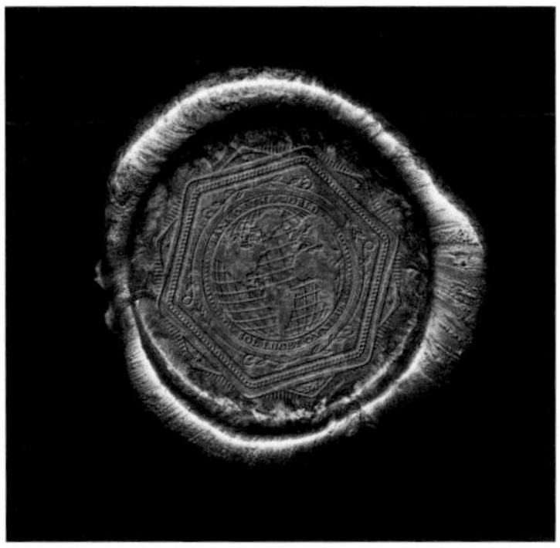

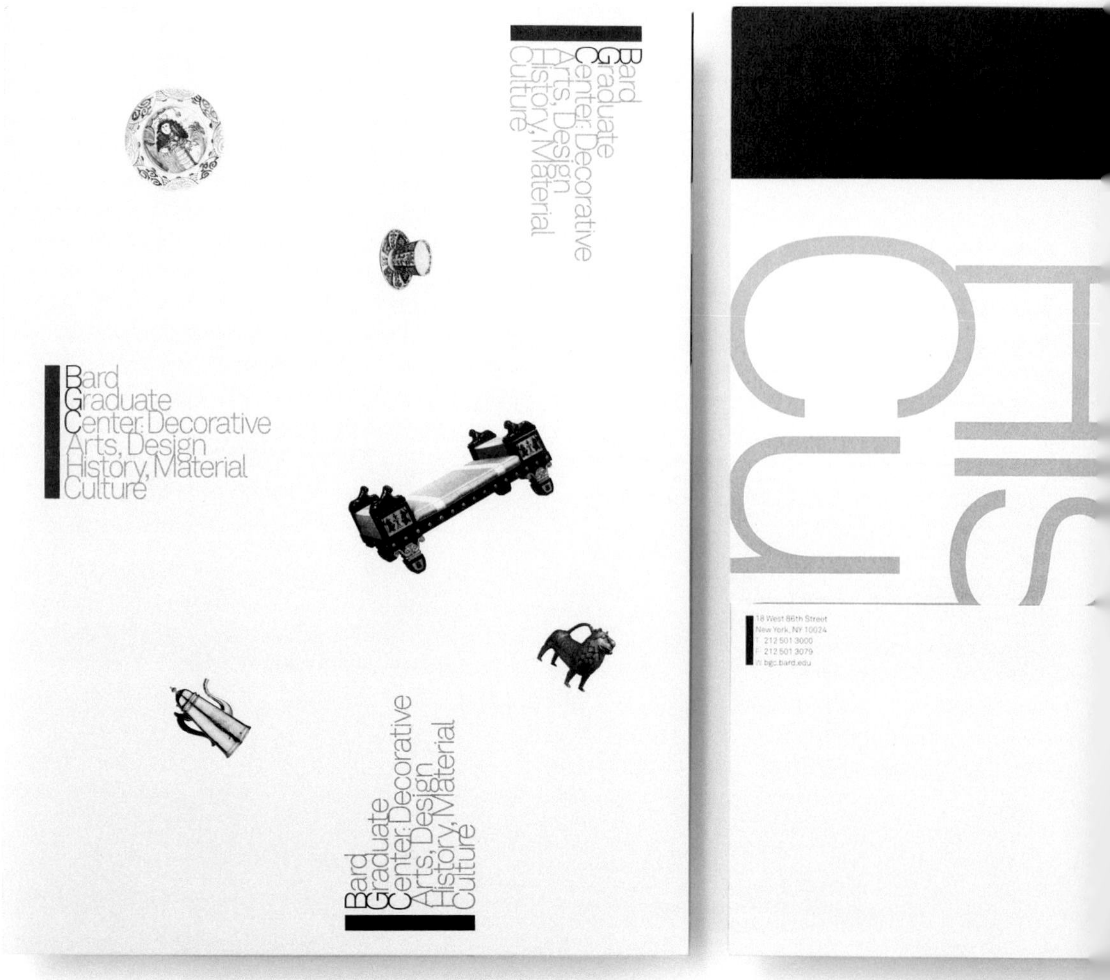

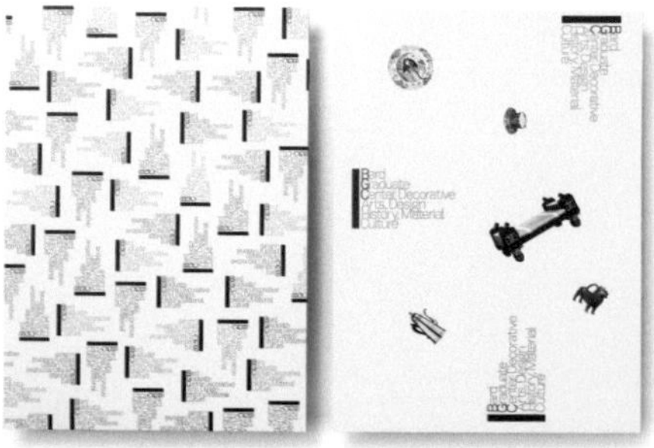

Client	Bard Graduate Center
Year	2009
Design	Pentagram

Bard
Graduate
Center Decorative
Arts, Design
History, Material
Culture
18 West 86th Street, New York, NY 10024
Michael W. Schnepf
Art Director
38 West 86th Street, New York, NY 10024
T 212 501 3048 F 212 501 3092
E schnepf@bgc.bard.edu
Back Cover, clockwise from top left
Front Cover, clockwise from top left

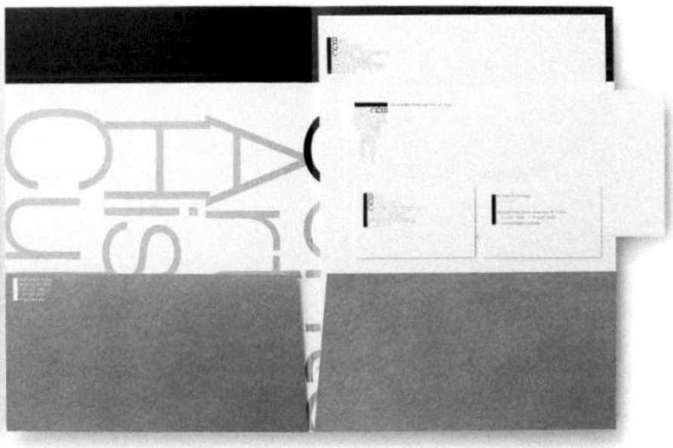

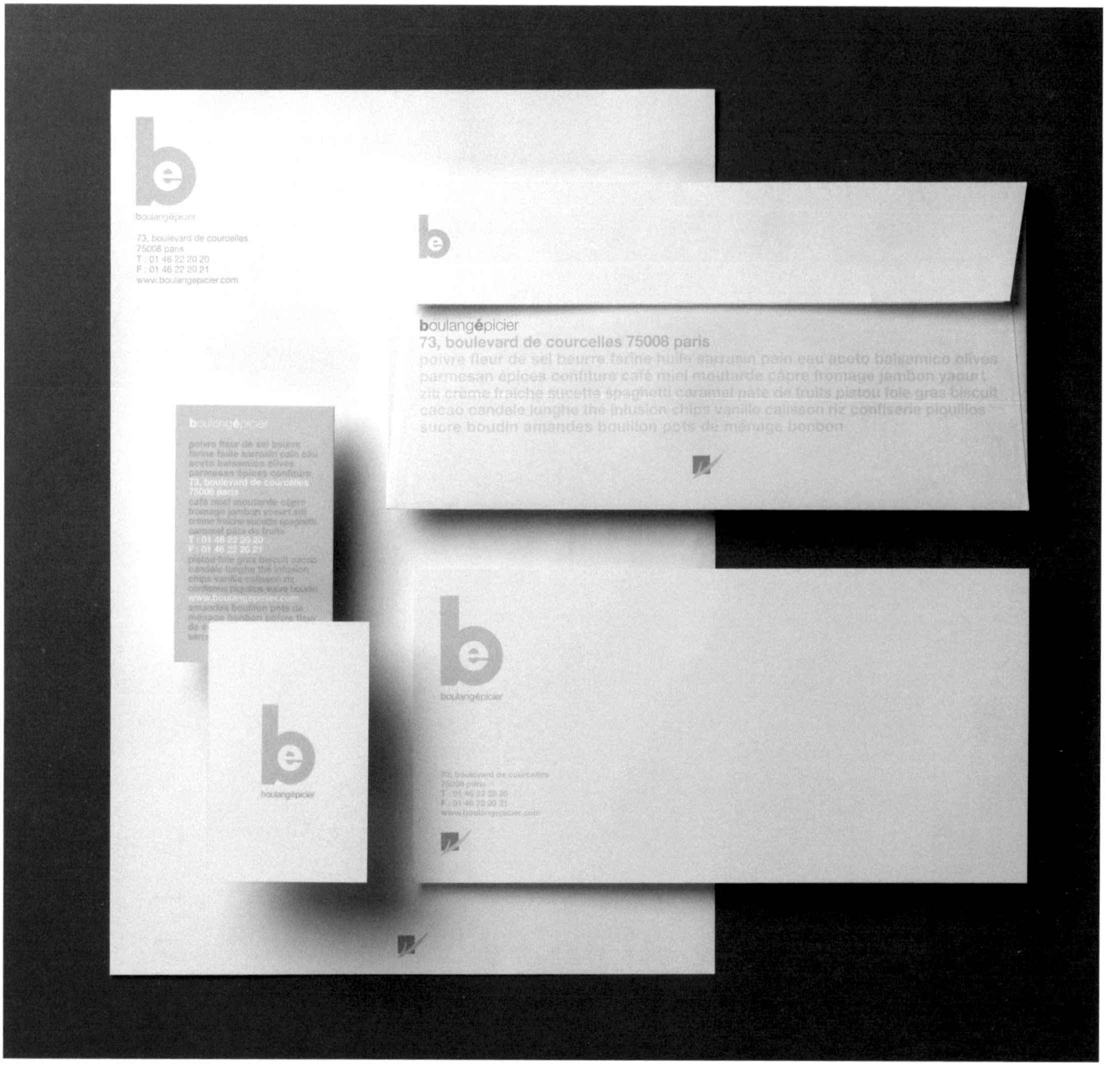

Client be boulangépicier
Year 2002
Design Philippe David

boulangépicier
poivre fleur de sel beurre
farine huile sarrasin pain eau
aceto balsamico olives
parmesan épices confiture
73, boulevard de courcelles
75008 paris
café miel moutarde câpre
fromage jambon yaourt ziti
crème fraîche sucette spaghetti
caramel pâte de fruits
T : 01 46 22 20 20
F : 01 46 22 20 21
pistou foie gras biscuit cacao
candele lunghe thé infusion
chips vanille calisson riz
confiserie
amandes
boulangépicier
73, boulevard de
poivre fleur de
parmesan
ziti crème
cacao candele
sucre boudin
boulangépicier

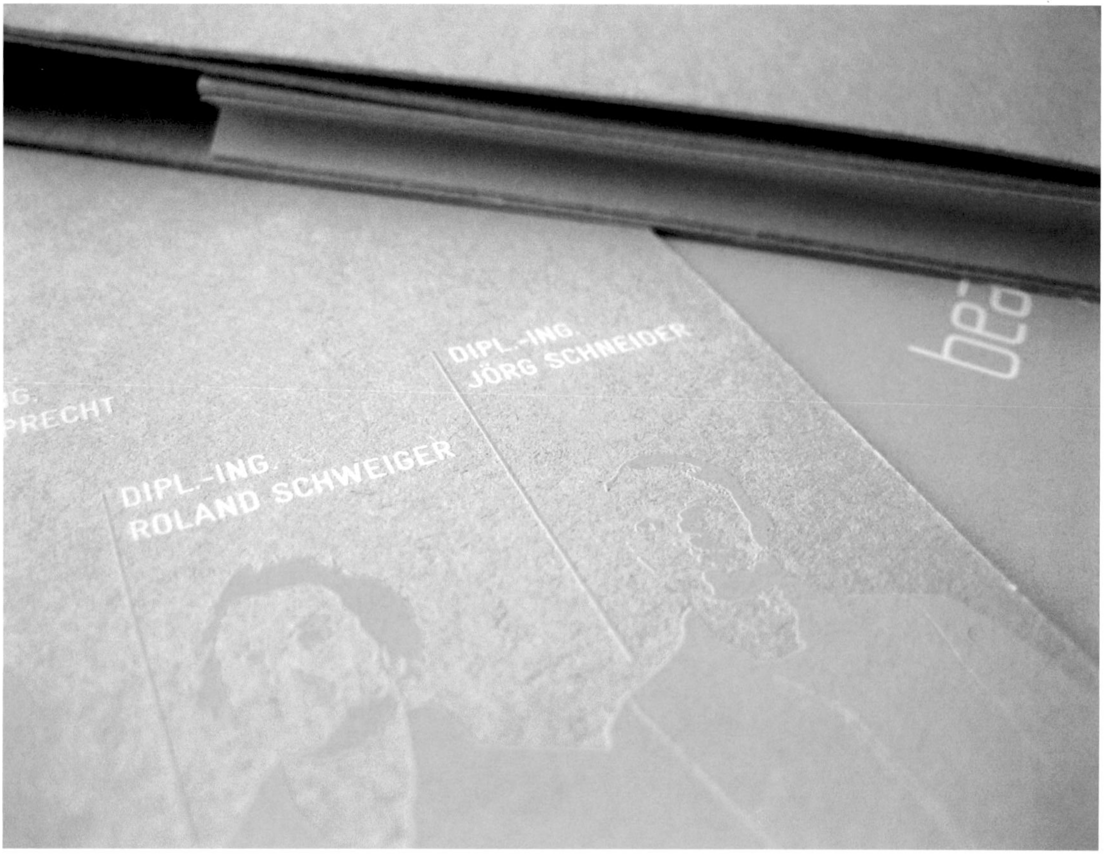

Client	Beaufort Architekten
Year	2006
Design	Transporter Visuelle Logistik

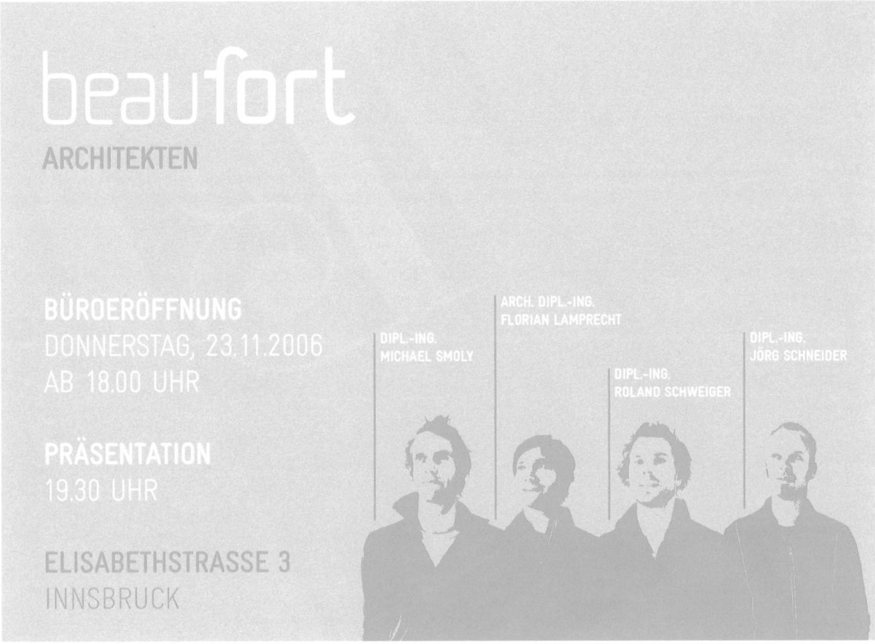
beaufort
ARCHITEKTEN
BÜROERÖFFNUNG
DONNERSTAG, 23.11.2006
AB 18.00 UHR
PRÄSENTATION
19.30 UHR
ELISABETHSTRASSE 3
INNSBRUCK
DIPL.-ING.
MICHAEL SMOLY
ARCH. DIPL.-ING.
FLORIAN LAMPRECHT
DIPL.-ING.
ROLAND SCHWEIGER
DIPL.-ING.
JÖRG SCHNEIDER

Becka Oakley
Jewelry
151 Fairmont Street
Manchester
M1 6HK
0161 748 8373
Becka Oakley
Jewelry
151 Fairmont Street
Manchester
M1 6HK
0161 748 8373

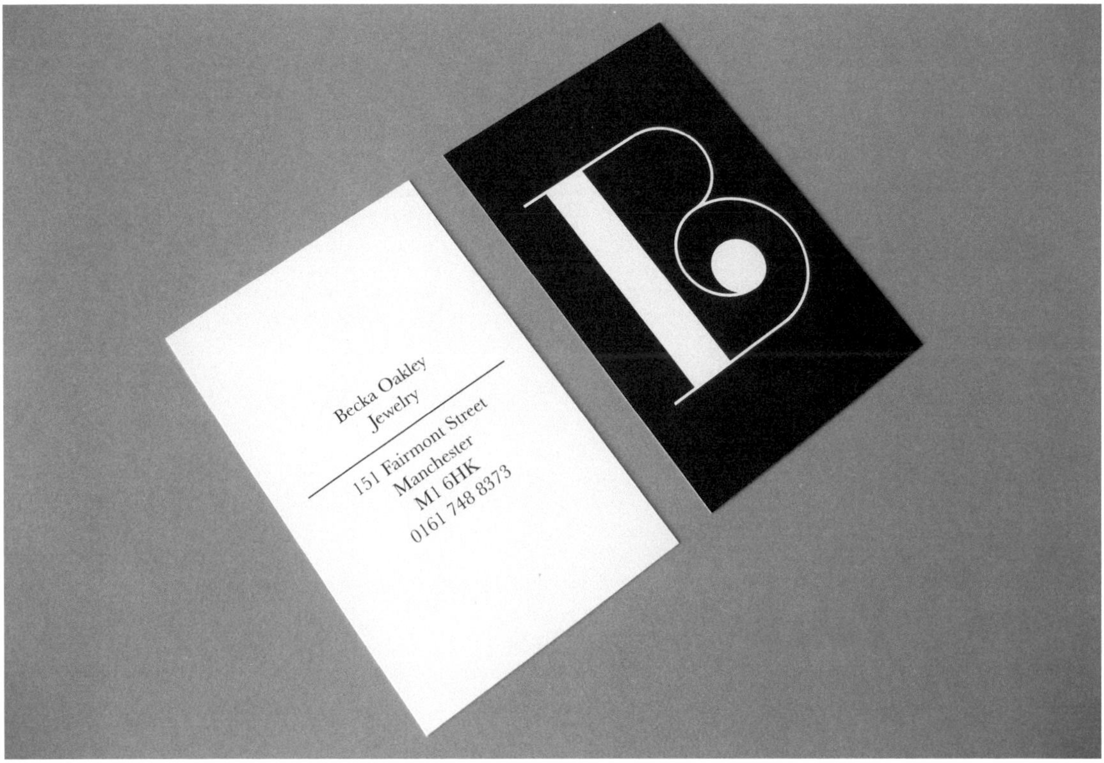

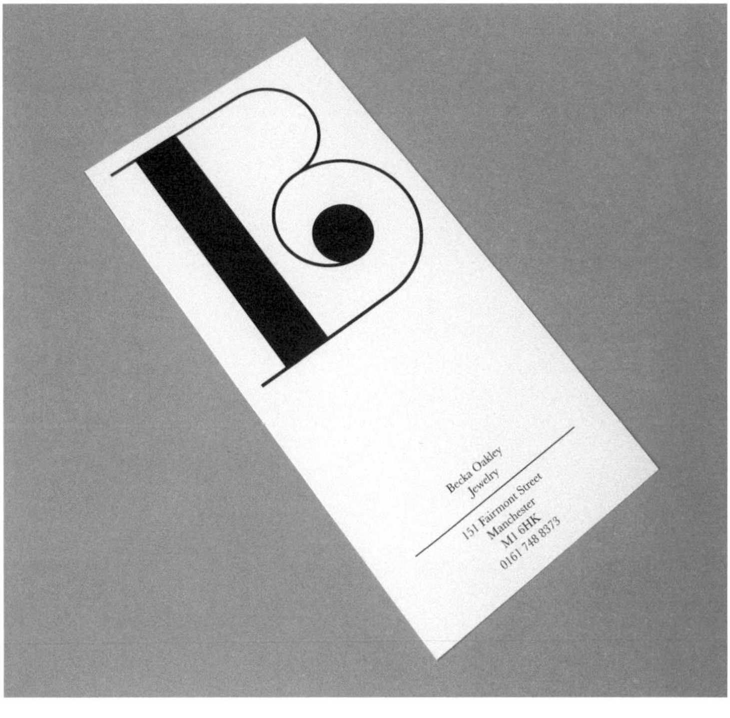

Client Becka Oakley
Year 2008
Design huvi

Client Benkiraï
Year 2006
Design Philippe David

BENKIRAÏ
SAINT-TROPEZ
LE RESTAURANT

Client Bernardes Jacobsen Arquitetura
Year 2007
Design 6D
Team Beto Martins, Emilio Rangel

Bernardes Jacobsen

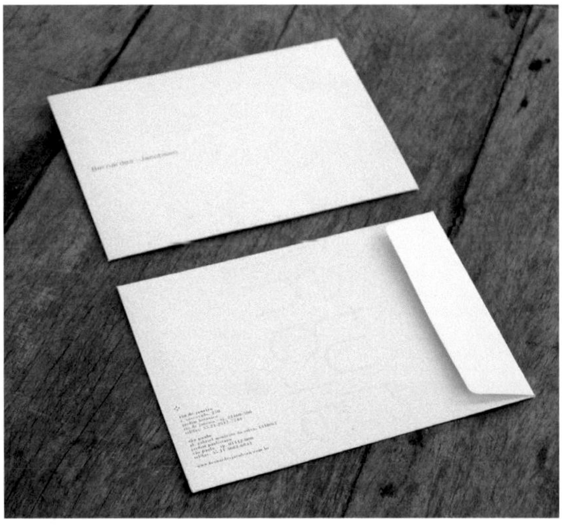

Client Betrix
Year 2009
Design huvi

Client Bicentenario Argentino
Year 2009
Design imagenHB

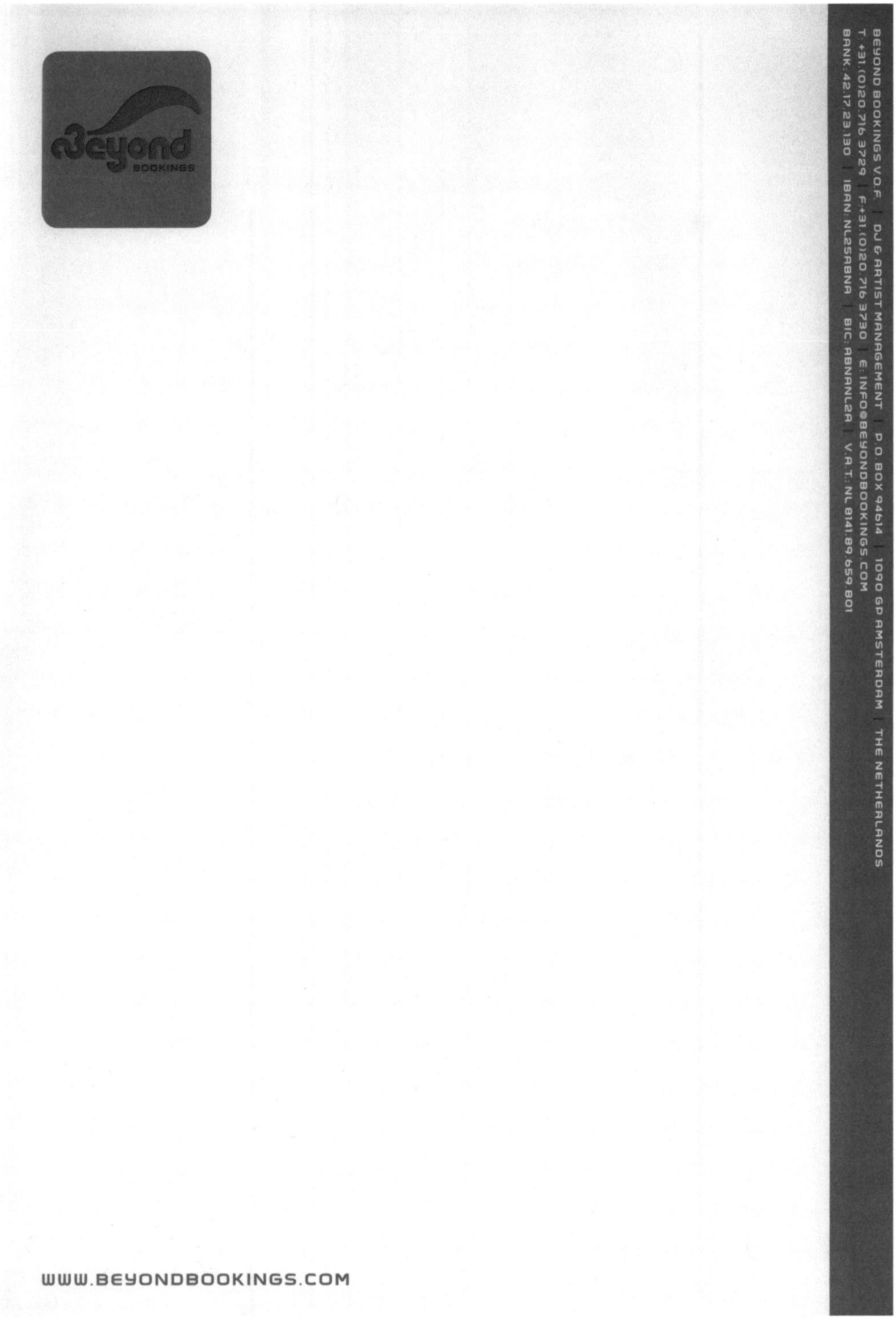
Beyond
BOOKINGS
BEYOND BOOKINGS V.O.F. | DJ & ARTIST MANAGEMENT | P.O. BOX 94614 | 1090 GP AMSTERDAM | THE NETHERLANDS
T: +31.(0)20.716 3729 | F: +31.(0)20.716 3730 | E: INFO@BEYONDBOOKINGS.COM
BANK: 42.17.23.130 | IBAN: NL25ABNA | BIC: ABNANL2A | V.A.T.: NL 8141.89.659.B01
WWW.BEYONDBOOKINGS.COM

Beyond
P.O. BOX 94614 | 1090 GP AMSTERDAM | THE NETHERLANDS
WWW.BEYONDBOOKINGS.COM

Client Beyond Bookings
Year 2008
Design DBXL

bideawee

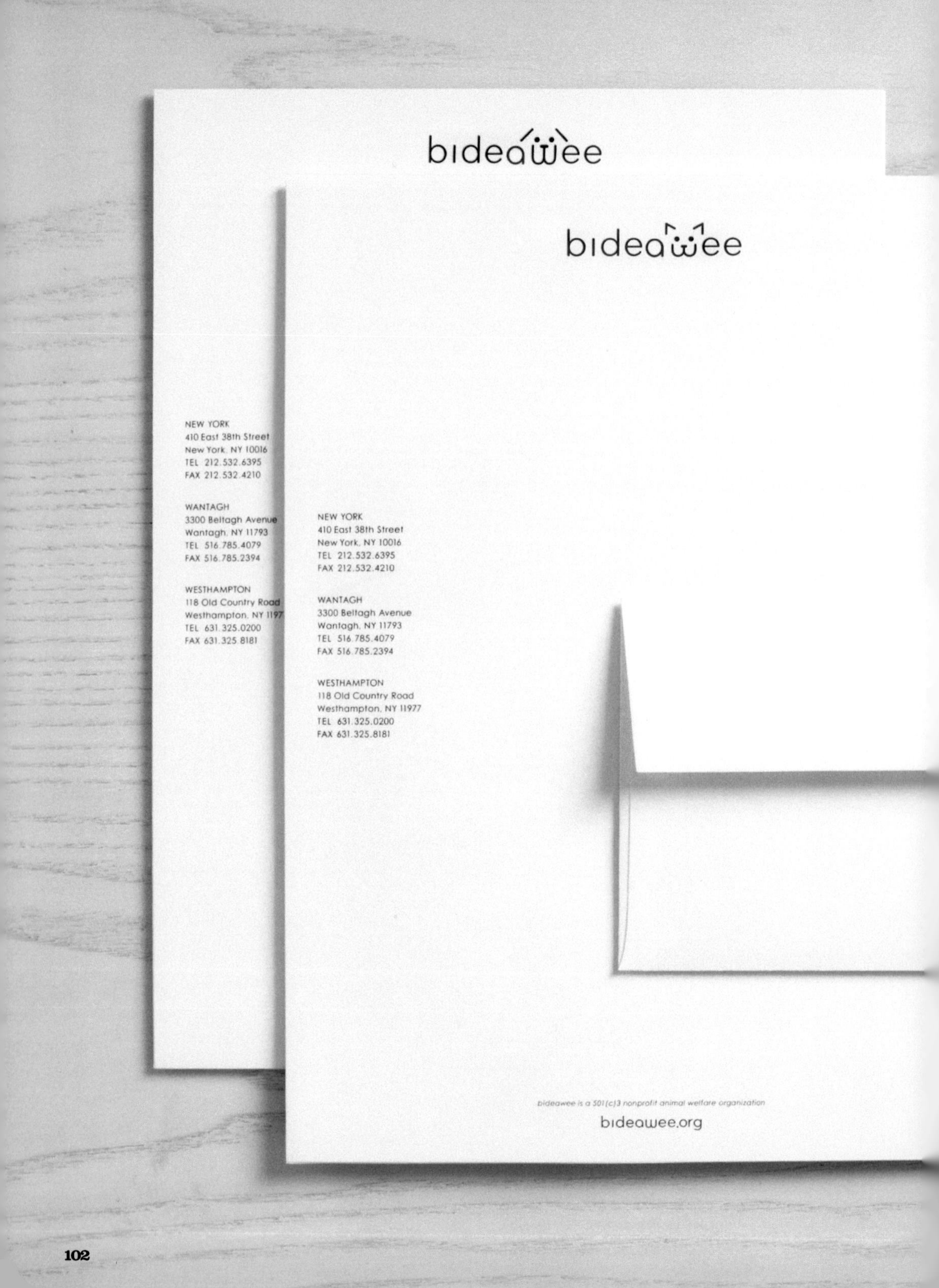

bideawee

NEW YORK
410 East 38th Street
New York, NY 10016
TEL 212.532.6395
FAX 212.532.4210

WANTAGH
3300 Beltagh Avenue
Wantagh, NY 11793
TEL 516.785.4079
FAX 516.785.2394

WESTHAMPTON
118 Old Country Road
Westhampton, NY 11977
TEL 631.325.0200
FAX 631.325.8181

NEW YORK
410 East 38th Street
New York, NY 10016
TEL 212.532.6395
FAX 212.532.4210

WANTAGH
3300 Beltagh Avenue
Wantagh, NY 11793
TEL 516.785.4079
FAX 516.785.2394

WESTHAMPTON
118 Old Country Road
Westhampton, NY 11977
TEL 631.325.0200
FAX 631.325.8181

bideawee is a 501(c)3 nonprofit animal welfare organization
bideawee.org

bideawee
bideawee
CODY McBURNETT
Development Associate,
Special Events & Sponsorships
410 East 38th Street, New York, NY 10016
cody.mcburnett@bideawee.org
TEL 212.532.6395 FAX 212.532.4210
bideawee.org
bideawee
bideawee

Client Bideawee
Year 2007
Design Carbone Smolan Agency
Team Leslie Smolan, Nina Masuda

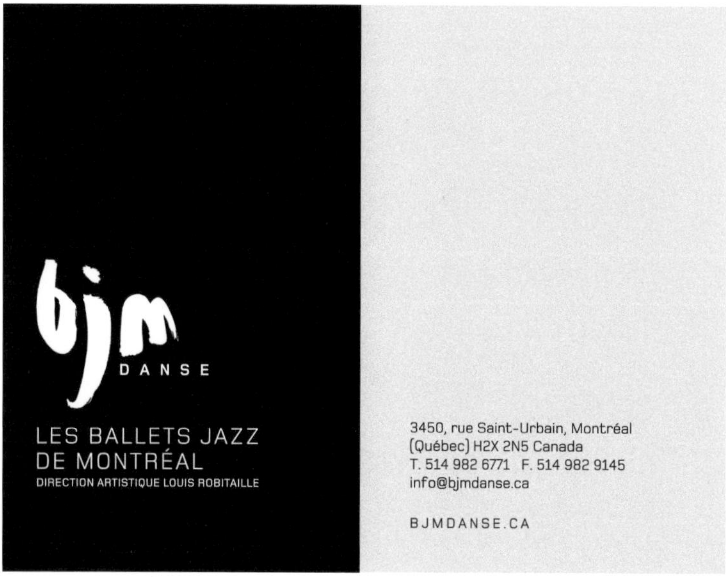

Client BJM Danse
Year 2009
Design Minimal Médias

Client BKRS Crane Systems
Year 2007
Design Edhv
Team Remco vd Craats, Jeroen Braspenning

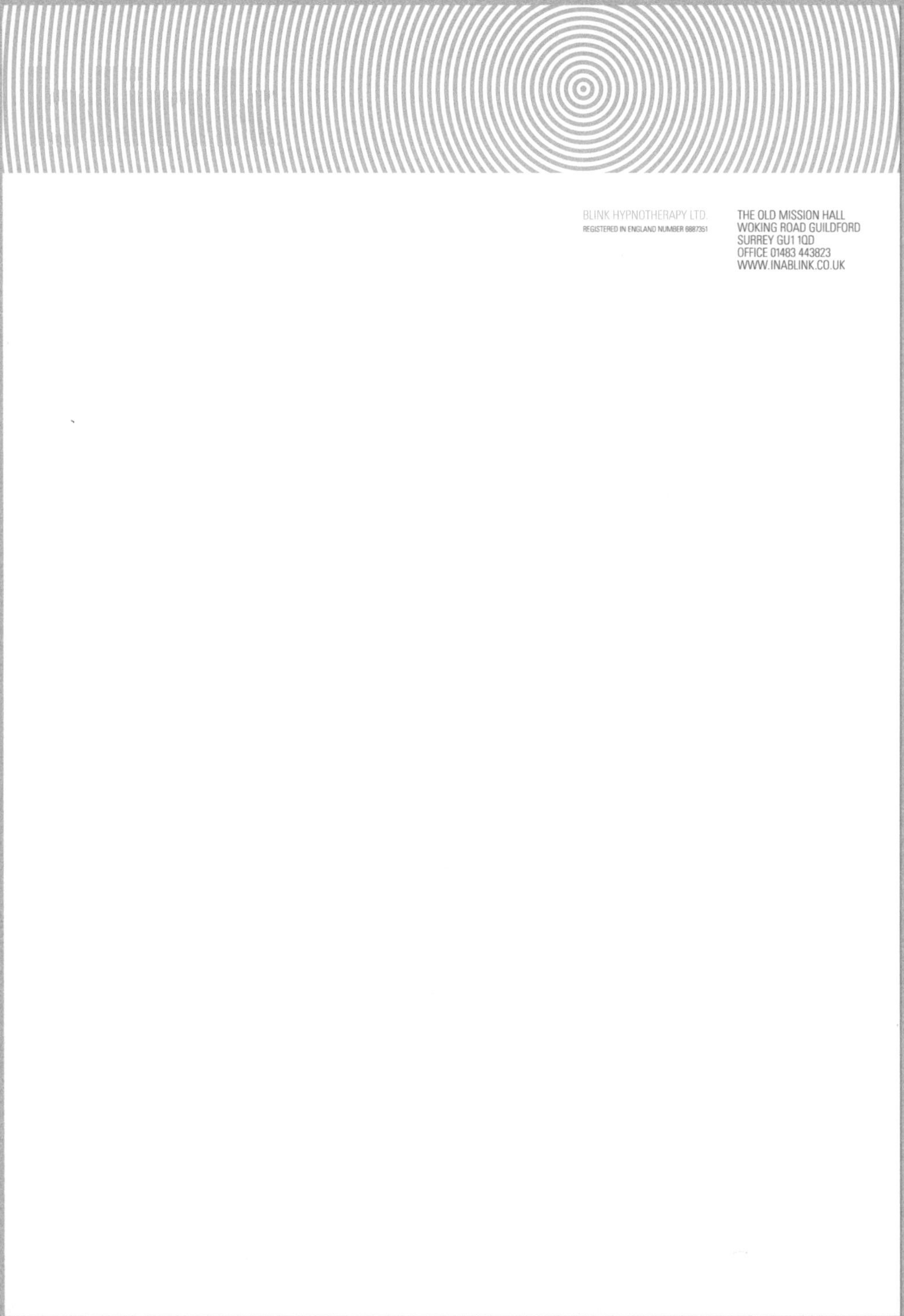

BLINK HYPNOTHERAPY LTD.
REGISTERED IN ENGLAND NUMBER 6887351
THE OLD MISSION HALL
WOKING ROAD GUILDFORD
SURREY GU1 1QD
OFFICE 01483 443823
WWW.INABLINK.CO.UK

Client Blink
Year 2009
Design Buddy

Client Bridges Magnes
Year 2007
Design Pentagram
Team Pentagram Design San Francisco

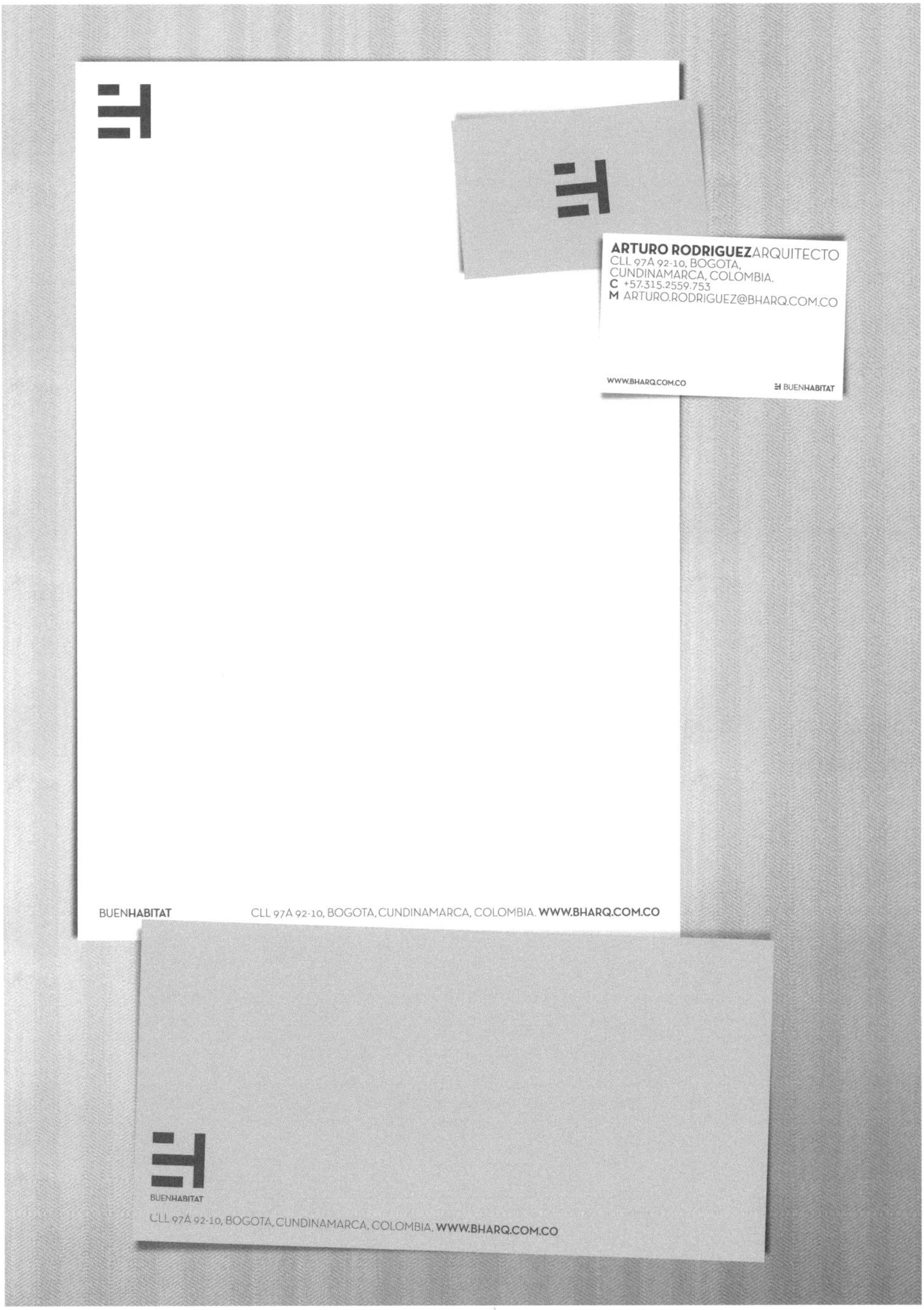

Client Buen Habitat
Year 2009
Design Dogo

Client Bullerei
Year 2009
Design weissraum.de(sign)°
Team Bernd Brink, Lucas Buchholz

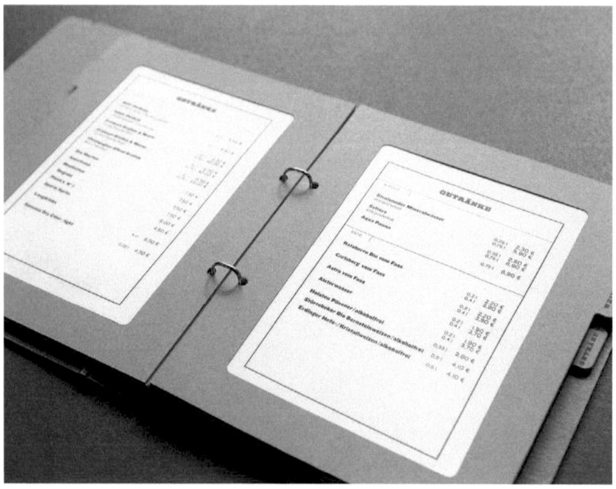

BULLEREI
BULLEREI
BULLEREI
Patrick Rüther, Tim Mälzer
AG Hamburg HRB 104903

BULLEREI
BULLEREI
BULLEREI
RESTAURANT / DELI
Bullerei
TELEFON, FAX
+49 - (0) 40 - 33 44 2 110
+49 - (0) 40 - 33 44 2 11 99
MAIL, INTERNET
www.bullerei.com
ADRESSE
Bullerei Lagerstraße 34 b 20357 Hamburg
ADRESSE
Bullerei GmbH & Co. KG
Lagerstraße 34 b, 20357 Hamburg
TELEFON, FAX
+49 - (0) 40 - 33 44 2 110
+49 - (0) 40 - 33 44 2 11 99
MAIL, INTERNET
info@bullerei.com
www.bullerei.com
BANKVERBINDUNG
Hamburger Sparkasse
BLZ 200 505 50, Konto 1268 144 910
GERICHTSSTAND, UST.-ID-NR.
AG Hamburg HRA 108216
DE 25960 8727
PERSÖNLICH HAFTENDE GESELLSCHAFTERIN
Bullerei Verwaltungs GmbH
GERICHTSSTAND DER P. H. G.
AG Hamburg HRB 104903
GESCHÄFTSFÜHRER
Patrick Rüther, Tim Mälzer

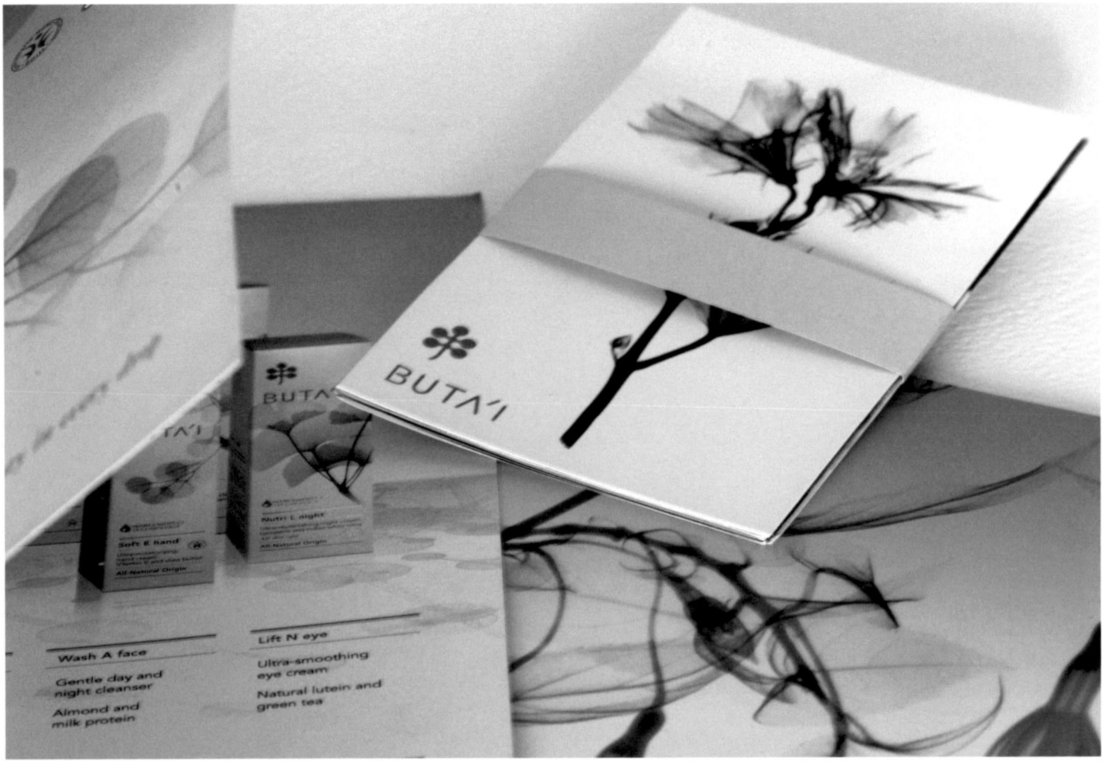
BUTA'I
Soft E hand
All Natural Origin
Nutri L night
All Natural Origin
Wash A face
Gentle day and night cleanser
Almond and milk protein
Lift N' eye
Ultra-smoothing eye cream
Natural lutein and green tea

BUTA'I
www.butaicosmetics.com
BUTA'I

Client BUTA'I
Year 2008
Design Dan Alexander & Co
Team Danny Goldberg, Michal Koll

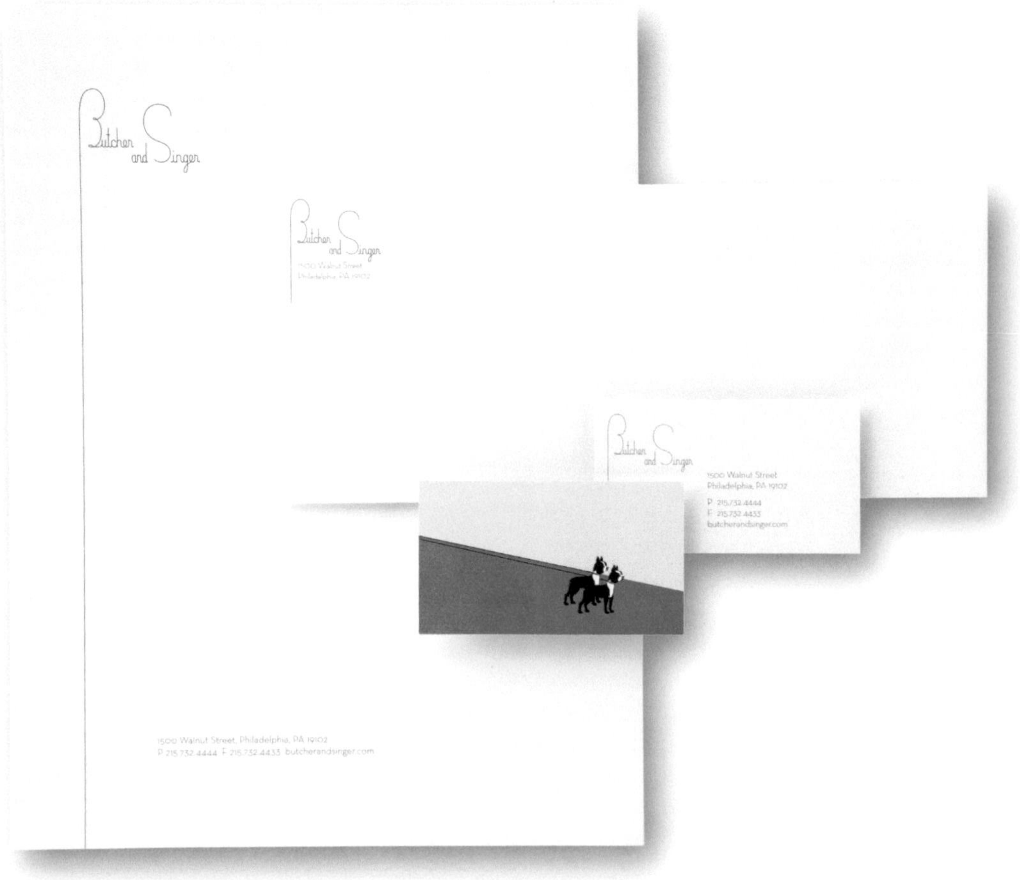
Butcher and Singer
Butcher and Singer
1500 Walnut Street
Philadelphia, PA 19102
Butcher and Singer
1500 Walnut Street
Philadelphia, PA 19102
P 215.732.4444
F 215.732.4433
butcherandsinger.com
1500 Walnut Street, Philadelphia, PA 19102
P 215.732.4444 F 215.732.4433 butcherandsinger.com

Butcher and Singer

Butcher and Singer

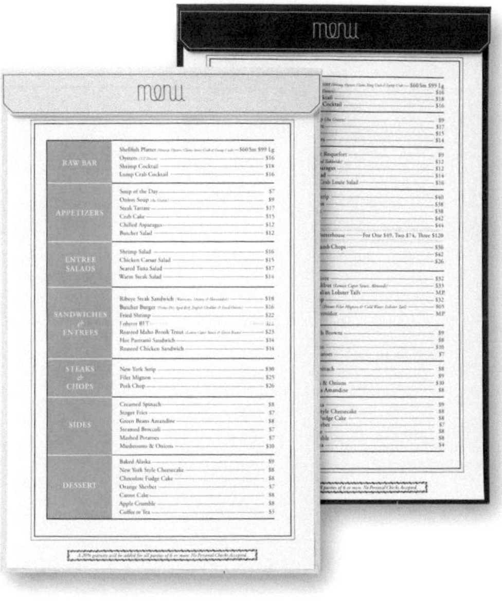

Client	Butcher and Singer
Year	2008
Design	Pentagram

California Academy of Sciences

Client	California Academy of Science
Year	2007
Design	Pentagram
Team	Pentagram Design San Francisco

Client CBF
Brazilian Football
Confederation

Year 2010

Design Monte Design

CBF
CBF
CBF
BRASIL
Gillette
TAM
TAM

BRASIL
BRASIL
BRASIL
BRASIL

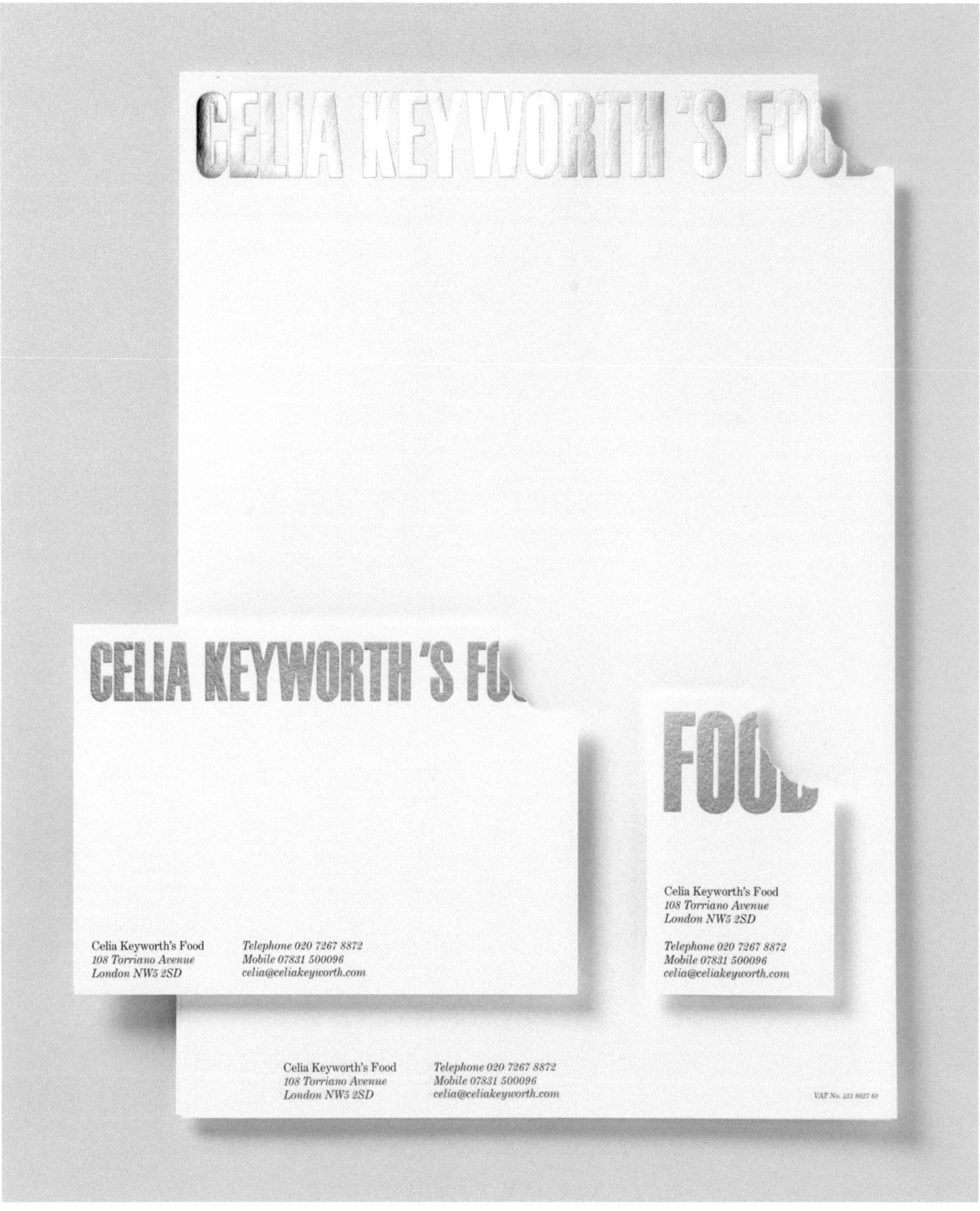

Client	Celia Keyworth's
Year	2007
Design	Pentagram
Team	Pentagram Design London

Client Chairman Ting Industries
Year 2010
Design Chairman Ting Industries

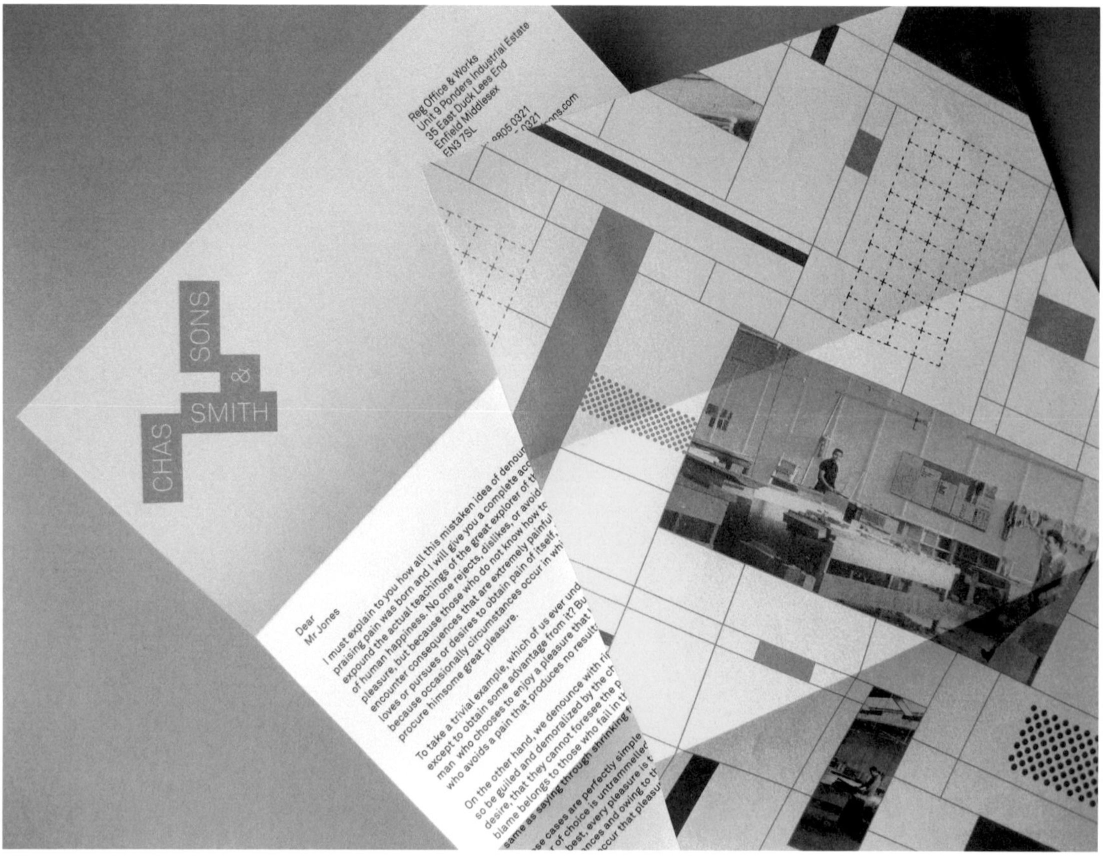

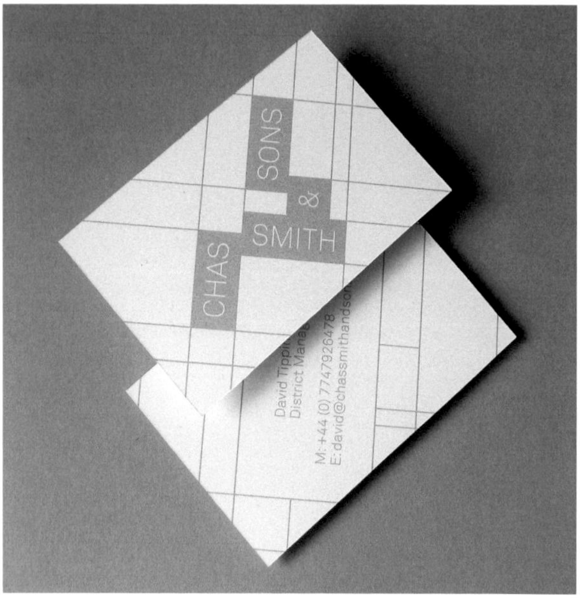

Client Chas Smith & Sons
Year 2009
Design huvi

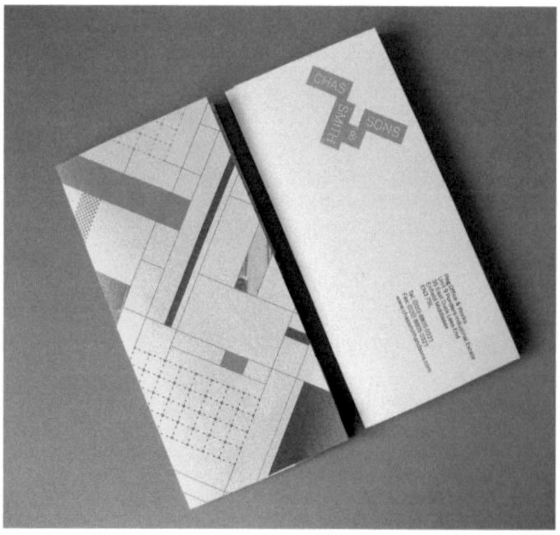

Client Chi Nar
Year 2009
Design huvi

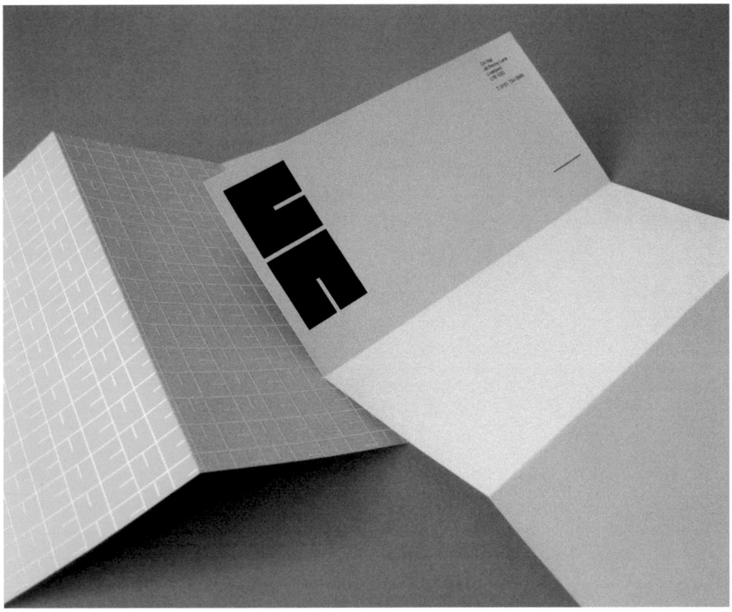

Client CINCO
Year 2009
Design CINCO

Client University of Arts London, Creative Connexions
Year 2009
Design SVIDesign

PC- und Netzwerksupport

079 735 23 93
Letzigraben 126
8047
Zürich

daniel fitzi
PC- und Netzwerksupport

079 735 23 93
Letzigraben 126
8047
Zürich

Sandra Schlittier
Russenweg 24
8050 Zürich

Sehr geehrte Frau Schlitter

Betriebssysteme können als das direkte E
ben betrachtet werden. Deshalb ist es une
den zugehörigen Systeme

Lochkarten gehören mitt
systems, queued system
wurden von nur einer Pe
Lochkarten an und überg
und händigte den Progra
den Programme übergab

Eine Weiterentwicklung
Daten im Speicher halte
Verwaltung, Speicherver
dem Beginn eines Betrie

Neben den klassischen Varianten gibt
zwischen dem logie Cray arbeiten nach
verteilte Systeme ist Amoeba.

Freundliche Grüsse

Daniel Fitzi

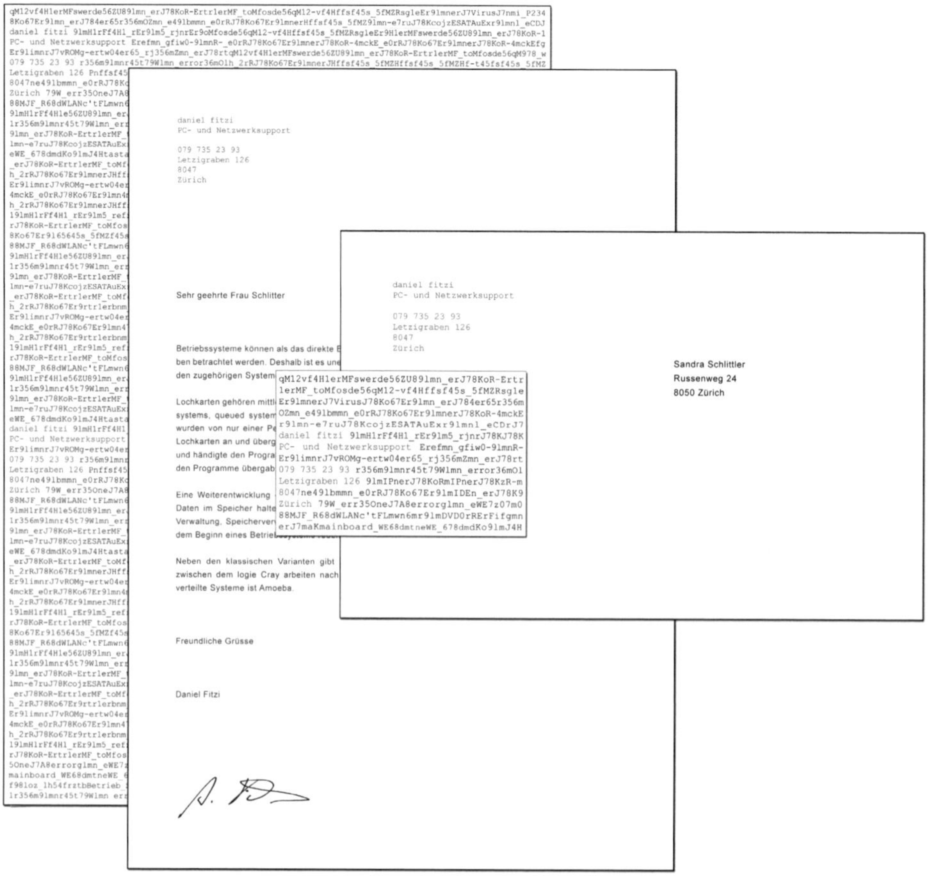

Client	Daniel Fitzi PC- und
	Netzwerksupport
Year	2009
Design	Silvia Gallart

daniel fitzi
PC- und Netzwerksupport

079 735 23 93
Letzigraben 126
8047
Zürich

-eWE7z07mori
rRErFifgmnerJ7m
E7z07m0M12-vf4Hf
2rRJ78Ko67Er91mn_
6q8Ko67Er91mn_e
mIDEn88MJF_R68
-eçSdghi91mH1r
CD daniel fitz
m2 PC- und Ne
6mZmn_erJ78rt
u9 079 735 2
5f Letzigra
R7o 8047ne4
c4D Zürich
5s_5fMjnr5s
VD0rRErFi
-eWE7z07m0
0lh_2rRJ78
de56q8Ko
91mIDEn

qM12vf4H
1erMF_to
Er91mne
OZmn_e4
r91mn-
daniel
PC- und Netz
Er91
079
Letzigrab
8047ne491
Zürich 79
88MJF_R6
erJ7maKmainboard_WE

qM12vf4H
1erMF_toM
Er91mnerJ7
OZmn_e491bm
r91mn-e7ru
daniel fitzi
PC- und Netz
Er91imnrJ7vRO
079 735 23 93
Letzigraben 126
8047ne491bmmn_e
Zürich 79W_err3
88MJF_R68dWLANc
erJ7maKmainboard

8047ne491
Zürich 79W_
88MJF_R68dW
erJ7maKmain

7E
ro
er9
cef
5_rj
5t79
5fM
7Er9
error
r91m
78KoR

Client De Buitenwereld
Year 2008
Design Edhv
Team Remco vd Craats,
Eric de Haas,
Jeroen Braspenning

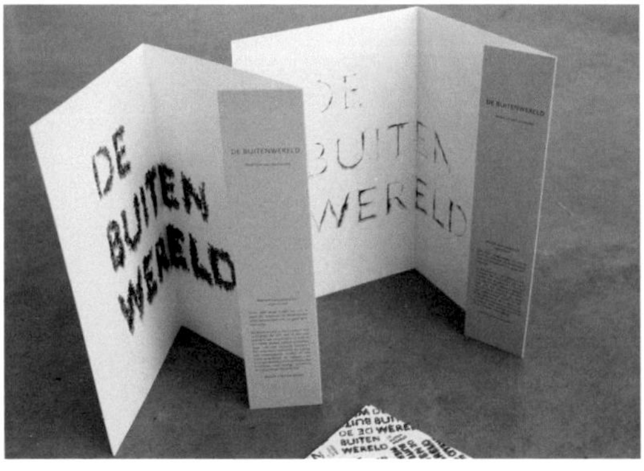

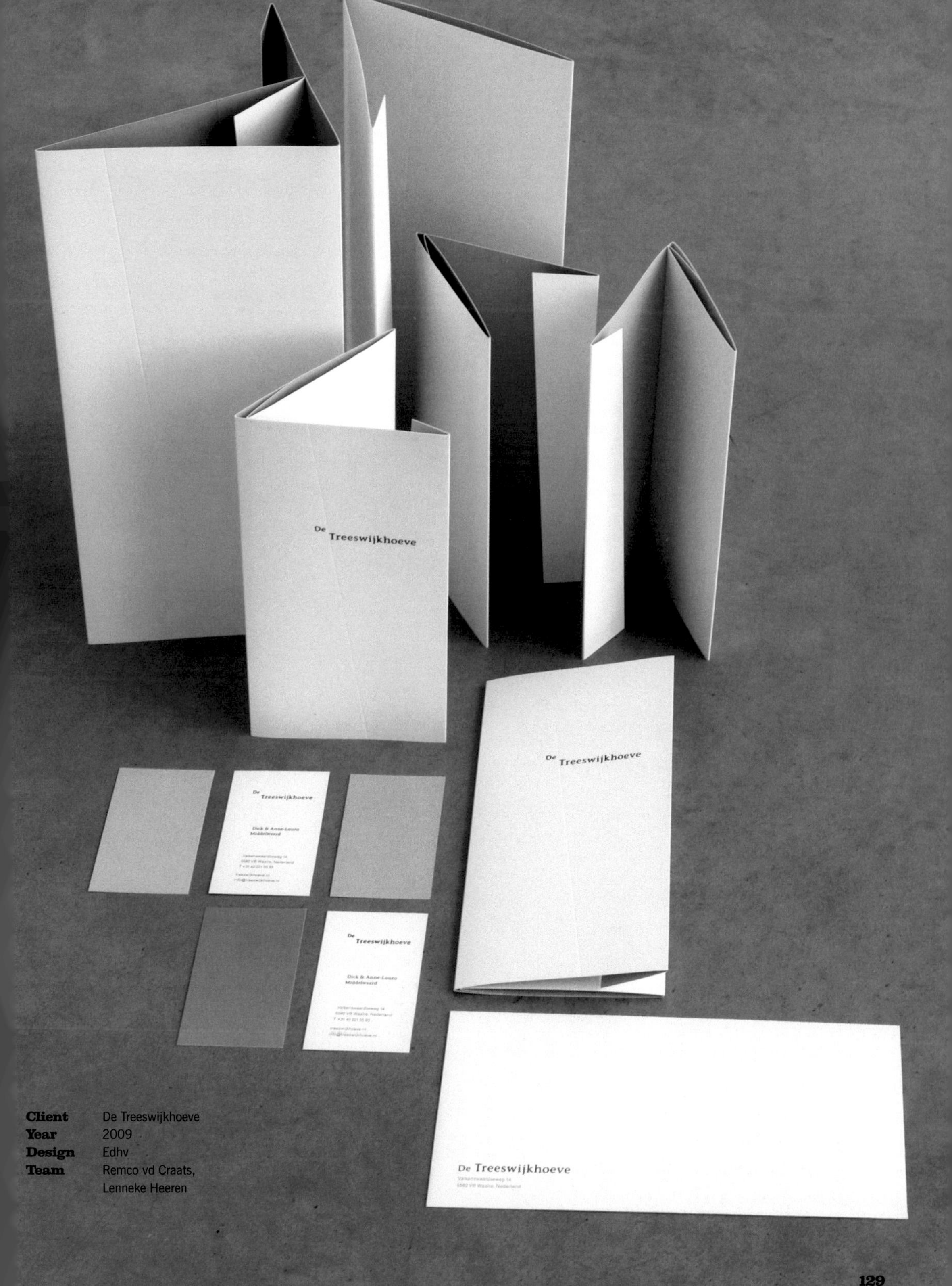

Client De Treeswijkhoeve
Year 2009
Design Edhv
Team Remco vd Craats, Lenneke Heeren

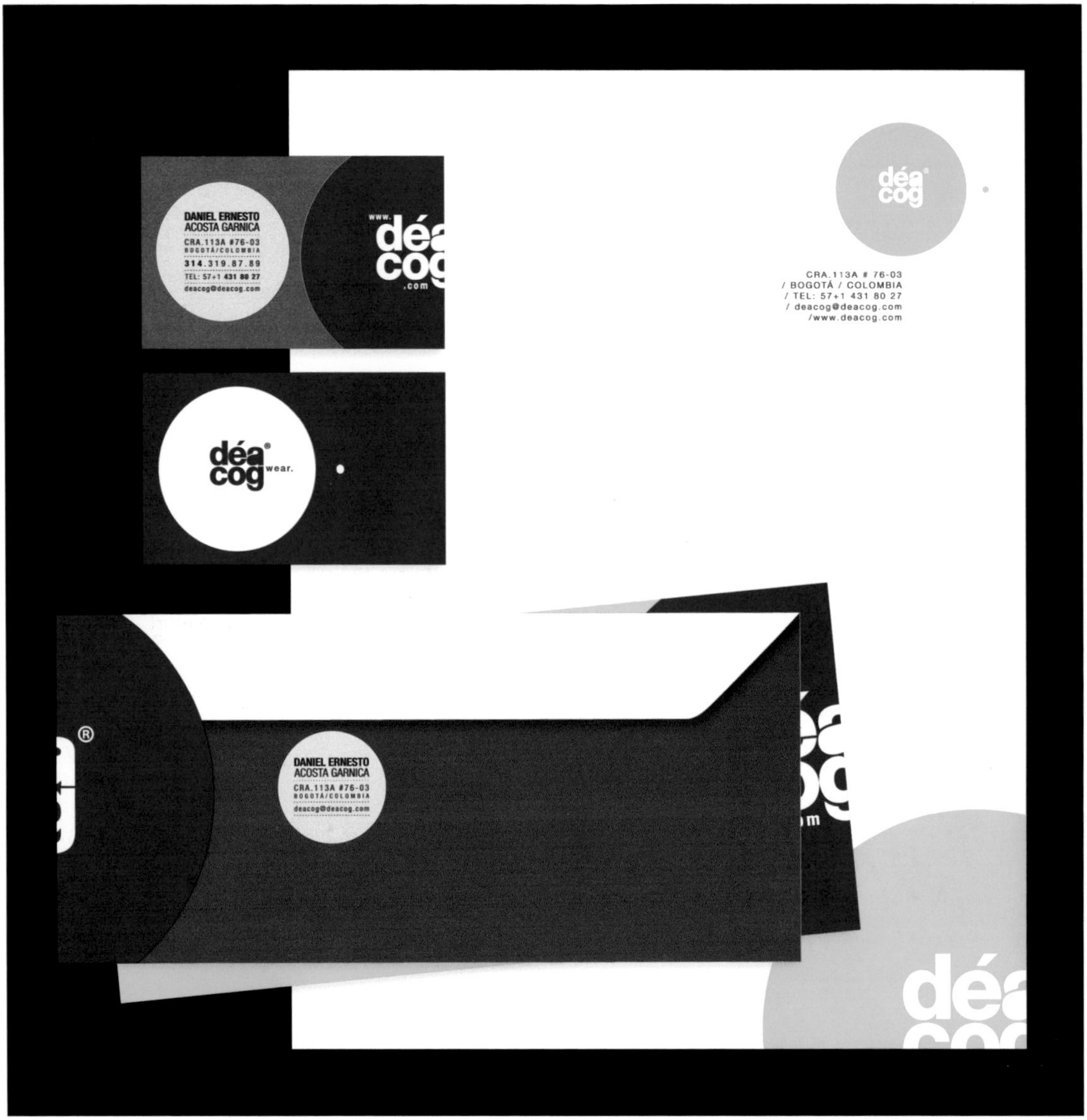

Client Déacog
Year 2010
Design Wonksite Studio
Team Jorge Restrepo

déa
cog
wear.

DANIEL ERNESTO
ACOSTA GARNICA
CRA.113A #76-03
BOGOTÁ/COLOMBIA
314.319.87.89
TEL: 57+1 431 80 27
deacog@deacog.com
www.
déa
cog
.com

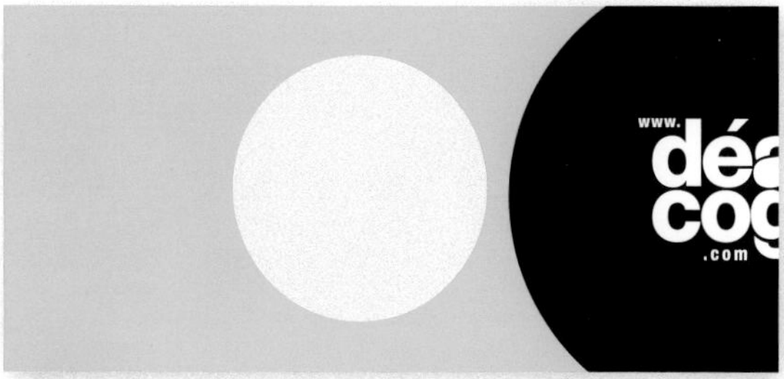
www.
déa
cog
.com

MR A.JOHNSON
ICP DIGITAL
12 G. TITCHFIELD HOUSE
GREAT TITCHFIELD ST
LONDON W1W 8BU
DESIGN ARRIVAL
IF UNDELIVERED PLEASE RETURN TO:
12 WATERSON STREET • SHOREDITCH • LONDON • E2 8HL
WWW.DESIGNARRIVAL.CO.UK

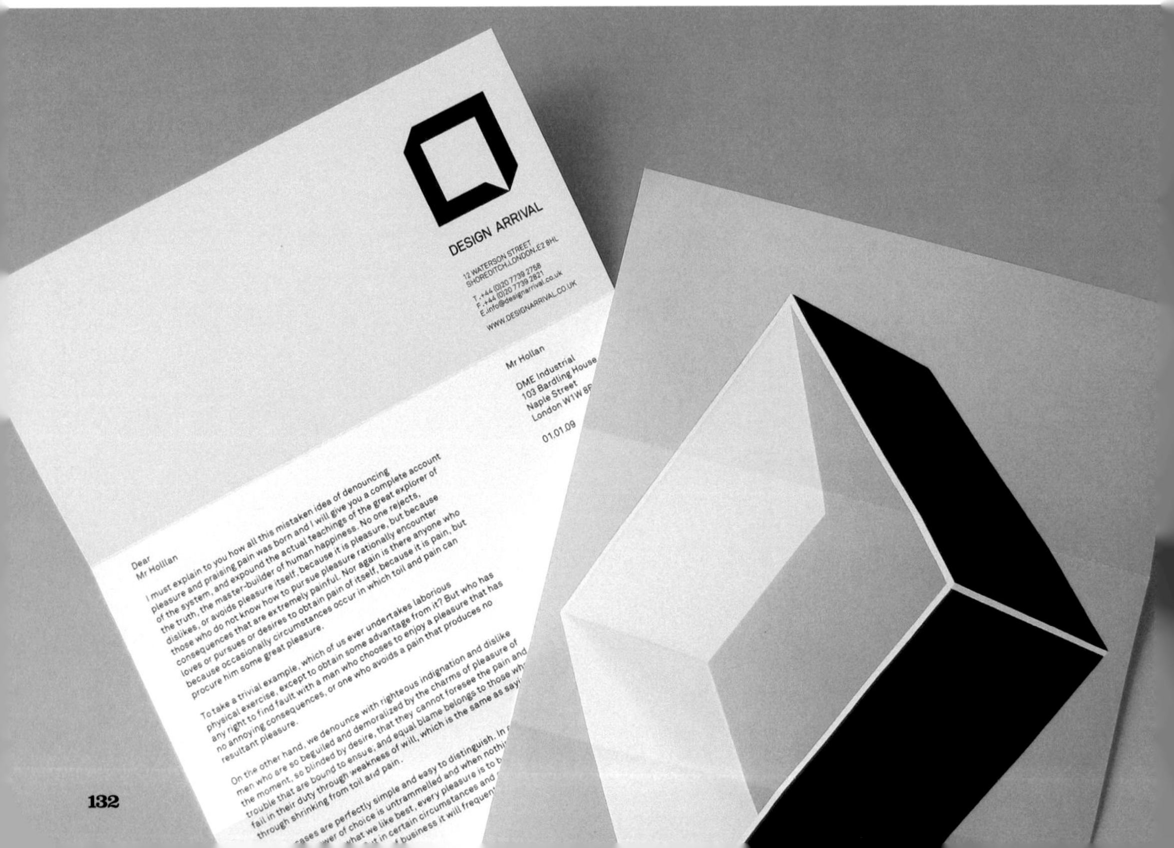
DESIGN ARRIVAL
12 WATERSON STREET
SHOREDITCH.LONDON.E2 8HL
T.+44 (0)20 7739 2768
F.+44 (0)20 7739 2621
E.info@designarrival.co.uk
WWW.DESIGNARRIVAL.CO.UK
Mr Hollan
DME Industrial
103 Bardling House
Naple Street
01.01.09
Dear
Mr Hollan

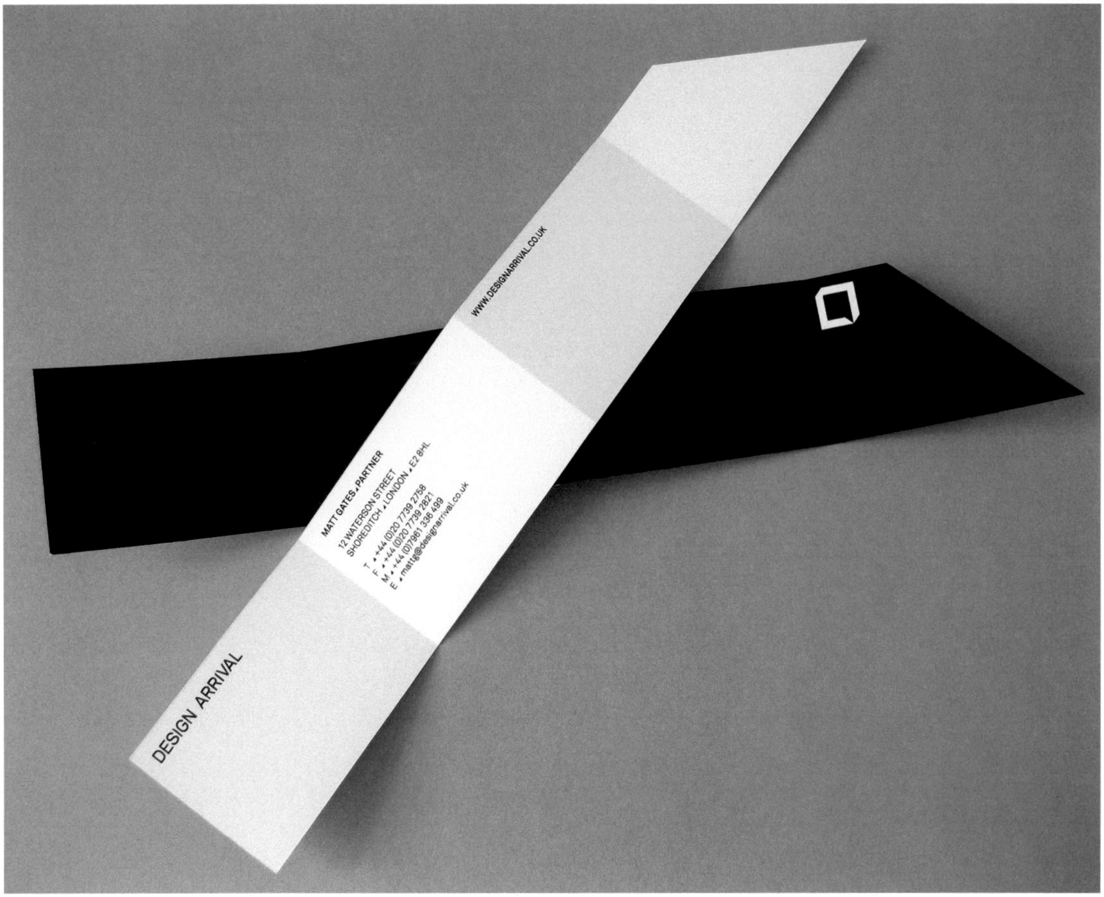

Client Design Arrival
Year 2009
Design huvi

Client	Design Factory Brainport
Year	2008
Design	Edhv
Team	Remco van de Craats, Jeroen Braspenning

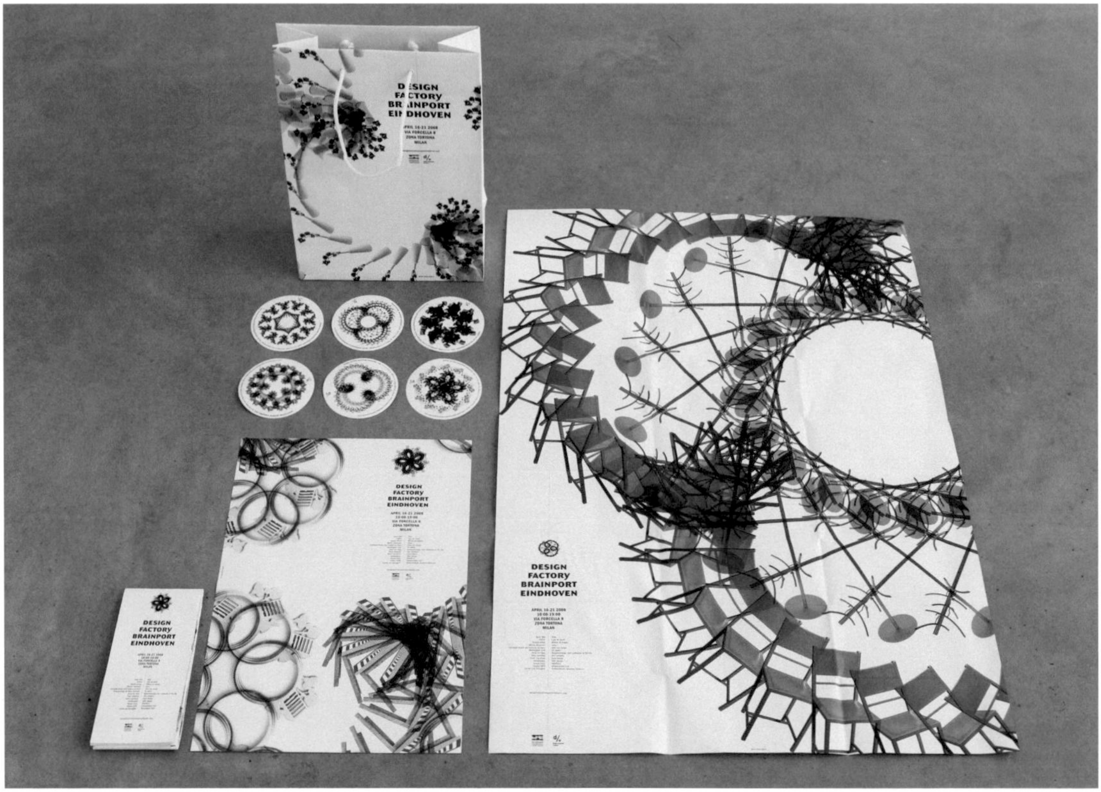

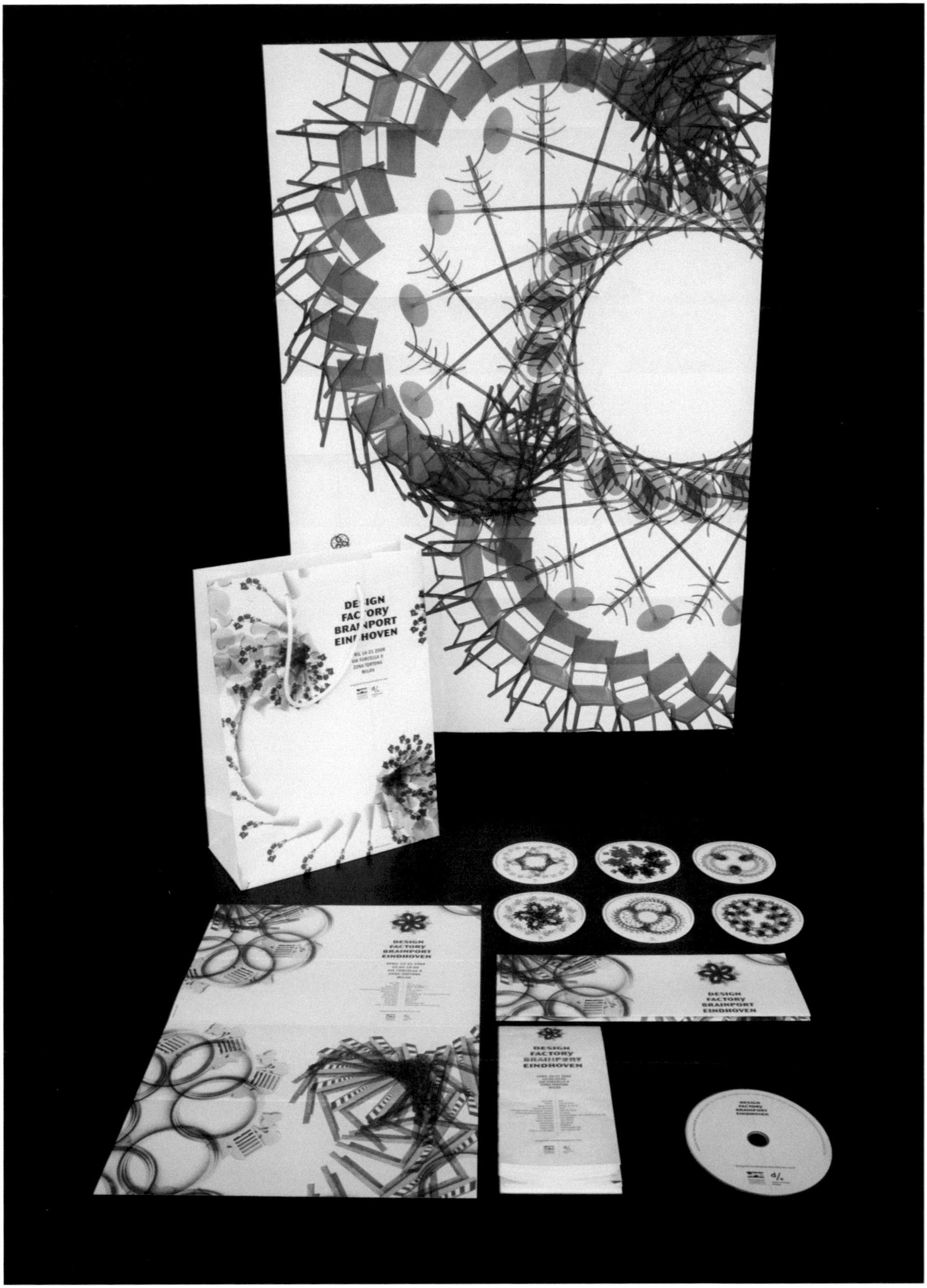
DESIGN FACTORY BRAINPORT EINDHOVEN

DESIGN IS PLAY
designer
ANGIE WANG
email
A@DESIGNISPLAY.COM
play
"YOU AND I KNOW THAT WONDER IS THE SECRET OF BLISS, AND THAT WITH REASON COMES THE DEATH OF THE BEAUTIFUL."

DESIGN IS PLAY
designer
MARK FOX
email
M@DESIGNISPLAY.COM
A BEE STAGGERS OUT OF THE PEONY.

DESIGN IS PLAY
designer ANGIE WANG
email A@DESIGNISPLAY.COM
"YOU AND I KNOW THAT WONDER IS THE SECRET OF BLISS, AND THAT WITH REASON COMES THE DEATH OF THE BEAUTIFUL."

Client Design is Play
Year 2008
Design Design is Play
Team Angie Wang, Mark Fox

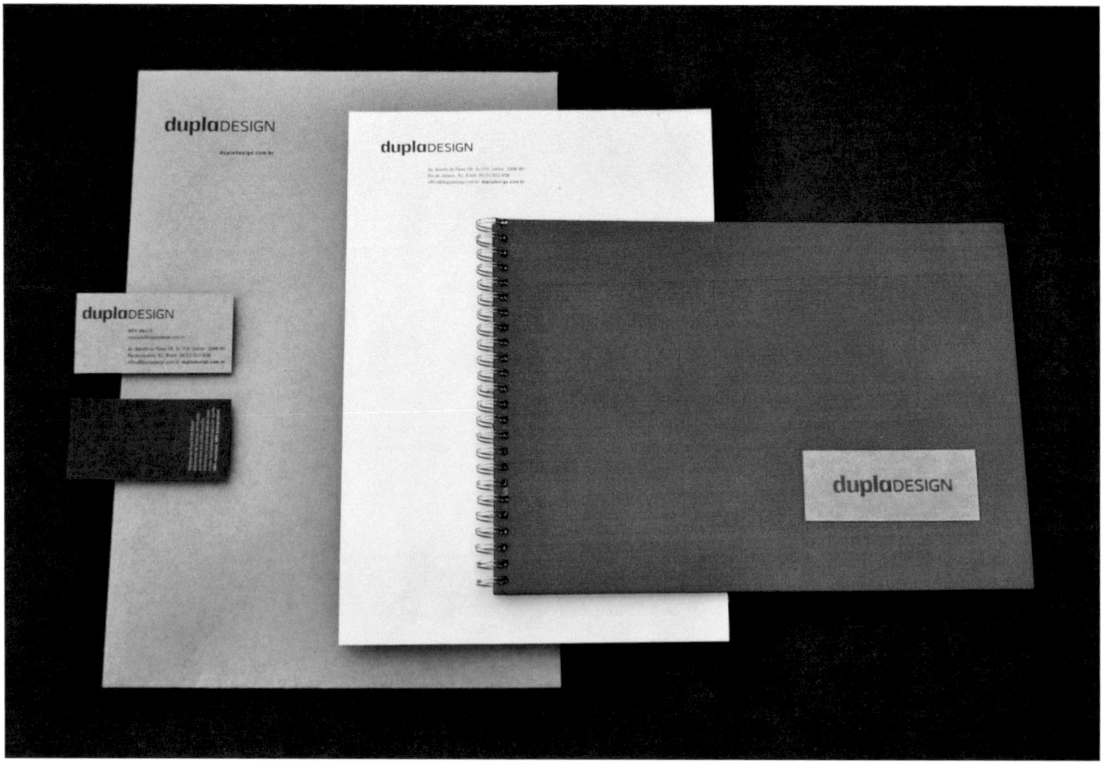

Client	Dupla Design
Year	2010
Design	Dupla Design
Team	Claudia Gamboa, Beatriz Abreu

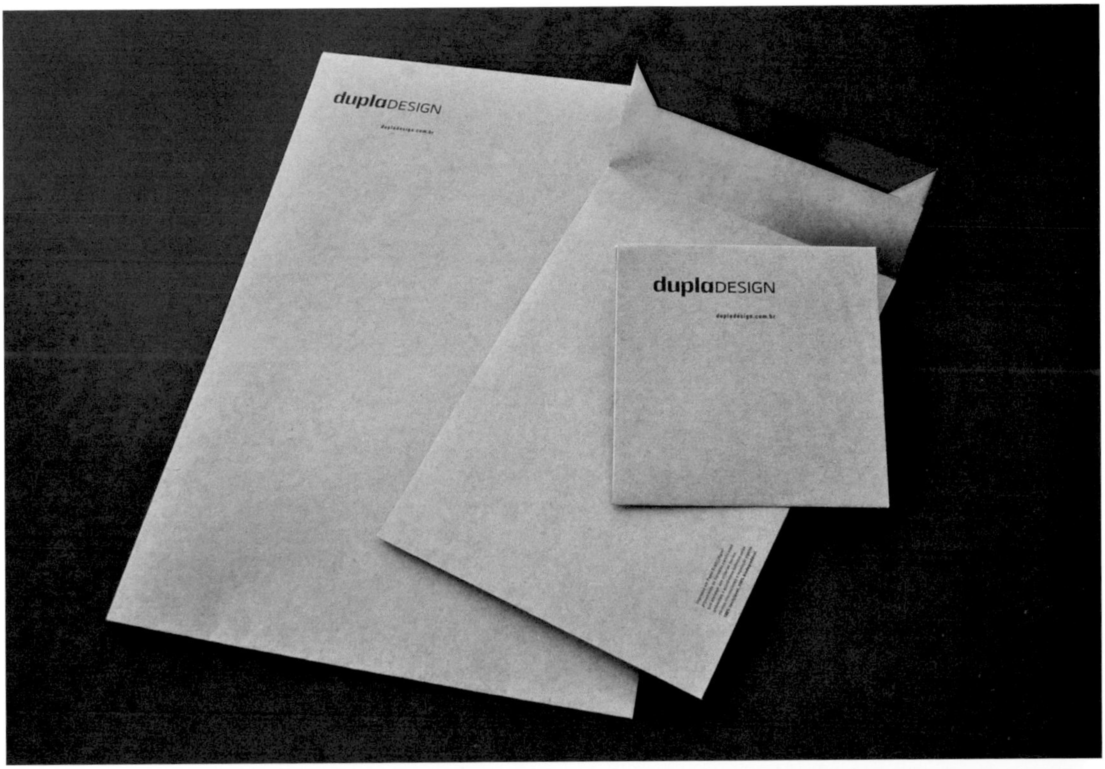
duplaDESIGN
duplaDESIGN

duplaDESIGN

EASTWEST מזרחמערב

EASTWEST מזרחמערב
www.east-west.co.il · info@east-west.co.il

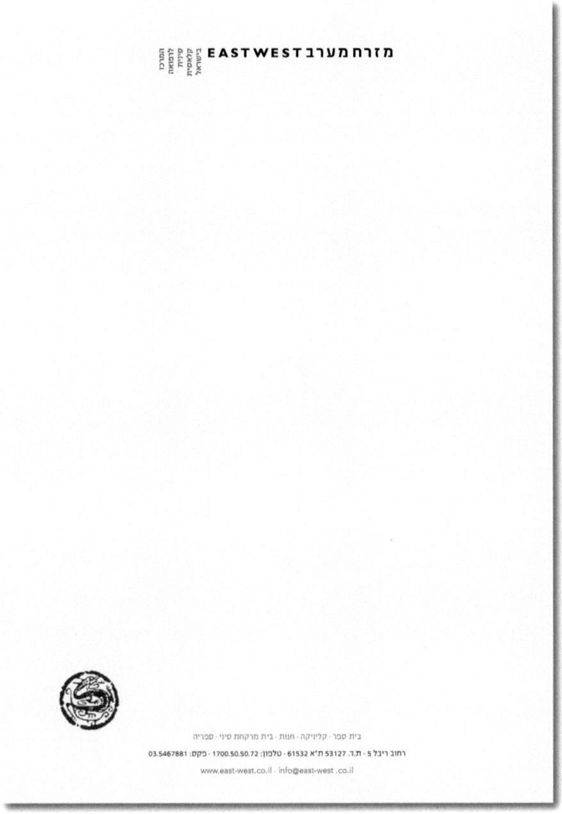

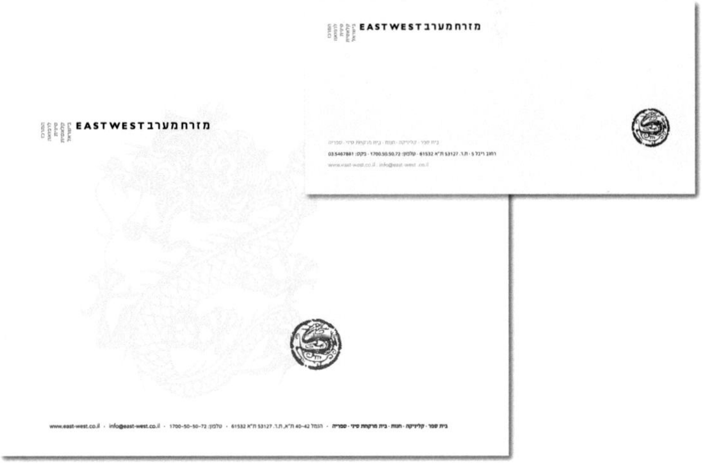

Client East-West
Year 2006
Design Dan Alexander & Co
Team Danny Goldberg, Michal Koll

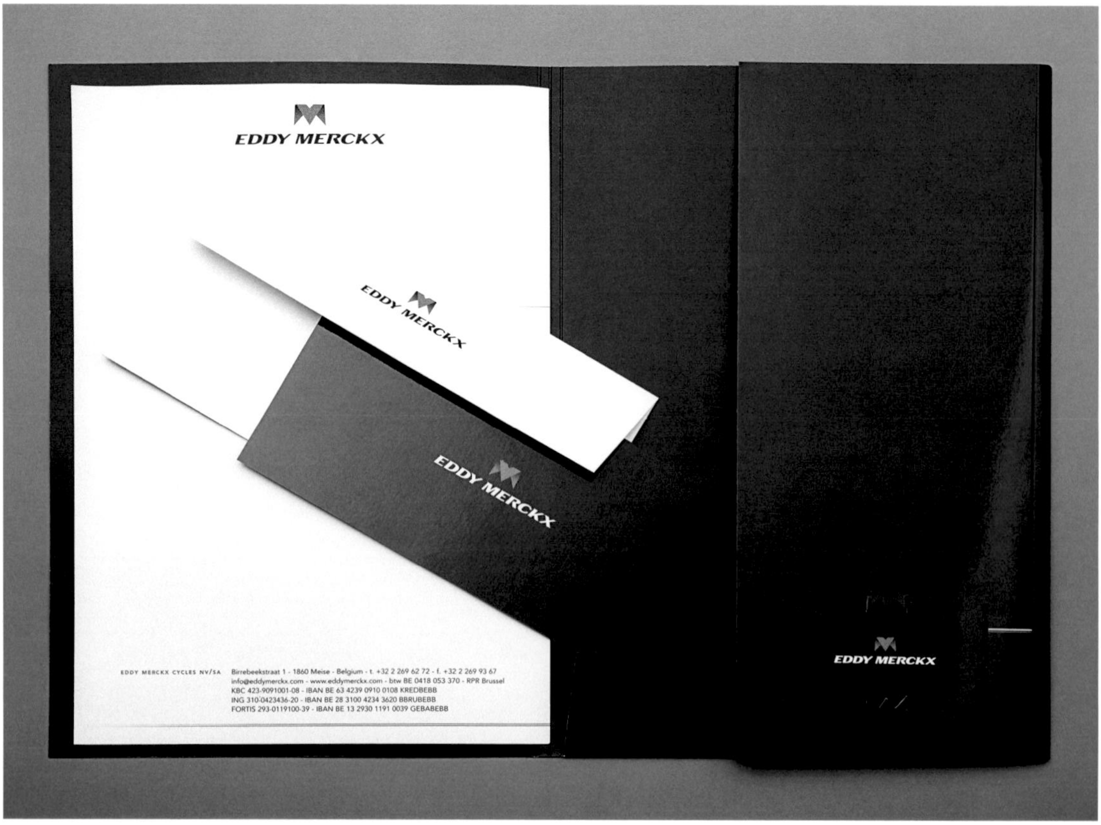

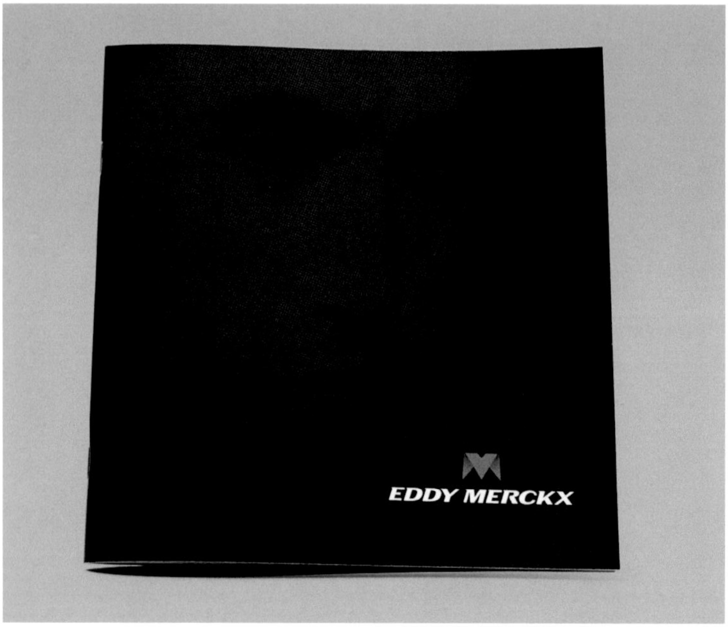

Client Eddy Merckx Cycles
Year 2009
Design Sign*
Team Cédric Aubrion, Franck Sarfati

Client Elk City Council
Year 2009
Design Papajastudio

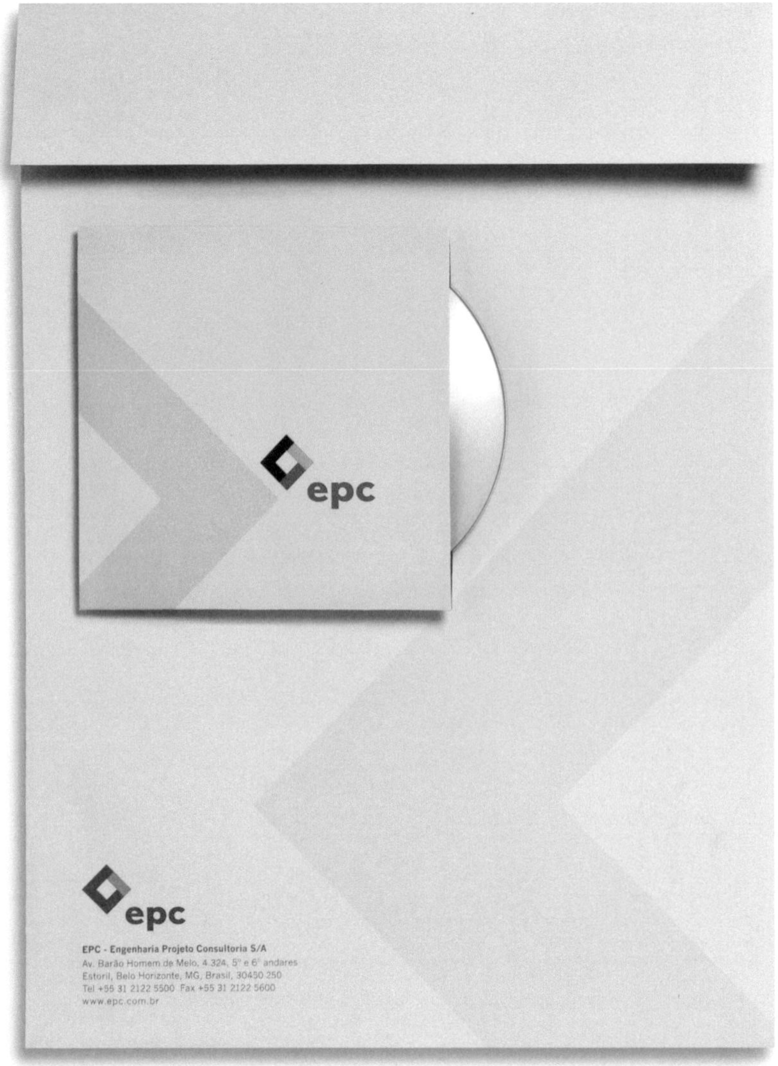
epc
epc
EPC - Engenharia Projeto Consultoria S/A
Av. Barão Homem de Melo, 4.324, 5º e 6º andares
Estoril, Belo Horizonte, MG, Brasil, 30450 250
Tel +55 31 2122 5500 Fax +55 31 2122 5600
www.epc.com.br

epc
André Victor de Mendonça Alves
Arquiteto
Architect
EPC Engenharia Projeto Consultoria S/A

Client EPC
Year 2008
Design Hardy Design

Client Et Voilà Zirkus Schule
Year 2006
Design Silvia Gallart

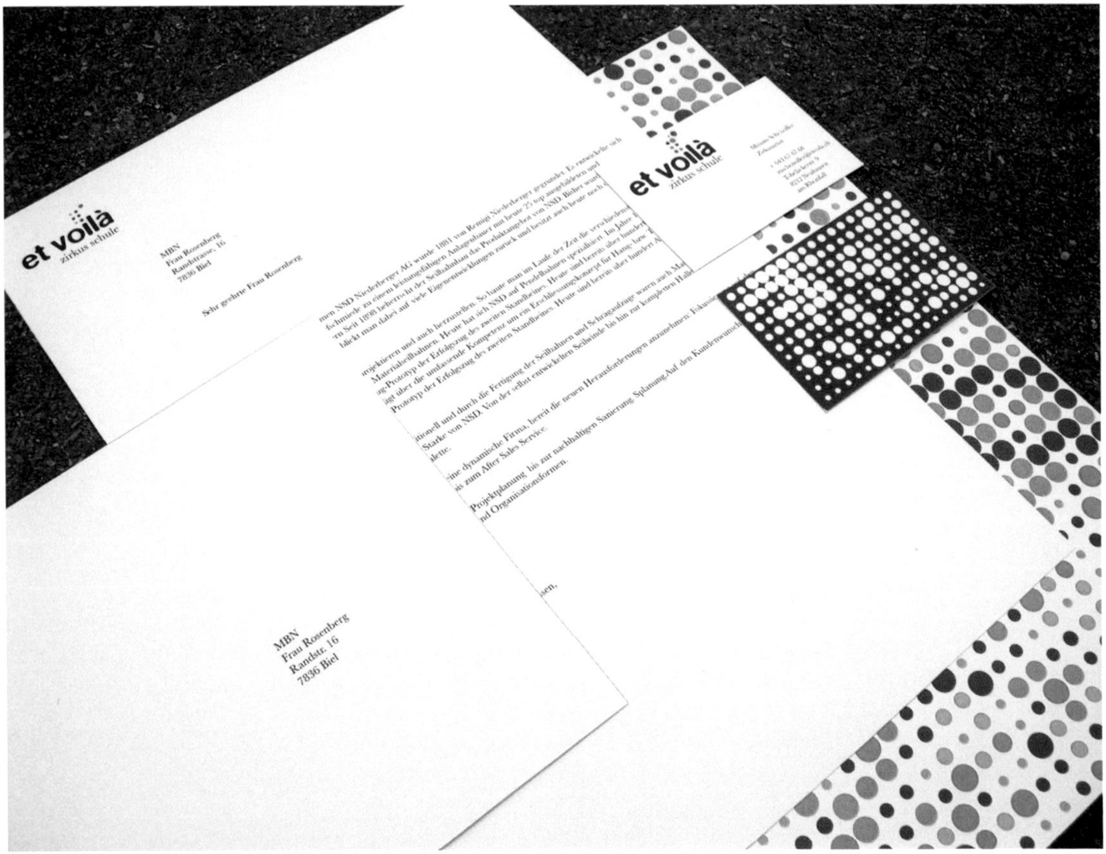

Client Existic
Year 2009
Design Kollor Design Agency

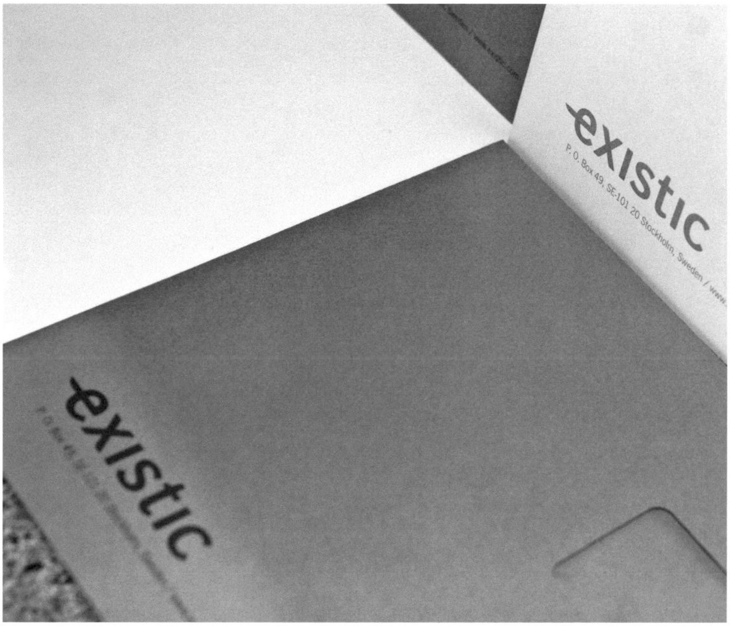

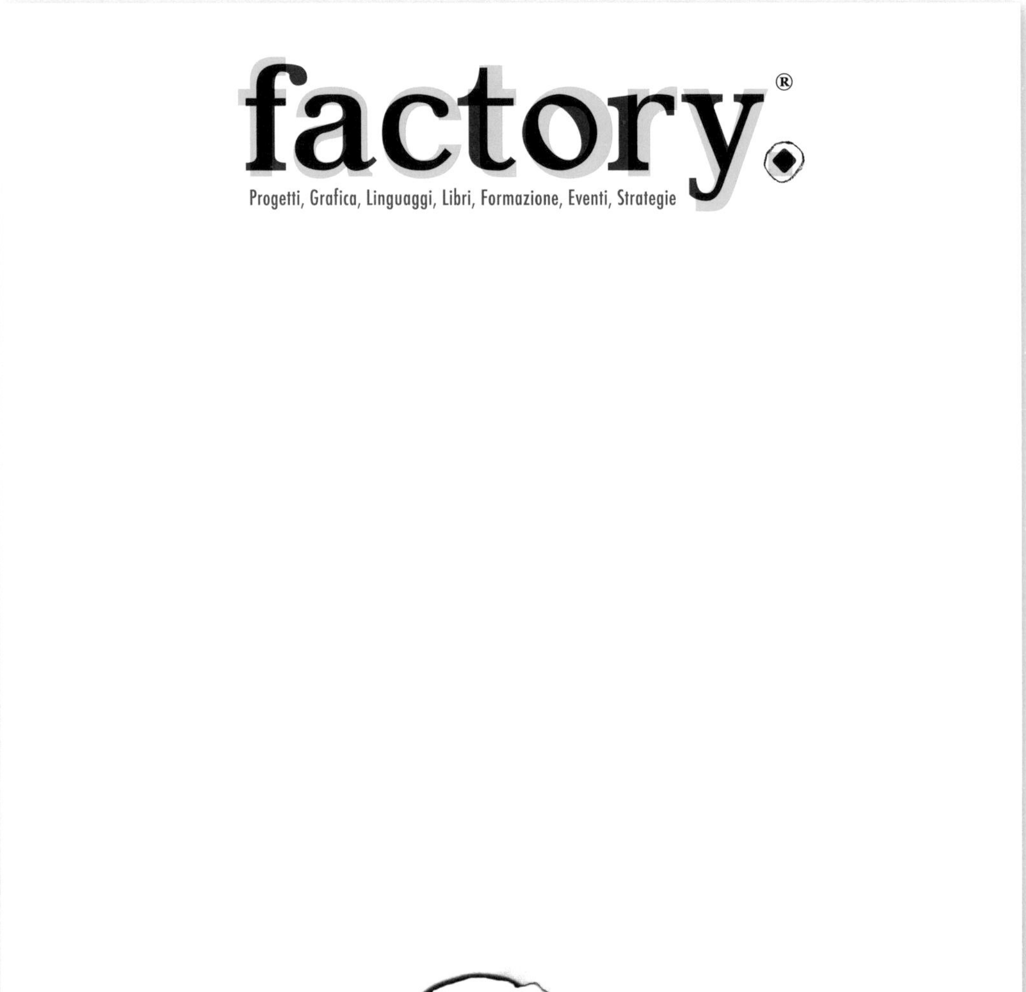
factory®
Progetti, Grafica, Linguaggi, Libri, Formazione, Eventi, Strategie
ho un'idea!
Michele Guidarini
www.micheleguidarini.com
Arca srl
www.arcafactory.it

Client Factory
Design Michele Guidarini

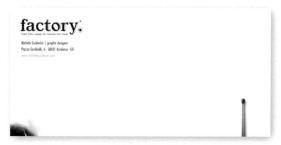

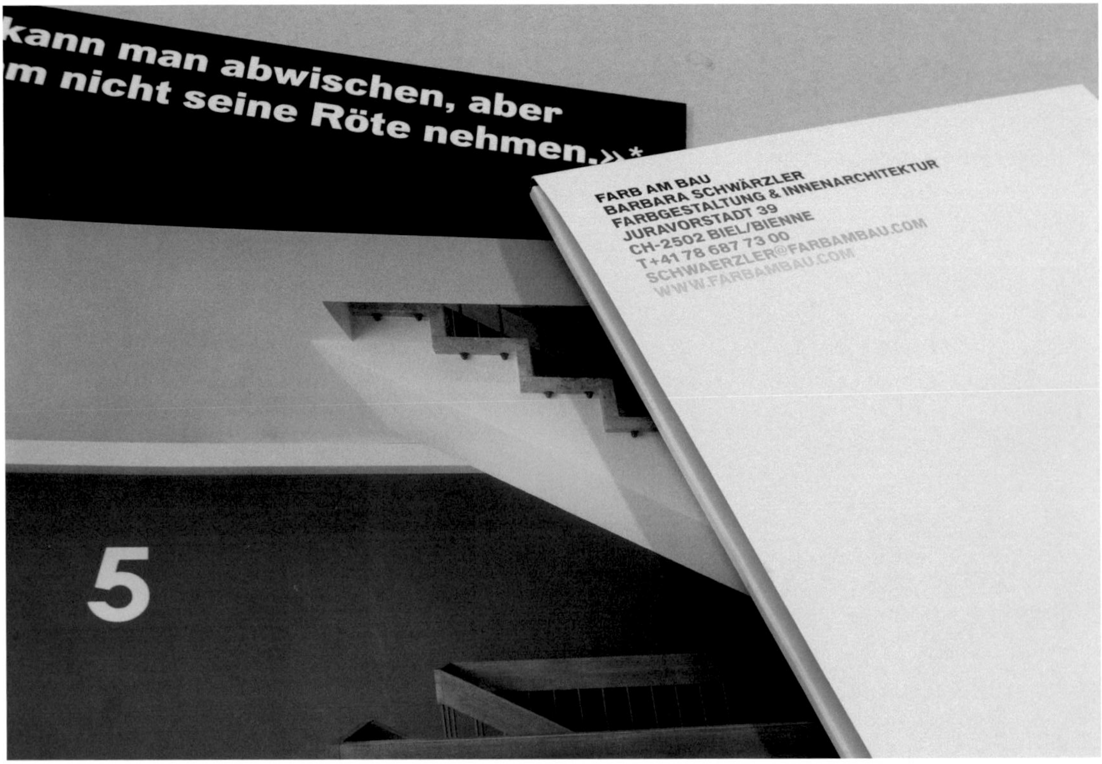

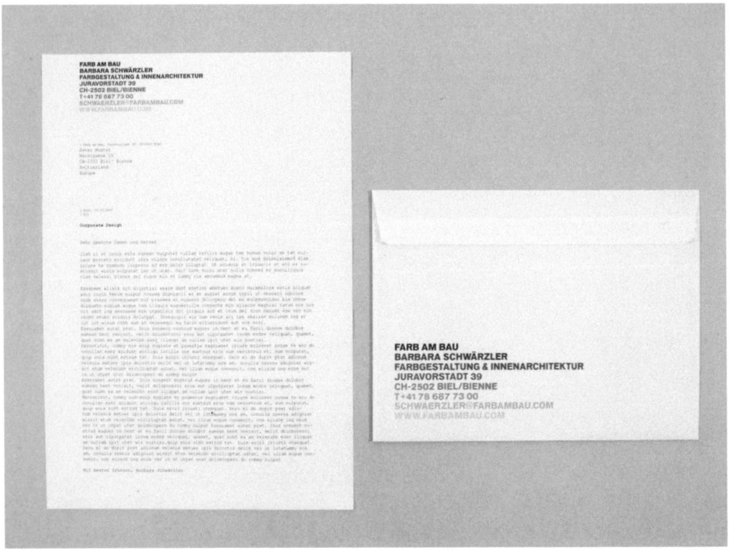

Client Farb am Bau
Year 2008
Design superbüro
Team Barbara Ehrbar

FARB AM BAU
BARBARA SCHWÄRZLER
FARBGESTALTUNG & INNENARCHITEKTUR
JURAVORSTADT 39
CH-2502 BIEL/BIENNE
T+41 78 687 73 00
SCHWAERZLER@FARBAMBAU.COM
WWW.FARBAMBAU.COM
«Zinnober kann man abwischen, aber man kann ihm nicht seine Röte nehmen.»*
5

FARB AM BAU
BARBARA SCHWÄRZLER
FARBGESTALTUNG & INNENARCHITEKTUR
JURAVORSTADT 39
CH-2502 BIEL/BIENNE
T+41 78 687 73 00
SCHWAERZLER@FARBAMBAU.COM
WWW.FARBAMBAU.COM

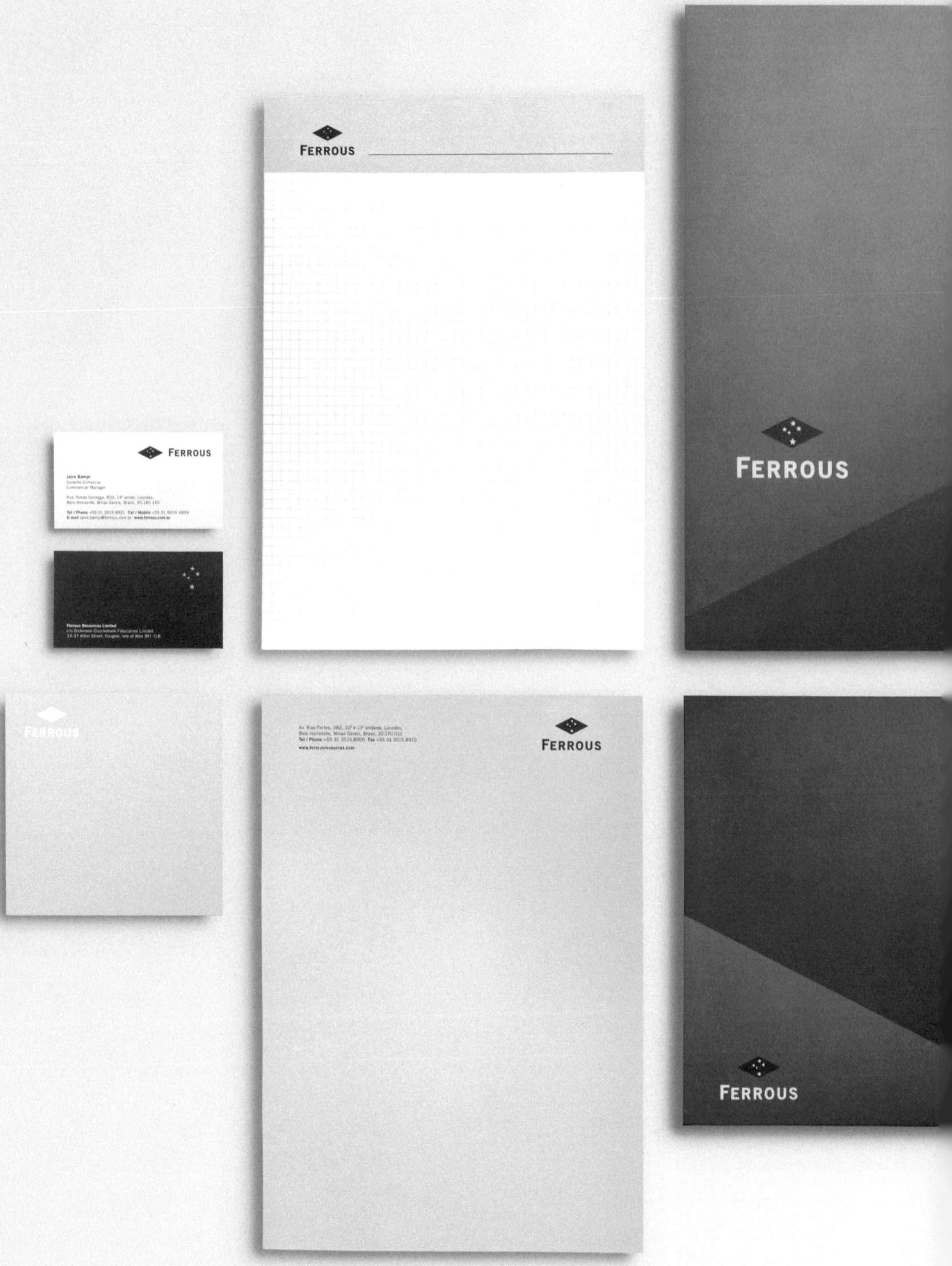
FERROUS
FERROUS
FERROUS
FERROUS
FERROUS
FERROUS

Client Ferrous
Year 2007
Design Hardy Design

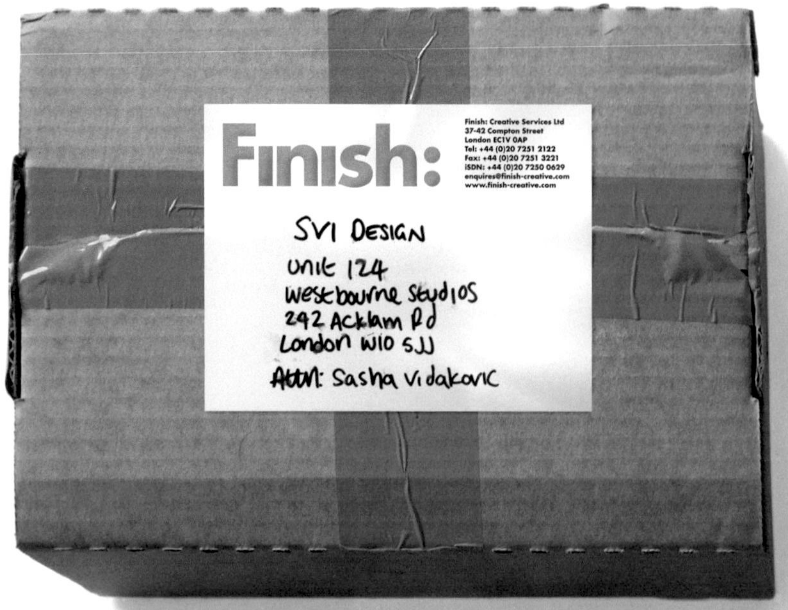
Finish:
Finish: Creative Services Ltd
37-42 Compton Street
London EC1V 0AP
Tel: +44 (0)20 7251 2122
Fax: +44 (0)20 7251 3221
iSDN: +44 (0)20 7250 0629
enquires@finish-creative.com
www.finish-creative.com
SVI DESIGN
Unit 124
Westbourne Studios
242 Acklam Rd
London W10 5JJ
Attn: Sasha Vidakovic

Finish:
Lee Robinson:
Director
Finish: Creative Services Ltd
37-42 Compton Street
London EC1V 0AP
Tel: +44 (0)20 7251 2122
Fax: +44 (0)20 7251 3221
iSDN: +44 (0)20 7250 0629
Lee@finish-creative.com
www.finish-creative.com

Artwork:Digital proofs:
Litho proofs:Silkscreen:
Foil-blocking:Embossing:
Debossing:Spraying:Cans:
Digital-cutting:Aerosols:
Dry tranfers:Shrinkwraps:
Flow wraps:3d rendering:
Bottles:Cartons:Tubes:Etc...

Client Finish
Year 2008
Design SVIDesign

Finish:
Finish: Creative Services Ltd
37-42 Compton Street
London EC1V 0AP
Tel: +44 (0)20 7251 2122
Fax: +44 (0)20 7251 3221
iSDN: +44 (0)20 7250 0629
enquires@finish-creative.com
www.finish-creative.com

Artwork: Digital proofs:
Litho proofs: Silkscreen:
Foil-blocking: Embossing:
Debossing: Spraying: Cans:
Digital-cutting: Aerosols:
Dry tranfers: Shrinkwraps:
Flow wraps: 3d rendering:
Bottles: Cartons: Tubes: Etc...

Finish:

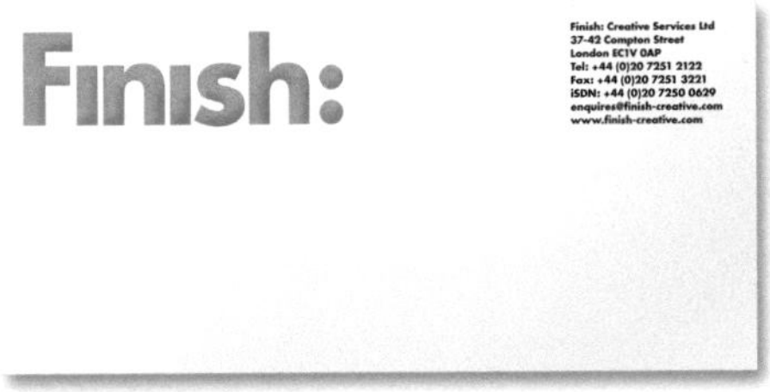
Finish:
Finish: Creative Services Ltd
37-42 Compton Street
London EC1V 0AP
Tel: +44 (0)20 7251 2122
Fax: +44 (0)20 7251 3221
iSDN: +44 (0)20 7250 0629
enquires@finish-creative.com
www.finish-creative.com

Artwork: Digital proofs: Litho proofs:
Debossing: Spraying: Cans:
Shrinkwraps:
Cartons: Tubes :Etc...

Client	First & 42nd
Year	2007
Design	Pentagram
Team	Pentagram Design London

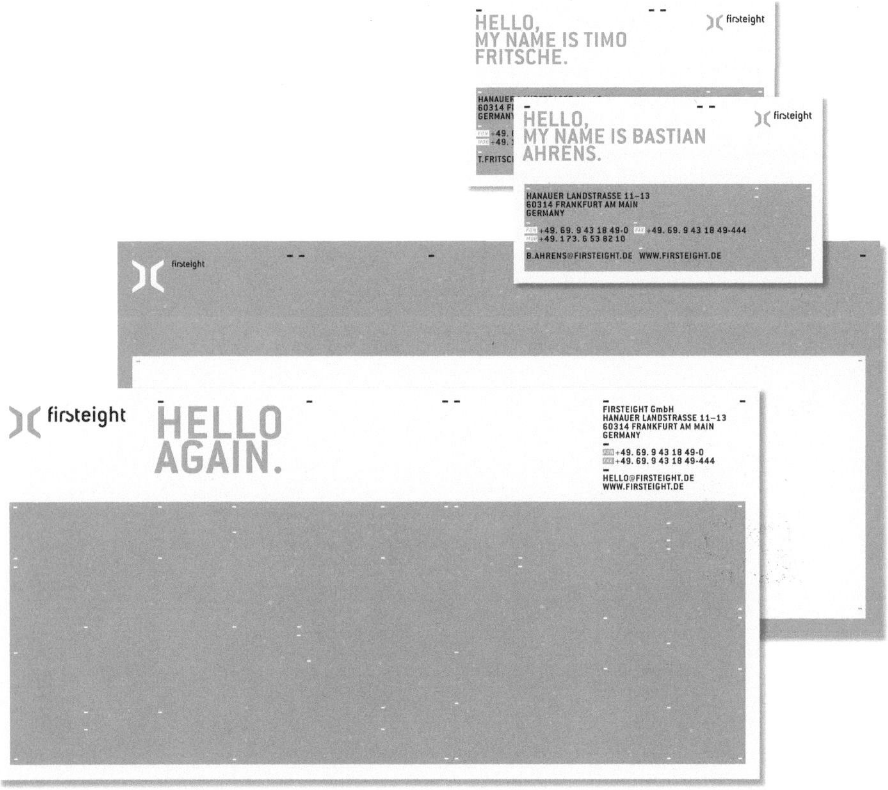

Client Firsteight
Year 2008
Design Falko Ohlmer

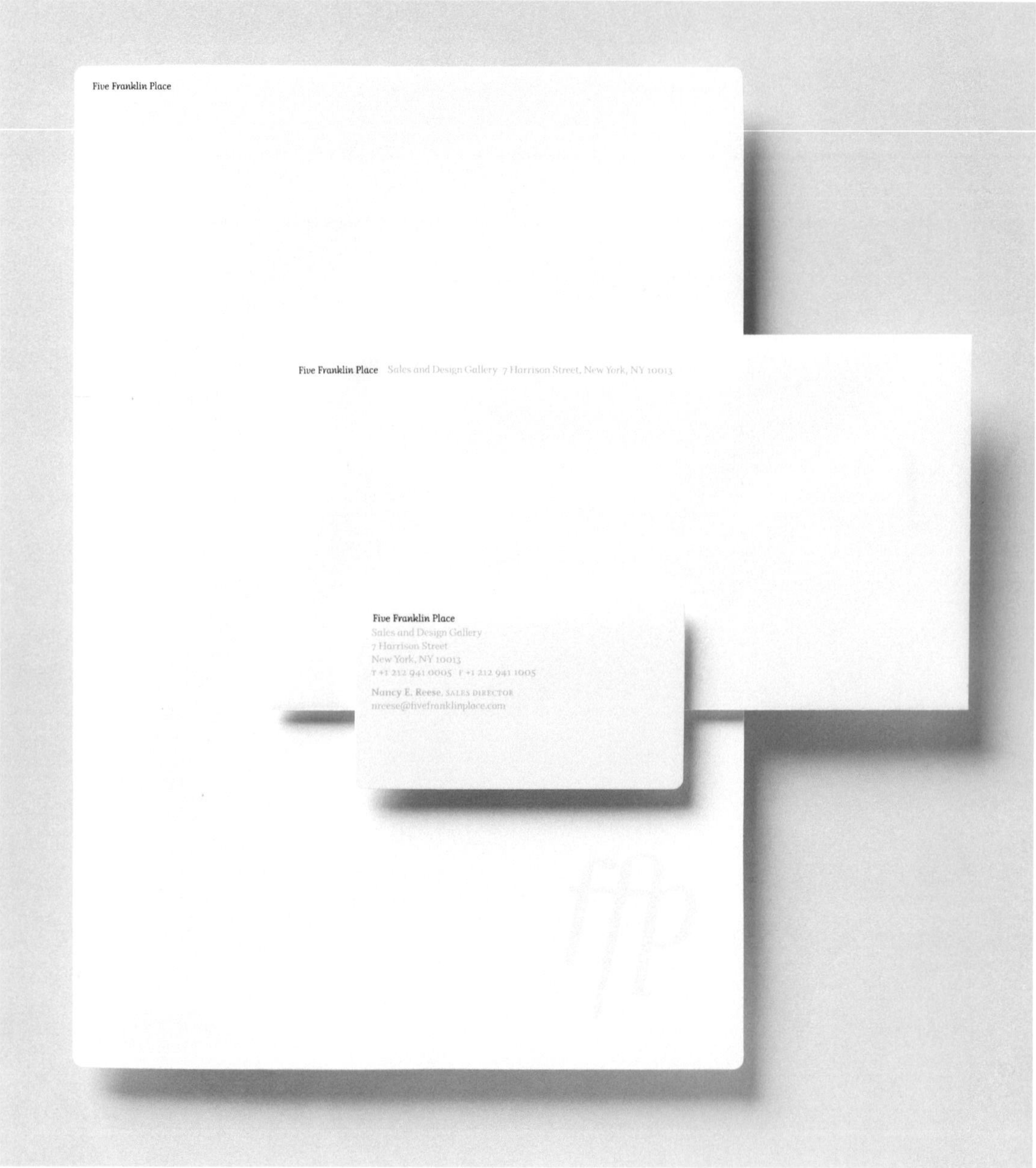

Client Five Franklin Place
Year 2009
Design Pentagram

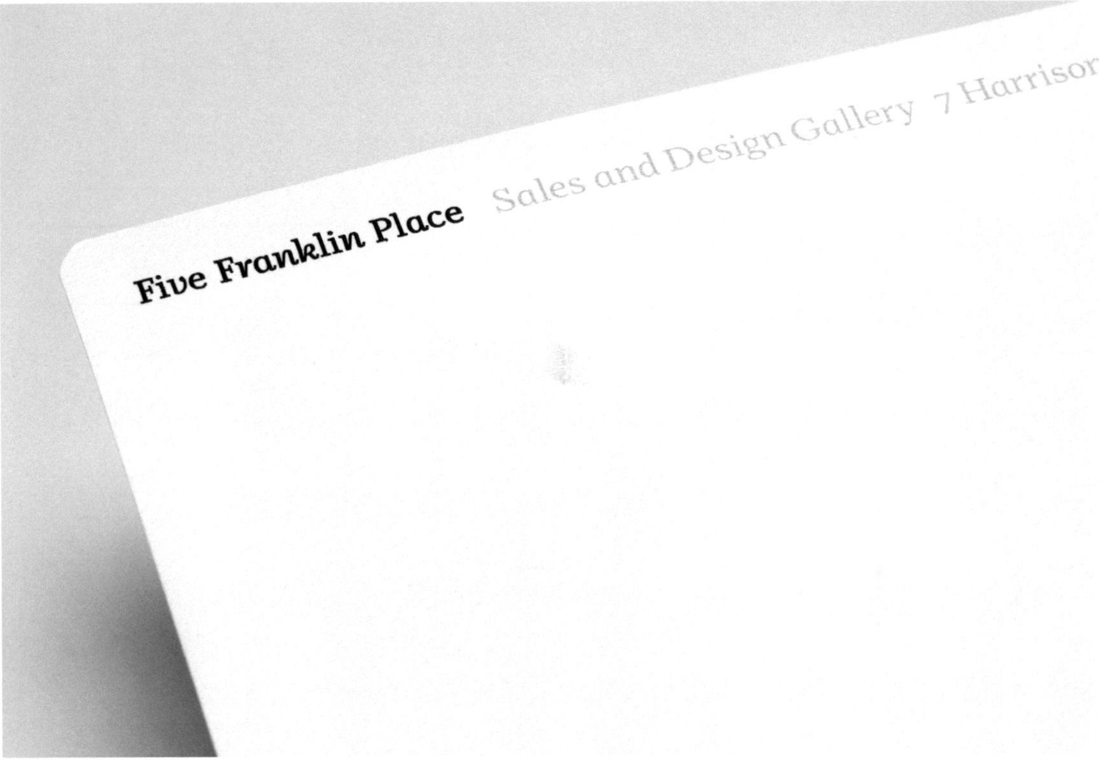
Five Franklin Place
Sales and Design Gallery 7 Harrison

Five Franklin Place

flow33 : waterlink : flow33 : waterlink : flow33 : waterlink : flow33 : wat
flow33 flow33 flow33
Flow Beyond 49 Karlibach st., Ramat Gan 96162, Israel Tel: +972(3) 688.7148 Fax: +972(3) 688.7149 Mobile: +972(54) 816.948 avnerg@flowbeyond.com

Client Flow 33
Year 2008
Design Dan Alexander & Co

Client Fragola
Year 2007
Design Zenteno Design Studio

Fragola
fashion store
Calle Velasco No. 45
Phone: (591) (33) 3303532
Bolivia - Santa Cruz,

Client	Frolic Contract
Year	2009
Design	Bilder Branding
Team	Ana Moriset, Matias Cageao

Client Fundación Boliviana para la Reforma Democrática
Year 2004
Design Asterisco Arte y Comunicación
Team Ernesto Azcuy

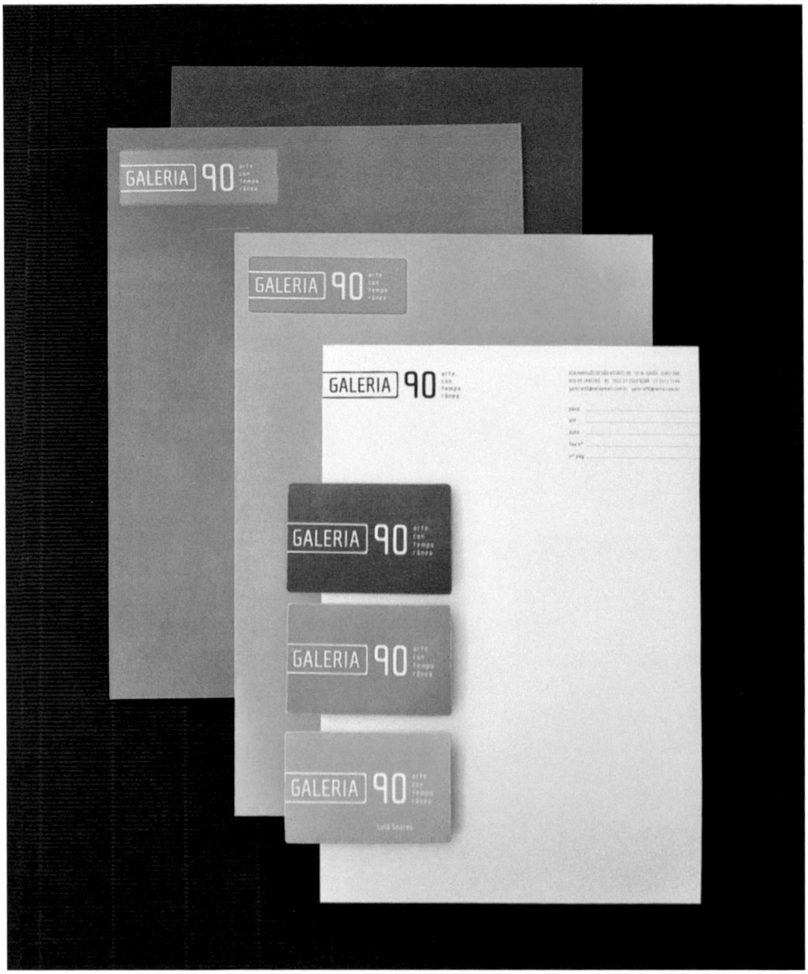

Client Galeria 90
Year 2007
Design Dupla Design
Team Claudia Gamboa, Ney Valle

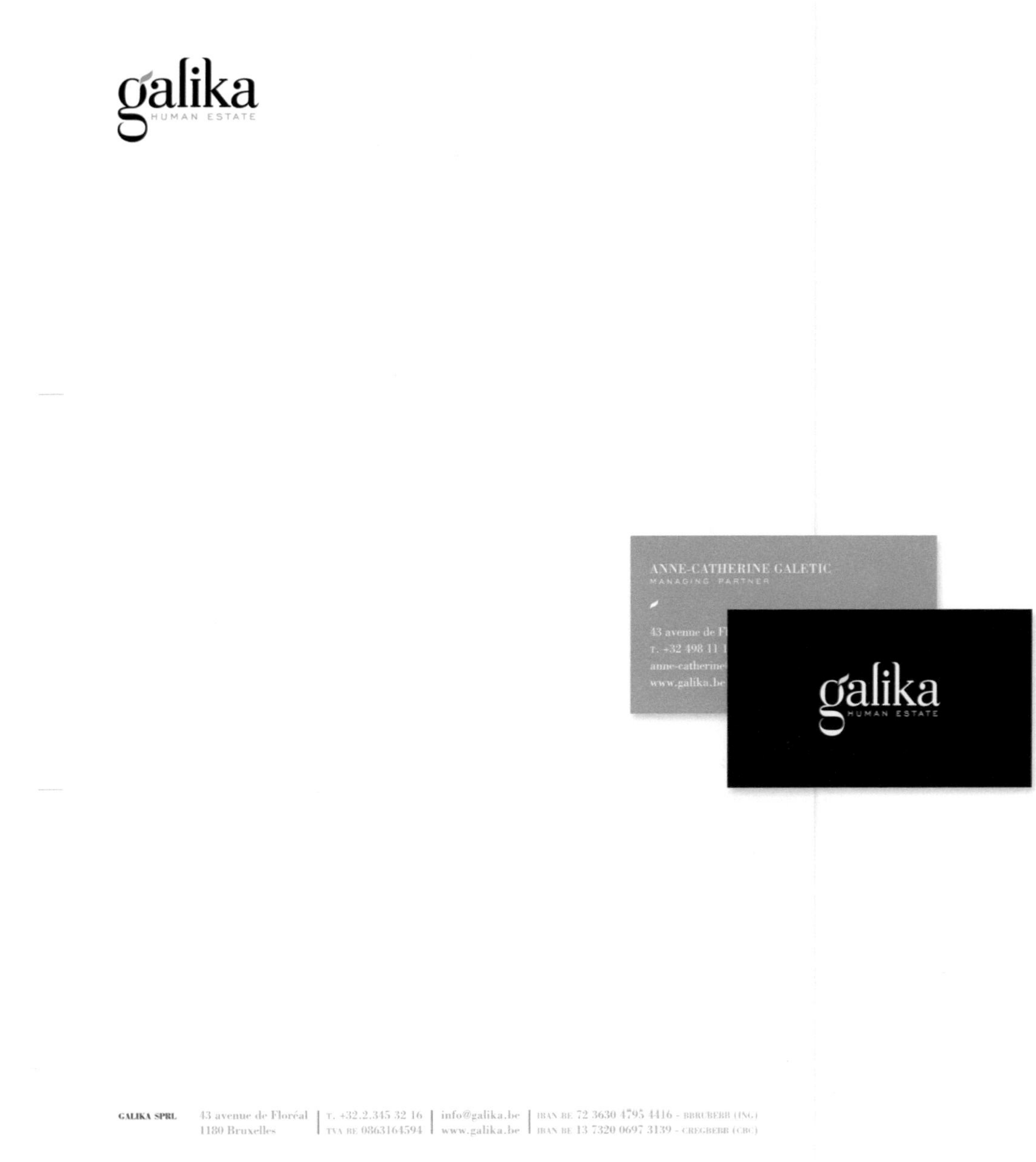

Client Galika
Year 2009
Design Sign*
Team Frédéric Chevalier

Client	Getxophoto
Year	2008
Design	Barfutura

Client Giralunas
Year 2009
Design Bilder Branding
Team Matias Cageao, Ana Moriset

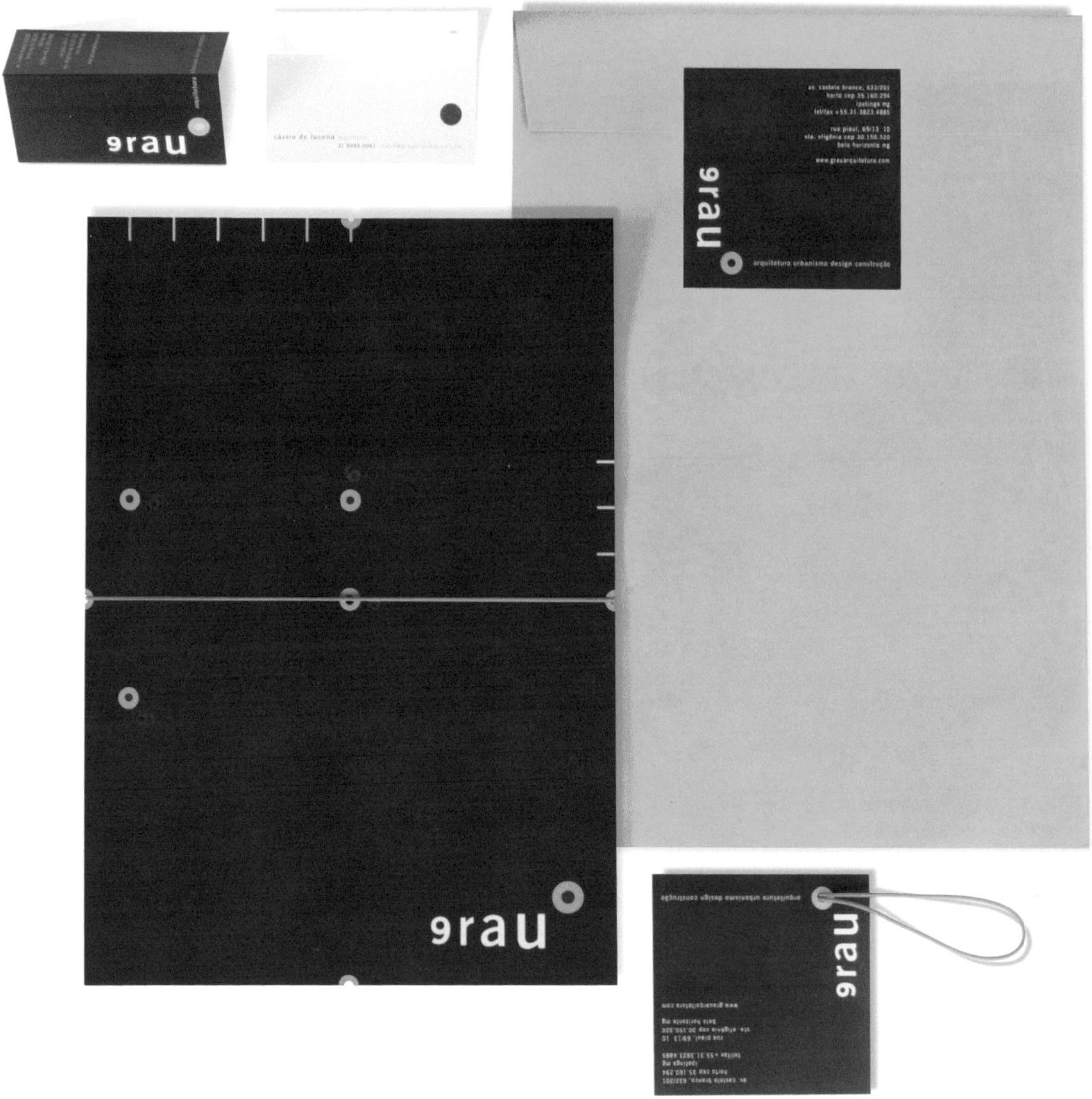
grau
av. castelo branco, 632/201
horto cep 35.160.294
ipatinga mg
tel/fax +55.31.3823.4885
rua piauí, 69/13 10
sta. efigênia cep 30.150.320
belo horizonte mg
www.grauarquitetura.com
arquitetura urbanismo design construção

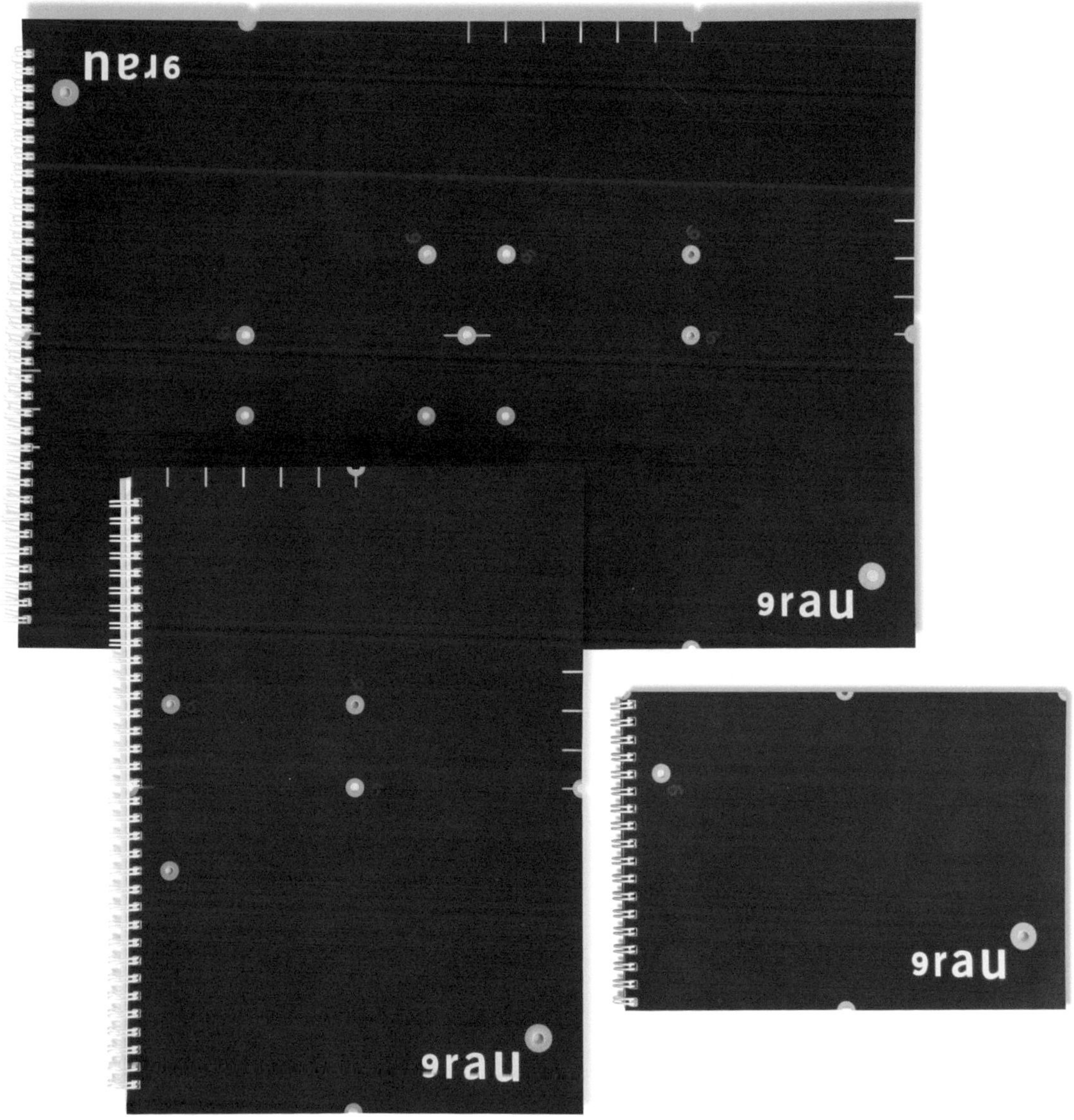

Client Grau
Year 2005
Design Hardy Design

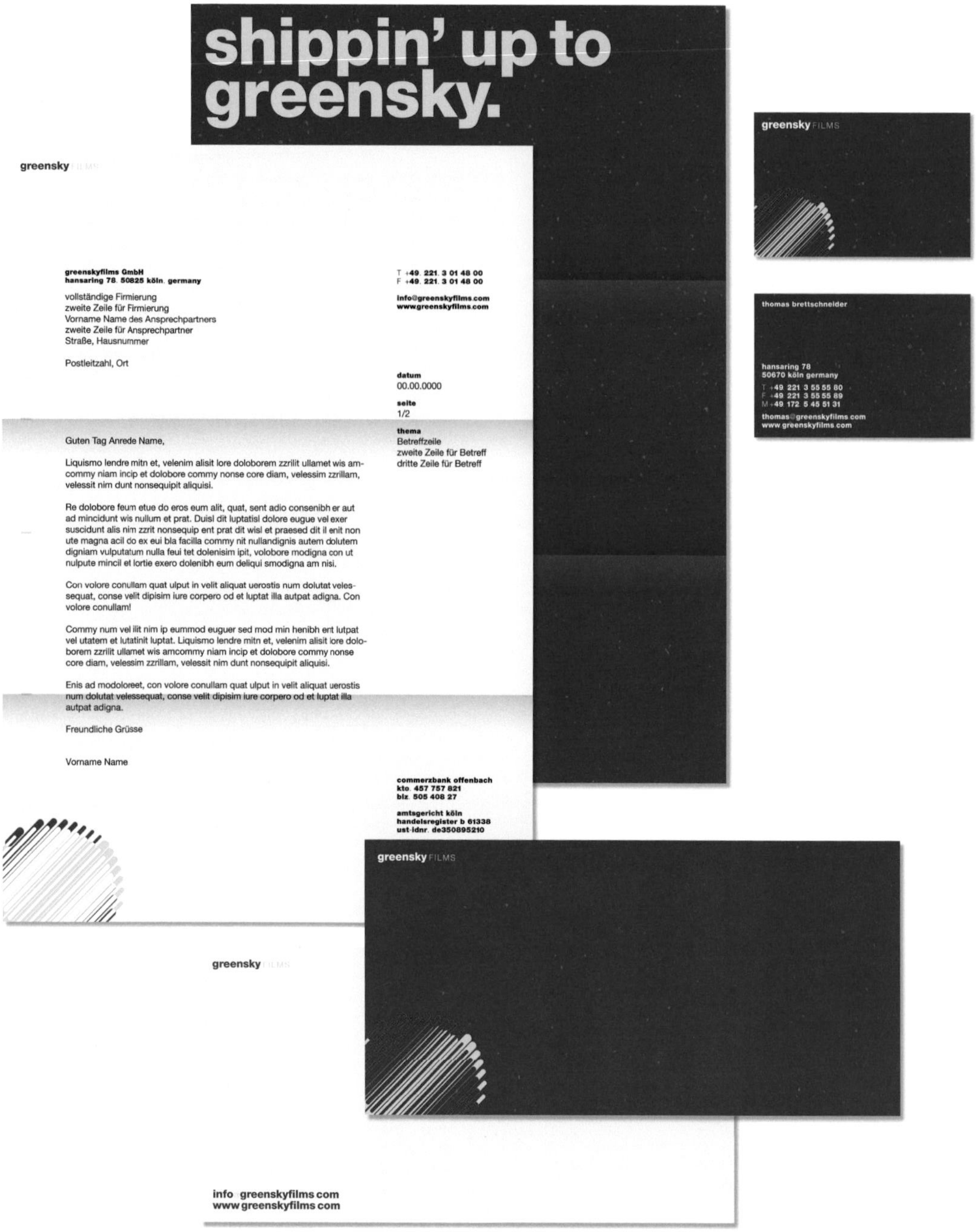

shippin' up to greensky.
greensky FILMS
greenskyfilms GmbH
hansaring 78. 50825 köln. germany
vollständige Firmierung
zweite Zeile für Firmierung
Vorname Name des Ansprechpartners
zweite Zeile für Ansprechpartner
Straße, Hausnummer
Postleitzahl, Ort
T +49. 221. 3 01 48 00
F +49. 221. 3 01 48 00
info@greenskyfilms.com
www.greenskyfilms.com
datum
00.00.0000
seite
1/2
thema
Betreffzeile
zweite Zeile für Betreff
dritte Zeile für Betreff
Guten Tag Anrede Name,
Liquismo lendre mitn et, velenim alisit lore doloborem zzrilit ullamet wis am-commy niam incip et dolobore commy nonse core diam, velessim zzrillam, velessit nim dunt nonsequipit aliquisi.
Re dolobore feum etue do eros eum alit, quat, sent adio consenibh er aut ad mincidunt wis nullum et prat. Duisl dit luptatisl dolore eugue vel exer suscidunt alis nim zzrit nonsequip ent prat dit wisl et praesed dit il enit non ute magna acil do ex eui bla facilla commy nit nullandignis autem dolutem digniam vulputatum nulla feui tet dolenisim ipit, volobore modigna con ut nulpute mincil et lortie exero dolenibh eum deliqui smodigna am nisi.
Con volore conullam quat ulput in velit aliquat uerostis num dolutat veles-sequat, conse velit dipisim iure corpero od et luptat illa autpat adigna. Con volore conullam!
Commy num vel ilit nim ip eummod euguer sed mod min henibh ent lutpat vel utatem et lutatinit luptat. Liquismo lendre mitn et, velenim alisit lore dolo-borem zzrilit ullamet wis amcommy niam incip et dolobore commy nonse core diam, velessim zzrillam, velessit nim dunt nonsequipit aliquisi.
Enis ad modoloreet, con volore conullam quat ulput in velit aliquat uerostis num dolutat velessequat, conse velit dipisim iure corpero od et luptat illa autpat adigna.
Freundliche Grüsse
Vorname Name
commerzbank offenbach
kto. 457 757 821
blz. 505 408 27
amtsgericht köln
handelsregister b 61338
ust-idnr. de350895210
greensky FILMS
thomas brettschneider
hansaring 78
50670 köln germany
T +49. 221. 3 55 55 80
F +49. 221. 3 55 55 89
M +49. 172. 5 45 51 31
thomas@greenskyfilms.com
www.greenskyfilms.com
greensky FILMS
greensky
info@greenskyfilms.com
www.greenskyfilms.com

Client Greensky Films
Year 2008
Design Falko Ohlmer

Client Haka Group
Year 2005
Design NNSS Visual Universes

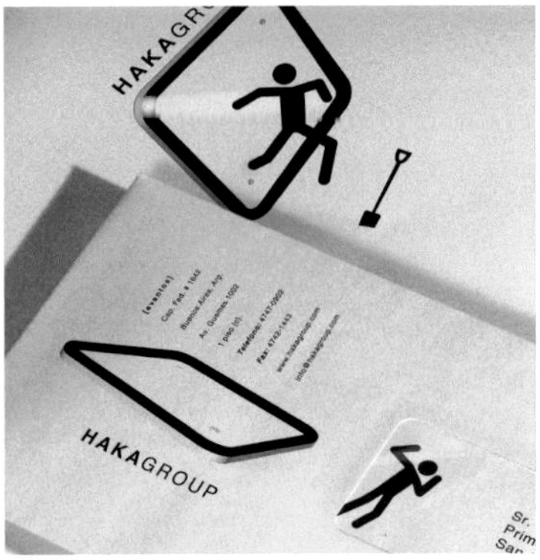

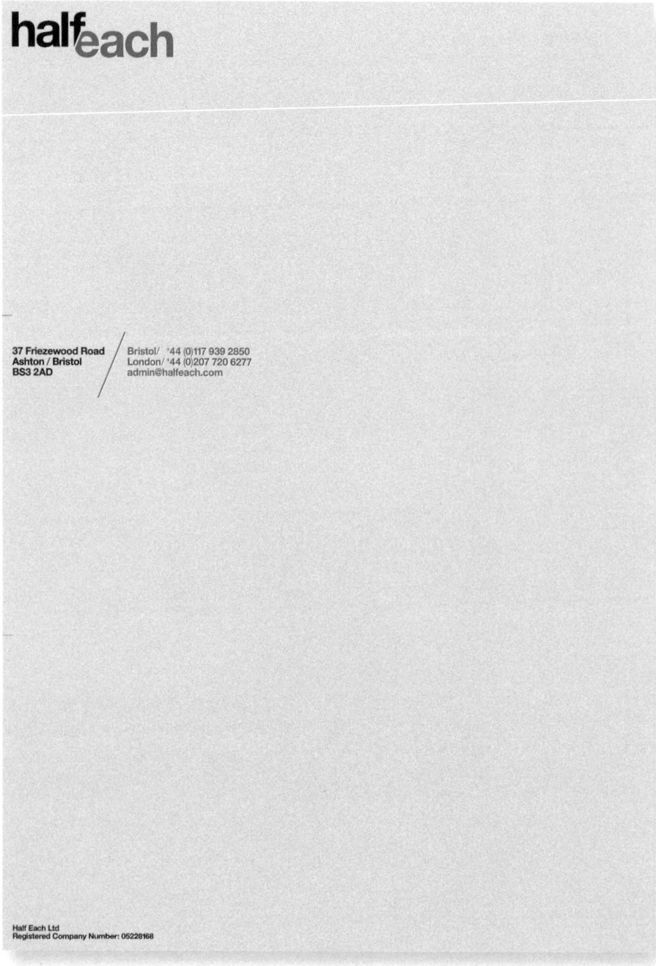
halfeach
37 Friezewood Road
Ashton / Bristol
BS3 2AD
Bristol/ +44 (0)117 939 2850
London/ +44 (0)207 720 6277
admin@halfeach.com
Half Each Ltd
Registered Company Number: 05228168

halfeach
London/ +44 (0)207 720 6277
Bristol/ +44 (0)117 939 2850
info@halfeach.com

halfeach

Half Each
Digital Communications
Hannah Cocks
Director
Bristol
T/ +44 (0)117 939 2850
M/ +44 (0)7855 504 263
hannah@halfeach.com
London
T/ +44 (0)207 720 6277
M/ +44 (0)7736 459 932
london@halfeach.com
www.halfeach.com

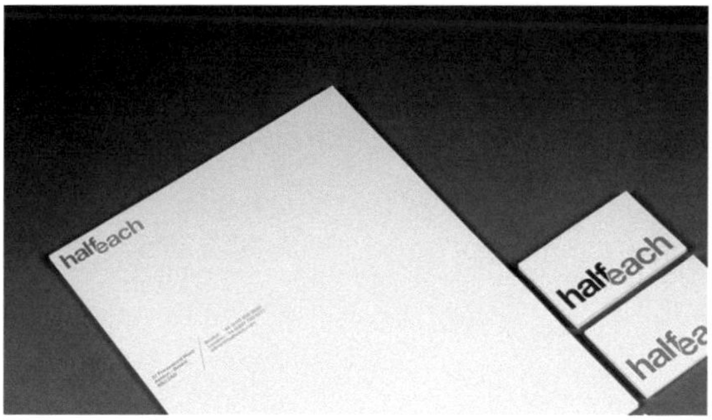

Client Half Each
Year 2008
Design Stereo

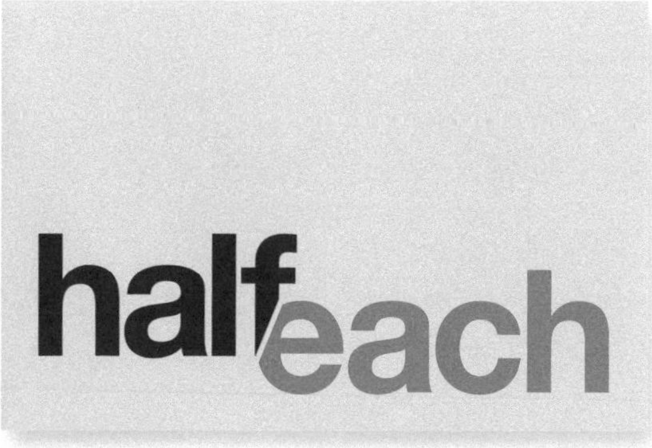

Client Haras Los Durmientes
Year 2010
Design Bilder Branding
Team Ana Moriset, Matias Cageao

RUTA N205 KM77/
1814.CANUELAS
/BUENOS AIRES/
ARGENTINA/
WWW.
LOSDURMIENTES.
COM.AR
HARAS
LOS
DUR
MIEN
TES

RUTA N205 KM77/
1814.CANUELAS
/BUENOS AIRES/
ARGENTINA/
LOSDURMIENTES.
COM.AR/
HARAS
LOS
DUR
MIEN
TES
ANA KOGAN/
T.5411.4784.8338
/15.5052.6242/
RUTA N205 KM77/
1814.CANUELAS
/BUENOS AIRES/
ARGENTINA/

HARRY WATTS
PHOTOGRAPHER
HARRY-WATTS.CO.UK
7764 906 885
HARRY-WATTS.CO.UK
WWW.
+44 (0)
STUDIO@
HARRY WATTS
BIRCH STUDIO
15 METROPOLIS
LONDON
SE11 5TF
HARRY WATTS
PHOTOGRAPHER
HARRY-WATTS.CO.UK
7764 906 885
HARRY-WATTS.CO.UK
WWW.
+44 (0)
STUDIO@
WWW.
+44 (0)
WATTS.CO.UK
HARRY WATTS
PHOTOGRAPHER
HARRY-WATTS.CO.UK
7764 906 885
STUDIO@HARRY-

Client	Harry Watts
Year	2010
Design	Birch Studio

Client Health & Safety
Year 2008
Design Truly Design
Team Rems182

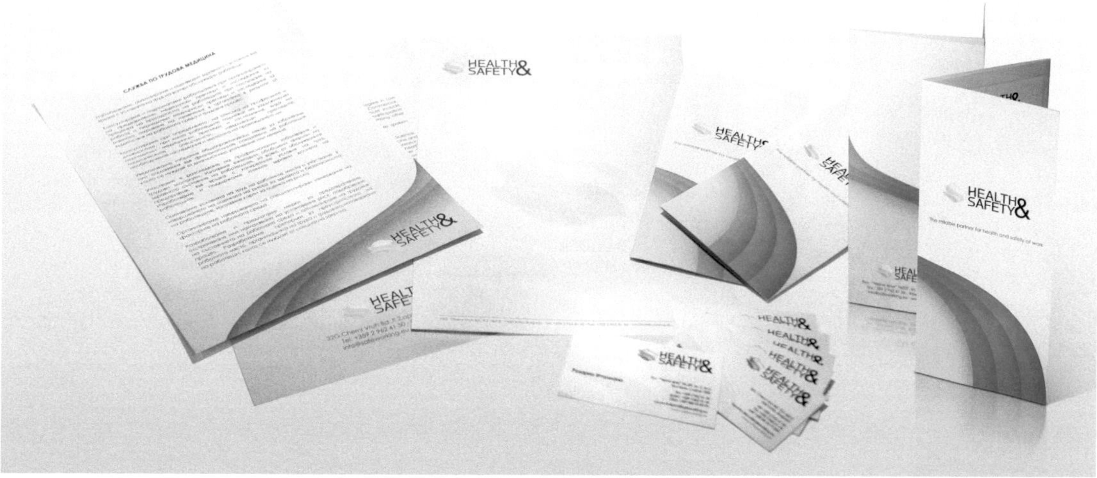

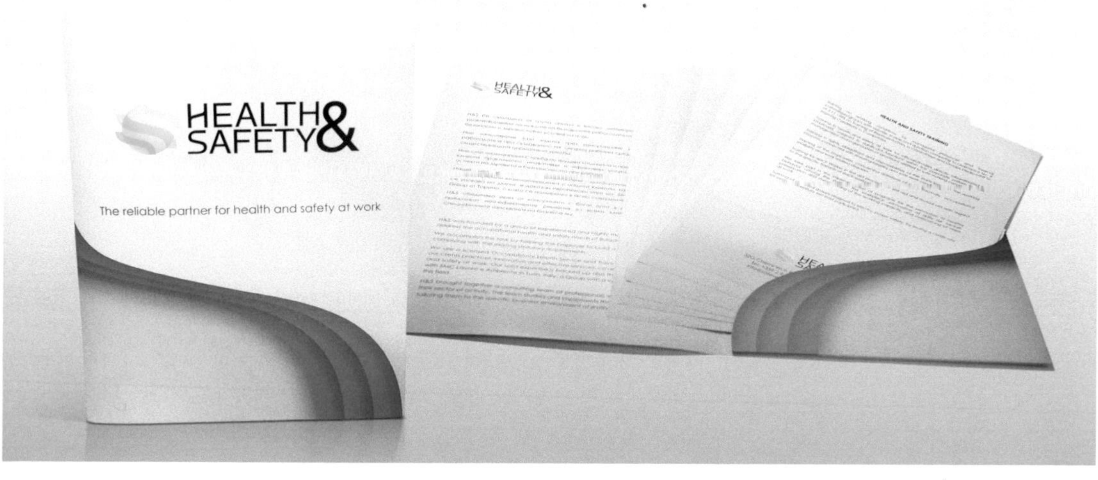

Client Hoax
Year 2009
Design huvi

Client	HTW Berlin, University of Applied Sciences
Year	2009
Design	Adler & Schmidt Kommunikations-Design
Team	Florian Adler, J. Strehmann, R. Engelkamp, Hans-Peter Schmidt

htw.
www.htw-berlin.de
Vielfältig und
innovativ –
die HTW Berlin
Masterstudiengang
Wirtschafts-
kommunikation
Masterstudiengang
Bauingenieurwesen
Das grafische
Erscheinungsbild
Masterstudiengang
Facility Management
Bachelorstudiengang
Betriebliche
Umweltinformatik
Hochschule für Technik
und Wirtschaft Berlin
Masterzeugnis
Master's Degree – Grade Transcript
Studienangebot
frischer!

huvi
Matt Keers
Creative Director
huvi
Sample Name
Audio, 10 Marine Parade,
Brighton, BN2 1TL
Graphic Design &
Art Direction
info@huvidesign.com
www.huvidesign.com
+44 (0)161 820 8545
huvi
Sample Name
Audio, 10 Marine Parade,
Brighton, BN2 1TL
Graphic Design &
Art Direction
info@huvidesign.com
www.huvidesign.com
+44 (0)161 820 8545
Invoice No: #000
Date: 00/00/0000
Your Ref: #000
Our Ref: #000
Service Details
Net Amount
£000.00
VAT Amount
£000.00
Print and production
Net Amount
£000.00
VAT Amount
£000.00
Total Net Amount
£000.00
Total VAT Amount
£000.00
Invoice Total
£000.00
Bank Details for immediate transfer
BANK / Sort Code: 00 00 00 / Account Number 1111111111
huvi
Graphic Design &
Art Direction
info@huvidesign.com
www.huvidesign.com
+44 (0)161 820 8545
With Compliments
huvi
With Compliments

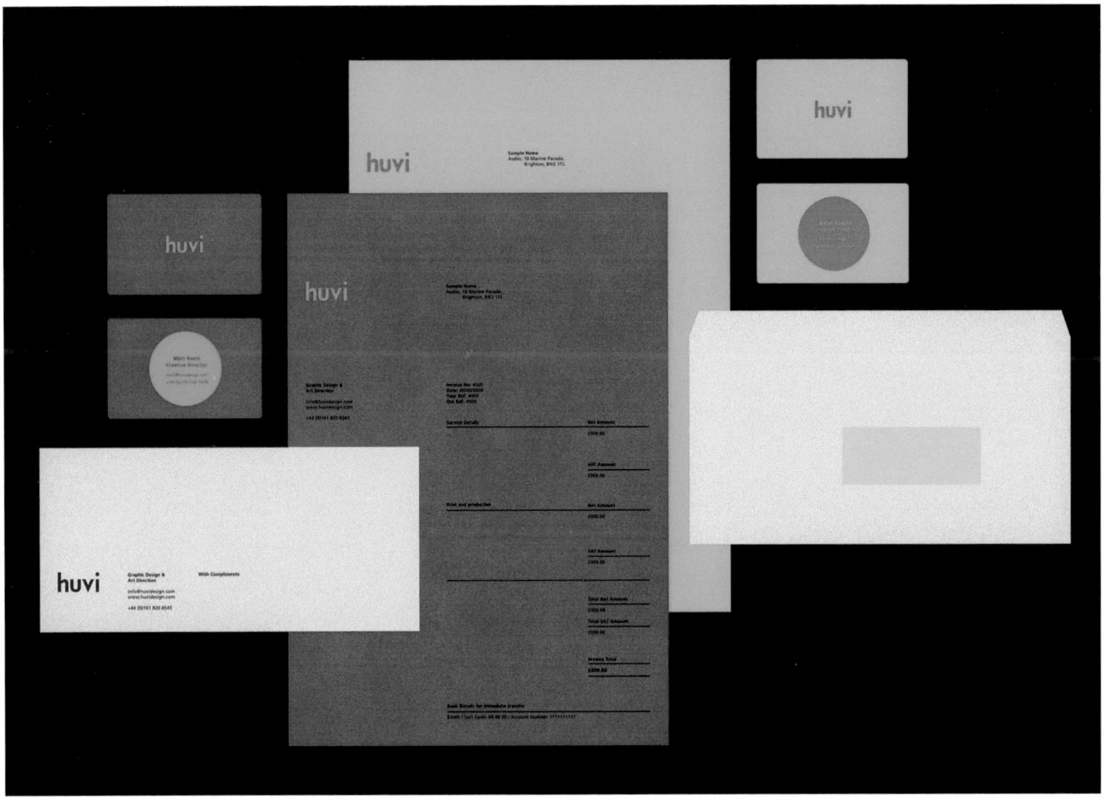

Client huvi
Year 2010
Design huvi

I+Drink
Cocktailing and more
Campoamor 27, 33001 Oviedo
+34 655 667 135
imasdrink@imasdrink.com
www.imasdrink.com
I+Yes!
I+Wow!
Cuba libre
Ron
Zumo de lima
Azúcar
Coca Cola
Angostura

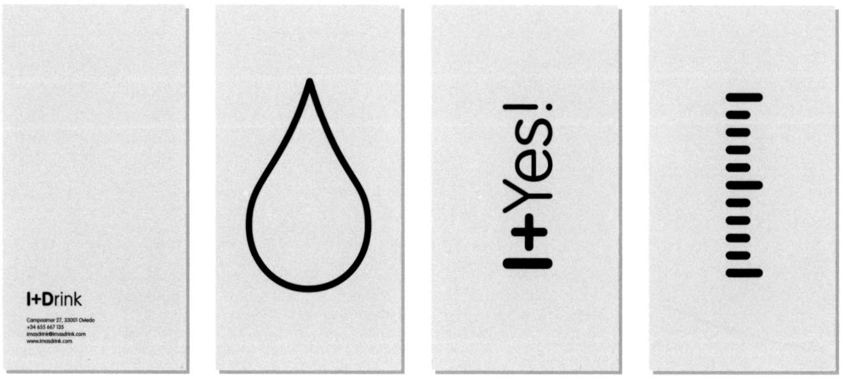
I+Drink
I+Yes!

Client I+Drink
Year 2009
Design m Barcelona
Team Marion Dönneweg

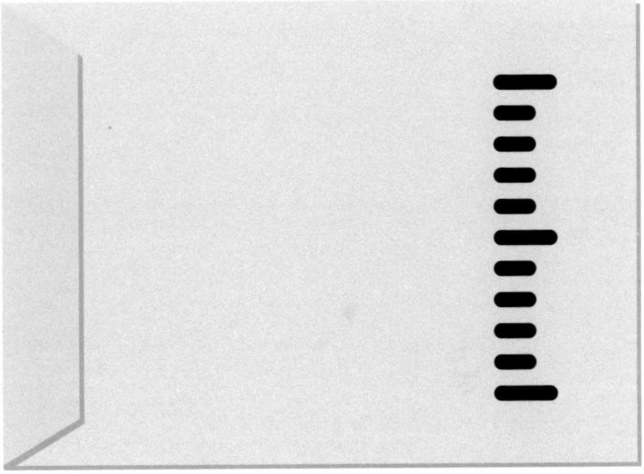

I-Estrategia
Fernando Moiguer
Director Grupo CCR
Profesor Universidad de San Andrés

Fernando Moiguer
Director Grupo CCR
Profesor Universidad de San Andrés
(54 11) 4546 7100
fmoiguer@i-estrategia.com.ar

I-Estrategia
Blanco Encalada 3202
Ciudad de Buenos Aires
C1428DED - Argentina
(54 11) 4546 7100
www.i-estrategia.com.ar
I-Es

Client I-Estrategia
Year 2007
Design másSustancia
Team Lucas D'Amore

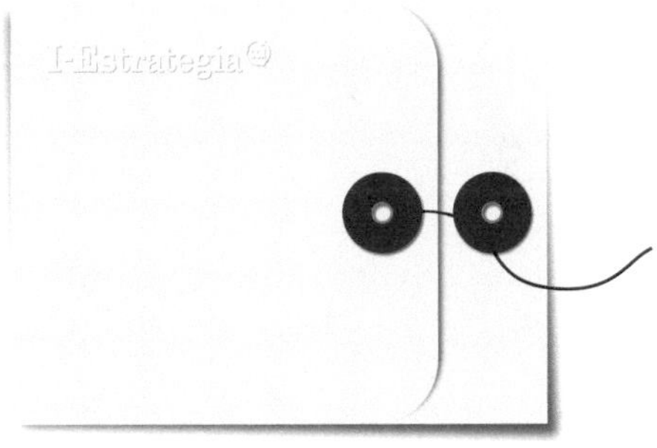

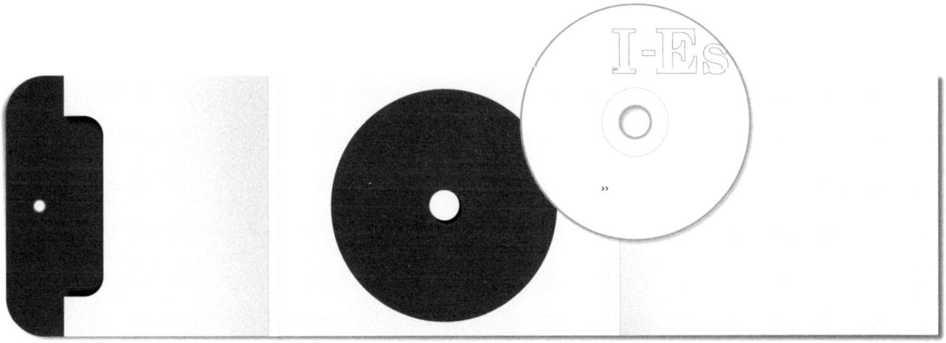

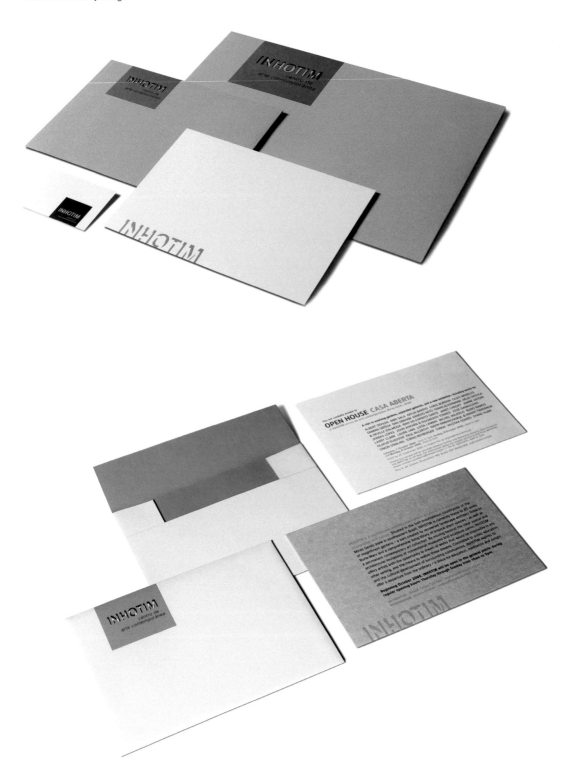

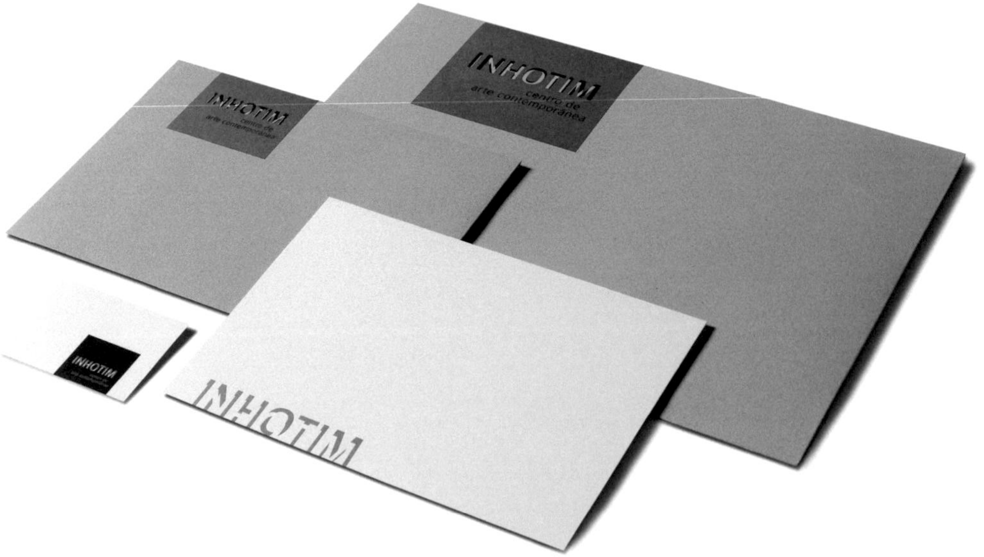
INHOTIM
centro de
arte contemporânea
INHOTIM
centro de
arte contemporânea
INHOTIM
INHOTIM

OPEN HOUSE CASA ABERTA
INHOTIM
centro de
arte contemporânea
INHOTIM

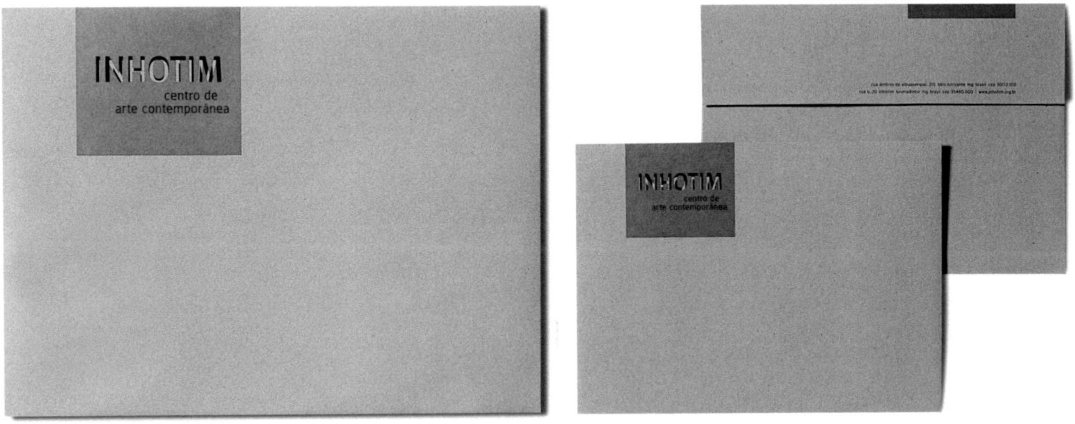

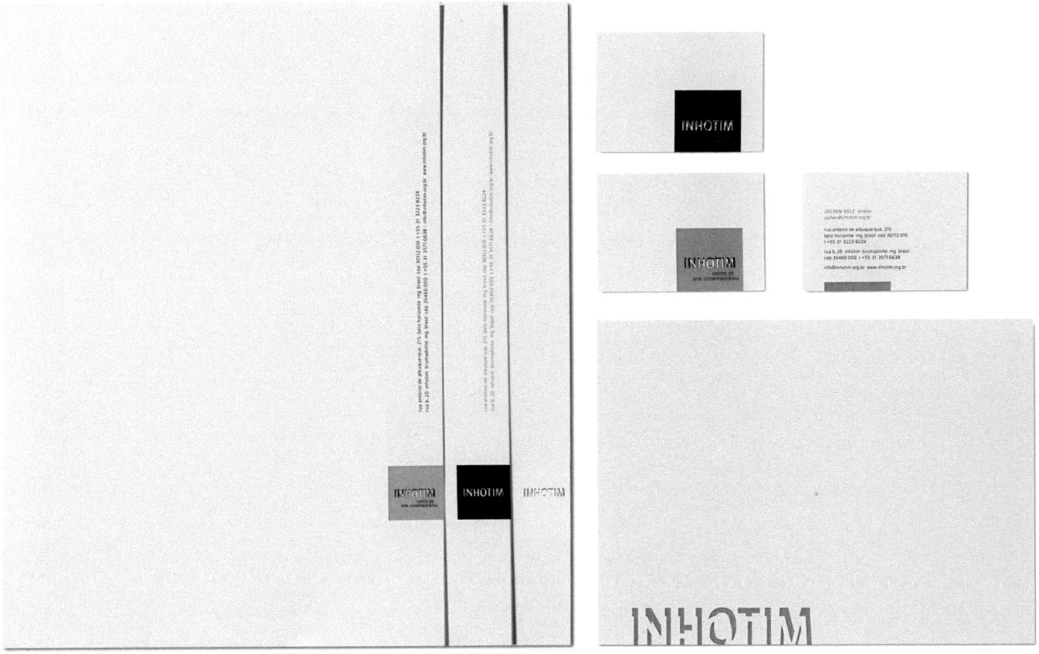

Client Inhotim
Year 2006
Design Hardy Design

INSTITUTO
artivisão
INSTITUTO
artivisão
R DOMINGOS VIEIRA, 273 SL 1002 CEP 30150-240 STA EFIGÊNIA BELO HORIZONTE MG TEL + 55 31 3241 5880 WWW.INSTITUTOARTIVISAO.ORG.BR

Client Instituto Artivisão
Year 2005
Design Hardy Design

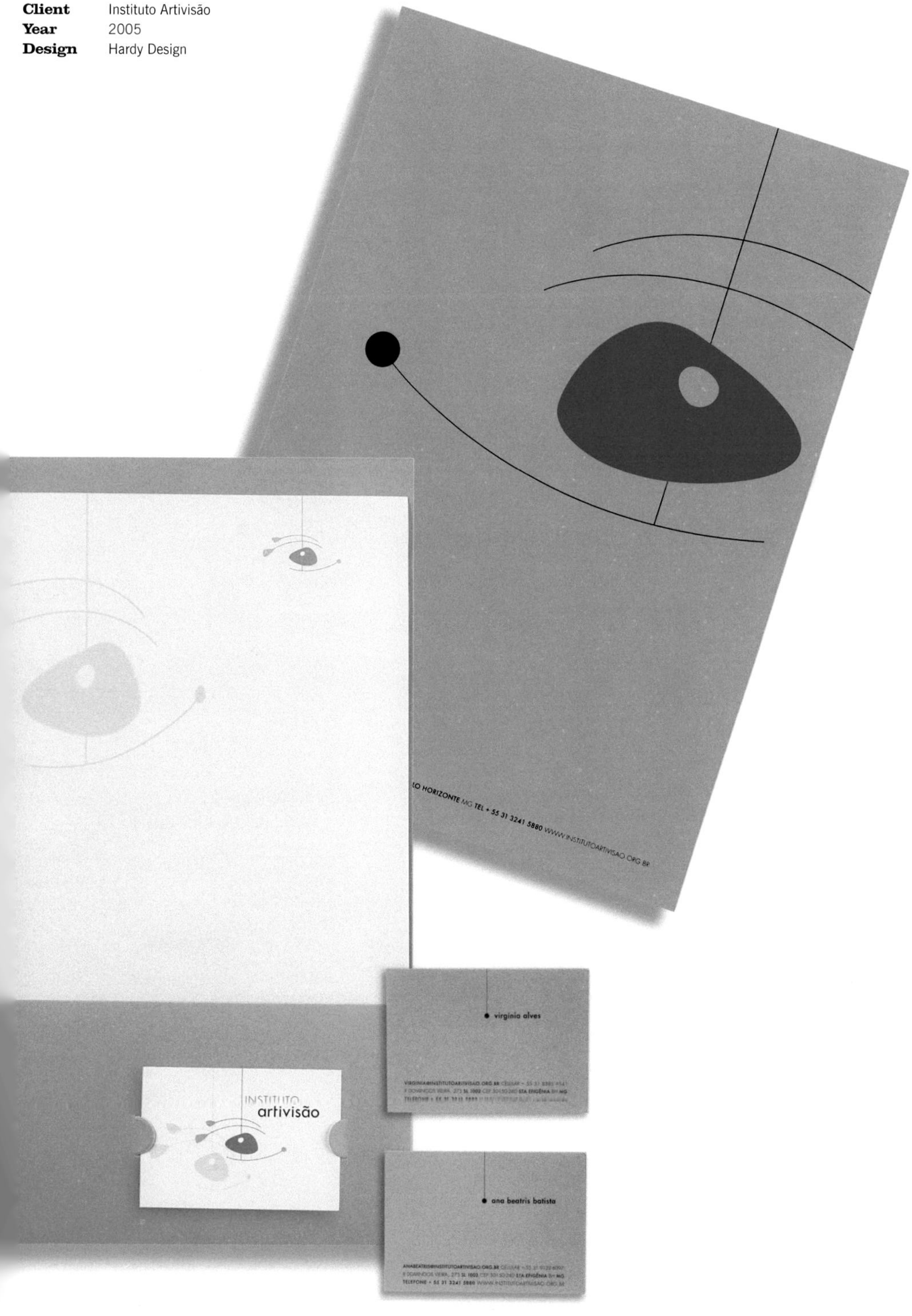

invensys
Steve Devany Head of Corporate Communications
T +44 (0)20 7821 3758 F +44 (0)20 7821 3709
M +44 (0)7970 59 39 41 E steve.devany@invensys.com
Invensys plc, Portland House, Bressenden Place
London SW1E 5BF, United Kingdom
www.invensys.com

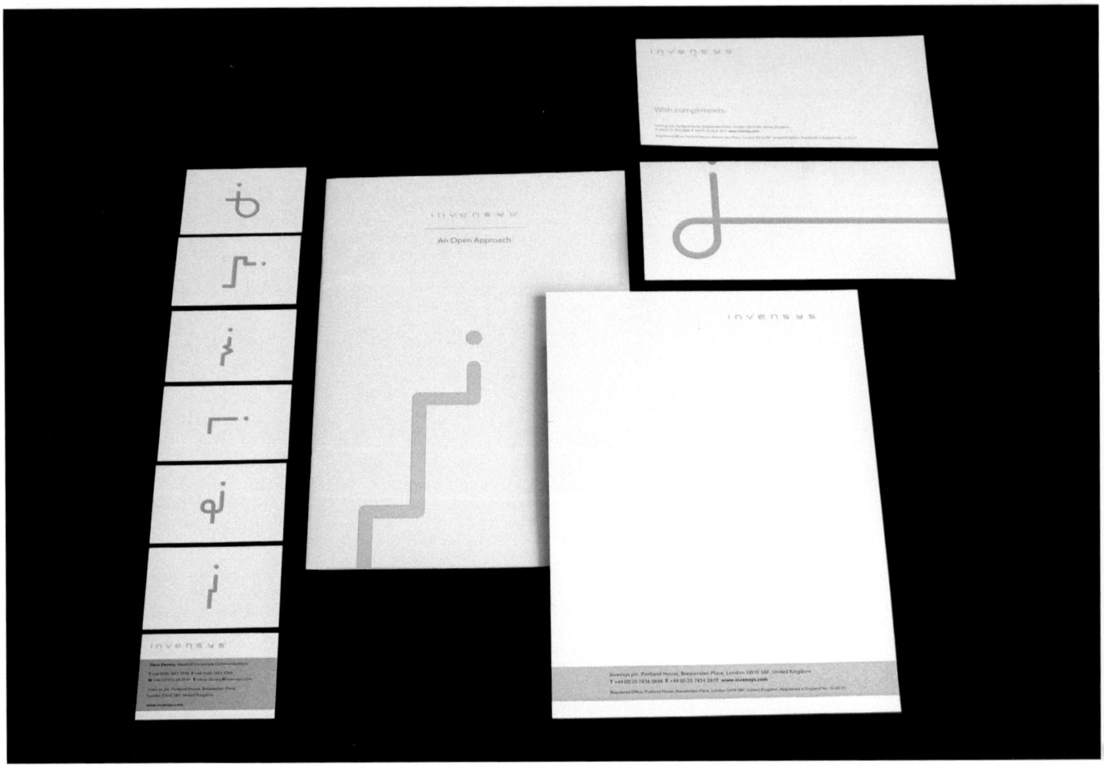
invensys
With compliments
invensys
An Open Approach
invensys

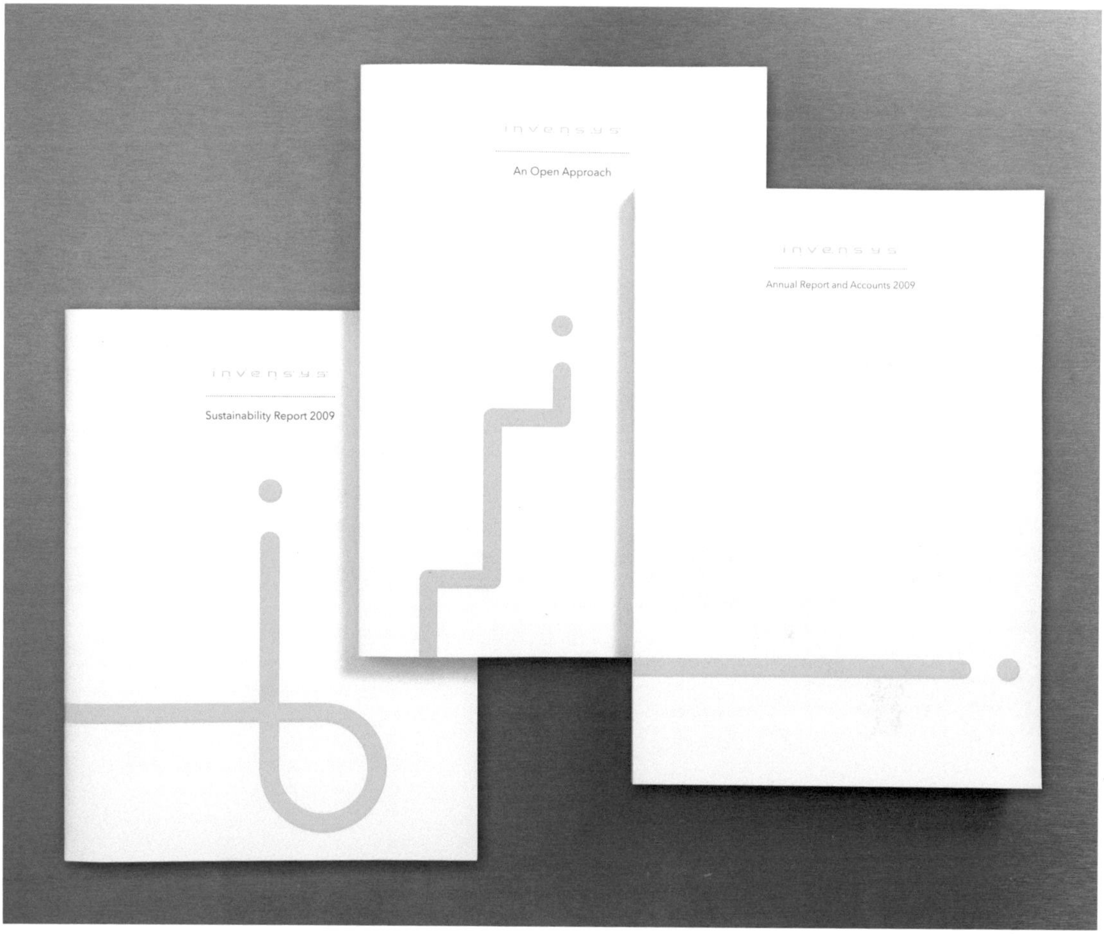

Client Invensys
Year 2009
Design Landor Associates

¡Come!
食べて!
¡Bebe!
飲んで!

IORI いおり
S1
TOKYO
東京スイート
HOMBRES
男
BAR
バー
DUCHA
シャワー
IORI いおり
S2
OSAKA
大阪スイート
MUJERES
女
DESAYUNO
朝食
P
PARKING
駐車場
IORI いおり
R1
SAKURA
桜ルーム
GUARDA ESQUI
スキールーム
COCINA
キッチン
H
HOTEL
ホテル

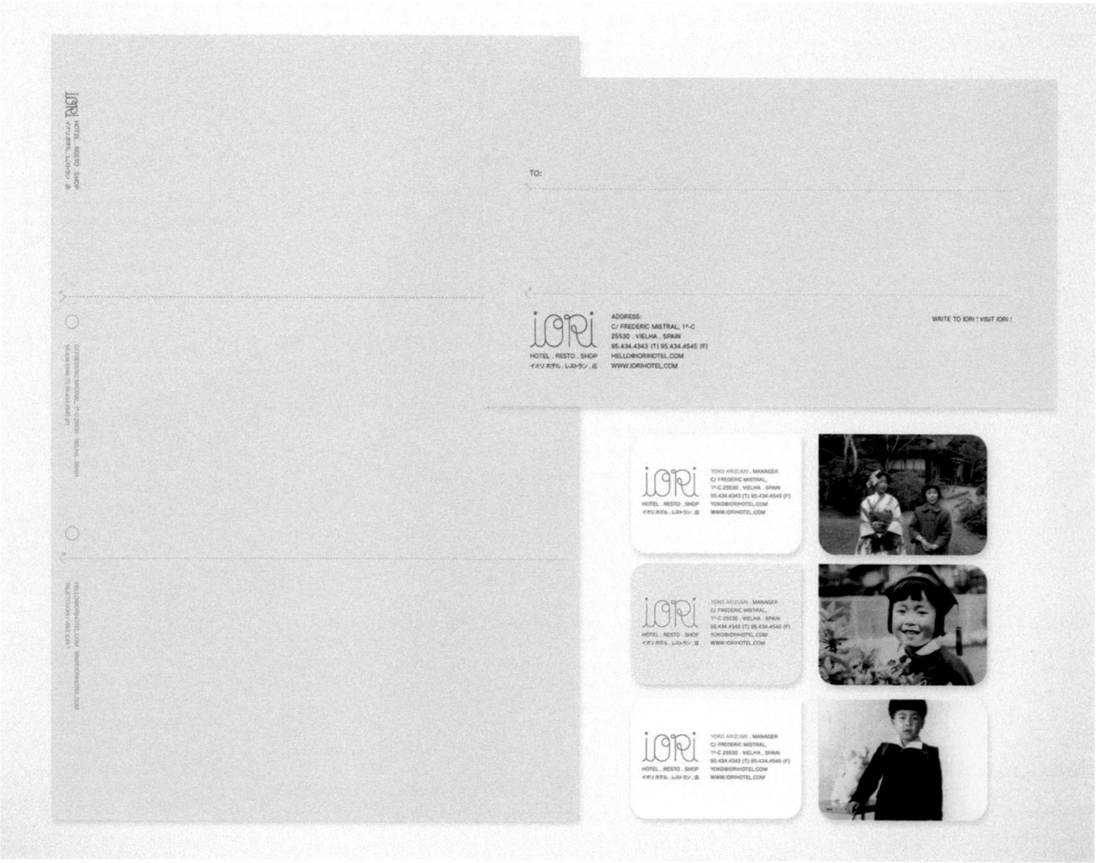

Client Iori Hotel Resto Shop
Year 2008
Design Tea Time Studio

Client Israeli Typography Reaserch Institute
Year 2009
Design Moshik Nadav
Material Enhanced matte 192 g/m2
Printing CMYK

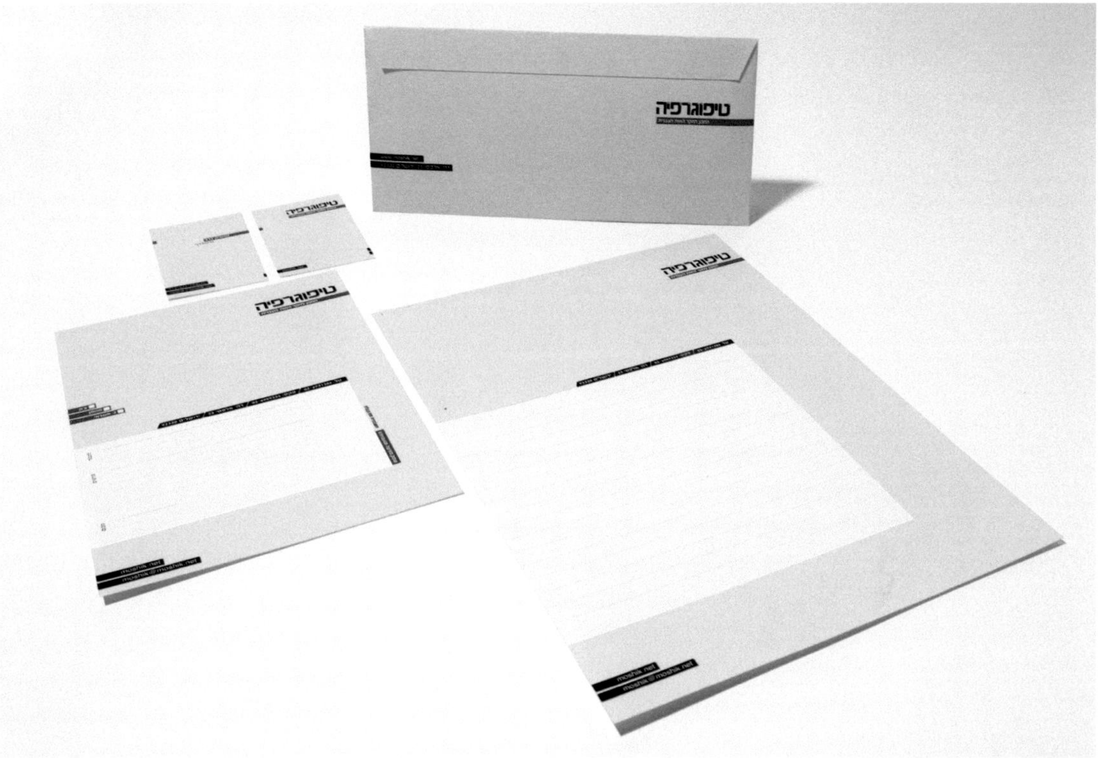
טיפוגרפיה

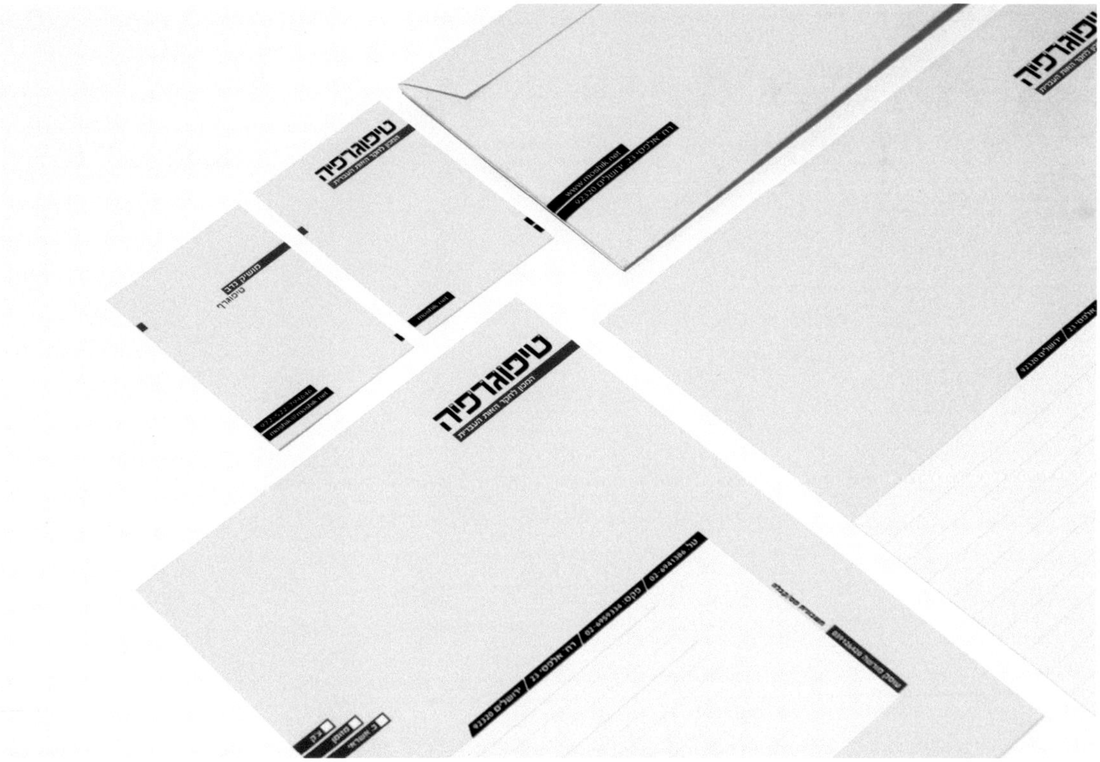
טיפוגרפיה
המכון לחקר האות העברית
www.moshik.net

Client	Festival Internacional Jazz Plaza
Year	2010
Design	Asterisco Arte y Comunicación
Team	Ernesto Azcuy

Client k.o.o.p architekten
Year 2007
Design superbüro
Team Barbara Ehrbar

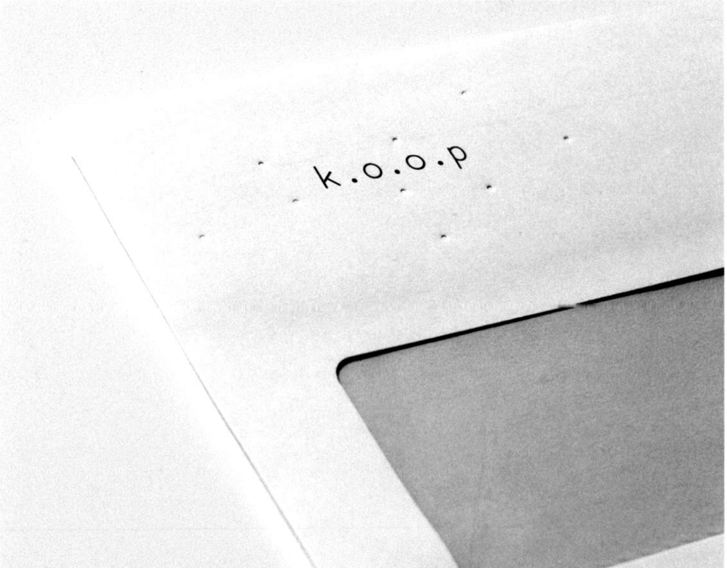

kalideen
acupuncture

kalideen
acupuncture
Shereen Kalideen
MA(hons), Dip Ac.
MBAcC
Contact
+44 (0)777 333 2864
shereen@kalideen.com
www.kalideen.com

Client Kalideen Acupuncture
Year 2007
Design Team Magpie Studio
Creative Directors:
David Azurdia, Ben Christie,
Jamie Ellul; Designer:
David Azurdia

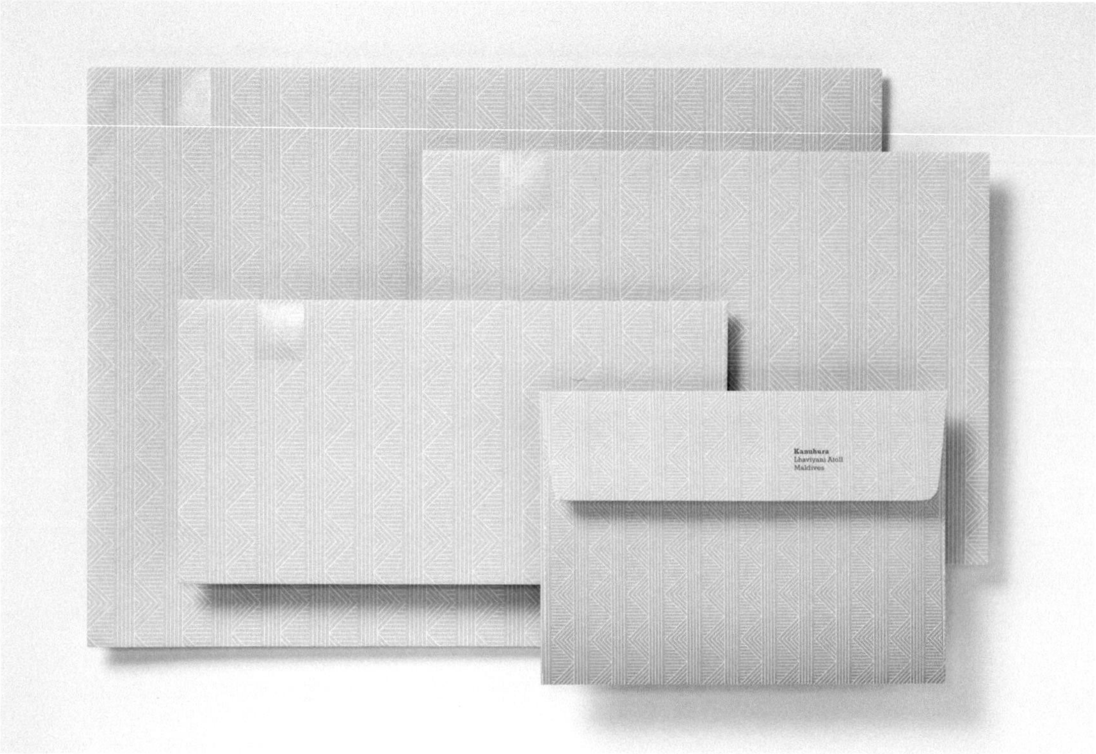

Client	Kanuhura
Year	2007
Design	Pentagram
Team	Pentagram Design London

Kanuhura
Lhaviyani Atoll
Maldives
Date
Guest 2
Kanuhura
Lhaviyani Atoll
Maldives
T +960 662 00 44
F +960 662 00 33
www.kanuhura.com
Kanuhura
Lhaviyani Atoll
Maldives
Name Nom
Room number Numéro de chambre
Despite our best efforts the stains could not be removed without damaging the garment.
Malgré tout le soin avec lequel nous avons traité ce vêtement, nous n'avo ns pu le détacher complètement sans risque de dégradation.
Kanuhura
Lhaviyani Atoll
Maldives

karenKARCH
240 Mulberry Street
betw. Spring & PRINCE
NEW YORK, NY. 10012
telephone. 212 965 9699
fax. 212 334 6947
www.karenkarch.com

KAREN KARCH
kk@karenkarch.com

karenKARCH
240 Mulberry Street
betw. Spring & PRINCE
NEW YORK, NY. 10012
telephone. 212 965 9699
fax. 212 334 6947
www.karenkarch.com
INFO@karenkarch.com

Client Karen Karch
Year 2006
Design Base Design

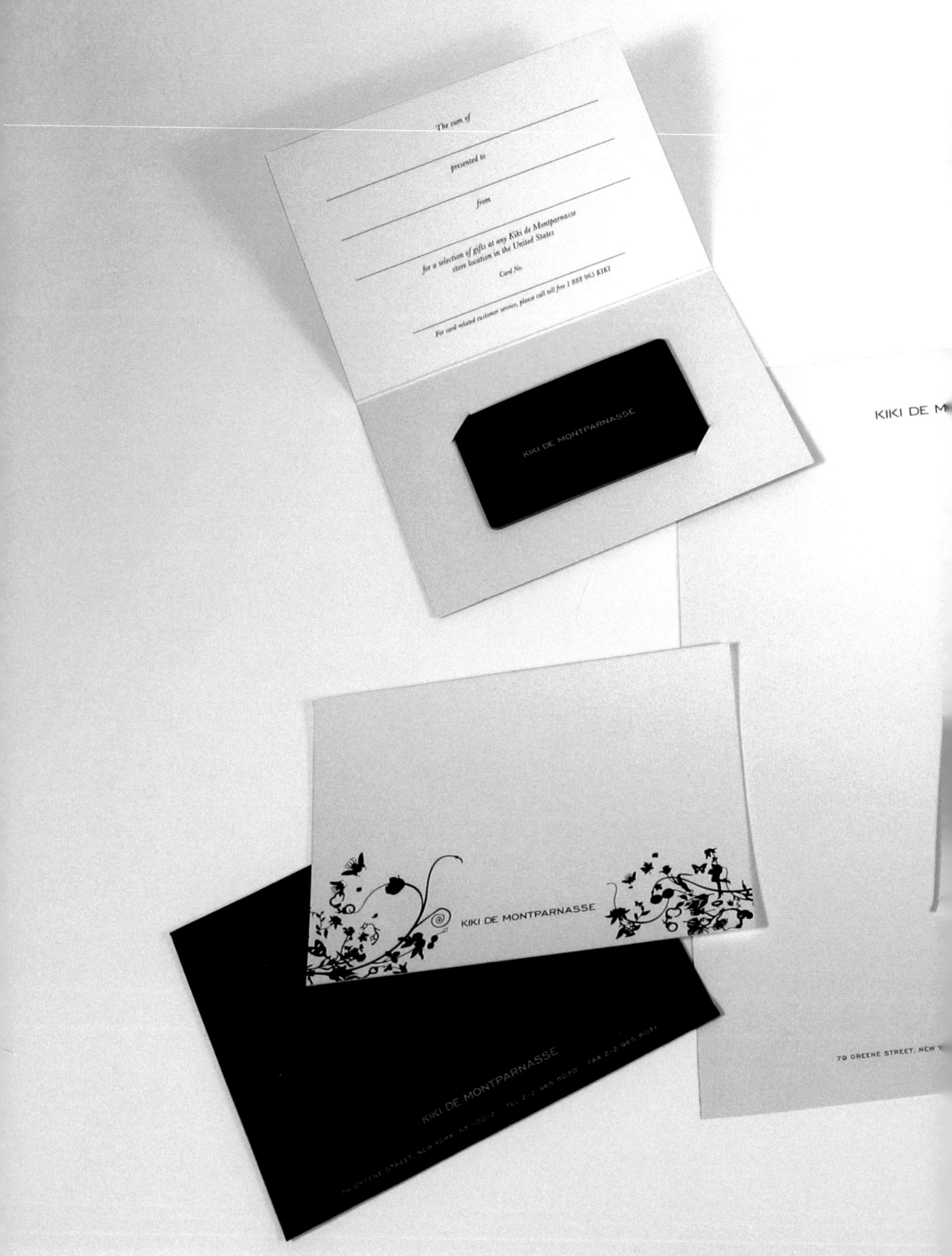
The sum of
presented to
from
for a selection of gifts at any Kiki de Montparnasse store location in the United States
Card No.
For card-related customer service, please call toll free 1 888 965 KIKI
KIKI DE MONTPARNASSE
KIKI DE MONTPARNASSE
KIKI DE MONTPARNASSE
79 GREENE STREET,

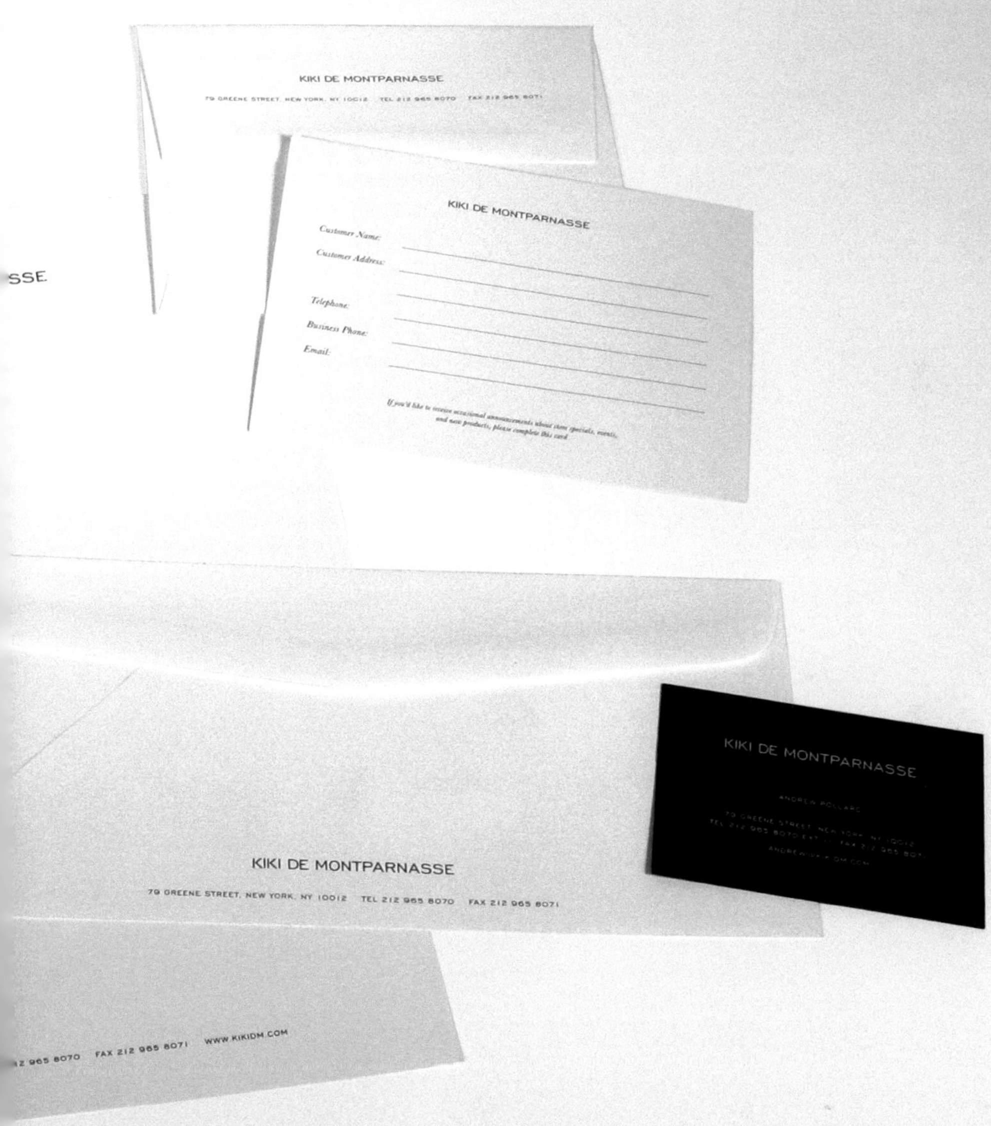

Client Kiki de Montparnasse
Year 2006
Design Base Design

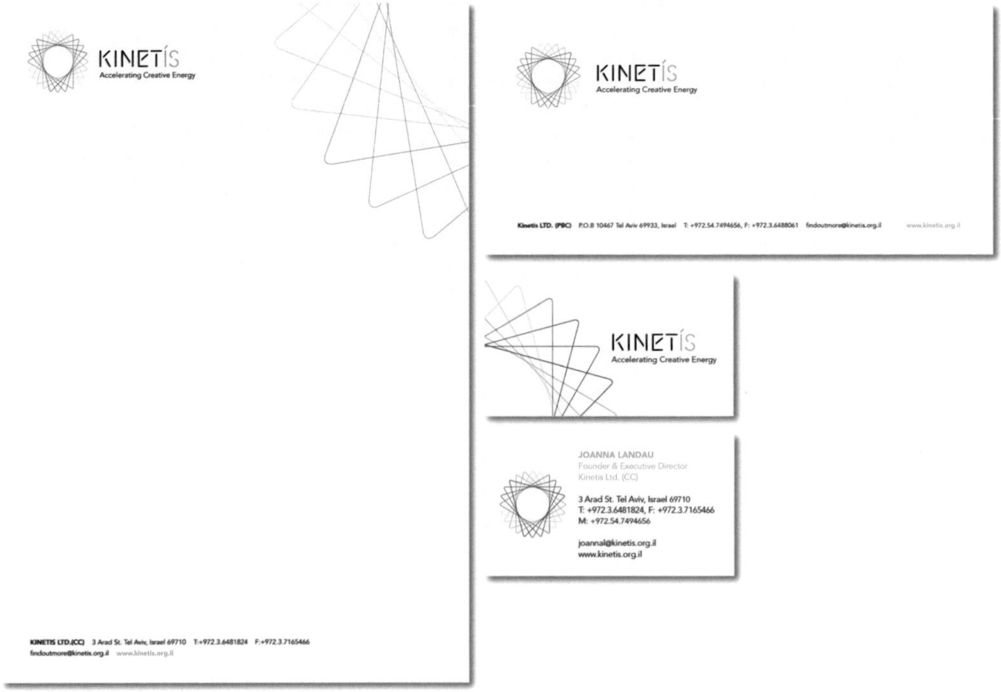

Client Kinetis
Year 2010
Design Dan Alexander & Co
Team Danny Goldberg, Michal Koll

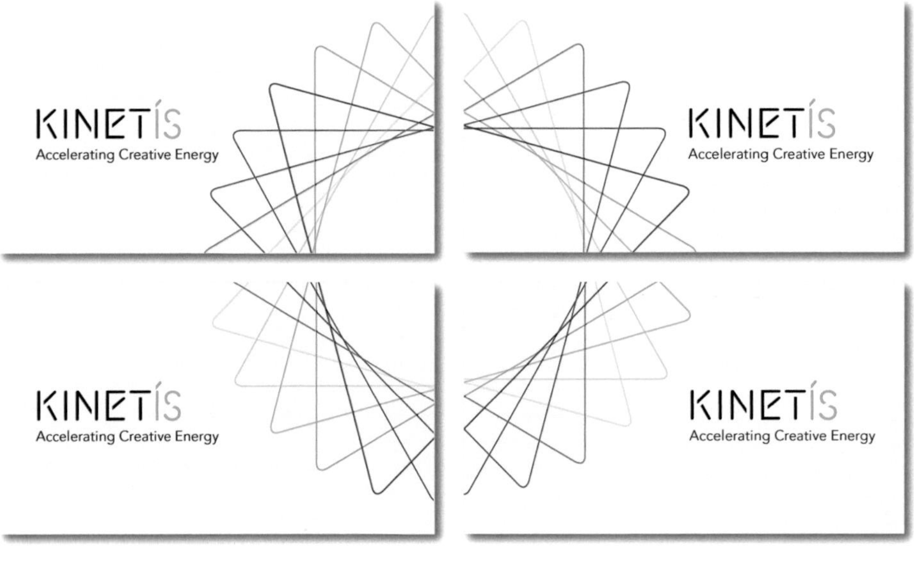

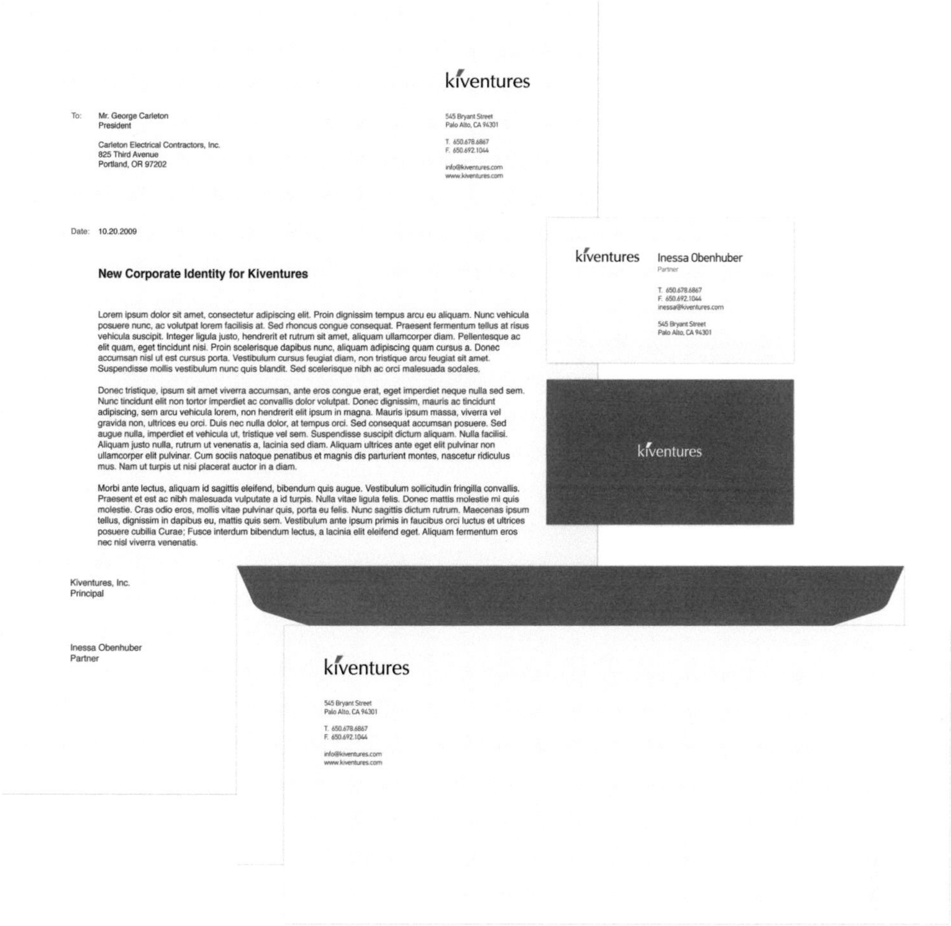

kiventures

545 Bryant Street
Palo Alto, CA 94301

T. 650.678.6867
F. 650.692.1044

info@kiventures.com
www.kiventures.com

To: Mr. George Carleton
President

Carleton Electrical Contractors, Inc.
825 Third Avenue
Portland, OR 97202

Date: 10.20.2009

New Corporate Identity for Kiventures

Lorem ipsum dolor sit amet, consectetur adipiscing elit. Proin dignissim tempus arcu eu aliquam. Nunc vehicula posuere nunc, ac volutpat lorem facilisis at. Sed rhoncus congue consequat. Praesent fermentum tellus at risus vehicula suscipit. Integer ligula justo, hendrerit et rutrum sit amet, aliquam ullamcorper diam. Pellentesque ac elit quam, eget tincidunt nisi. Proin scelerisque dapibus nunc, aliquam adipiscing quam cursus a. Donec accumsan nisl ut est cursus porta. Vestibulum cursus feugiat diam, non tristique arcu feugiat sit amet. Suspendisse mollis vestibulum nunc quis blandit. Sed scelerisque nibh ac orci malesuada sodales.

Donec tristique, ipsum sit amet viverra accumsan, ante eros congue erat, eget imperdiet neque nulla sed sem. Nunc tincidunt elit non tortor imperdiet ac convallis dolor volutpat. Donec dignissim, mauris ac tincidunt adipiscing, sem arcu vehicula lorem, non hendrerit elit ipsum in magna. Mauris ipsum massa, viverra vel gravida non, ultrices eu orci. Duis nec nulla dolor, at tempus orci. Sed consequat accumsan posuere. Sed augue nulla, imperdiet et vehicula ut, tristique vel sem. Suspendisse suscipit dictum aliquam. Nulla facilisi. Aliquam justo nulla, rutrum ut venenatis a, lacinia sed diam. Aliquam ultrices ante eget elit pulvinar non ullamcorper elit pulvinar. Cum sociis natoque penatibus et magnis dis parturient montes, nascetur ridiculus mus. Nam ut turpis ut nisi placerat auctor in a diam.

Morbi ante lectus, aliquam id sagittis eleifend, bibendum quis augue. Vestibulum sollicitudin fringilla convallis. Praesent et est ac nibh malesuada vulputate a id turpis. Nulla vitae ligula felis. Donec mattis molestie mi quis molestie. Cras odio eros, mollis vitae pulvinar quis, porta eu felis. Nunc sagittis dictum rutrum. Maecenas ipsum tellus, dignissim in dapibus eu, mattis quis sem. Vestibulum ante ipsum primis in faucibus orci luctus et ultrices posuere cubilia Curae; Fusce interdum bibendum lectus, a lacinia elit eleifend eget. Aliquam fermentum eros nec nisl viverra venenatis.

Kiventures, Inc.
Principal

Inessa Obenhuber
Partner

kiventures Inessa Obenhuber
Partner
T. 650.678.6867
F. 650.692.1044
inessa@kiventures.com
545 Bryant Street
Palo Alto, CA 94301

kiventures

kiventures
545 Bryant Street
Palo Alto, CA 94301
T. 650.678.6867
F. 650.692.1044
info@kiventures.com
www.kiventures.com

Client Kiventures
Year 2010
Design Uber Experience

Client Kudo
Year 2010
Design Buddy

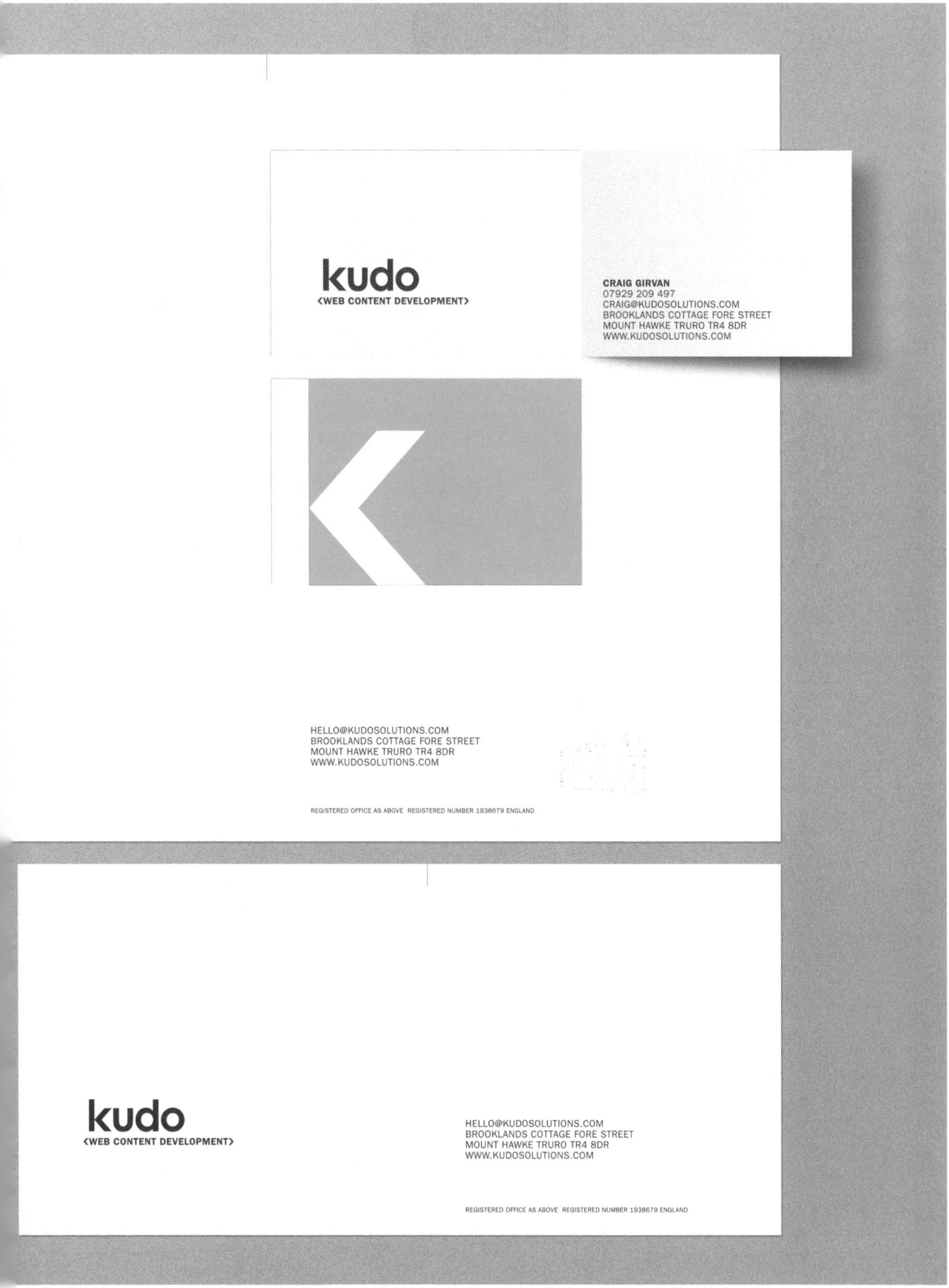
kudo
<WEB CONTENT DEVELOPMENT>
CRAIG GIRVAN
07929 209 497
CRAIG@KUDOSOLUTIONS.COM
BROOKLANDS COTTAGE FORE STREET
MOUNT HAWKE TRURO TR4 8DR
WWW.KUDOSOLUTIONS.COM
HELLO@KUDOSOLUTIONS.COM
BROOKLANDS COTTAGE FORE STREET
MOUNT HAWKE TRURO TR4 8DR
WWW.KUDOSOLUTIONS.COM
REGISTERED OFFICE AS ABOVE REGISTERED NUMBER 1938679 ENGLAND
kudo
<WEB CONTENT DEVELOPMENT>
HELLO@KUDOSOLUTIONS.COM
BROOKLANDS COTTAGE FORE STREET
MOUNT HAWKE TRURO TR4 8DR
WWW.KUDOSOLUTIONS.COM
REGISTERED OFFICE AS ABOVE REGISTERED NUMBER 1938679 ENGLAND

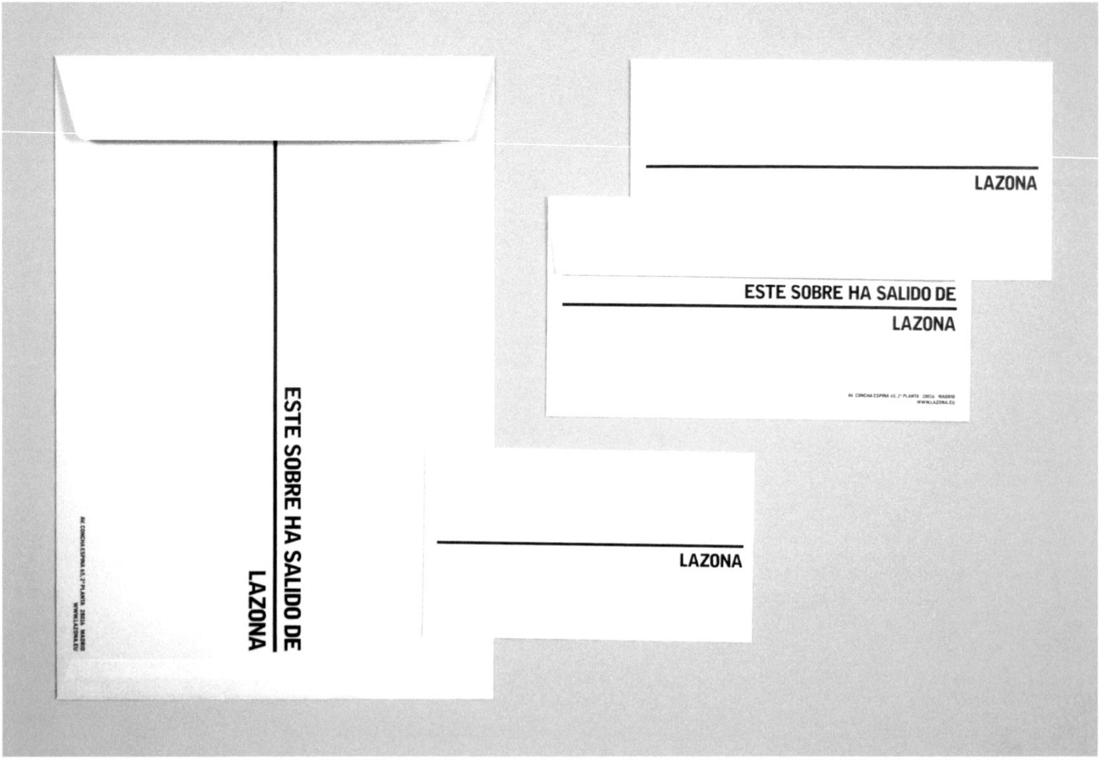

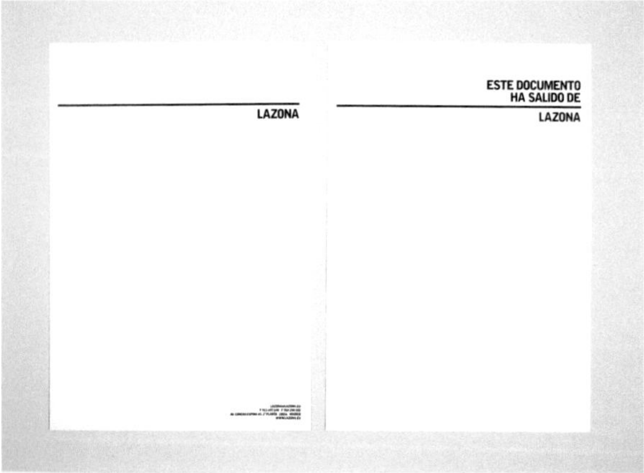

Client Lazona
Year 2009
Design Barfutura

Client Le Immobiliari
Year 2009
Design Dogo

Client	Le Touessrok
Year	2007
Design	Pentagram
Team	Pentagram Design London

210 Grafton Road
London NW5 4AX
T: +44 207 428 0748
www.leave2remain.org

Bruce Goodison
Director
210 Grafton Road
London NW5 4AX
M: +44 7711 141 301
T: +44 207 428 0748
E: brucegoodison@googlemail.com
www.leave2remain.org

Kate Cook
Producer
210 Grafton Road
London NW5 4AX
M: +44 7711 141 301
T: +44 207 428 0748
E: katecook@googlemail.com
www.leave2remain.org

Client Leave to Remain
Year 2010
Design SVIDesign

LEAVE TO REMAIN

210 Grafton Road
London NW5 4AX

M: +44 7711 141 301
T: +44 207 428 0748

E: brucegoodison@googlemail.com
www.leave2remain.org

Client Lebesque
Year 2007
Design Edhv
Team Remco vd Craats, Kim Hemmes

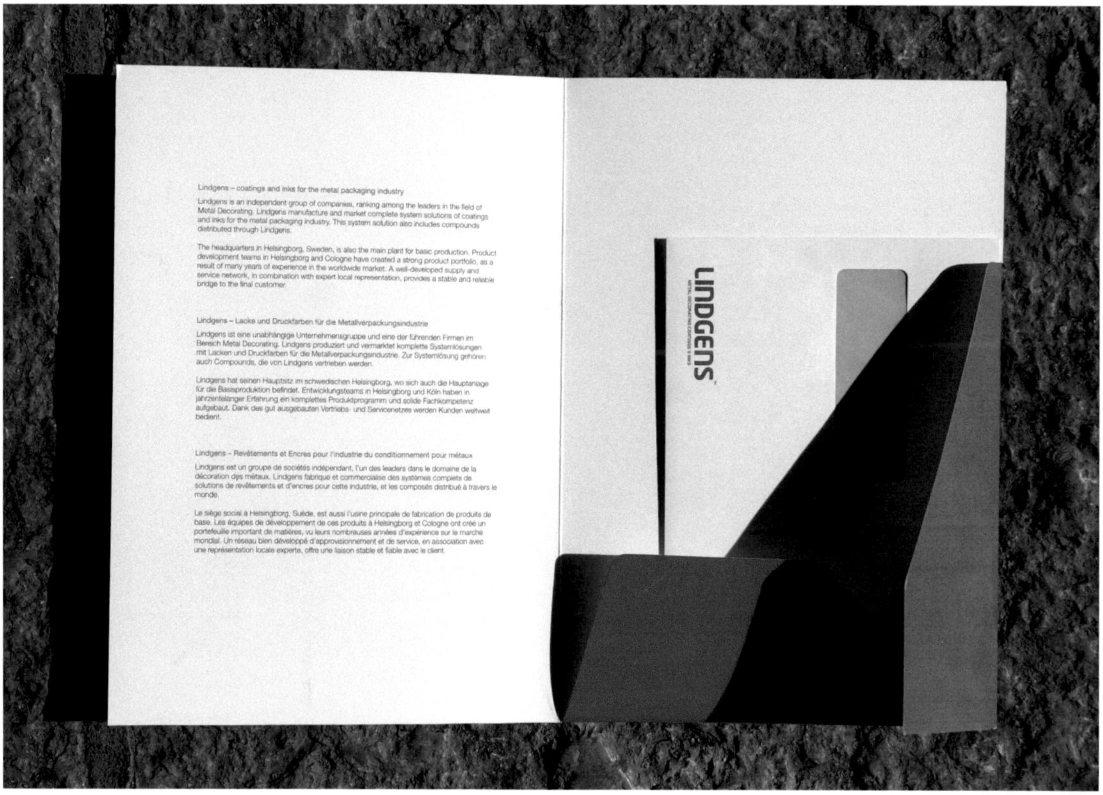
Lindgens – coatings and inks for the metal packaging industry
Lindgens is an independent group of companies, ranking among the leaders in the field of Metal Decorating. Lindgens manufacture and market complete system solutions of coatings and inks for the metal packaging industry. This system solution also includes compounds distributed through Lindgens.
The headquarters in Helsingborg, Sweden, is also the main plant for basic production. Product development teams in Helsingborg and Cologne have created a strong product portfolio, as a result of many years of experience in the worldwide market. A well-developed supply and service network, in combination with expert local representation, provides a stable and reliable bridge to the final customer.
Lindgens – Lacke und Druckfarben für die Metallverpackungsindustrie
Lindgens ist eine unabhängige Unternehmensgruppe und eine der führenden Firmen im Bereich Metal Decorating. Lindgens produziert und vermarktet komplette Systemlösungen mit Lacken und Druckfarben für die Metallverpackungsindustrie. Zur Systemlösung gehören auch Compounds, die von Lindgens vertrieben werden.
Lindgens hat seinen Hauptsitz im schwedischen Helsingborg, wo sich auch die Hauptanlage für die Basisproduktion befindet. Entwicklungsteams in Helsingborg und Köln haben in jahrzentelanger Erfahrung ein komplettes Produktprogramm und solide Fachkompetenz aufgebaut. Dank des gut ausgebauten Vertriebs- und Servicenetzes werden Kunden weltweit bedient.
Lindgens – Revêtements et Encres pour l'industrie du conditionnement pour métaux
Lindgens est un groupe de sociétés indépendant, l'un des leaders dans le domaine de la décoration des métaux. Lindgens fabrique et commercialise des systèmes complets de solutions de revêtements et d'encres pour cette industrie, et les composés distribué à travers le monde.
Le siège social à Helsingborg, Suède, est aussi l'usine principale de fabrication de produits de base. Les équipes de développement de ces produits à Helsingborg et Cologne ont créé un portefeuille important de matières, vu leurs nombreuses années d'expérience sur le marché mondial. Un réseau bien développé d'approvisionnement et de service, en association avec une représentation locale experte, offre une liaison stable et fiable avec le client.
LINDGENS

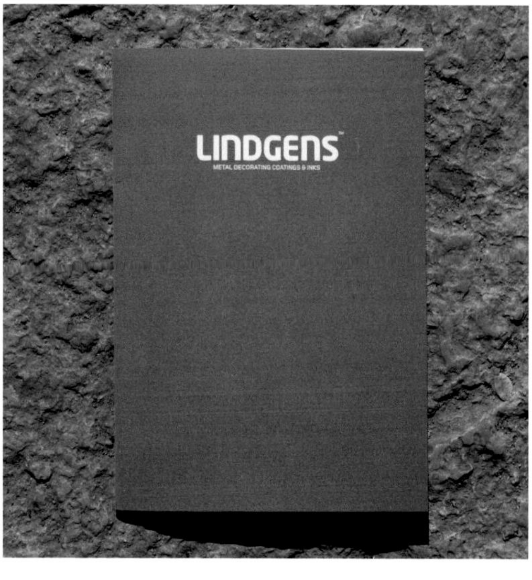

Client Lindgens
Year 2006
Design Kollor Design Agency

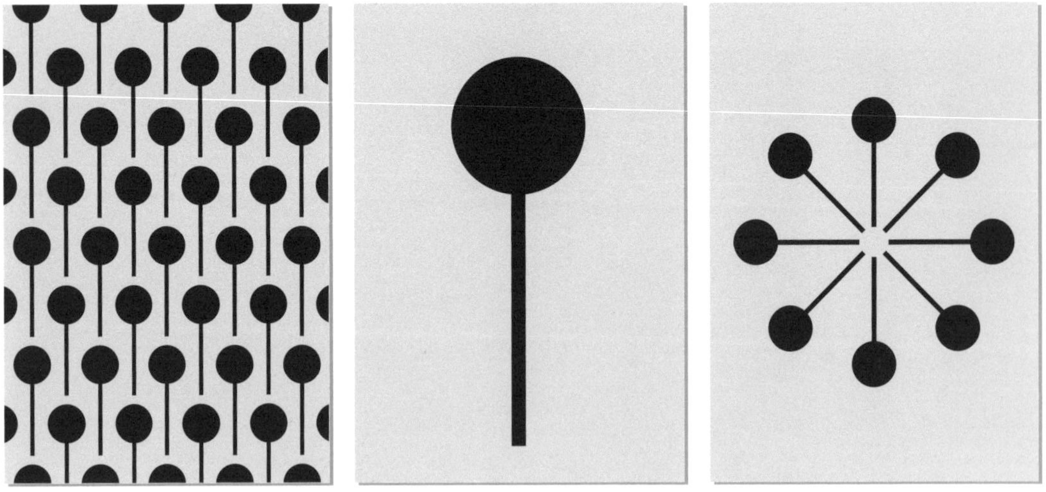

lollipop
+34 679 49 26 21
www.lollipopagency.com
info@ lollipopagency.com

lollipop
+34 679 49 26 21
www.lollipopagency.com
info@ lollipopagency.com

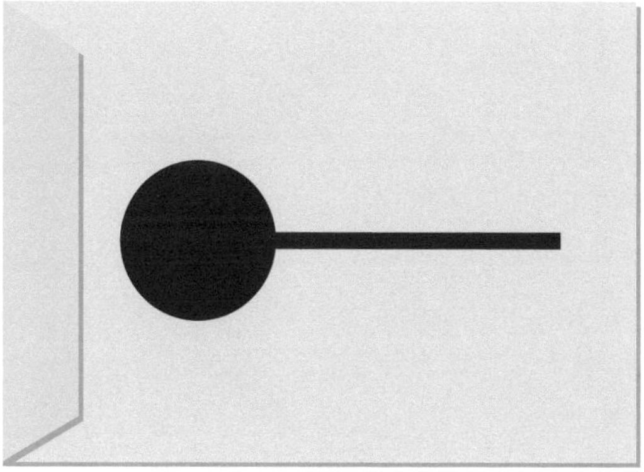

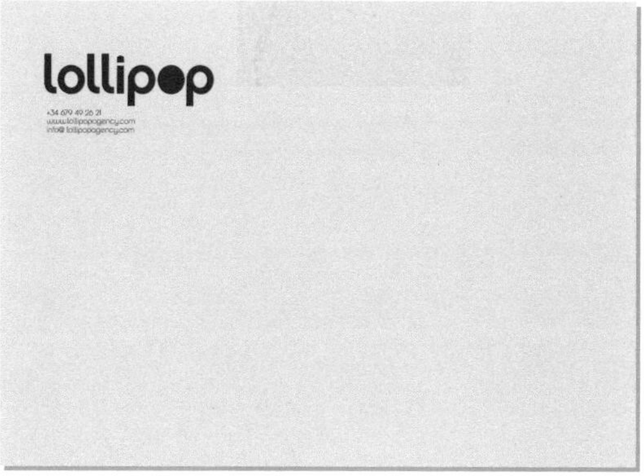

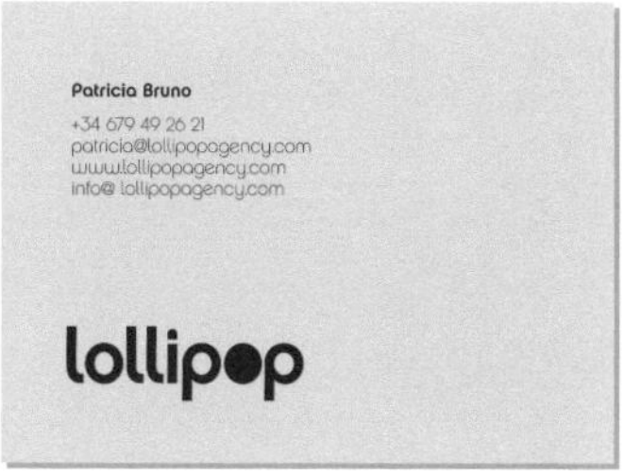

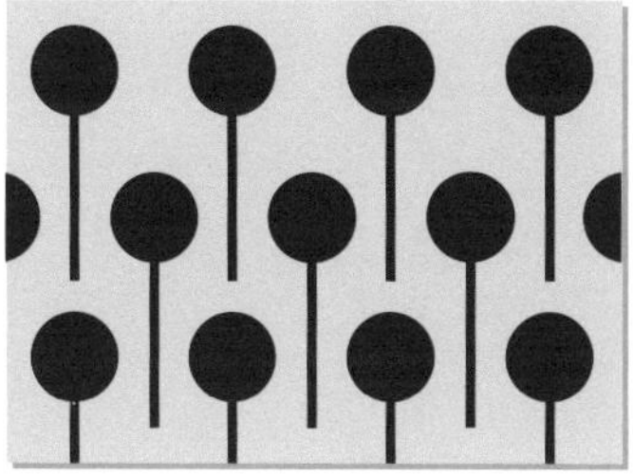

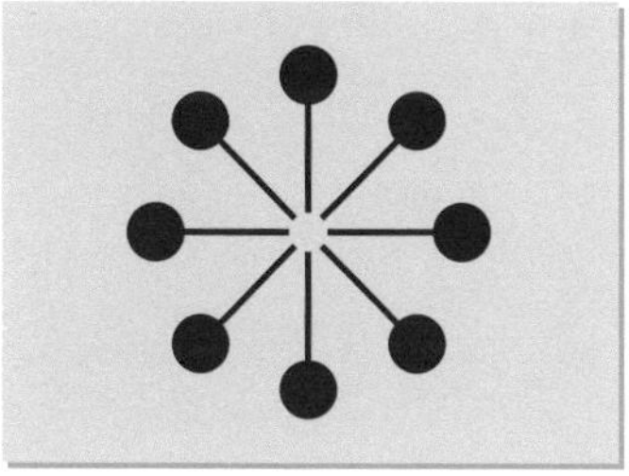

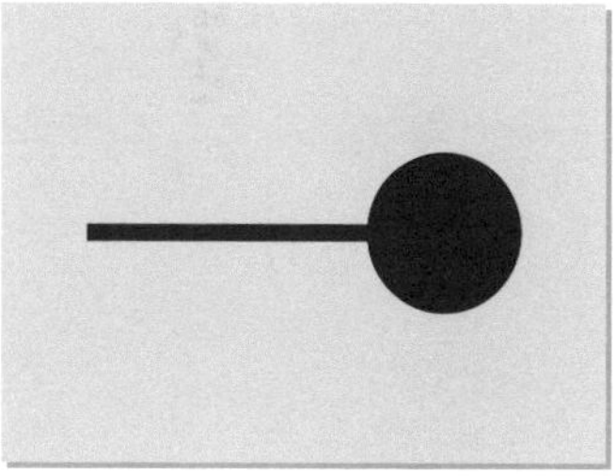

Client Lollipop
Year 2007
Design m Barcelona
Team Marion Dönneweg

Client Lyris
Year 2005
Design Hardy Design

LYRIS
LYRIS
LYRIS

Client Machicao Design
Year 2009
Design Machicao Design

machicaodesign
machicaodesign
MACHICAO PACHECO
esemepe@pobox.com
machicaodesign
machicaodesign
comunicación visual // communication design
artista gráfica // graphic artist
susana
MACHICAO PACHECO
C. (+591) 715 48460
T. (+591-2) 277 0996
esemepe@pobox.com
Casilla 8193/La Paz/Bolivia
skype/msn/yahoo ID: esemepe
machicaodesign

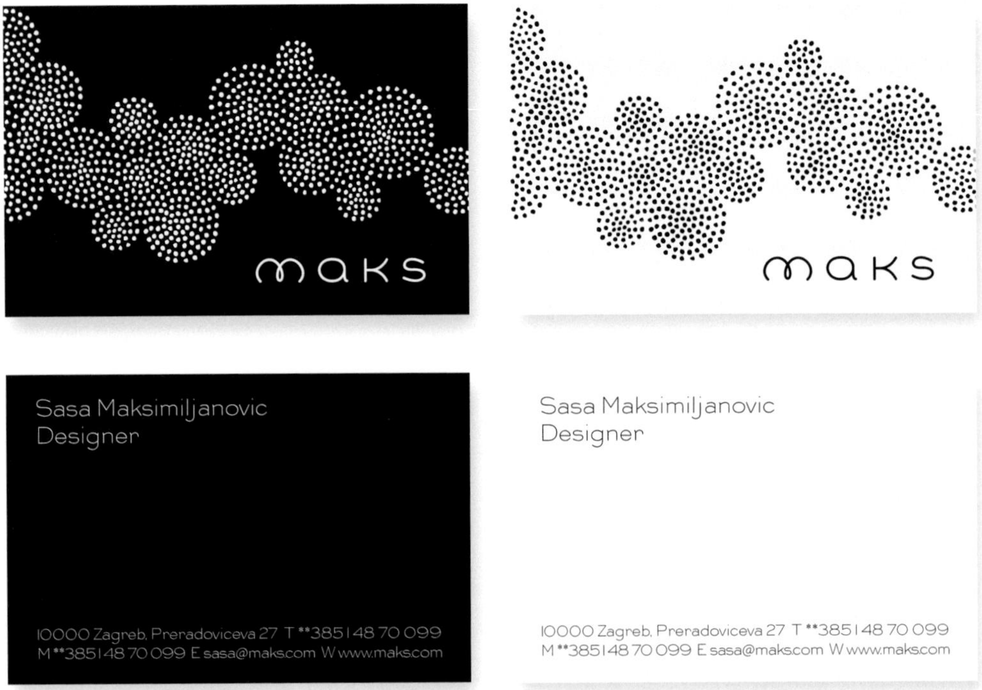

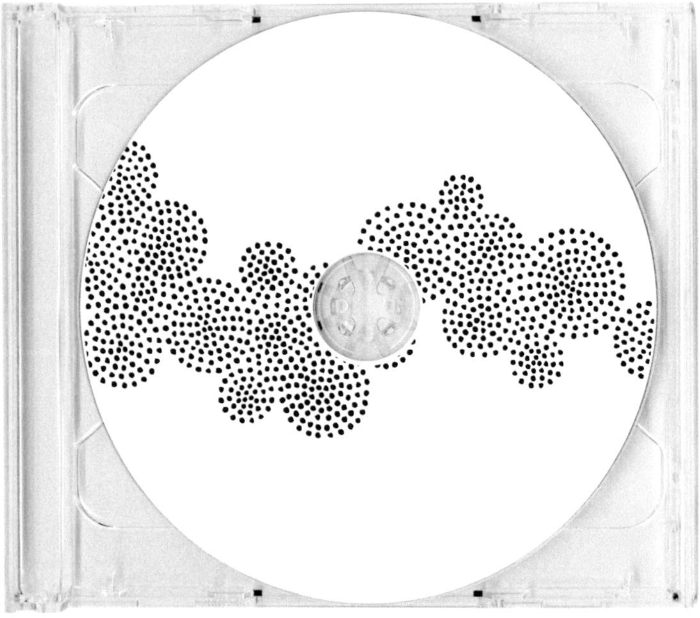

Client Maks
Year 2007
Design SVIDesign

maks
10000 Zagreb, Preradoviceva 27 T **385 1 48 70 099 W www.maks.com

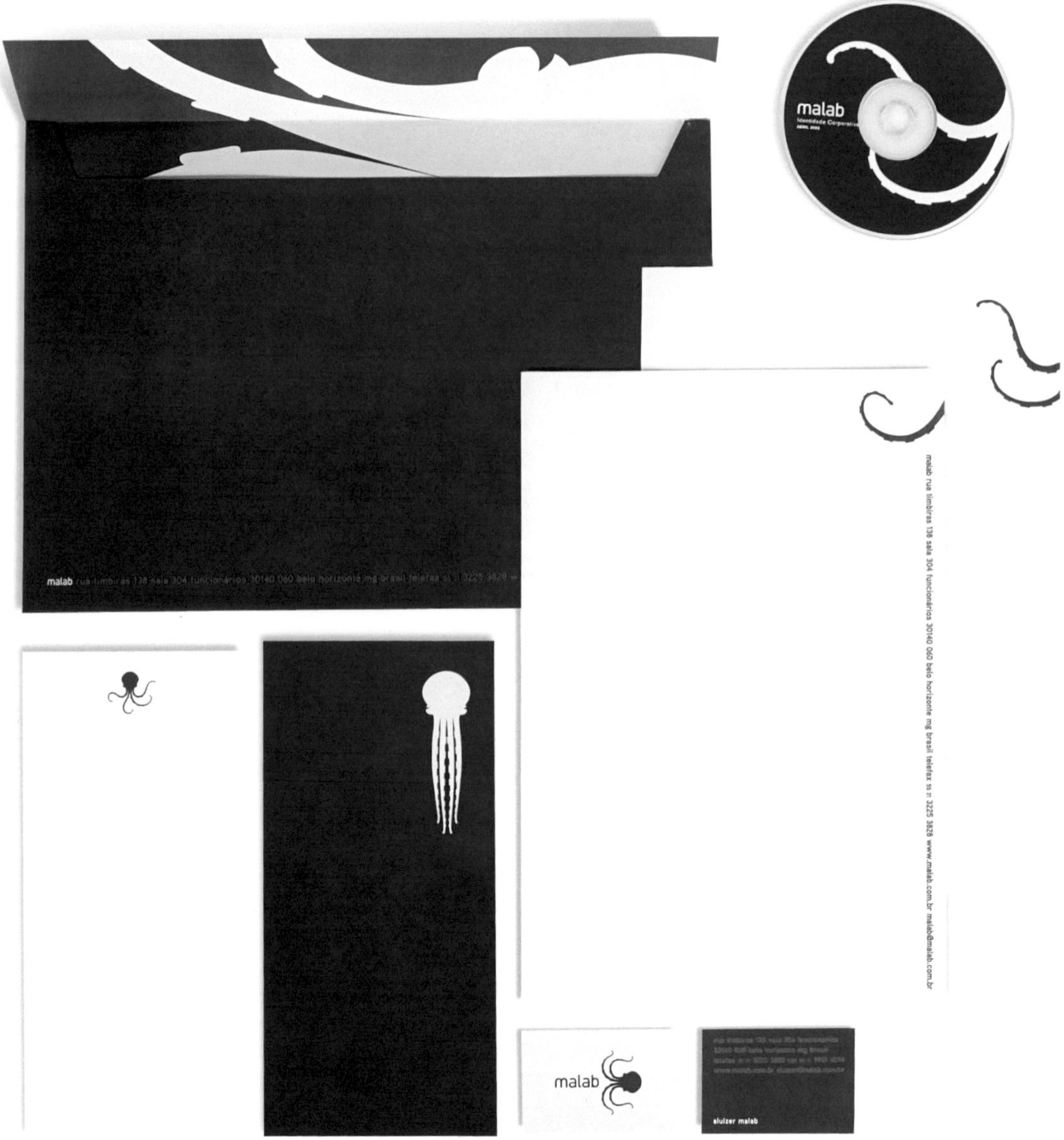

Client	Malab
Year	2006
Design	Hardy Design

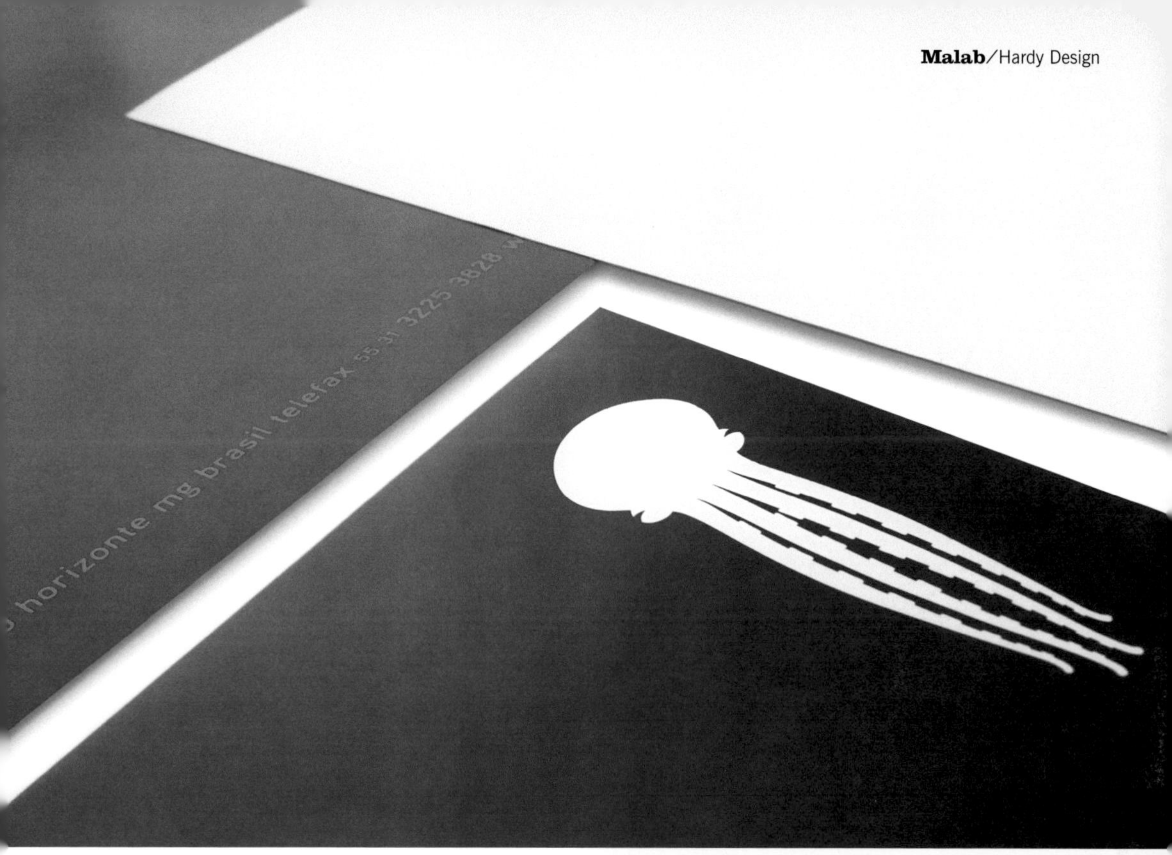
horizonte mg brasil telefax 55 31 3225 3828

malab

MARCUS
170 New Bond Street
London W1Y 9PB
Telephone: 020 7290 6500
Facsimile: 020 7290 6501
MARCUS
MARCUS
with compliments
Marcus J Margulies
MARCUS
170 New Bond Street
London W1Y 9PB
Telephone: 020 7290 6500
Facsimile: 020 7290 6501
170 New Bond Street
London W1Y 9PB
Telephone: 020 7290 6500
Facsimile: 020 7290 6501

Client Marcus
Year 2007
Design Pentagram
Team Pentagram Design London

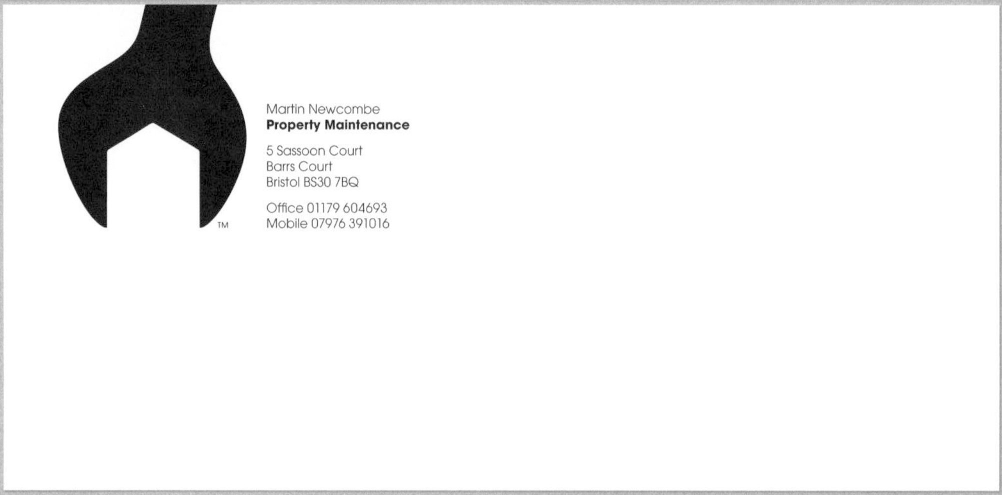

Client Martin Newcombe Property Maintenance
Year 2009
Design Buddy

TM
Martin Newcombe
Property Maintenance
5 Sassoon Court
Barrs Court
Bristol BS30 7BQ
Office 01179 604693
Mobile 07976 391016

Client Matizar Filmes
Year 2008
Design Dupla Design
Team Claudia Gamboa, Fabiana Takeda, Ney Valle

matizarfilmes
matizarfilmes
matizarfilmes

matizarfilmes

matter

matter

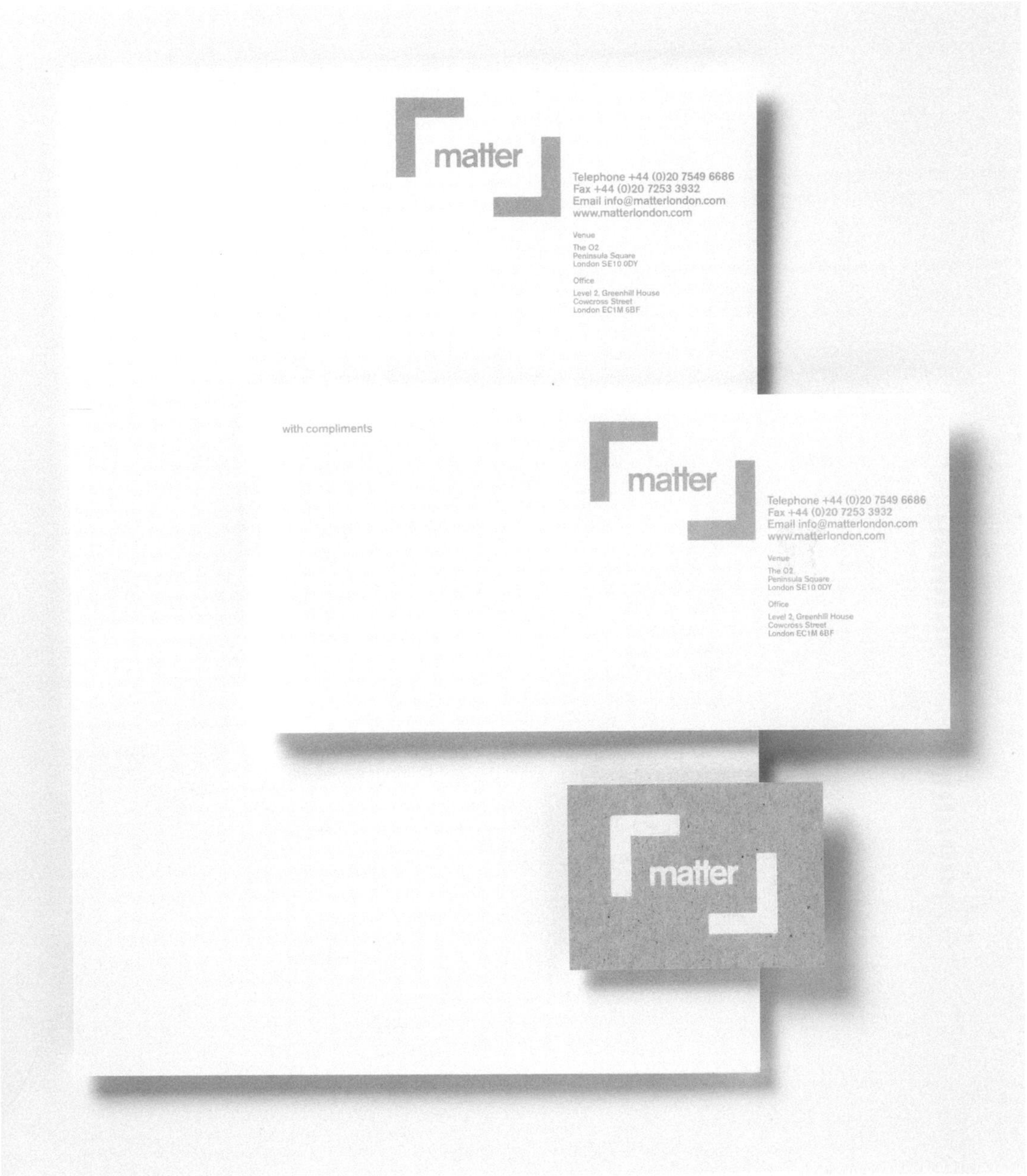

Client Matter
Year 2007
Design Pentagram
Team Pentagram Design London

MAUD
Maud
L +61 (0)2 9029 6497
contact@maud.com.au
S3, L3, 2-12 Foveaux St,
Surry Hills, Sydney, 2010
maud.com.au

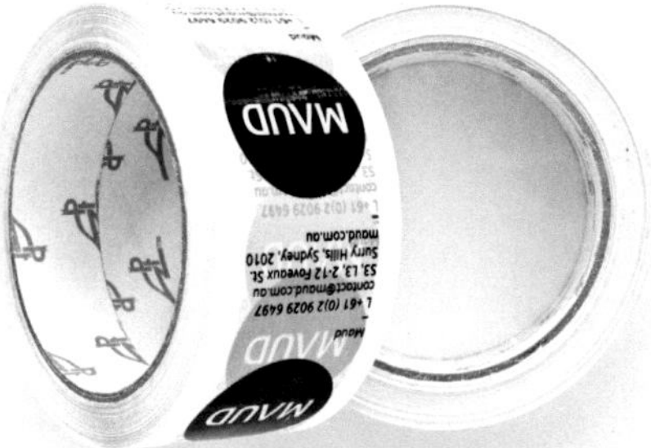

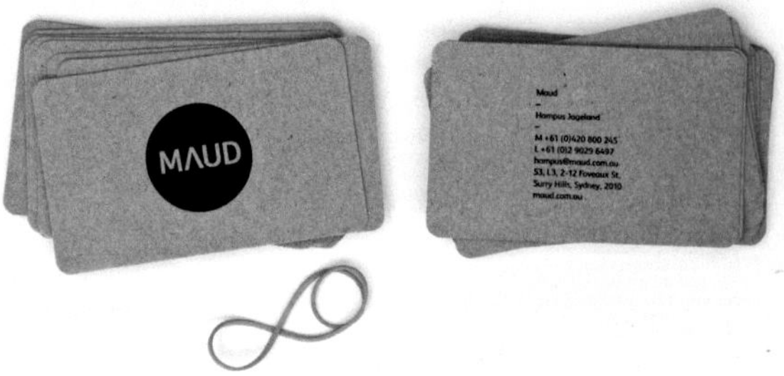

Client Maud
Year 2009
Design Maud
Team Hampus Jageland, David Park

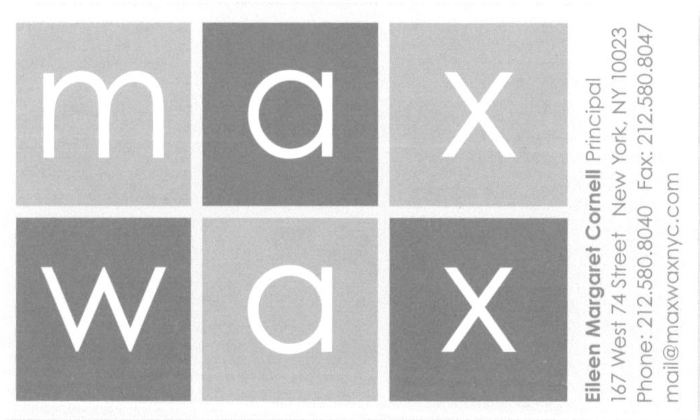

Client Maxwax
Year 2003
Design Anke Stohlmann Design

Client Metamorphosis Salon
Year 2006
Design Uber Experience

metamorphosis
salon
415 252 1020
1841 Market St., San Francisco, CA 94103
www.metasalon.com
New Corporate Identity for Metamorphosis
Lorem ipsum dolor sit amet, consectetur adipiscing elit. Proin dignissim tempus arcu eu aliquam. Nunc vehicula posuere nunc, ac volutpat lorem facilisis at. Sed rhoncus congue consequat. Praesent fermentum tellus at risus vehicula suscipit. Integer ligula justo, hendrerit et rutrum sit amet, aliquam ullamcorper diam. Pellentesque ac elit quam, eget tincidunt nisi. Proin scelerisque dapibus nunc, aliquam adipiscing quam cursus a. Donec accumsan nisl ut est cursus porta. Vestibulum cursus feugiat diam, non tristique arcu feugiat sit amet. Suspendisse mollis vestibulum nunc quis blandit. Sed scelerisque nibh ac orci malesuada sodales.
Donec tristique, ipsum sit amet viverra accumsan, ante eros congue erat, eget imperdiet neque nulla sed sem. Nunc tincidunt elit non tortor imperdiet ac convallis dolor volutpat. Donec dignissim, mauris ac tincidunt adipiscing, sem arcu vehicula lorem, non hendrerit elit ipsum in magna. Mauris ipsum massa, viverra vel gravida non, ultrices eu orci. Duis nec nulla dolor, at tempus orci. Sed consequat accumsan posuere. Sed augue nulla, imperdiet et vehicula ut, tristique vel sem. Suspendisse suscipit dictum aliquam. Nulla facilisi. Aliquam justo nulla, rutrum ut venenatis a, lacinia sed diam. Aliquam ultrices ante eget elit pulvinar non ullamcorper elit pulvinar. Cum sociis natoque penatibus et magnis dis parturient montes, nascetur ridiculus mus. Nam ut turpis ut nisi placerat auctor in a diam.
Morbi ante lectus, aliquam id sagittis eleifend, bibendum quis augue. Vestibulum sollicitudin fringilla convallis. Praesent et est ac nibh malesuada vulputate a id turpis. Nulla vitae ligula felis. Donec mattis molestie mi quis molestie. Cras odio eros, mollis vitae pulvinar quis, porta eu felis. Nunc sagittis dictum rutrum. Maecenas ipsum tellus, dignissim in dapibus eu, mattis quis sem. Vestibulum ante ipsum primis in faucibus orci luctus et ultrices posuere cubilia Curae; Fusce interdum bibendum lectus, a lacinia elit eleifend eget. Aliquam fermentum eros nec nisl viverra venenatis.
STAS M.
agent of transformation
415 252 1020
metamorphosis
salon
metamorphosis
salon
415 252 1020
1841 Market St., San Francisco, CA 94103
www.metasalon.com
415 252 1020
1841 Market St., San Francisco, CA 94103
www.metasalon.com
metamorphosis
salon

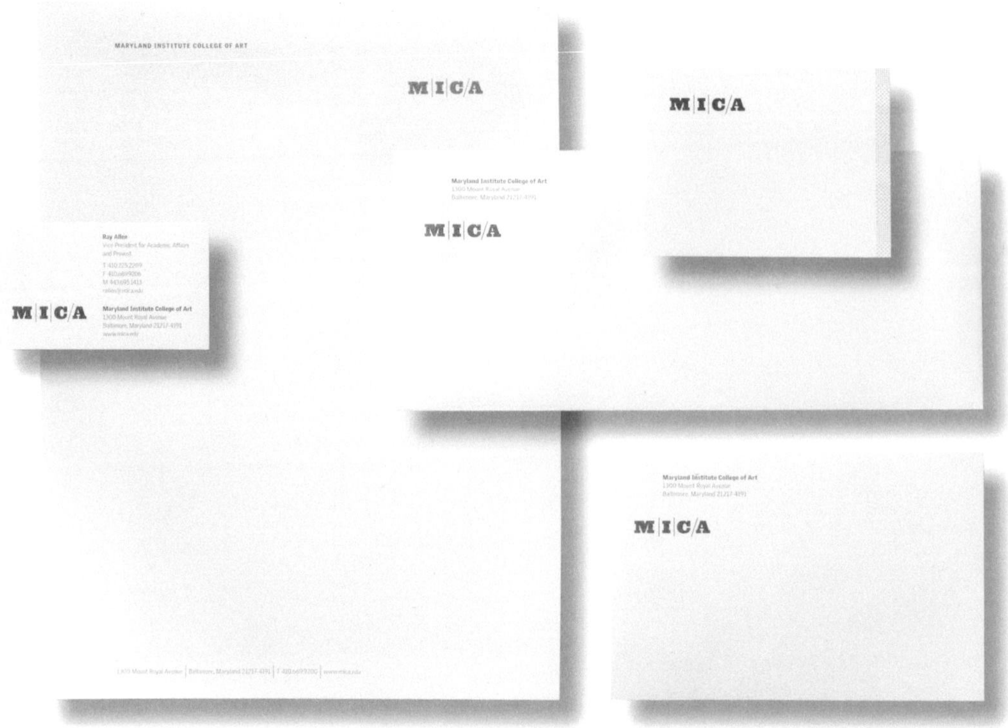

Client MICA – Maryland Institute College of Art
Year 2007
Design Pentagram

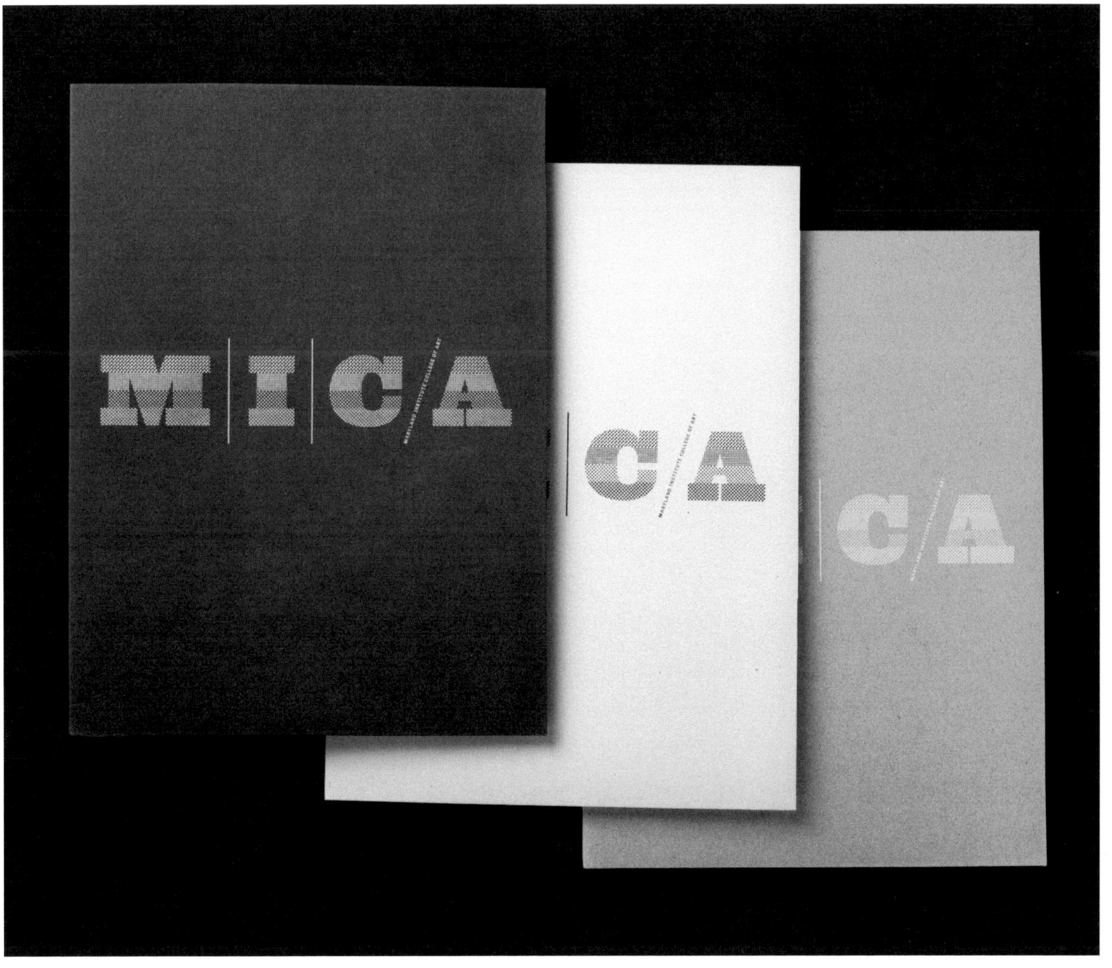
M|I|C/A
MARYLAND INSTITUTE COLLEGE OF ART
C/A
MARYLAND INSTITUTE COLLEGE OF ART
C/A

M|I|C/A
M|I|C/A
MARYLAND INSTITUTE COLLEGE OF ART
M|I|C/A

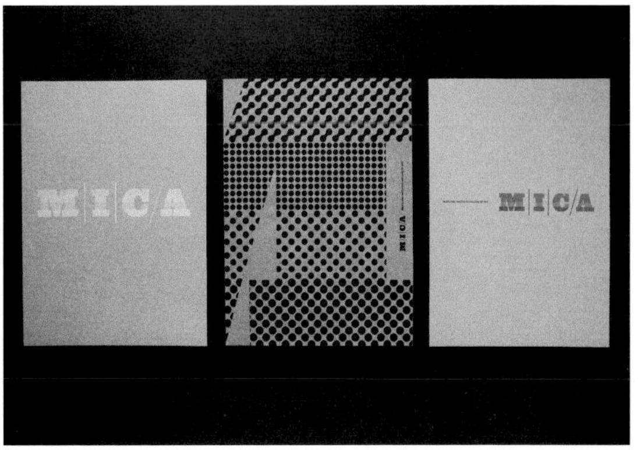
M|I|C/A
M|I|C/A

Client Milk
Year 2006
Design Base Design

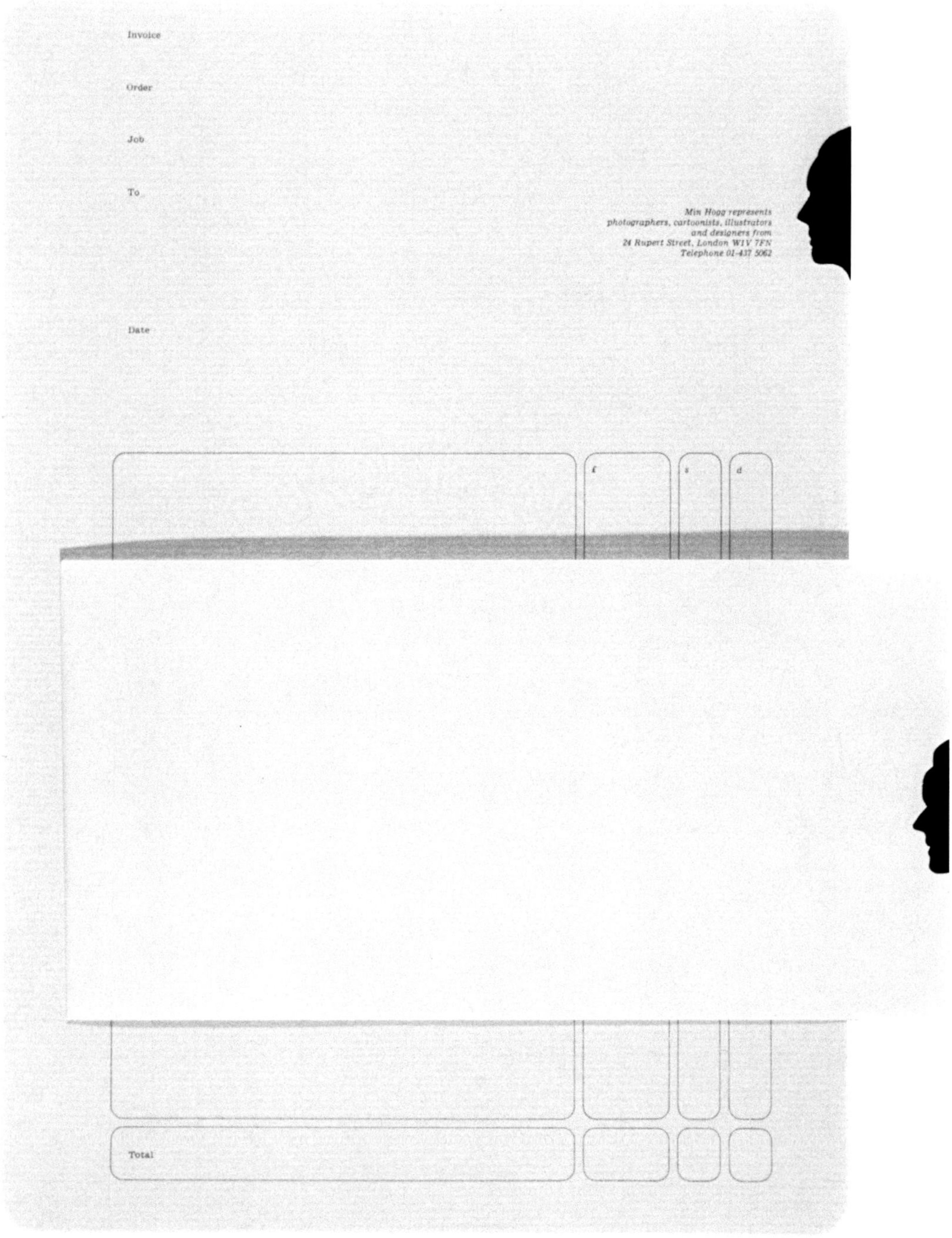
Invoice
Order
Job
To
Min Hogg represents
photographers, cartoonists, illustrators
and designers from
24 Rupert Street, London W1V 7FN
Telephone 01-437 5062
Date
£
s
d
Total

Client Min Hogg
Year 2007
Design Pentagram
Team Pentagram Design London

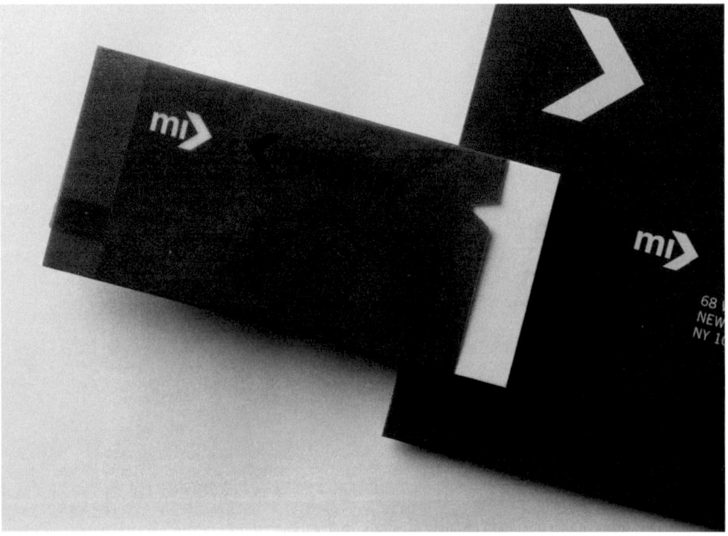

Client Mix in New York
Year 2003
Design Philippe David

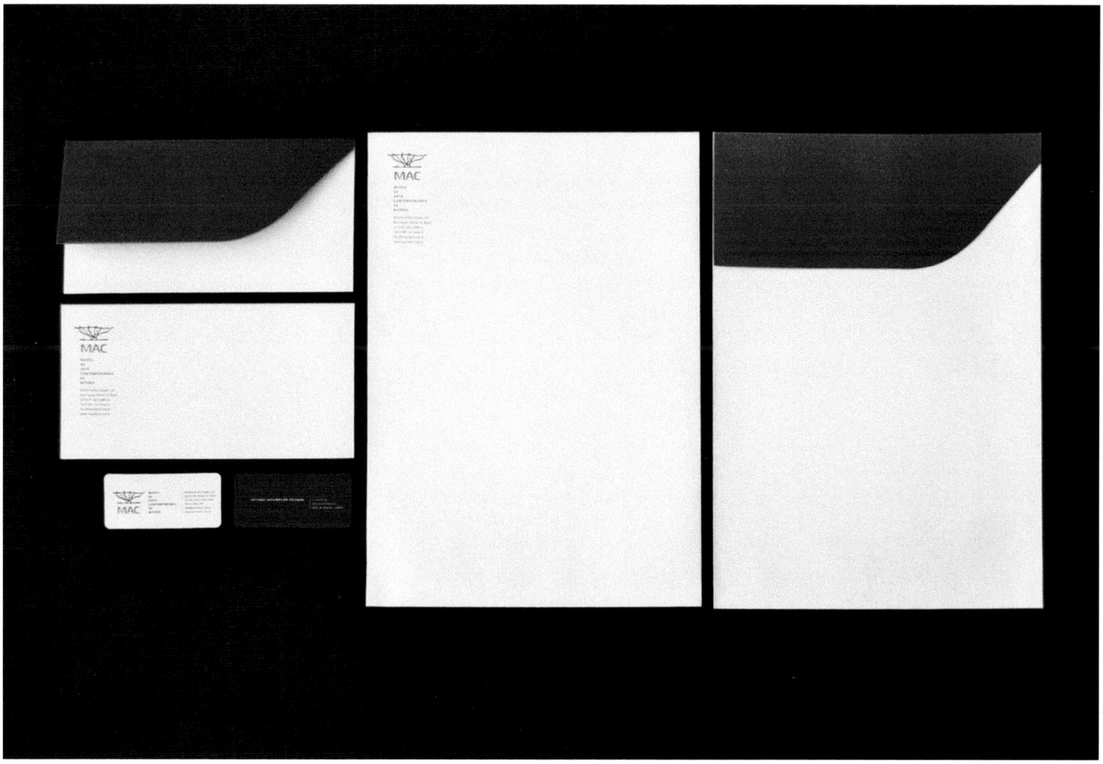

Client Museu de Arte Contemporânea de Niterói
Year 2006
Design Dupla Design
Team Claudia Gamboa, Fabiana Takeda

KAISER-JOSEPH-STRASSE
79098 FREIBURG
MORTON-AND-PEPLOW.COM
MORTON & PEPLOW
MORTON & PEPLOW
MORTON & PEPLOW
MORTON & PEPLOW'S
FINE LONDON FOOD
FREIBURG MARKTHALLE

MORTON & PEPLOW

Client Morton & Peplow
Year 2008
Design Team Magpie Studio
Creative Directors:
David Azurdia,
Ben Christie, Jamie Ellul;
Designer: David Azurdia

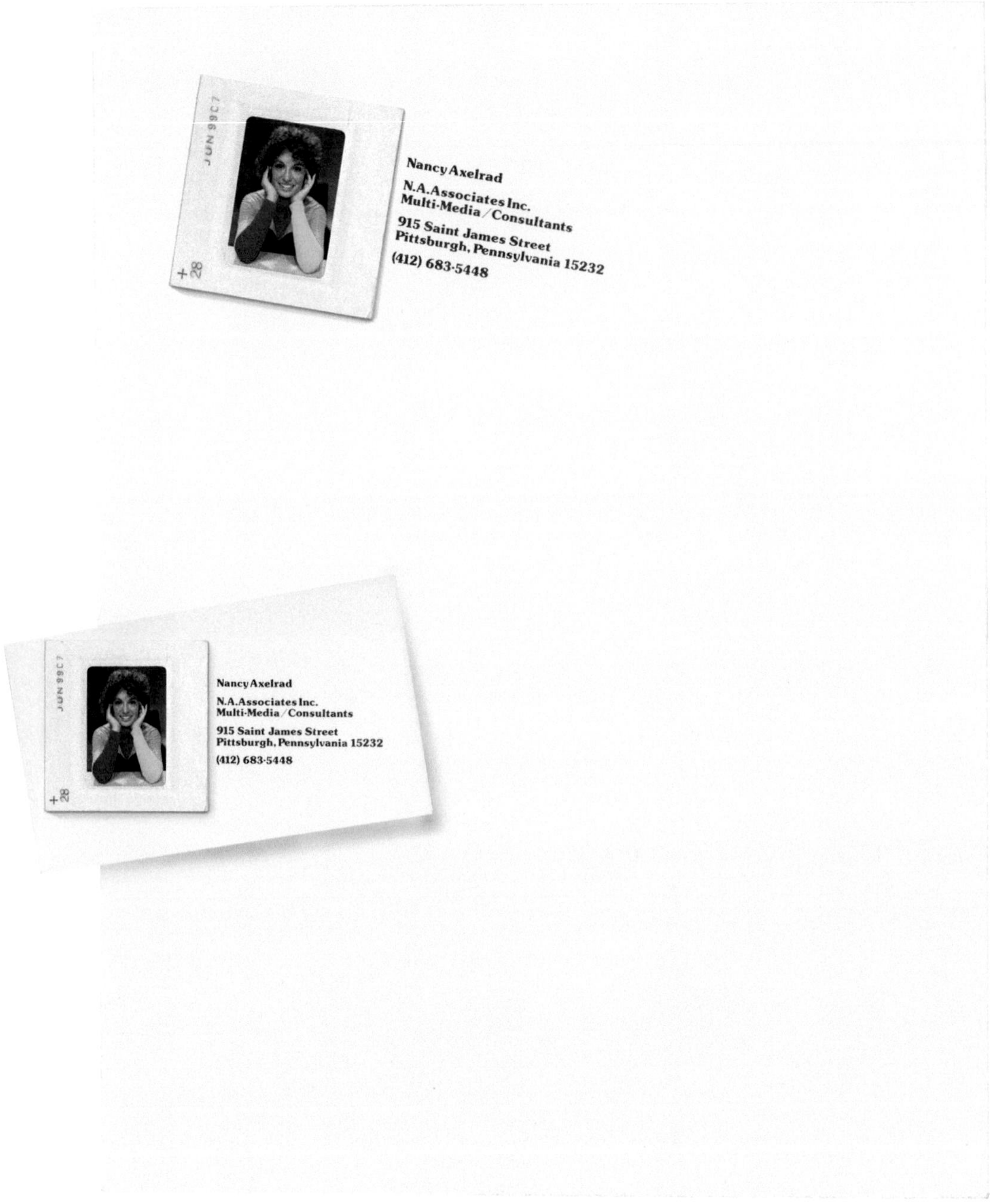

Client	Nancy Axelrad
Year	2000
Design	SX2

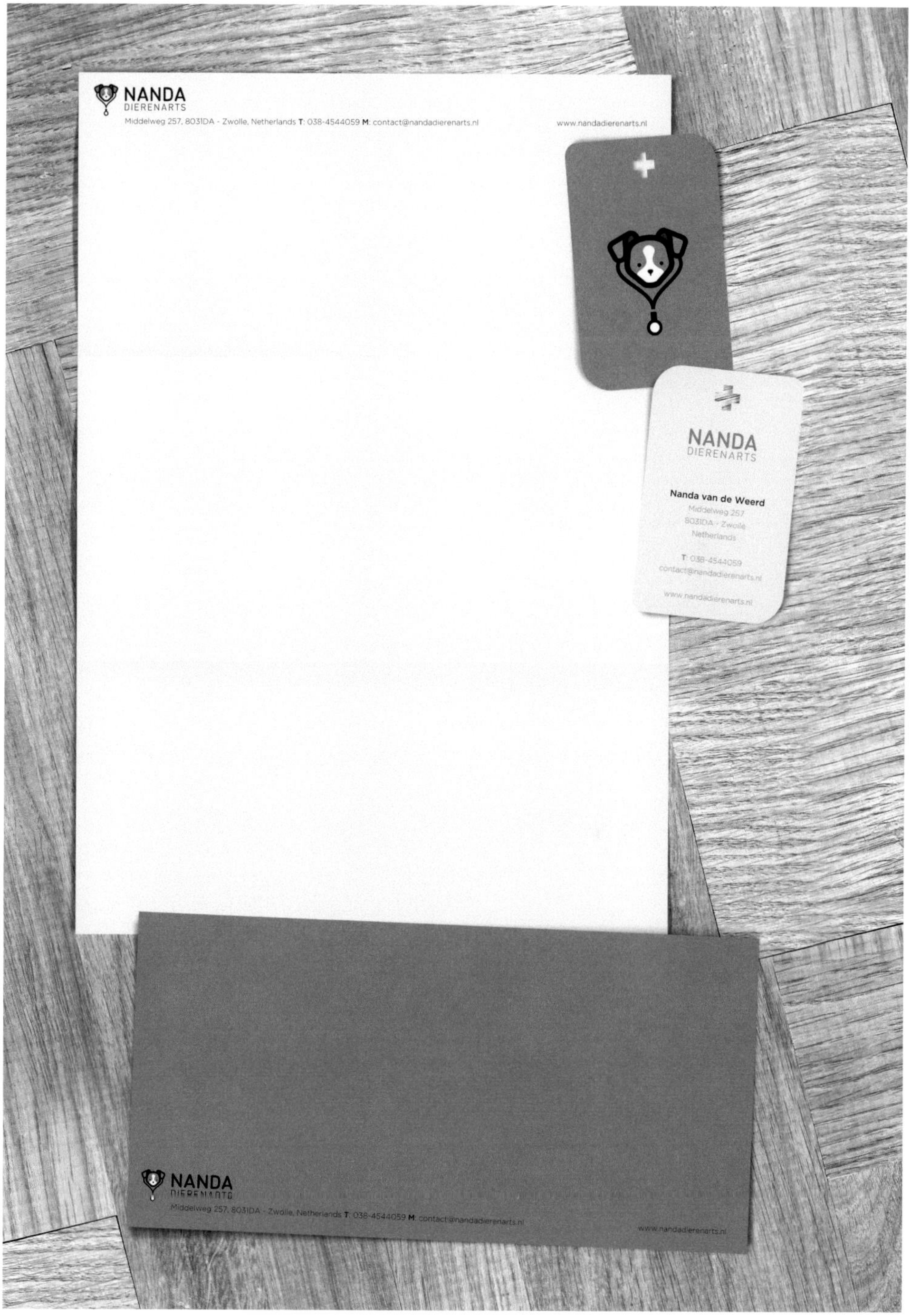

Client Nanda Dierenarts
Year 2010
Design Dogo

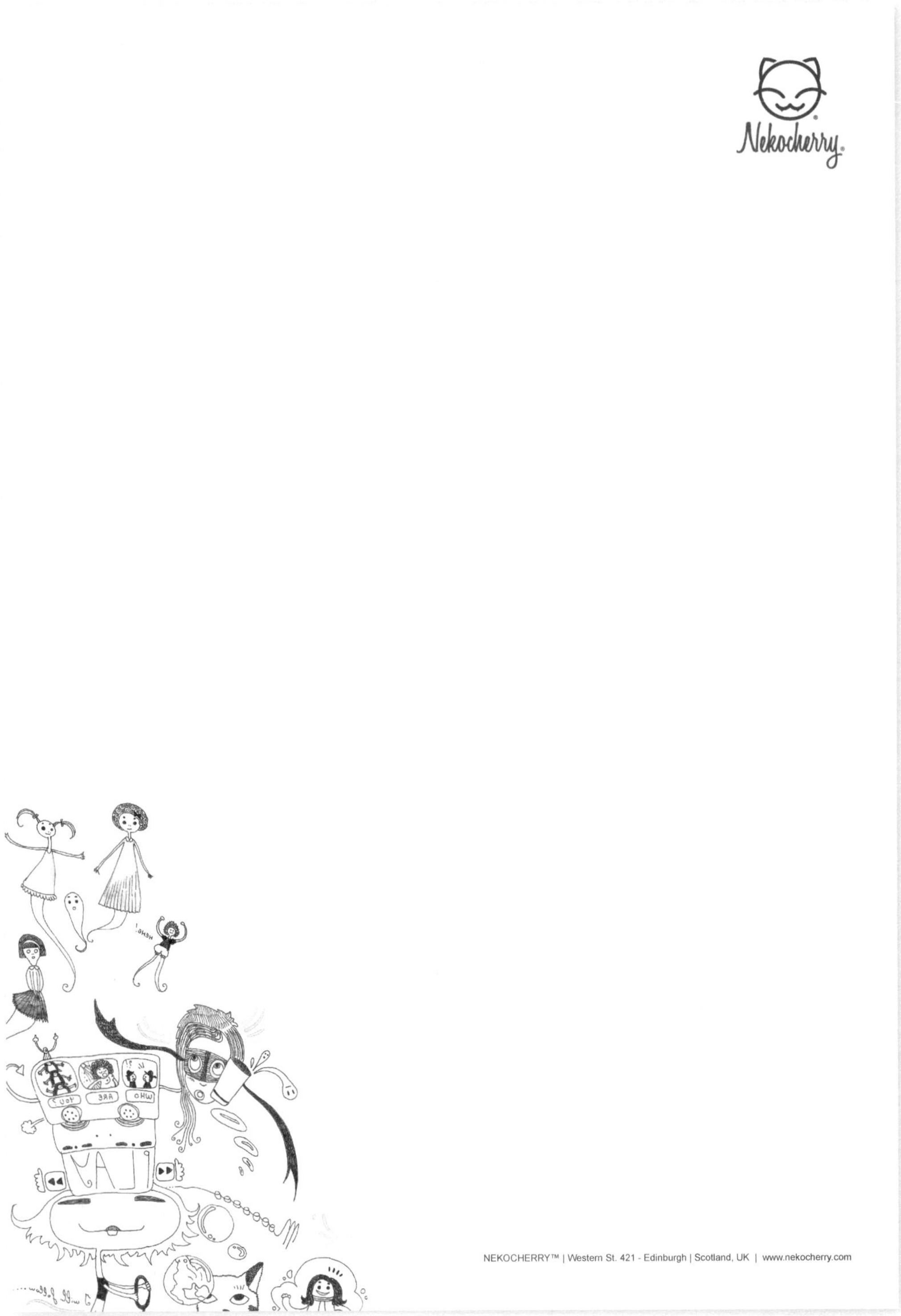
Nekocherry

NEKOCHERRY™ | Western St. 421 - Edinburgh | Scotland, UK | www.nekocherry.com

Nekocherry.
NEKOCHERRY™ | Western St. 421 - Edinburgh | Scotland, UK | www.nekocherry.com

Nekocherry.
NEKOCHERRY™ | Western St. 421 - Edinburgh | Scotland, UK | www.nekocherry.com

Client NekoCherry
Year 2009
Design DavGraficArts

New State Entertainment/Zip Design

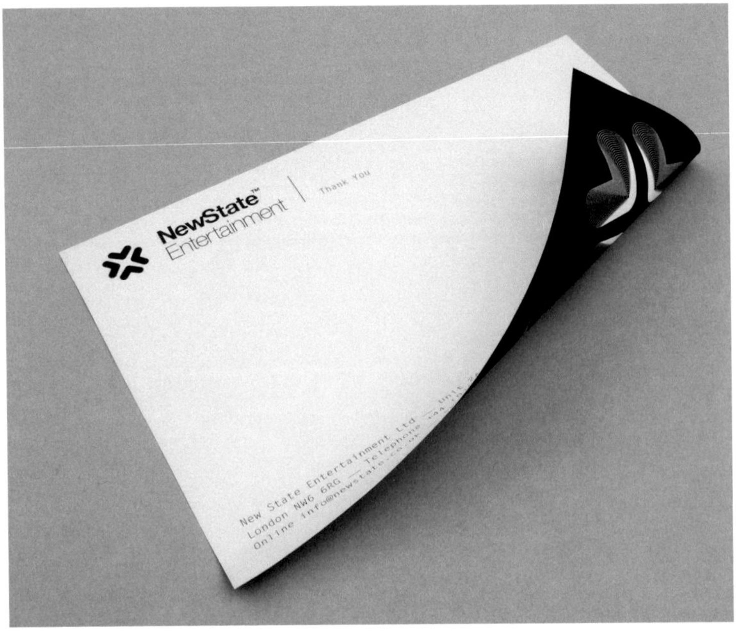

Client	New State Entertainment
Year	2009
Design	Zip Design
Team	David Bowden

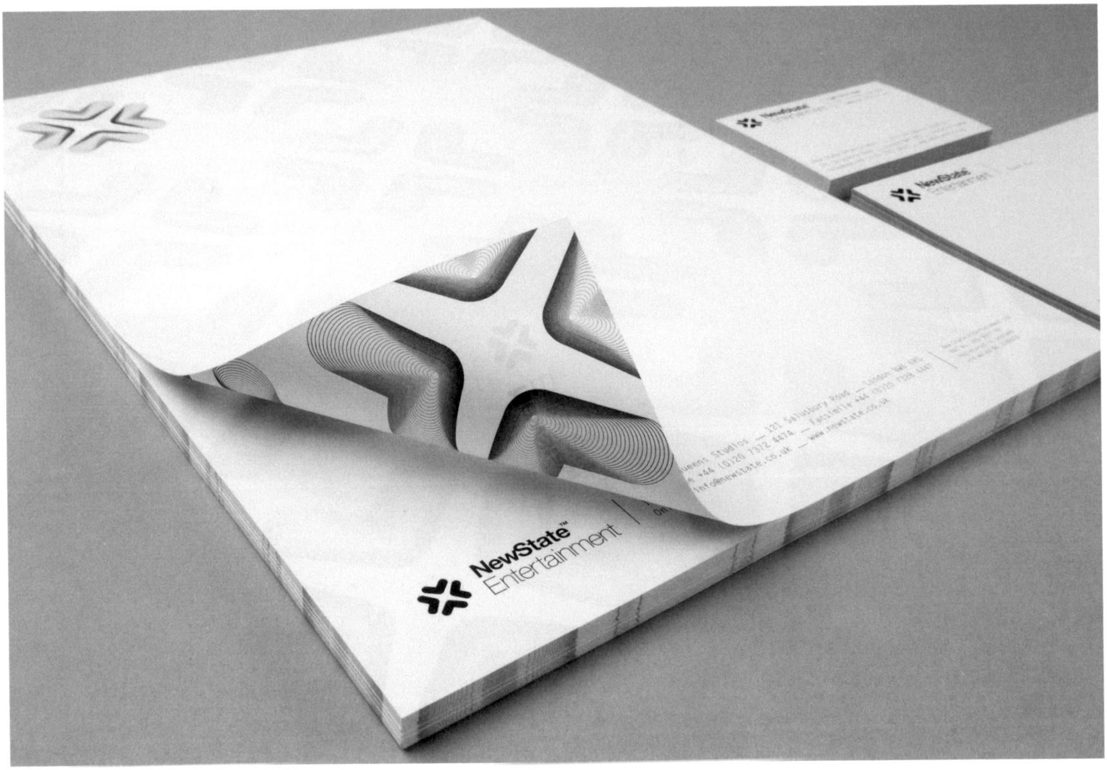

NewState™
Entertainment
Tom Parkinson
+44 (0)7970 004 651
tom@newstate.co.uk
New State Entertainment — Unit 2A Queens Studios
121 Salusbury Road — London NW6 6RG — United Kingdom
Telephone +44 (0)20 7372 4474 — www.newstate.co.uk

We are Nice Agency
We love all things RIA
1 Spital Yard, Spital Square
London E1 6ED
Call us: +44 (0)203 008 4443
Mail us: info@niceagency.co.uk
Web: www.niceagency.co.uk
nice®
working
with you.
Nice is the trading name of Nice Agency Ltd.
Registered address: 1 Spital Yard, Spitalfields
London E1 6ED.
Registered in England and Wales Number:
06919885. VAT Number: 978 4902 62
We are Nice Agency.
nice®
you.
Ryan Hall
Nice Director
RIA

We love all things RIA.
1 Spital Yard, Spitalfields
London E1 6ED
Call us: +44 (0)7872 565 990
Mail us: info@niceagency.co.uk
Web: www.niceagency.co.uk
nice®
talking to you.
CD/DVD
nice®
data.
Contents:
We love all things RIA
Nice Rich Internet Applications
Call us: +44 (0)203 008 4443
Mail us: info@niceagency.co.uk
Web: www.niceagency.co.uk
Tweet: twitter.com/niceagency
nice®
surprise.
If undelivered please return to:
Nice Agency, 1 Spital Yard, Spitalfields
London E1 6ED

Client	Nice Agency
Year	2009
Design	Socio Design
Team	Nigel Bates

Client Nizuc resort and private residences
Year 2007
Design Carbone Smolan Agency
Team Leslie Smolan, Carla Miller, Melissa Laux

nizuc

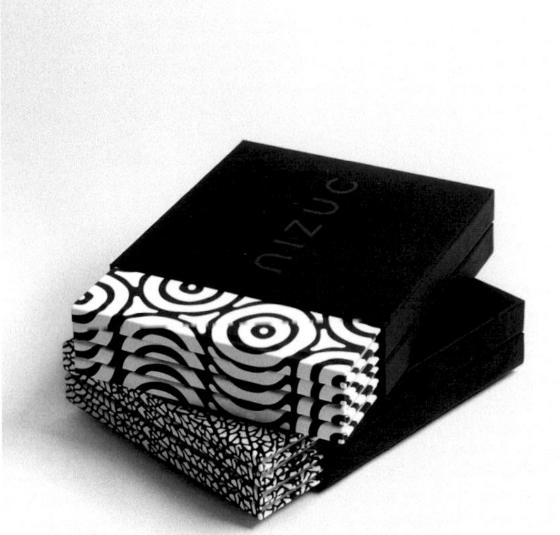
nizuc

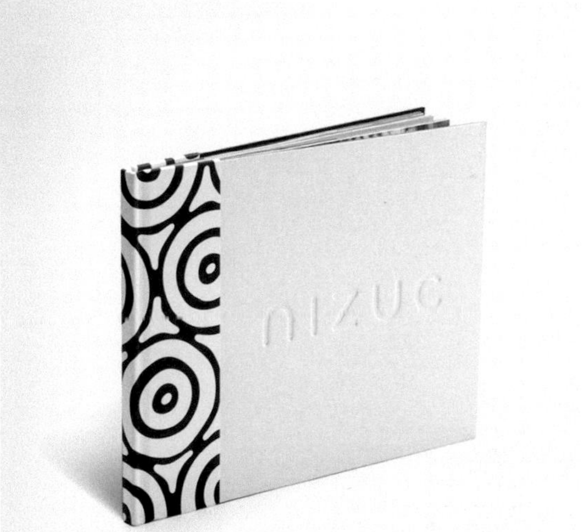
nizuc

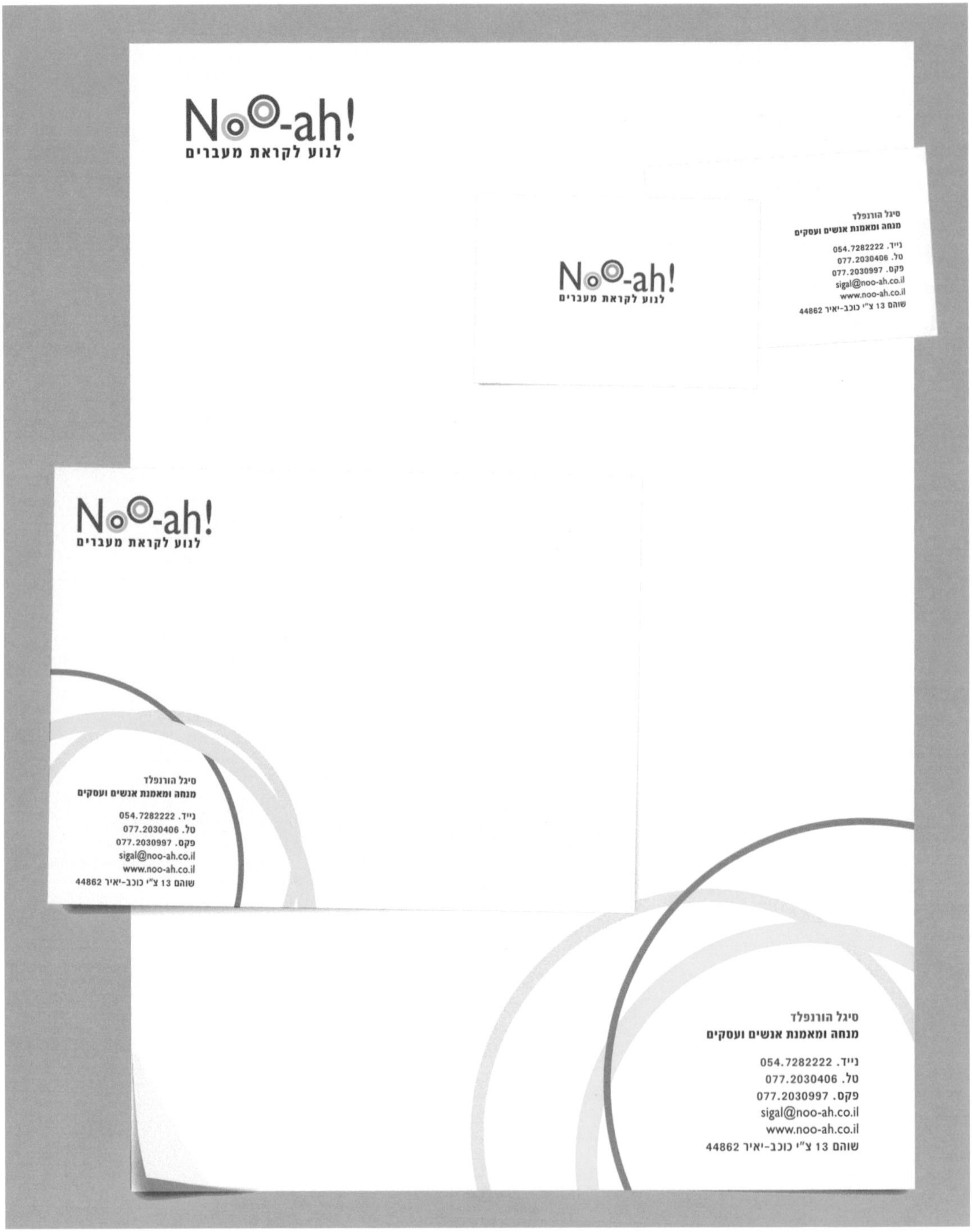

Client Noo-ah!
Year 2008
Design AbadiGuard

Client Nowy Sacz City Council
Year 2010
Design Papajastudio

OBENHUBER PARTNERS
1045 Mason Street, Suite 202 | San Francisco, CA 94108
New Corporate Identity for Obenhuber Partners
Lorem ipsum dolor sit amet, consectetur adipiscing elit. Phasellus congue nunc sit amet elit ultrices iaculis. Vivamus ullamcorper lobortis risus sed gravida. Sed eget tellus sed sapien imperdiet rhoncus id a elit. Sed condimentum congue justo nec mollis. Lorem ipsum dolor sit amet, consectetur adipiscing elit. Praesent lobortis congue ornare. In sit amet dui lorem. Donec viverra mauris id tellus faucibus sollicitudin. Sed imperdiet libero a dui sollicitudin nec laoreet mauris dapibus. Pellentesque sit amet dolor lacus. Donec cursus libero in nulla sagittis elementum.
Donec semper tellus in dui feugiat vitae cursus velit bibendum. Suspendisse eros nisl, suscipit id viverra vel, ornare vel lorem. Ut rutrum ante vitae sapien eleifend elementum. Lorem ipsum dolor sit amet,
adipiscing elit. Vivamus consequat, nisl non pellentesque convallis, risus ante bibendum
leo lorem quis urna. Praesent et ipsum enim. Nulla eu condimentum ante.
justo felis, lobortis sodales lobortis tincidunt, volutpat quis risus.
ornare neque imperdiet. Pellentesque tincidunt, tellus eu
diam odio nec augue. Mauris sodales dolor et
felis quam, eleifend sed ultrices a,
non ligula semper vestibulum.
Nunc sagittis, enim vitae fringilla
dolor vel odio sodales vulputate
Mauris in ligula purus, vel
eros auctor ut suscipit dolor
Donec quam purus, rhoncus non
malesuada condimentum.
Obenhuber Partners, Inc.
Principal
Inessa Obenhuber
Partner
OBENHUBER PARTNERS
1045 Mason Street, Suite 202 | San Francisco, CA 94108
Inessa Obenhuber
Managing partner
Office (415) 931 6422
Fax (650) 854 4069
Mobile (650) 678 6867
Email inessa@obenhuberpartners.com
1045 Mason Street, Suite 202 | San Francisco, CA 94108
OBENHUBER PARTNERS

Client Obenhuber Partners
Year 2008
Design Uber Experience

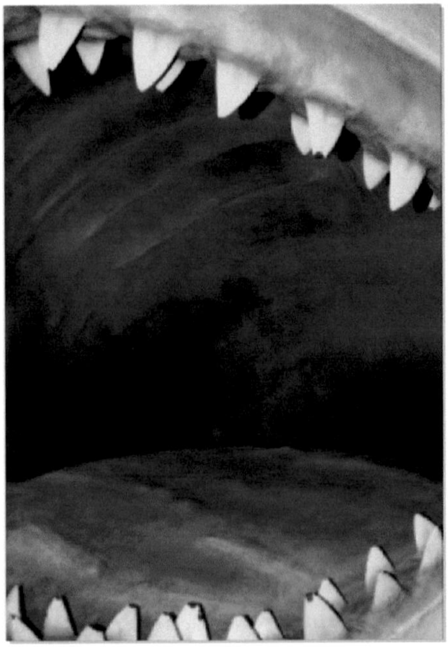

Client OCU
Year 2008
Design m Barcelona
Team Marion Dönneweg

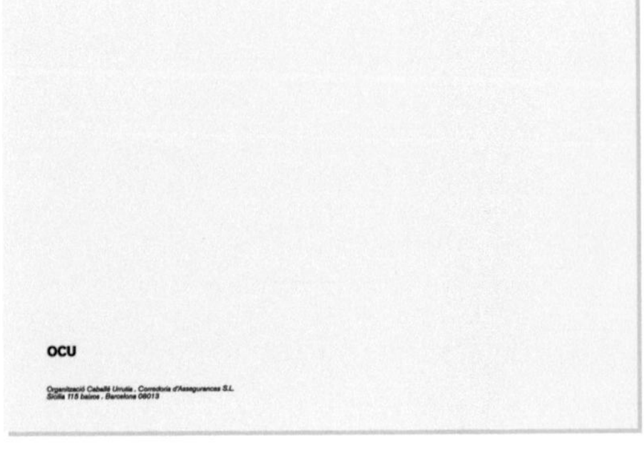

OCU

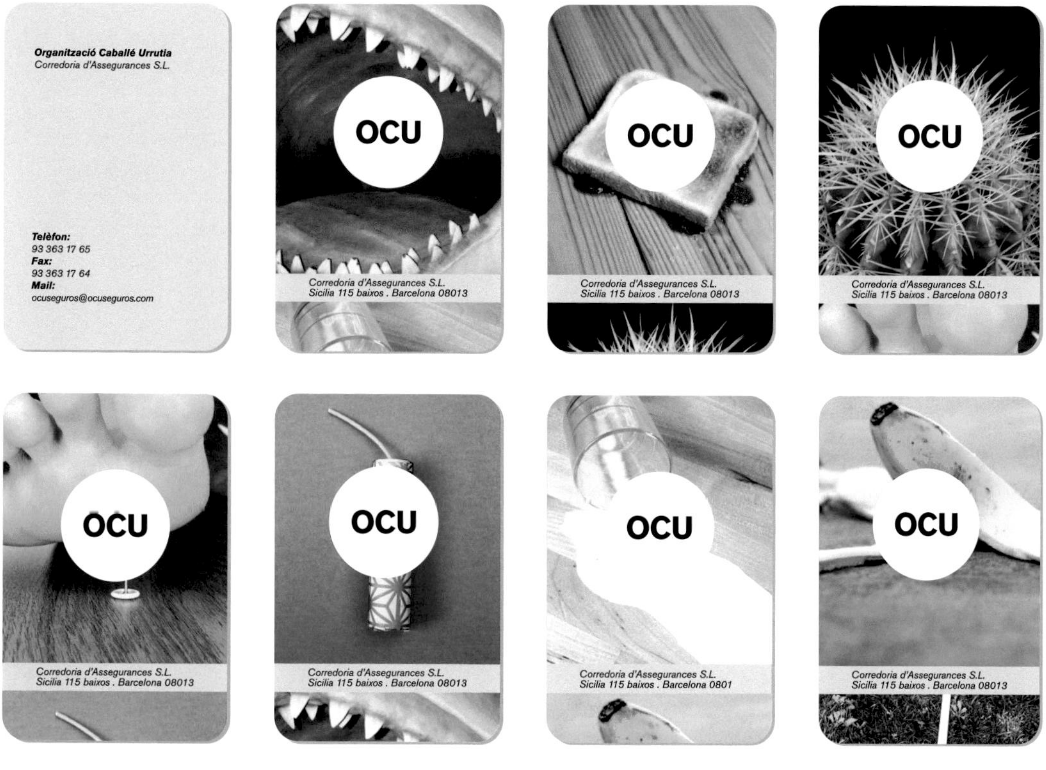
Organització Caballé Urrutia
Corredoria d'Assegurances S.L.
Telèfon:
93 363 17 65
Fax:
93 363 17 64
Mail:
ocuseguros@ocuseguros.com
OCU
Corredoria d'Assegurances S.L.
Sicilia 115 baixos . Barcelona 08013
OCU
Corredoria d'Assegurances S.L.
Sicilia 115 baixos . Barcelona 08013
OCU
Corredoria d'Assegurances S.L.
Sicilia 115 baixos . Barcelona 08013
OCU
Corredoria d'Assegurances S.L.
Sicilia 115 baixos . Barcelona 08013
OCU
Corredoria d'Assegurances S.L.
Sicilia 115 baixos . Barcelona 08013
OCU
Corredoria d'Assegurances S.L.
Sicilia 115 baixos . Barcelona 0801
OCU
Corredoria d'Assegurances S.L.
Sicilia 115 baixos . Barcelona 08013

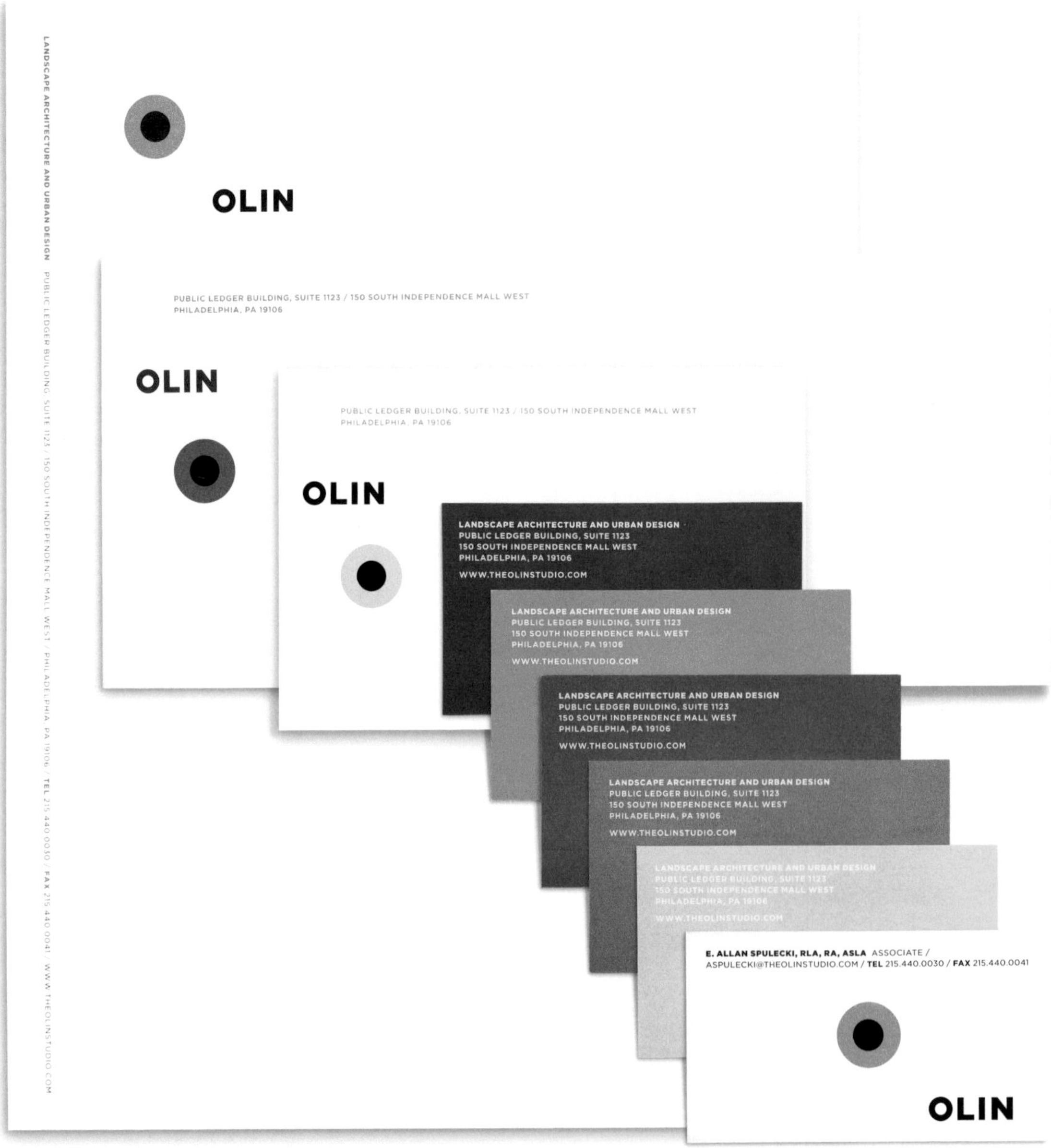

Client OLIN
Year 2009
Design Pentagram

ANDREW LEACH / ALEACH@THEOLINSTUDIO.COM /
TEL 215 440 0030 / FAX 215 440 0041
OLIN
LANDSCAPE ARCHITECTURE AND URBAN DESIGN
PUBLIC LEDGER BUILDING, SUITE 1123
150 SOUTH INDEPENDENCE MALL WEST
PHILADELPHIA, PA 19106
WWW.THEOLINSTUDIO.COM
GREG BURRELL, RLA, ASLA
DANEIL MAZONE DIRECTOR OF MARKETING
YUE LI, RLA, ASLA ASSOCIATE
JUDITH VENONSKY, AFFILATE MEMBER, ASLA

the whole is equal
to the sum of its parts
ONE MAN SHOW
illustrator + graphic designer + comic artist + publisher + journalist + e-radio producer + photographer + decoration designer + more = Tassos Papaioannou
the whole is equal
to the sum of its parts
Tassos Papaioannou
P.O. box 113, 190.04
Spata Attikis, Greece
mobile: +30.6974.88.38.35
email: info@onemanshowstudio.com
website: www.onemanshowstudio.com
illustrator / graphic designer / comic artist / publisher / journalist / e-radio producer / photographer / decoration designer / more
POPLIE.EU
WEB RADIO
P.O. box 113, 190.04, Spata Attikis, Greece, mobile: +30.6974.88.38.35, email: info@onemanshowstudio.com, website: www.onemanshowstudio.com

Client One Man Show
Year 2010
Design One Man Show

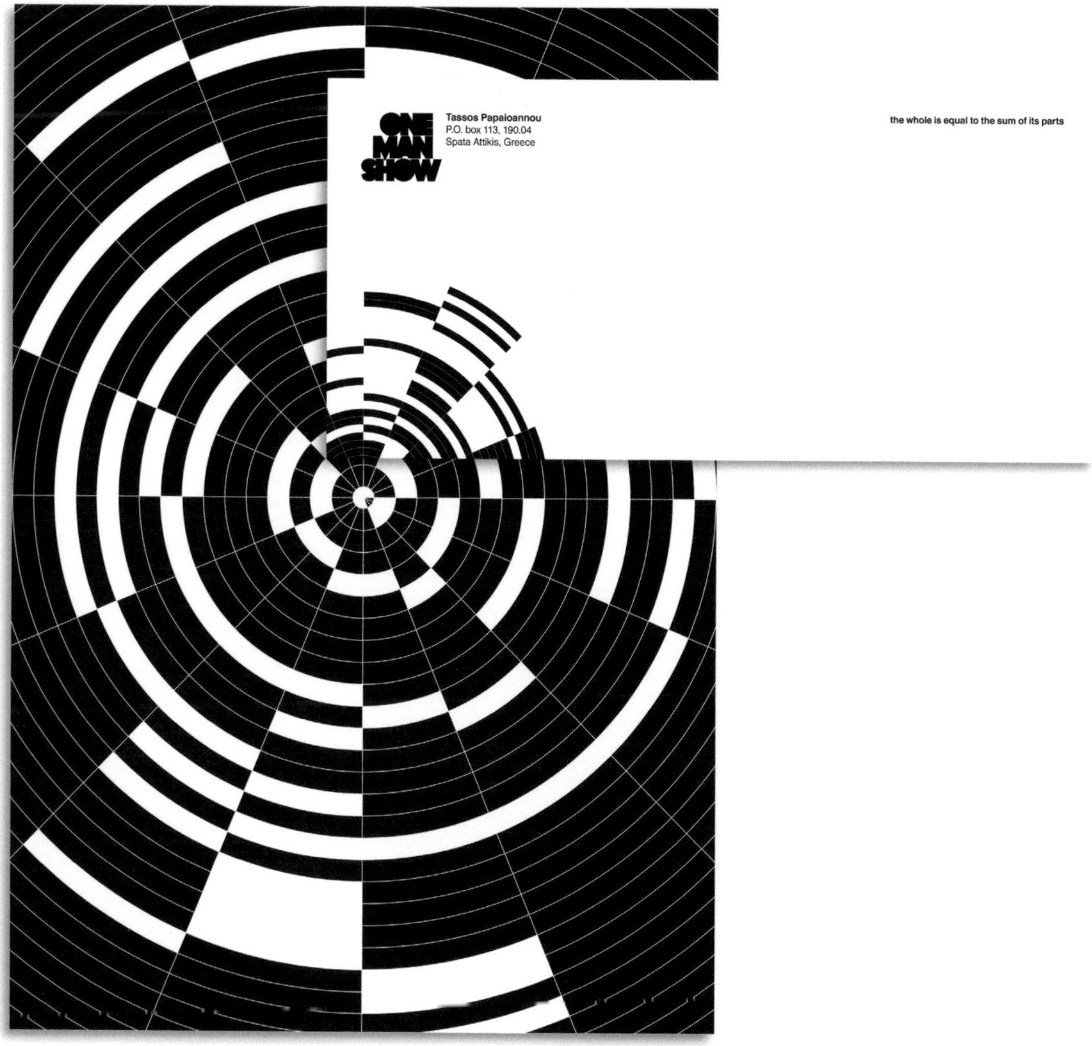
ONE
MAN
SHOW
Tassos Papaioannou
P.O. box 113, 190.04
Spata Attikis, Greece
the whole is equal to the sum of its parts

Client	Ossie Clark
Year	2007
Design	SVIDesign

OSSIE
CLARK
Islington House, Suite 5 & 6, 313 - 314 Upper Street, London N1 2XQ, UK, Tel: +44 (0)20 7354 5000, Fax: +44 (0)20 7354 0555,
www.ossieclarklondon.com

OSSIE
CLARK
A.V. Gur
Creative Director
Islington House, Suite 5 & 6
313 - 314 Upper Street
London N1 2XQ, UK
M: +44 (0)7740 676 579
E: av.gur@ossieclarklondon.com
T: +44 (0)20 7354 5000
F: +44 (0)20 7354 0555
www.ossieclarklondon.com

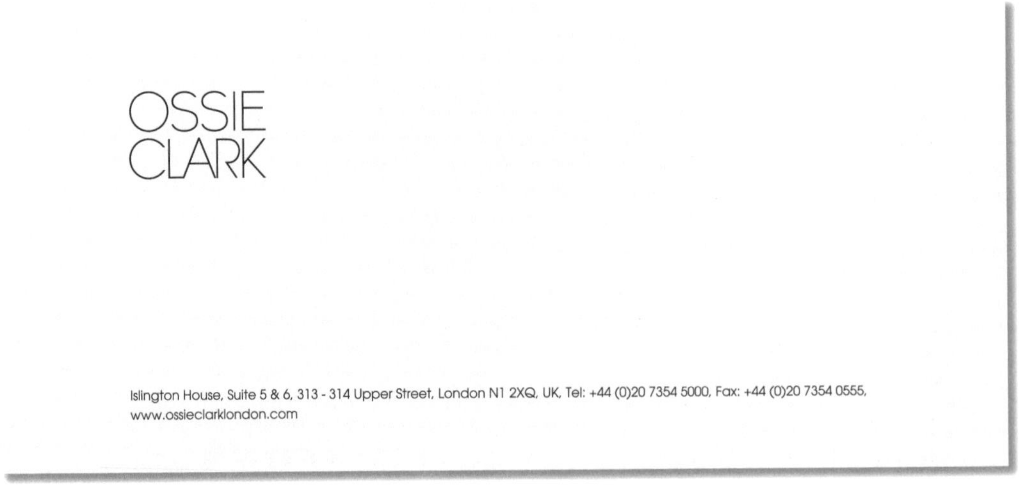
OSSIE
CLARK
Islington House, Suite 5 & 6, 313 - 314 Upper Street, London N1 2XQ, UK, Tel: +44 (0)20 7354 5000, Fax: +44 (0)20 7354 0555,
www.ossieclarklondon.com

OSSIE
CLARK

OSSIE
CLARK
Fiona Ennis
Sales Director
Islington House, Suite 5 & 6
313 - 314 Upper Street
London N1 2XQ, UK

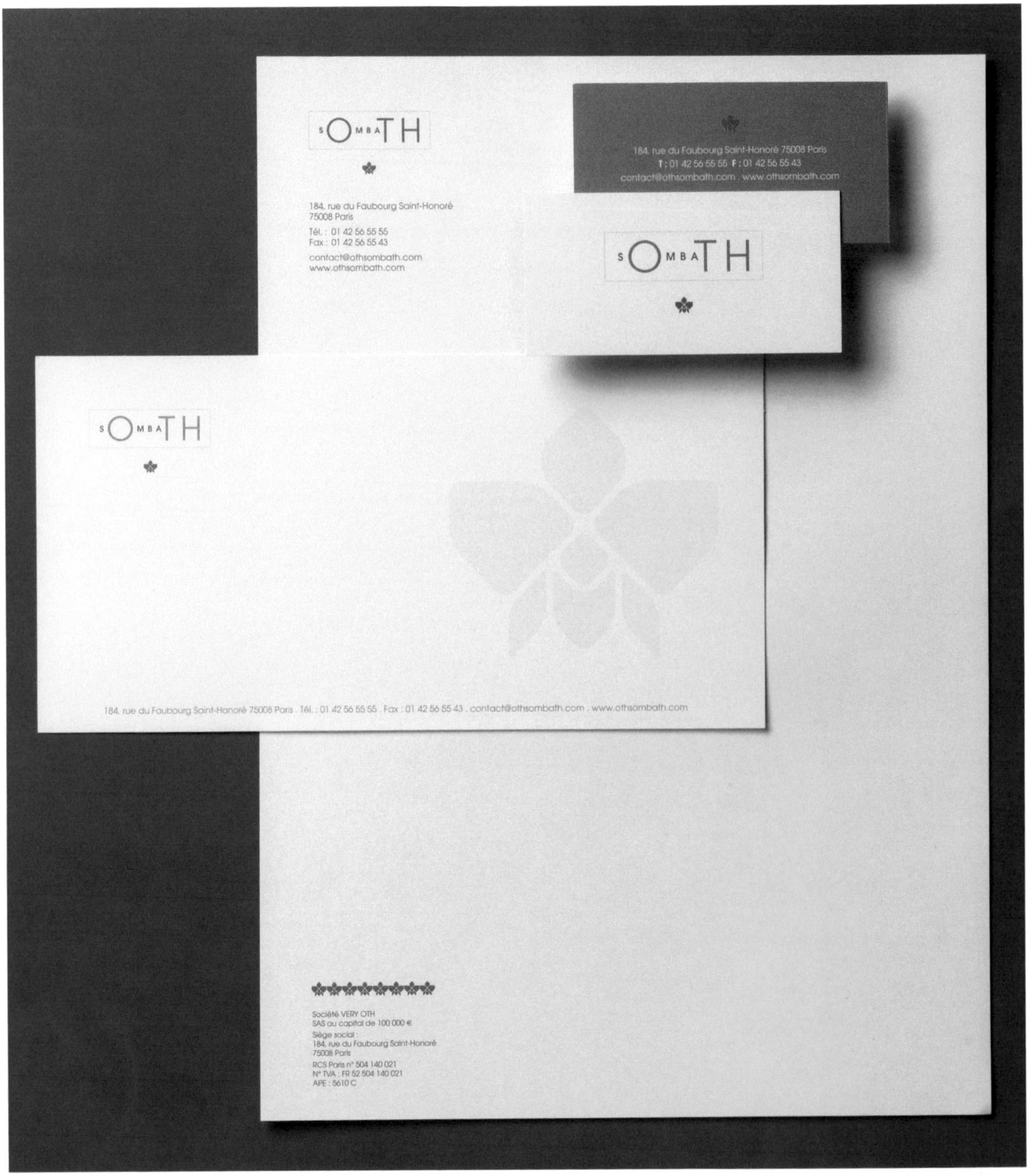

Client Oth Sombath
Year 2008
Design Philippe David

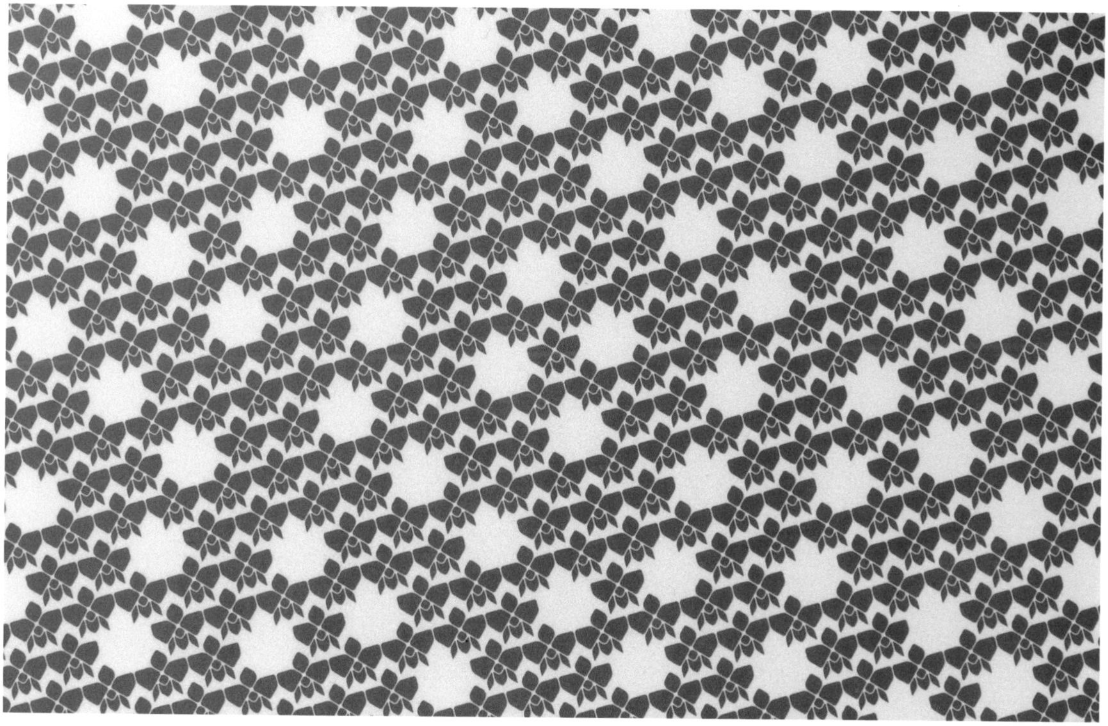

SOMBATH
184, rue du Faubourg Saint-Honoré 75008 Paris
T : 01 42 56 55 55 F : 01 42 56 55 43
contact@othsombath.com . www.othsombath.com

Outward Bound
Peacebuilding
Outward Bound
Peacebuilding

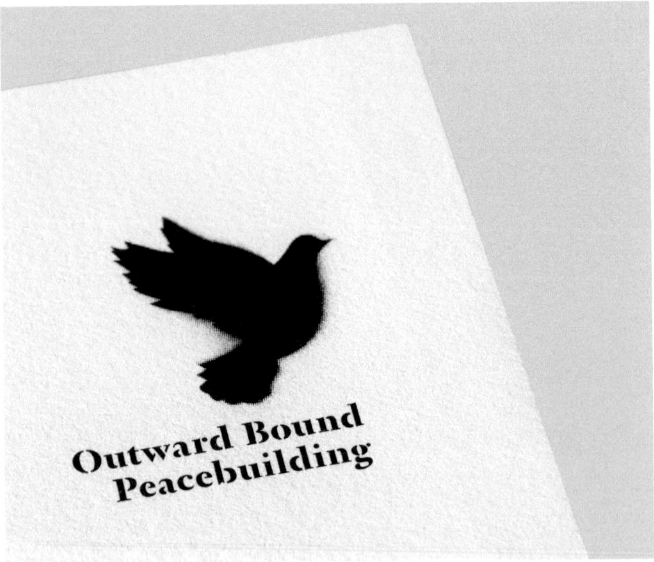
Outward Bound
Peacebuilding

Client Outward Bound Center for Peacebuilding
Year 2007
Design Pentagram

The Drill Hall
643 Park Avenue New York, NY 10065 T 212 616 3939
643 Park Avenue New York, NY 10065

Client The Park Avenue Armory Conservancy – The Drill Hall
Year 2007
Design Pentagram

Park Avenue Armory Conservancy/Pentagram

Client	The Park Avenue Armory Conservancy
Year	2007
Design	Pentagram

Park Avenue
Armory
Park Avenue
Armory

Park Avenue
Armory

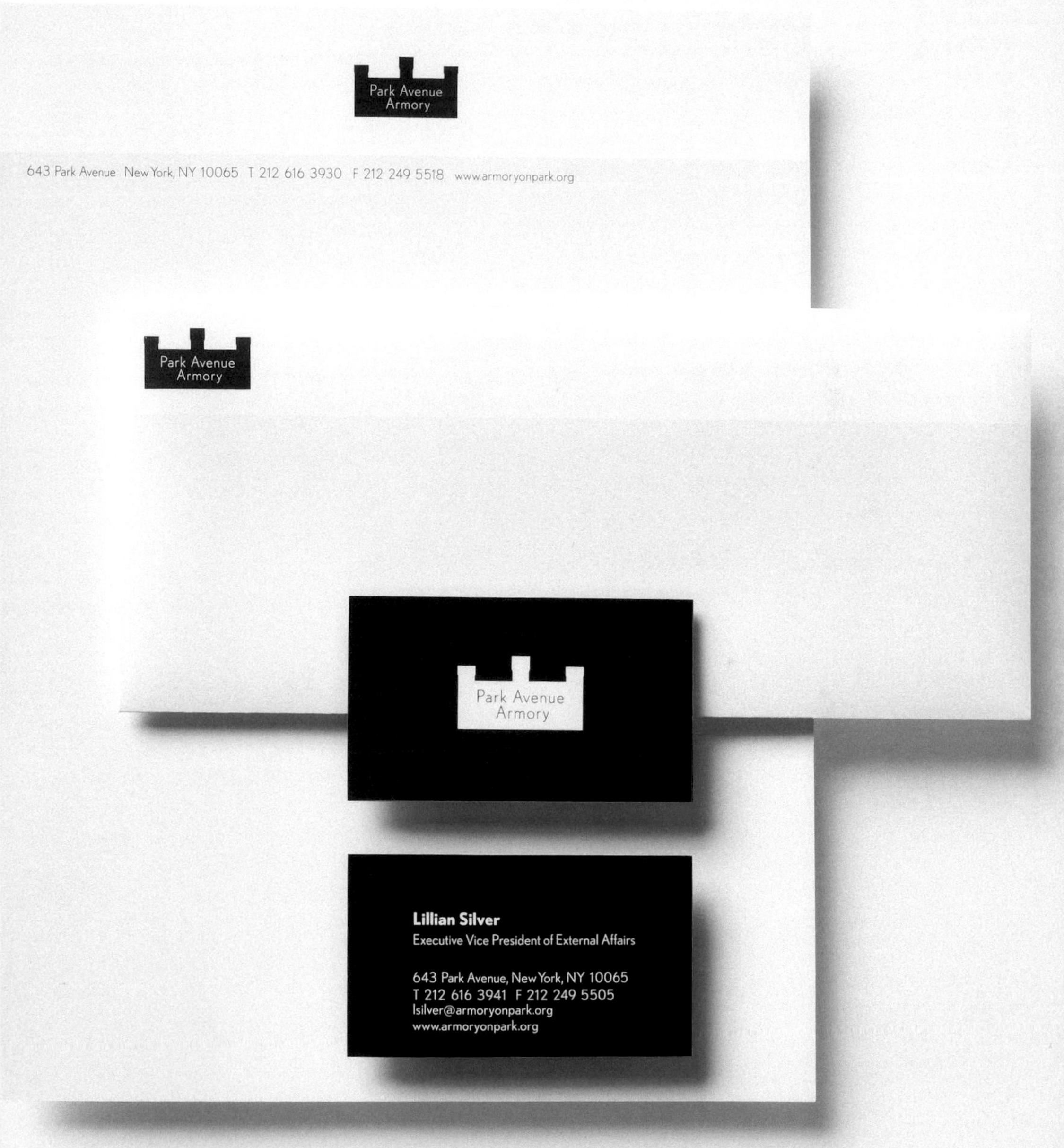
Park Avenue Armory
643 Park Avenue New York, NY 10065 T 212 616 3930 F 212 249 5518 www.armoryonpark.org
Park Avenue Armory
Park Avenue Armory
Lillian Silver
Executive Vice President of External Affairs
643 Park Avenue, New York, NY 10065
T 212 616 3941 F 212 249 5505
lsilver@armoryonpark.org
www.armoryonpark.org

passion for fashion®
Λουκάρεως & Κενδρινού 21-23, 106 78, Γκύζη, Αθήνα
t. 210.64.68.307 | e. passionforfashion@gmail.com
passion for fashion®
Λουκάρεως & Κενδρινού 21-23
10678, Γκύζη, Αθήνα
t. 210.64.68.307
passionforfashion@gmail.com
passion for fashion®
Λουκάρεως & Κενδρινού 21-23
10678, Γκύζη, Αθήνα
t. 210.64.68.307
passionforfashion@gmail.com

Client Passion for Fashion
Year 2010
Design One Man Show

passion for fashion
Λουκάρεως & Κενδρινού 21-23
10678, Γκύζη, Αθήνα

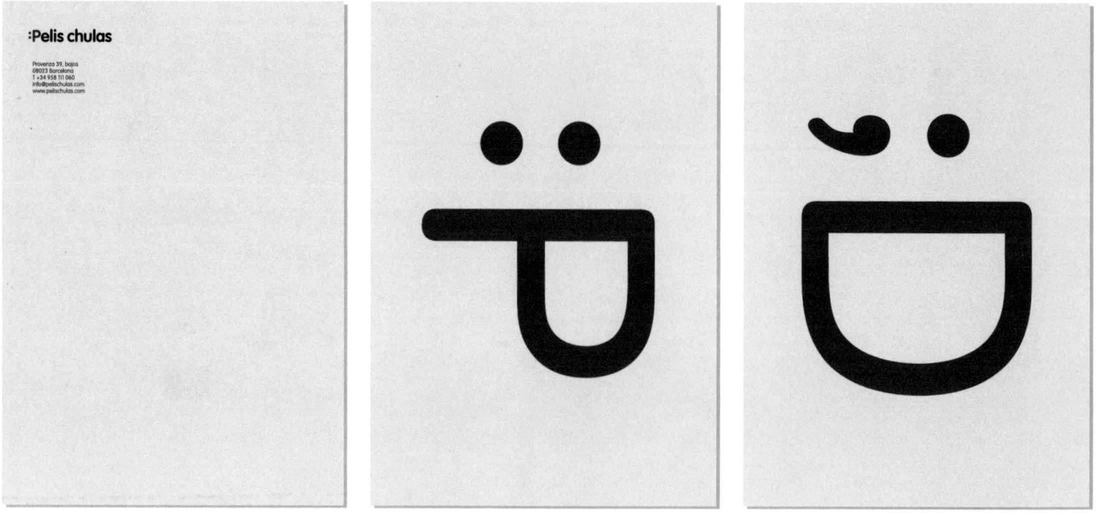
:Pelis chulas
Provenza 39, bajos
08023 Barcelona
T +34 958 111 060
info@pelischulas.com
www.pelischulas.com

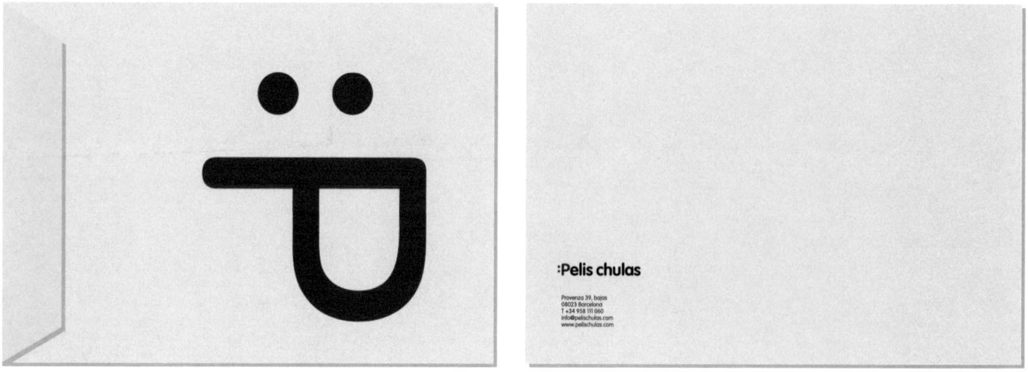
:Pelis chulas
Provenza 39, bajos
08023 Barcelona
T +34 958 111 060
info@pelischulas.com
www.pelischulas.com

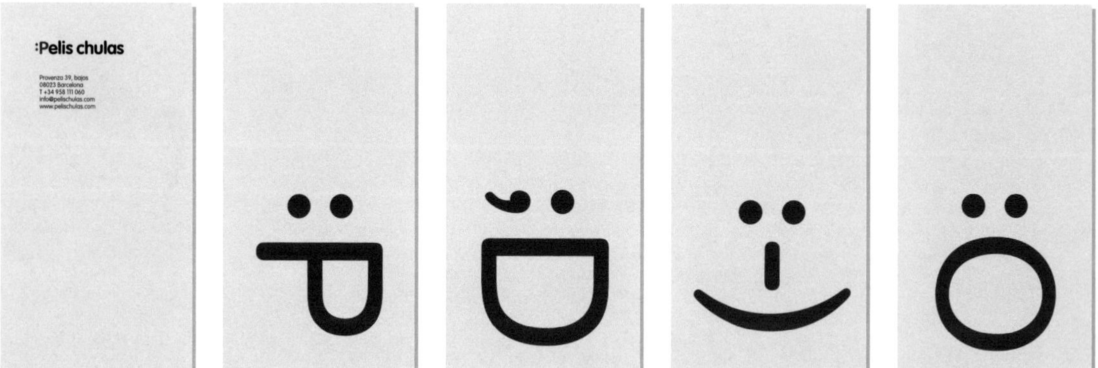
:Pelis chulas
Provenza 39, bajos
08023 Barcelona
T +34 958 111 060
info@pelischulas.com
www.pelischulas.com

Client Pelis chulas
Year 2010
Design m Barcelona
Team Marion Dönneweg

:Pelis chulas
Félix Fernández de Castro
Provenza 39, bajos
08023 Barcelona
T +34 958 111 060
info@pelischulas.com
www.pelischulas.com

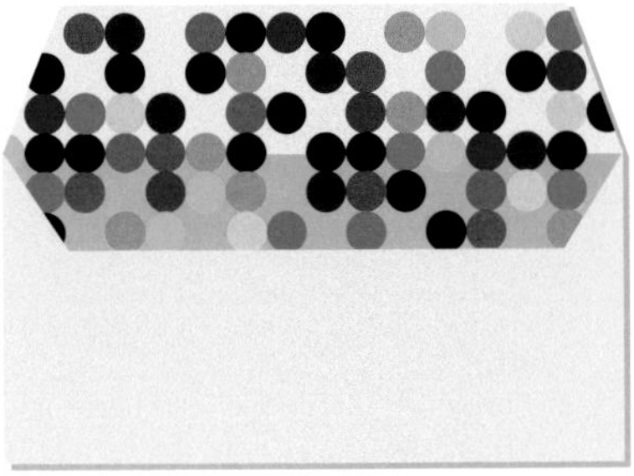

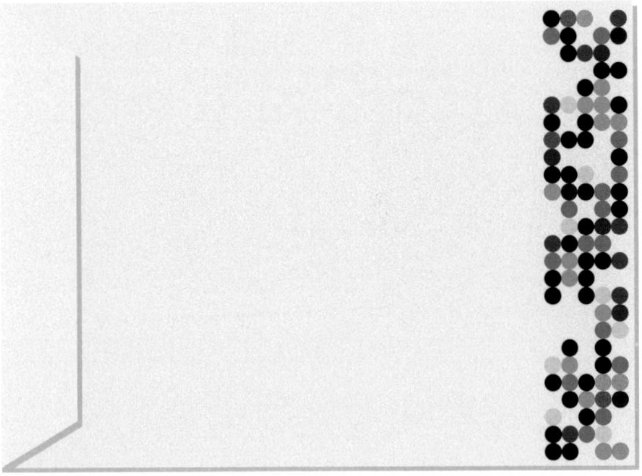

Client POK
Year 2007
Design m Barcelona
Team Marion Dönneweg, Mireia Roda

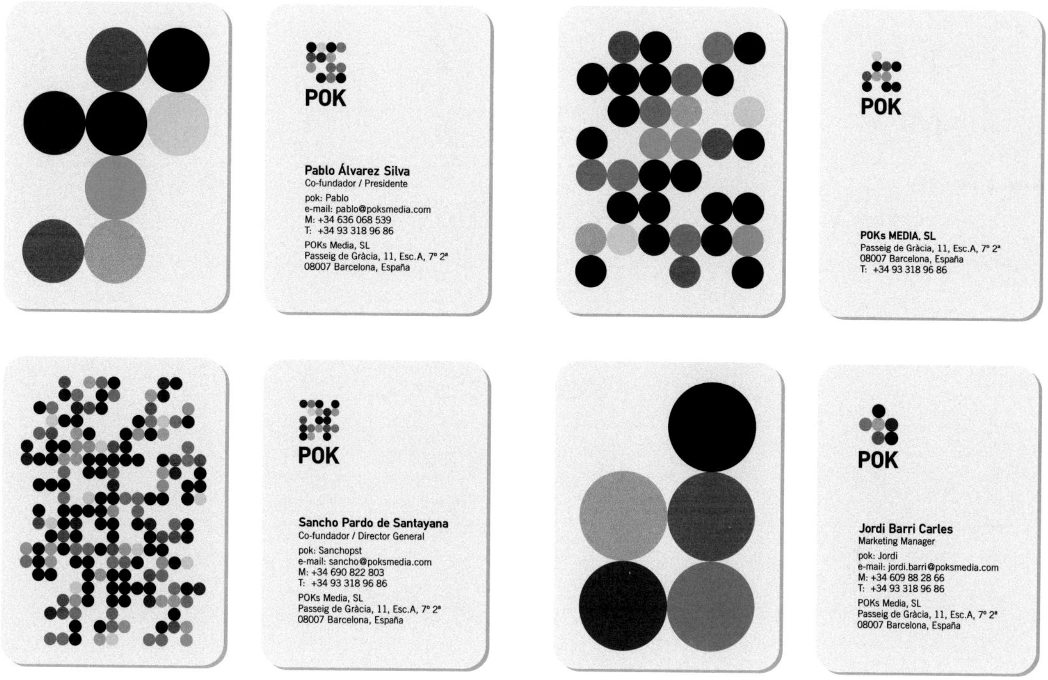
POK
Pablo Álvarez Silva
Co-fundador / Presidente
pok: Pablo
e-mail: pablo@poksmedia.com
M: +34 636 068 539
T: +34 93 318 96 86
POKs Media, SL
Passeig de Gràcia, 11, Esc.A, 7º 2ª
08007 Barcelona, España
POK
POKs MEDIA, SL
Passeig de Gràcia, 11, Esc.A, 7º 2ª
08007 Barcelona, España
T: +34 93 318 96 86
POK
Sancho Pardo de Santayana
Co-fundador / Director General
pok: Sanchopst
e-mail: sancho@poksmedia.com
M: +34 690 822 803
T: +34 93 318 96 86
POKs Media, SL
Passeig de Gràcia, 11, Esc.A, 7º 2ª
08007 Barcelona, España
POK
Jordi Barri Carles
Marketing Manager
pok: Jordi
e-mail: jordi.barri@poksmedia.com
M: +34 609 88 28 66
T: +34 93 318 96 86
POKs Media, SL
Passeig de Gràcia, 11, Esc.A, 7º 2ª
08007 Barcelona, España

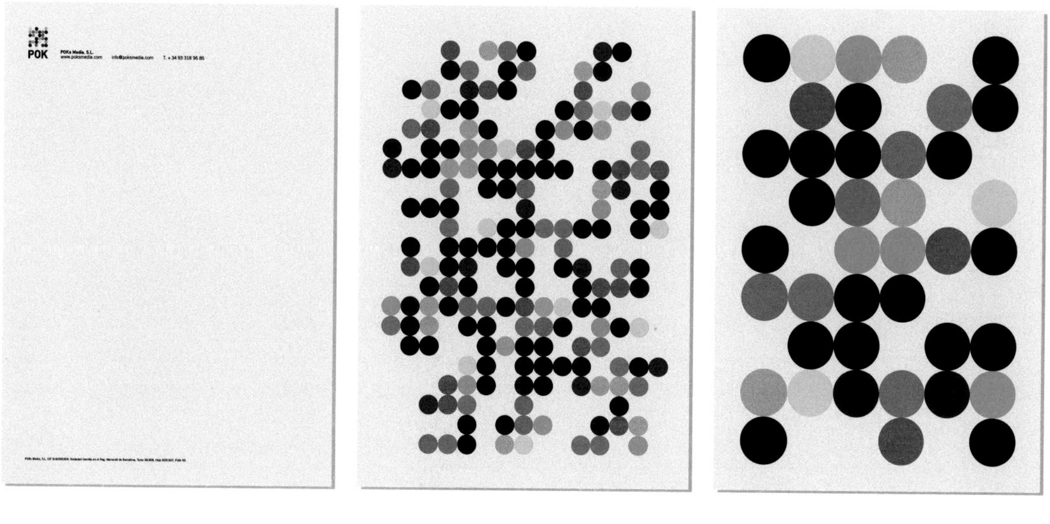
POK
POKs Media, S.L.
www.poksmedia.com
info@poksmedia.com
T. + 34 93 318 96 86

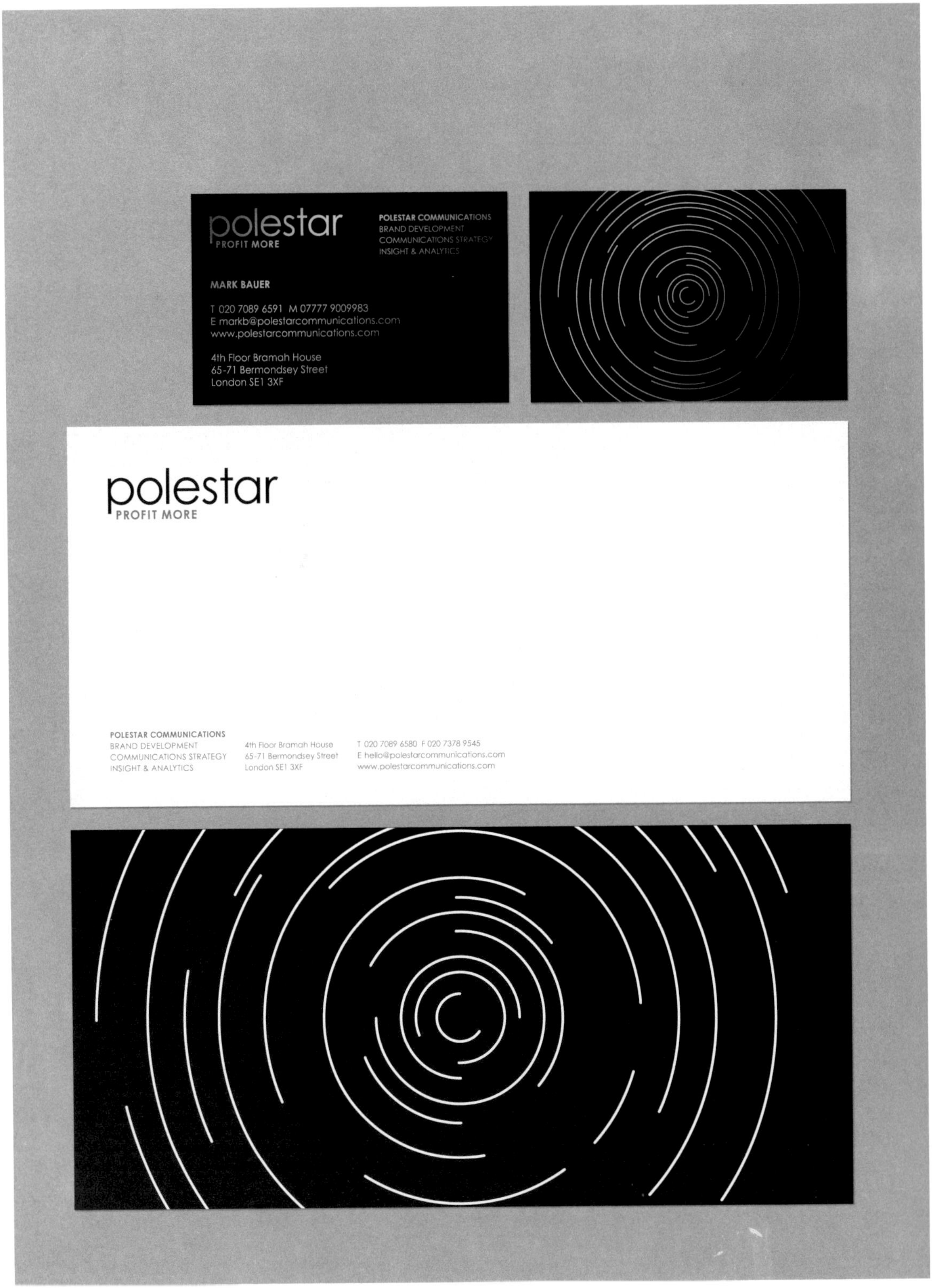
polestar
PROFIT MORE
POLESTAR COMMUNICATIONS
BRAND DEVELOPMENT
COMMUNICATIONS STRATEGY
INSIGHT & ANALYTICS
MARK BAUER
T 020 7089 6591 M 07777 9009983
E markb@polestarcommunications.com
www.polestarcommunications.com
4th Floor Bramah House
65-71 Bermondsey Street
London SE1 3XF
polestar
PROFIT MORE
POLESTAR COMMUNICATIONS
BRAND DEVELOPMENT
COMMUNICATIONS STRATEGY
INSIGHT & ANALYTICS
4th Floor Bramah House
65-71 Bermondsey Street
London SE1 3XF
T 020 7089 6580 F 020 7378 9545
E hello@polestarcommunications.com
www.polestarcommunications.com

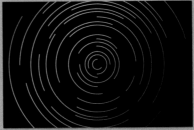

Client Polestar
Year 2009
Design Buddy

Pont-Aven School of Contemporary Art/Pentagram

Central Office
269 South Main Street
Providence, RI 02903
USA
Tel. 401.272.5445
Fax. 401.272.5448
www.pontaven.org
Main Campus
Pension Gloanec
5 Place Paul Gaugin
29930 Pont-Aven
France
Tel. 33 (0)2.98.09.10.45
Fax. 33 (0)2.98.06.17.38
Pont-Aven School of Contemporary Art
Pont-Aven School of Contemporary Art
Central Office
269 South Main Street
Providence, RI 02903
USA
Pont-Aven School of Contemporary Art
Ann Li
Director of Administration and Admissions
a.li@pontaven.org
Central Office
269 South Main Street
Providence, RI 02903
USA
Tel. 401.272.5445
Fax. 401.272.5448
Main Campus
Pension Gloanec
5 Place Paul Gaugin
29930 Pont-Aven
France
Tel. 33 (0)2.98.09.10.45
Fax. 33 (0)2.98.06.17.38
Board of Trustees
Jean R. Perrette
Chairman
Louis Urvois
President & Treasurer
Suzanne Deal Booth
Nana Gregory
Jill Jordon
Pierre Louis Roederer
Nicole de Montmorin
Shelley de Rouvray
Jennifer Sevaux
Caroline Boyle-Turner
Founder, Director of School Development

Client Pont-Aven School of Contemporary Art
Year 2008
Design Pentagram

Client Portfolio Advice Day
University of the Arts
London
Year 2009
Design Magpie Studio
Team Creative Directors:
David Azurdia, Ben Christie,
Jamie Ellul;
Designer: Jamie Ellul

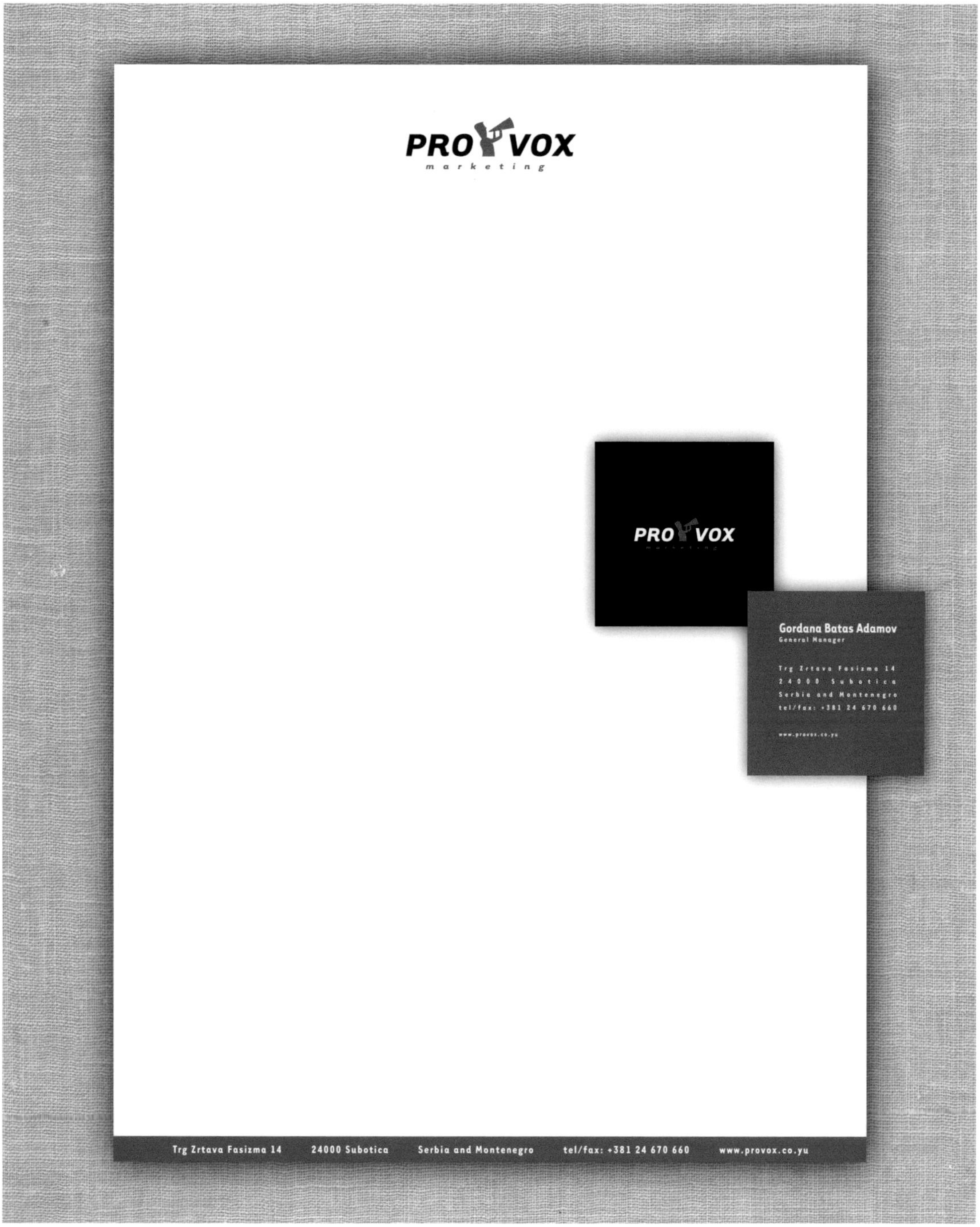

Client Provox Marketing
Year 2008
Design Heavyform

Client	Ralf Obergfell Photography
Year	2007
Design	Magpie Studio
Team	Creative Directors: David Azurdia, Ben Christie, Jamie Ellul; Designer: David Azurdia

Ralf Obergfell
Photography
+44 (0)7985 711 881
shoot@ralfobergfell.com
www.ralfobergfell.com

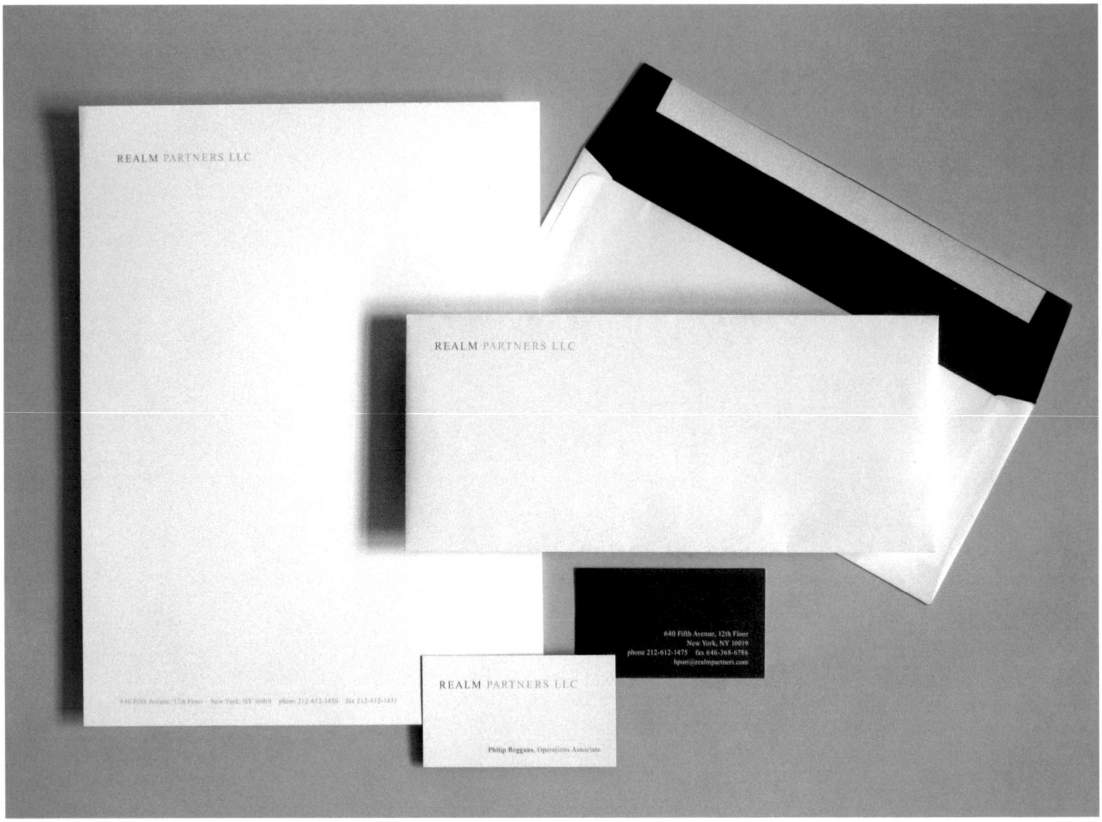

Client Realm Partners
Year 2010
Design Anke Stohlmann Design

Client Rebel Organization
Year 2004
Design BLK/MRKT

Client Red Photographic
Year 2008
Design SVIDesign

RED
PHOTOGRAPHIC

CORPORATE
FASHION
PORTRAIT
WEDDING

PRODUCT
SPORT
PARTY

126 Westbourne Studios
242 Acklam Road
London W10 5JJ
UK

Call 020 7524 7800
Fax 020 7524 7801
enquiry@red-photographic.com
www.red-photographic.com

Part of the Red Group Red Photographic Limited Company Registration: 06416560 Registered Address: 126 Westbourne Studios, 242 Acklam Road, London W10 5JJ

COMITÊ ORGANIZADOR
JOGOS PAN-AMERICANOS
RIO 2007
Rua da Assembléia, 10
Sala 2911 Centro
Rio de Janeiro RJ Brasil
Cep 20011 901
Tel. 55 21 3806 2338
Fax 55 21 2531 1116
renata.santiago@cob.org.br
www.rio2007.org.br
CELSO SCHVARTZER
Gen Bda R-1
SERGIO L. V. ROSÁRIO
RENATA SANTIAGO
COMITÊ ORGANIZADOR
RIO 2007
Sala 2920 Centro
Cep 20011 901
Tel. 55 21 3806 2422
Fax 55 21 3806 2426

Client XV Pan American Games Rio 2007
Year 2007
Design Dupla Design
Team Claudia Gamboa, Ney Valle

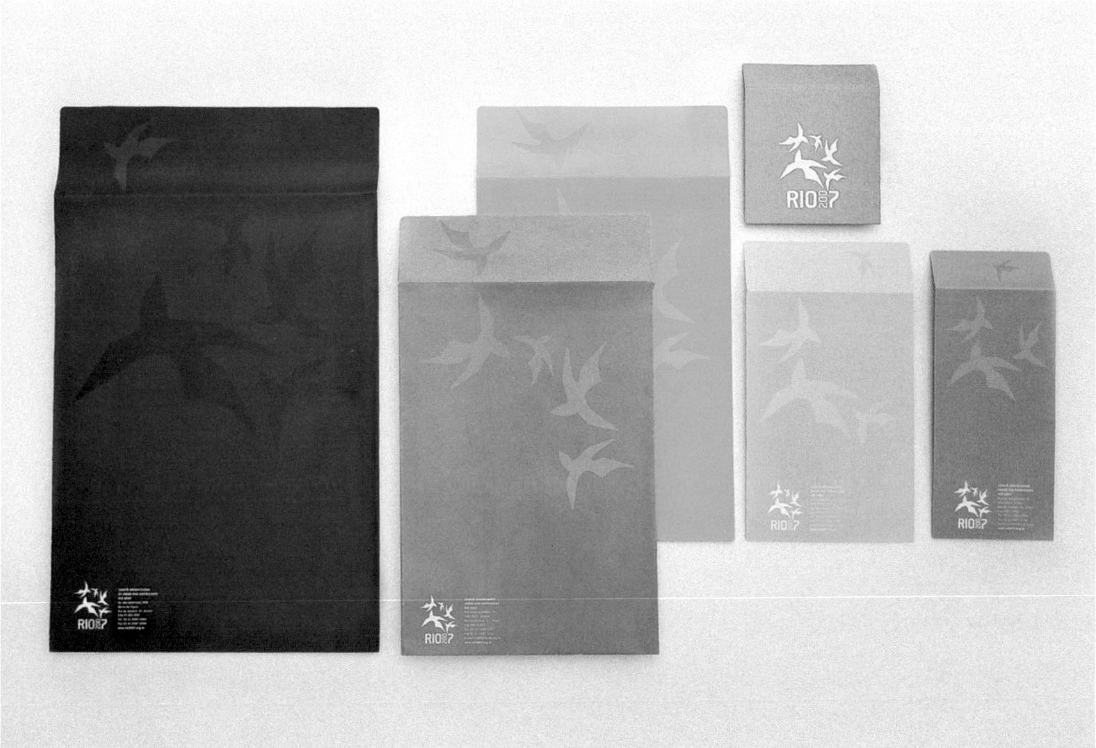

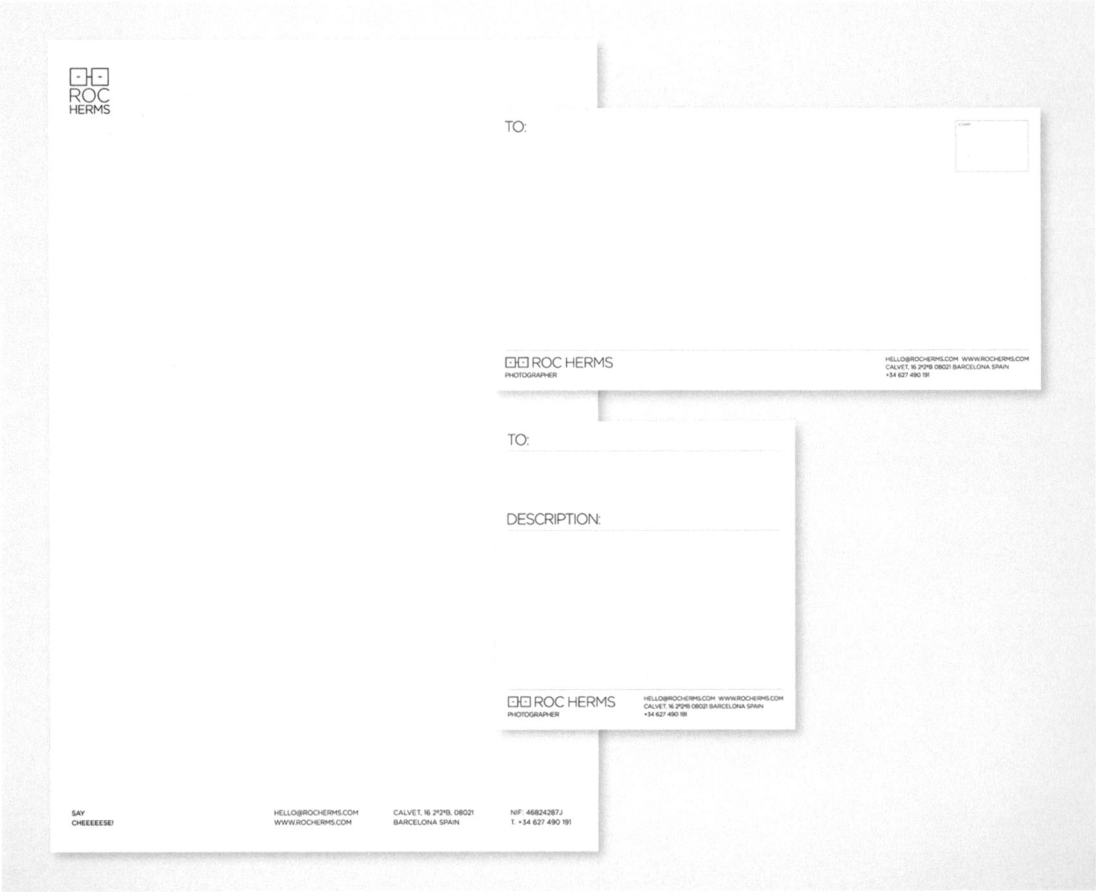

Client Roc Herms
Year 2009
Design Tea Time Studio

MERRY
CHRISISTMAS!

TO:

NAME

ADDRESS

CITY

POSTAL CODE

COUNTRY

□□ ROC HERMS
PHOTOGRAPHER

HELLO@ROCHERMS.COM
WWW.ROCHERMS.COM
+34 627 490 191

STAMP

SAY
CHEEEESE!

TO:

STAMP

NAME

ADDRESS

CITY POSTAL CODE

COUNTRY

□□ ROC HERMS
PHOTOGRAPHER

HELLO@ROCHERMS.COM
WWW.ROCHERMS.COM
+34 627 490 191

PROFESIONAL
VOYEUR

TO:

STAMP

NAME

ADDRESS

CITY POSTAL CODE

COUNTRY

□□ ROC HERMS
PHOTOGRAPHER

HELLO@ROCHERMS.COM
WWW.ROCHERMS.COM
+34 627 490 191

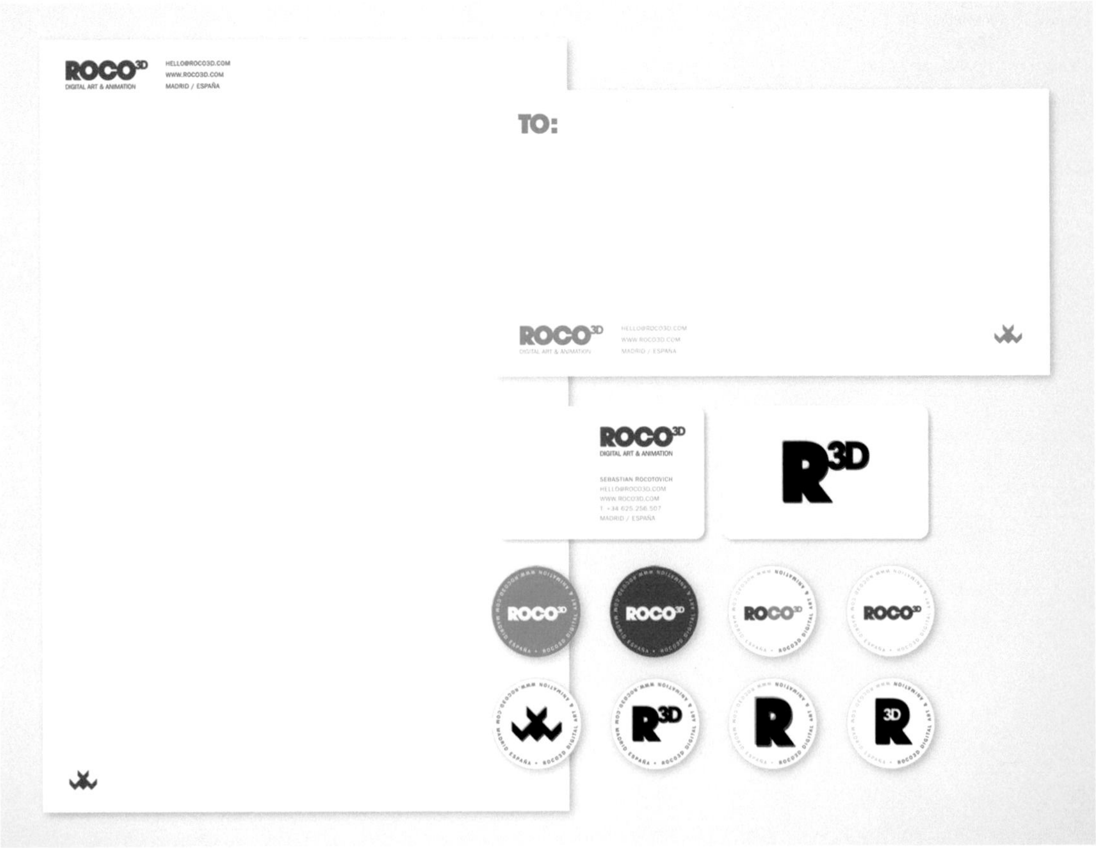
ROCO3D
DIGITAL ART & ANIMATION
HELLO@ROCO3D.COM
WWW.ROCO3D.COM
MADRID / ESPAÑA
TO:
SEBASTIAN ROCOTOVICH
R3D

ROCO3D
WWW.ROCO3D.COM MADRID ESPAÑA • ROCO3D DIGITAL ART & ANIMATION
R3D
R
3D

Client Roco3D
Year 2009
Design Tea Time Studio

ROCO3D
DIGITAL ART & ANIMATION
SEBASTIAN ROCOTOVICH
HELLO@ROCO3D.COM
WWW.ROCO3D.COM
T. +34 625.256.507
MADRID / ESPAÑA
ROCO3D
DIGITAL ART & ANIMATION
SEBASTIAN ROCOTOVICH
HELLO@ROCO3D.COM
WWW.ROCO3D.COM
T. +34 625.256.507
MADRID / ESPAÑA
R3D

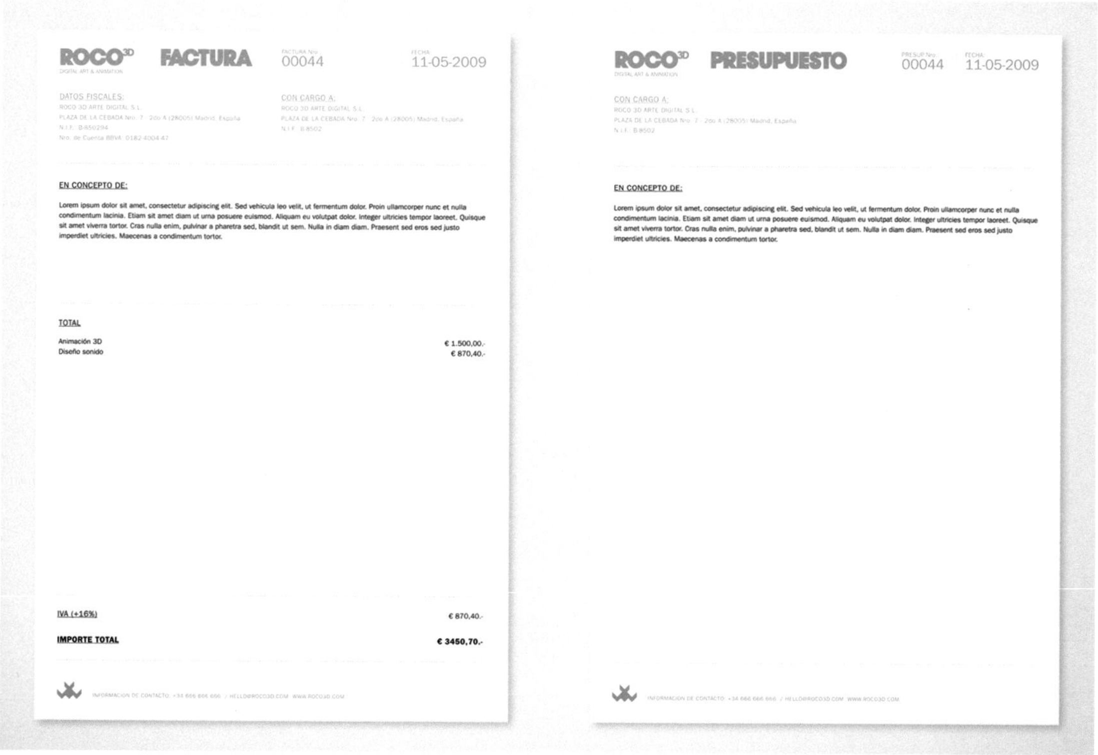
ROCO3D
FACTURA
00044
11-05-2009
DATOS FISCALES:
CON CARGO A:
EN CONCEPTO DE:
Lorem ipsum dolor sit amet, consectetur adipiscing elit. Sed vehicula leo velit, ut fermentum dolor. Proin ullamcorper nunc et nulla condimentum lacinia. Etiam sit amet diam ut urna posuere euismod. Aliquam eu volutpat dolor. Integer ultricies tempor laoreet. Quisque sit amet viverra tortor. Cras nulla enim, pulvinar a pharetra sed, blandit ut sem. Nulla in diam diam. Praesent sed eros sed justo imperdiet ultricies. Maecenas a condimentum tortor.
TOTAL
Animación 3D € 1.500,00.-
Diseño sonido € 870,40.-
IVA (+16%) € 870,40.-
IMPORTE TOTAL € 3450,70.-
ROCO3D
PRESUPUESTO
00044
11-05-2009
CON CARGO A:
EN CONCEPTO DE:
Lorem ipsum dolor sit amet, consectetur adipiscing elit. Sed vehicula leo velit, ut fermentum dolor. Proin ullamcorper nunc et nulla condimentum lacinia. Etiam sit amet diam ut urna posuere euismod. Aliquam eu volutpat dolor. Integer ultricies tempor laoreet. Quisque sit amet viverra tortor. Cras nulla enim, pulvinar a pharetra sed, blandit ut sem. Nulla in diam diam. Praesent sed eros sed justo imperdiet ultricies. Maecenas a condimentum tortor.

ROSE&
BLOOM
לימור רוזנר מוג'ה וגילת בלום
Limor Rosner Muggia & Gilat Blum
Architecture & Design
T +972 3 5279175 | F +972 3 5279176
8 Sgula st. Tel-Aviv-jaffa, Israel 68116
סגולה 8 תל־אביב־יפו, 68116
office@roseandbloom.net
www.roseandbloom.net

ROSE&
BLOOM
לימור רוזנר מוג'ה וגילת בלום
Limor Rosner Muggia & Gilat Blum
Architecture & Design
T +972 3 5279175 | F +972 3 5279176
8 Sgula st. Tel-Aviv-jaffa, Israel 68116
סגולה 8 תל־אביב-יפו, 68116
office@roseandbloom.net
www.roseandbloom.net

ROSE&
BLOOM
Limor Rosner Muggia & Gilat Blum
Architecture & Design

לימור רוזנר מוג'ה
Limor Rosner Muggia
8 Sgula st. Tel-Aviv-jaffa, Israel 68116 סגולה 8 תל־אביב-יפו,
T + 972 3 5279175 | M + 972 50 5409641 | F + 972 3 5279176
limor@roseandbloom.net | www.roseandbloom.net

Client Rose & Bloom
Year 2009
Design Dan Alexander & Co
Team Danny Goldberg, Michal Koll

שרגא פ. בירן Shraga F. Biran
בעז בירן Boaz Biran
גדעון חתוכה Gideon Hatuka
דויד אמיד David Amid
מאיר פורגס Meir Porges
תמי אבשלום Tami Avshalom
אמיר ליסטונד Amir Listwand
אפרת כראזי Efrat Karazi
יעל זפיר-אביגדור Yael Zafir-Avigdor
יפעת ארנון Yifat Arnon
עדנה ברסלר-לוין Edna Bresler-Levin
לילך שאולי Lilach Shauly
שני רביב-משה Shani Raviv-Moshe
אורית אביטבול Orit Abitbul
קרן זוקין Keren Zukin
דרור רוזנבלום Dror Rosenblum
LAW FIRM
S.Biran&Co
ש.בירן ושות'
Tel-Aviv : תל־אביב
מגדל המוזיאון, רח' ברקוביץ' 4, תל־אביב 64238
Museum Tower, 4 Berkowitz St., Tel-Aviv 64238
F 972.3.7773900 פ : T 972.3.7773939 ט
Jerusalem : ירושלים
מגדל העיר, רח' בן־יהודה 34, ירושלים 94230
City Tower, 34 Ben-Yehuda St., Jerusalem 94230
F 972.2.6258161 פ : T 972.2.6259284 ט
www.biranlaw.com : mail@biranlaw.com
LAW FIRM
S.Biran&Co
ש.בירן ושות'
Shraga F. Biran, Adv.
MJ
Museum Tower
4 Berkowitz St.
Tel-Aviv 64238
T +972.3.7773939
F +972.3.7773900
www.biranlaw.com
shraga@biranlaw.com
LAW FIRM
S.Biran&Co
ש.בירן ושות'
Jerusalem : ירושלים
City Tower, 34 Ben-Yehuda St., Jerusalem 94230
Tel-Aviv : תל־אביב
Museum Tower, 4 Berkowitz St., Tel-Aviv 64238
www.biranlaw.com

Client S.Biran & Co
Year 2009
Design Dan Alexander & Co
Team Danny Goldberg

LAW FIRM
S.Biran&Co
ש.בירן ושות'
With Compliments

LAW FIRM
S.Biran&Co
ש.בירן ושות'

Client Sanctuary
Year 2009
Design Design Positive
Team Scott Lambert, George McIntosh

SANCTUARY
WITH COMPLIMENTS
SANCTUARY
HO TRAM VIETNAM

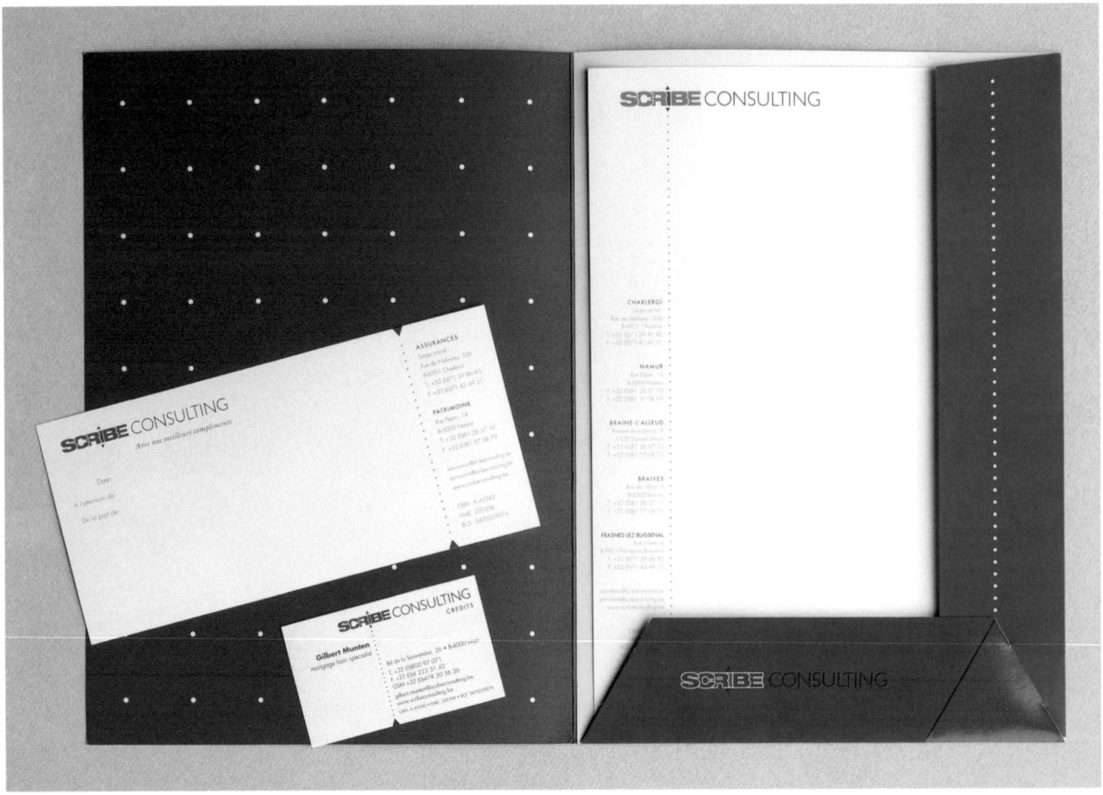

Client Scribe Consulting
Year 2008
Design Roland Henrion Design

SCRIBE CONSULTING
ASSURANCES
GESTION DE PATRIMOINE
SCRIBE

SHL
Telemedicine
SHL
World Leader in Telemedicine
www.shahal.co.il
info@cardiocare.com
East Coast HQ
77 South Palm Avenue,
Sarasota, Fl 34236-7724
Tel: (264)-5446-348
Fax: (264)-5446-349
West Coast HQ
1200 River Road - Suite 1302,
Conshohocken, Pa 19428
Tel: (254)-4416-348
Fax: (254)-4416-349
D-223-1

Client Shahal Telemedicine
Year 2010
Design Dan Alexander & Co
Team Danny Goldberg

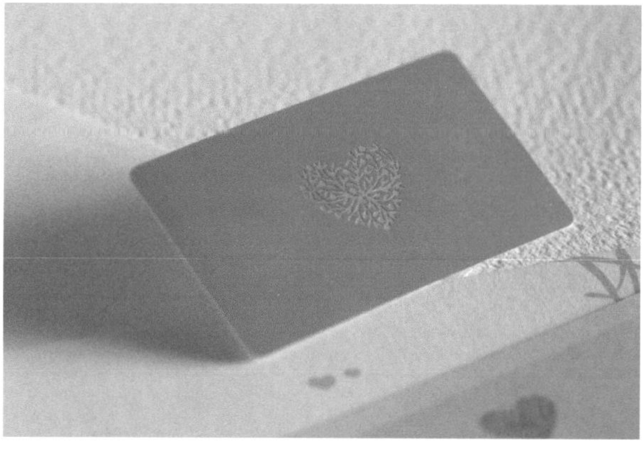

Client Smart
Year 2010
Design Machicao Design

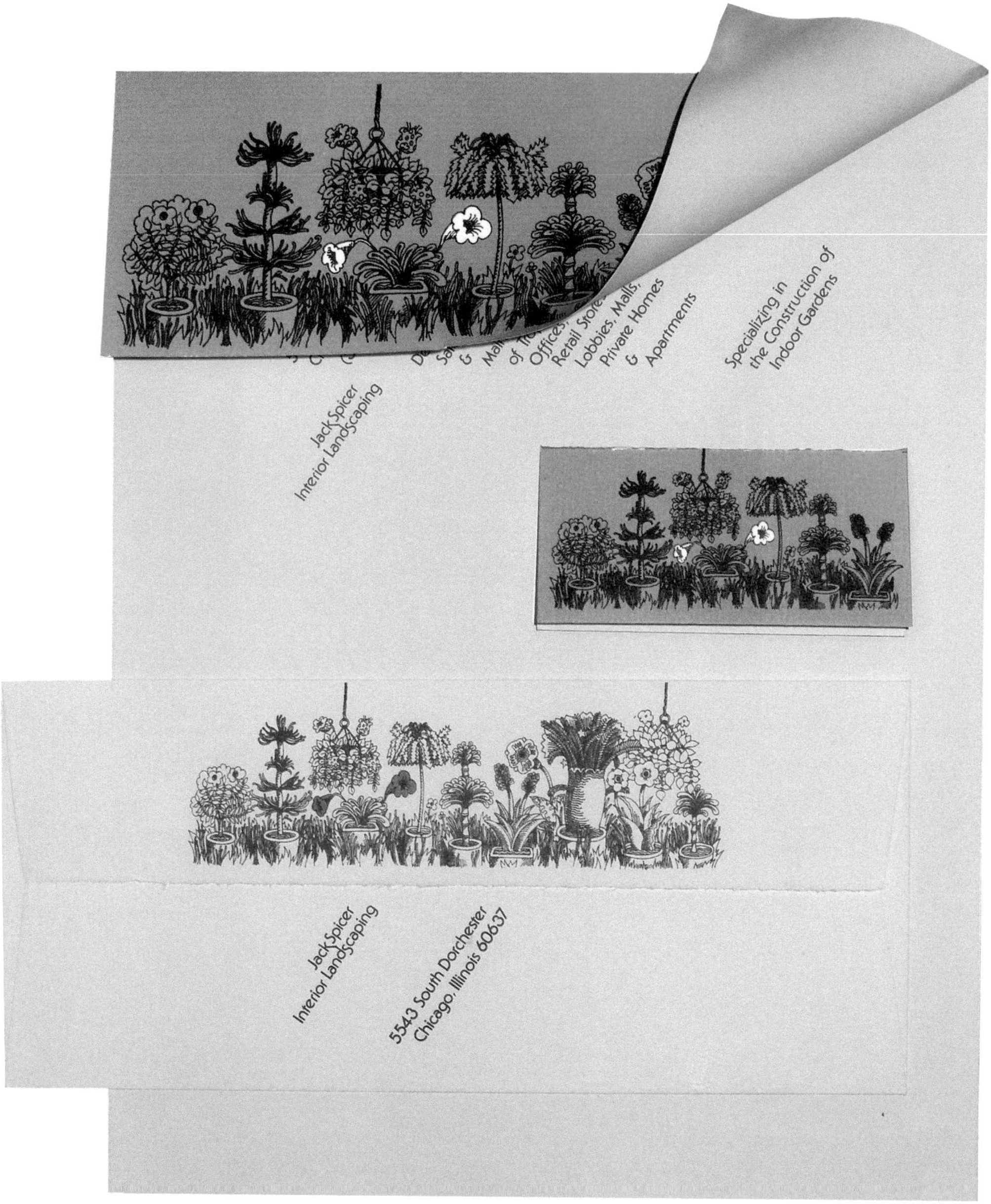
Jack Spicer
Interior Landscaping
Offices,
Retail Stores
Lobbies, Malls,
Private Homes
&
Apartments
Specializing in
the Construction of
Indoor Gardens
Jack Spicer
Interior Landscaping
5543 South Dorchester
Chicago, Illinois 60637

Client Spicer
Year 2000
Design SX2

With Thanks
+44 (0)161 452 7965
Spry Boutique,
23 Oldham Street, Manchester, M1 1JR
+44 (0)161 452 7965

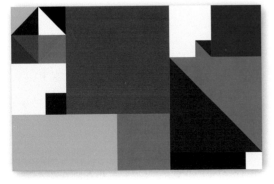

Matt Collins
Sales Manager
+44 (0)786 6011 137
m.collins@spryboutique.co.uk
www.spryboutique.co.uk

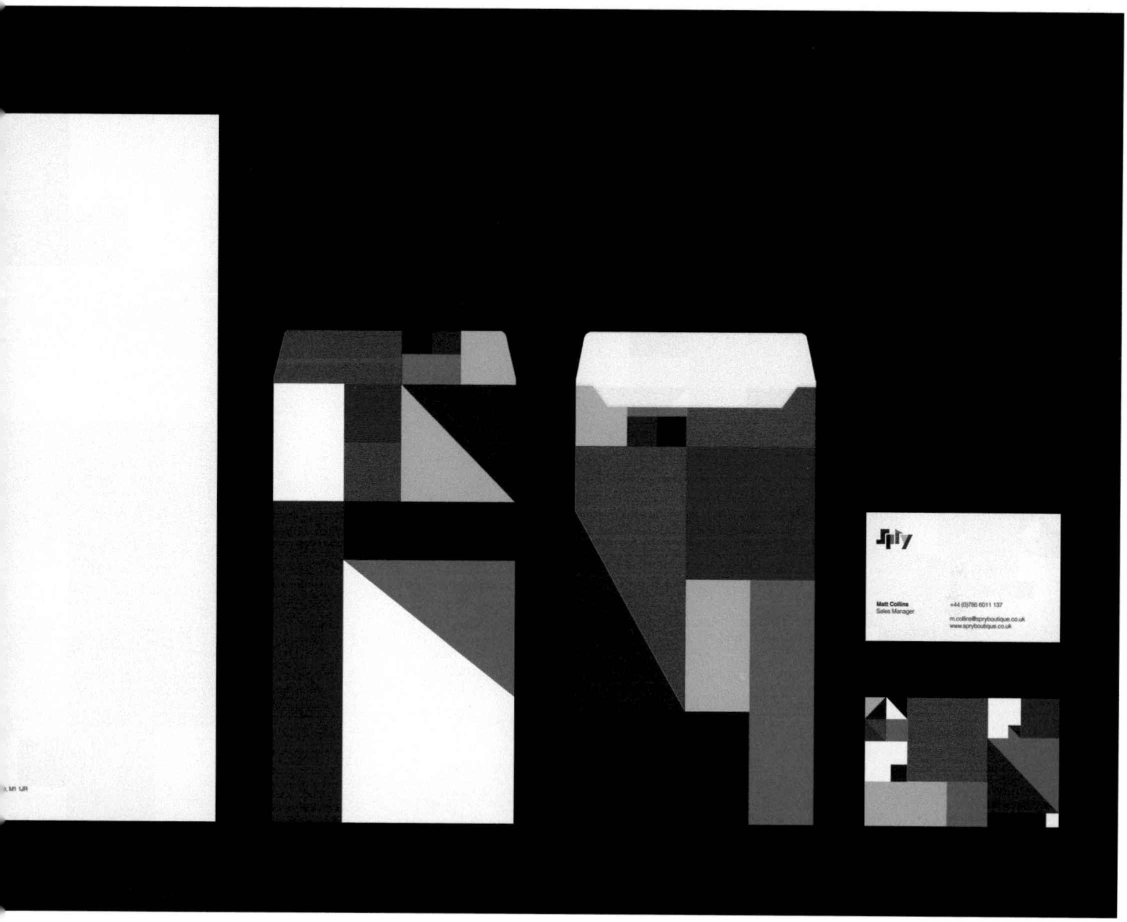

Client Spry Boutique
Year 2009
Design huvi

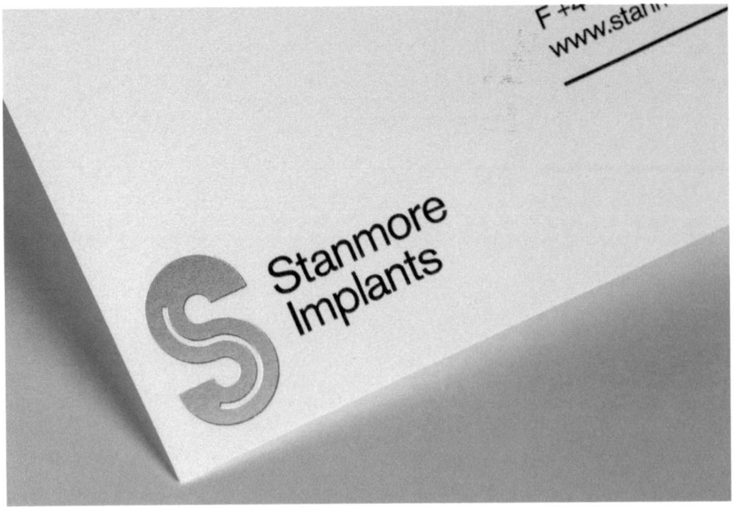

Client	Stanmore Implants
Year	2007
Design	Pentagram
Team	Pentagram Design London

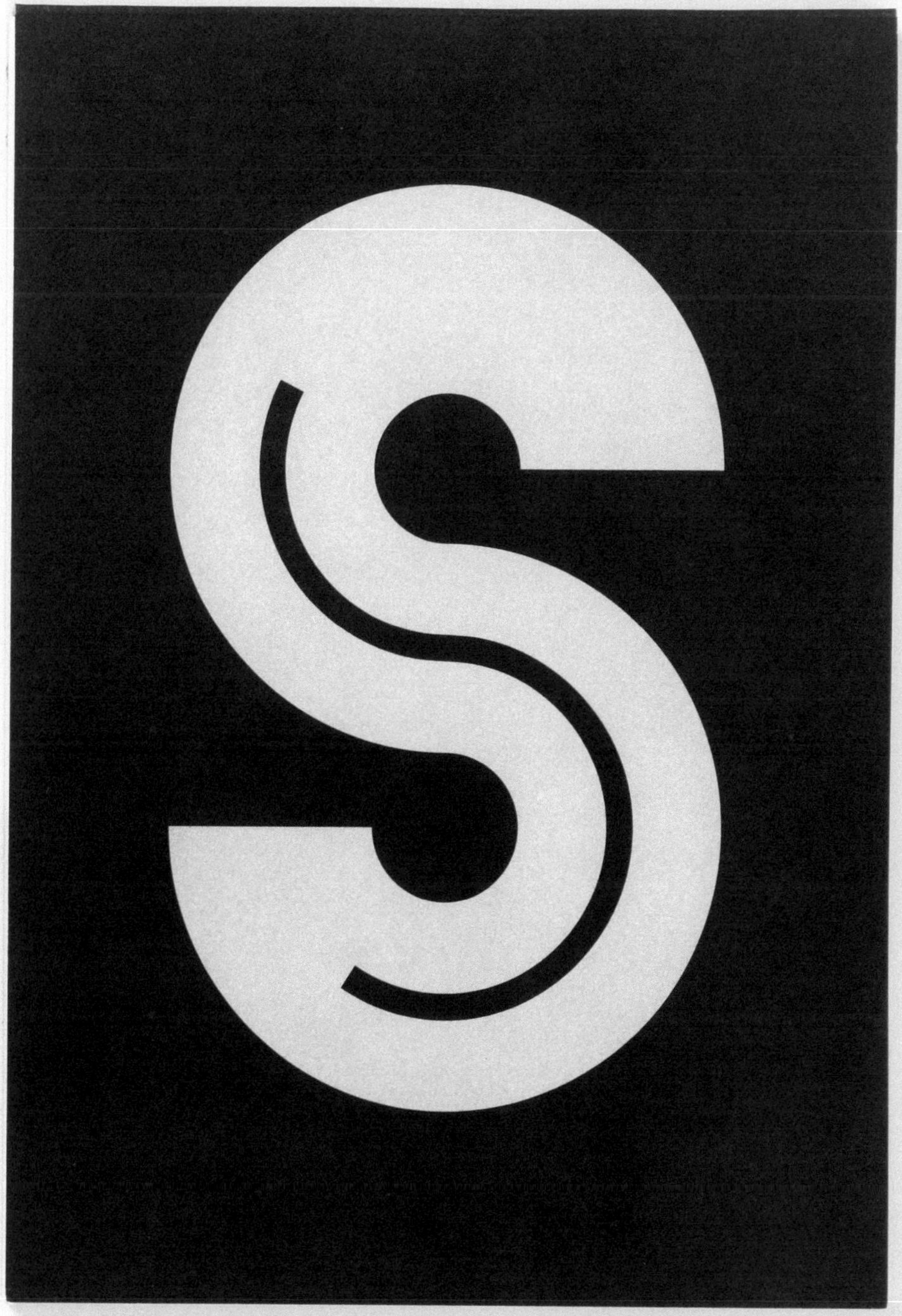

Client Stary Piec
Year 2009
Design Papajastudio

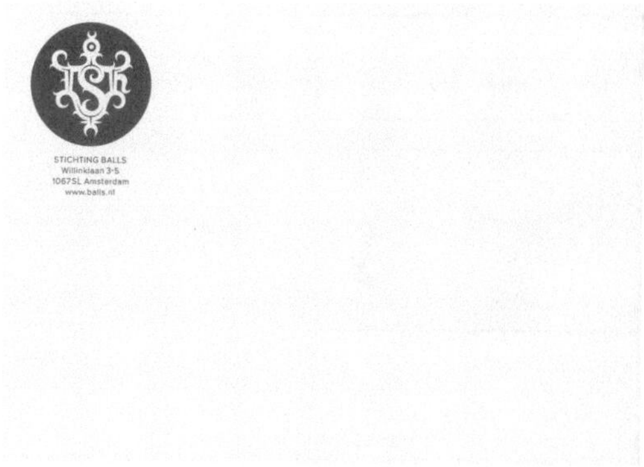

Client Stichting Balls
Year 2009
Design DBXL

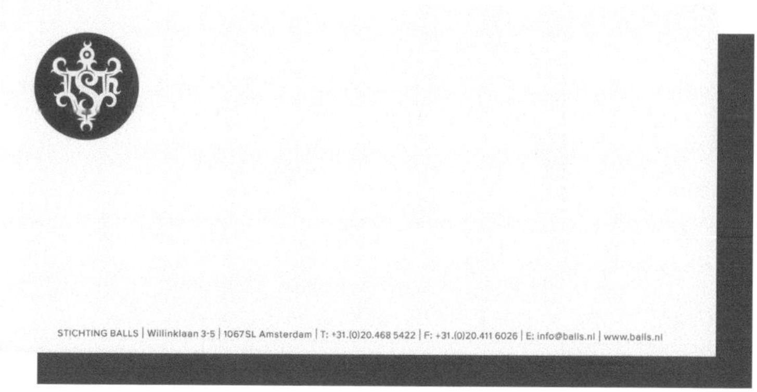

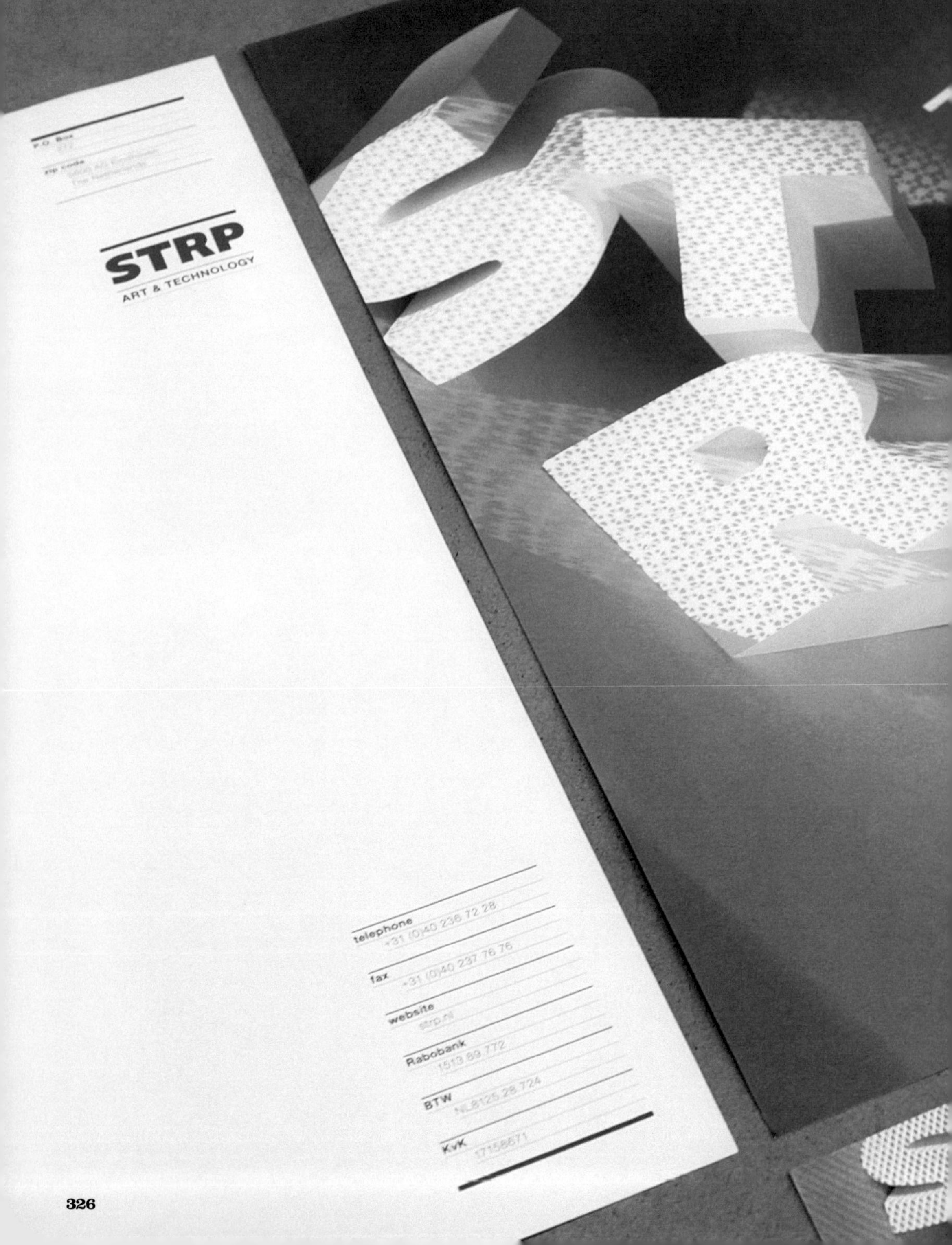
P.O. Box
STRP
ART & TECHNOLOGY
telephone
+31 (0)40 236 72 28
fax
+31 (0)40 237 76 76
website
strp.nl
Rabobank
1513 89 772
BTW
NL8125.28.724
KvK
17158671

Client STRP
Year 2009
Design Edhv
Team Remco vd Craats,
Sjoerd Koopmans

Client Strube GmbH
Year 2009
Design Adler & Schmidt Kommunikations-Design
Team Florian Adler, Katrin Schirmer, Hans-Peter Schmidt

strube
innovativ aus Tradition
strube
Mit freundlicher Empfehlung
Kind regards
WIE DIE SAAT · SO DIE ERNTE · SEIT 1877
strube
vertrieb.de@strube.net
www.strube.net
strube
strube
Sina Isabel Strube
M.sc.agr
Geschäftsführerin
Managing Director
Strube GmbH & Co. KG
Hauptstraße 1
38387 Söllingen | Germany
T +49 (0) 53 54 / 809 - 903
F +49 (0) 53 54 / 809 - 937
M +49 (0) 170 / 301 60 86
s.strube@strube.net
www.strube.net
struberesearch
Forschung und Entwicklung
Weizen
Research and Development
Wheat
Strube Research GmbH & Co. KG
Hauptstraße 1
38387 Söllingen | Germany
T +49 (0) 53 54 / 809 - 602
F +49 (0) 53 54 / 809 - 937
info@strube.net

STUDIO
apollo
4454 AVENUE PAPINEAU, MONTRÉAL
QUÉBEC, H2H 1T8, CANADA
WWW.STUDIOAPOLLO.COM
INFO@STUDIOAPOLLO.COM
[T] 514 524-9995
[F] 514 524-8621
A HIGH FIDELITY STEREOPHONIC MUSIC WORKSHOP

apollo
STUDIOS
4454, AVENUE PAPINEAU, MONTRÉAL
QUÉBEC, H2H 1T8, CANADA
WWW.STUDIOSAPOLLO.COM
INFO@STUDIOSAPOLLO.COM
A HIGH FIDELITY STEREOPHONIC MUSIC WORKSH

Client Studio Apollo
Year 2009
Design Minimal Médias

SUPERIEUR GRAPHIQUE

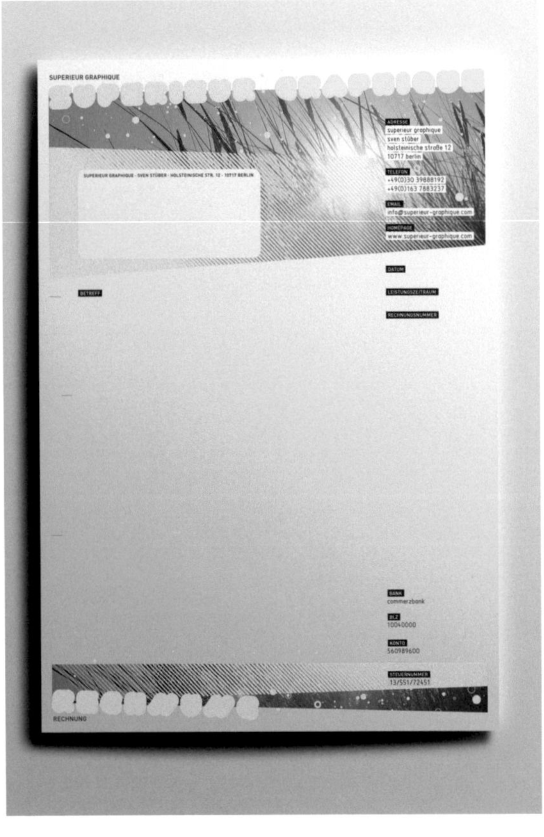
SUPERIEUR GRAPHIQUE
SUPERIEUR GRAPHIQUE · SVEN STÜBER · HOLSTEINISCHE STR. 12 · 10717 BERLIN
ADRESSE
superieur graphique
sven stüber
holsteinische straße 12
10717 berlin
TELEFON
+49(0)30 39888192
+49(0)163 7883237
EMAIL
info@superieur-graphique.com
HOMEPAGE
www.superieur-graphique.com
DATUM
BETREFF
LEISTUNGSZEITRAUM
RECHNUNGSNUMMER
BANK
commerzbank
BLZ
10040000
KONTO
560989600
STEUERNUMMER
13/551/72451
RECHNUNG

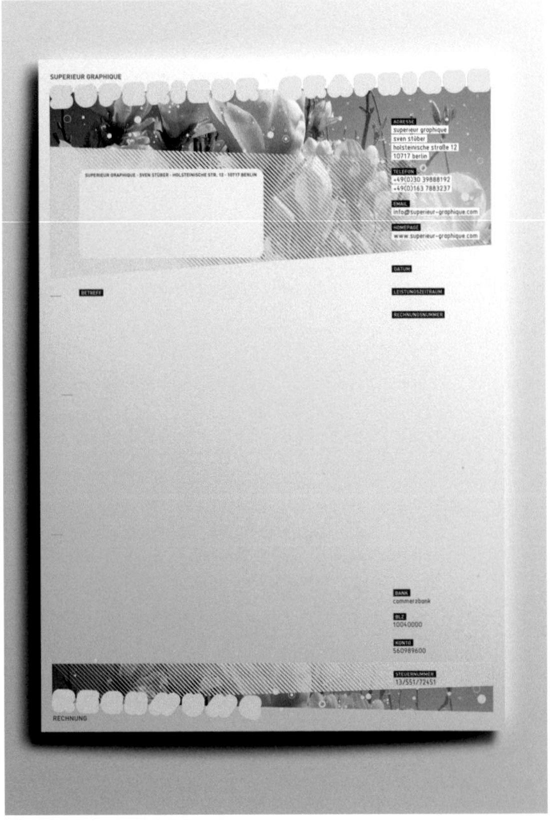
SUPERIEUR GRAPHIQUE
SUPERIEUR GRAPHIQUE · SVEN STÜBER · HOLSTEINISCHE STR. 12 · 10717 BERLIN
ADRESSE
superieur graphique
sven stüber
holsteinische straße 12
10717 berlin
TELEFON
+49(0)30 39888192
+49(0)163 7883237
EMAIL
info@superieur-graphique.com
HOMEPAGE
www.superieur-graphique.com
DATUM
BETREFF
LEISTUNGSZEITRAUM
RECHNUNGSNUMMER
BANK
commerzbank
BLZ
10040000
KONTO
560989600
STEUERNUMMER
13/551/72451
RECHNUNG

Client	Superieur Graphique
Year	2009
Design	Superieur Graphique
Team	Sven Stüber

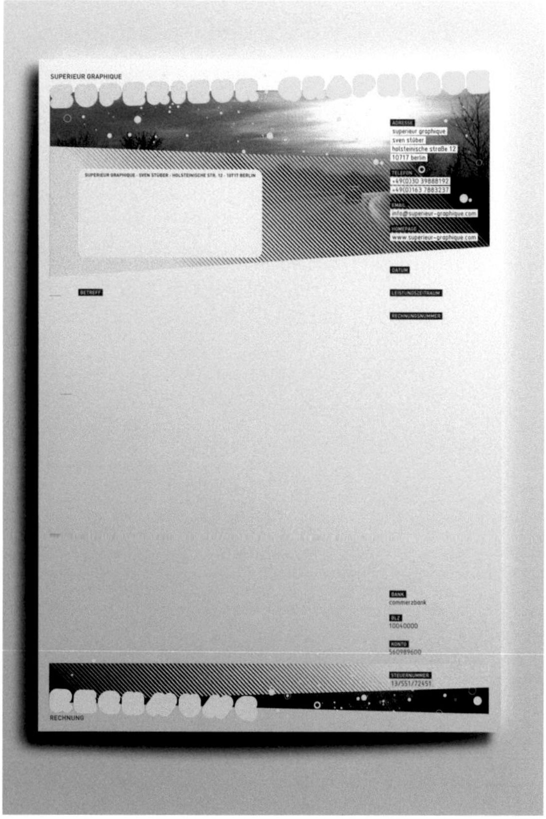

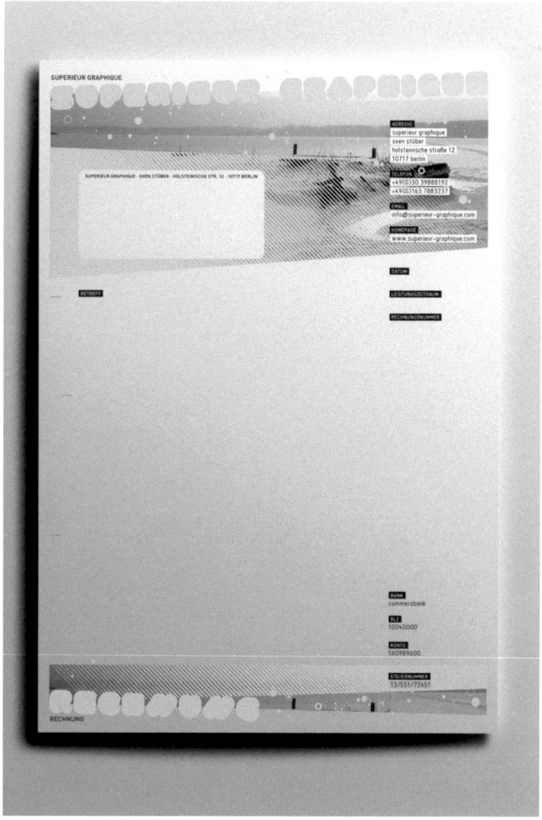

Client Supervixen
Year 2010
Design Supervixen

Client Svenska Stadsnät
Year 2006
Design Kollor Design Agency

Client Susannah Fone
Year 2009
Design Magpie Studio
Team Creative Directors: David Azurdia, Ben Christie, Jamie Ellul; Designer: Aimi Awang

4 Chapel Hill, Tilehurst, Reading,
Telephone 0118 986 6140 Mobile
info@susannah-fone.co.uk

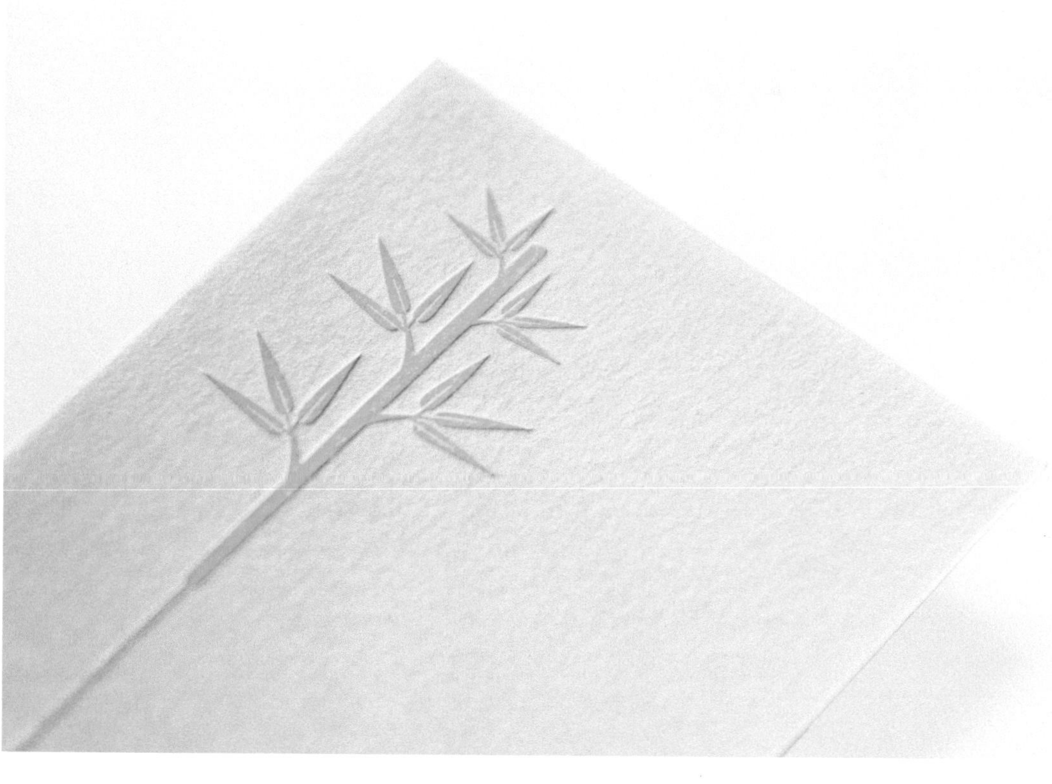

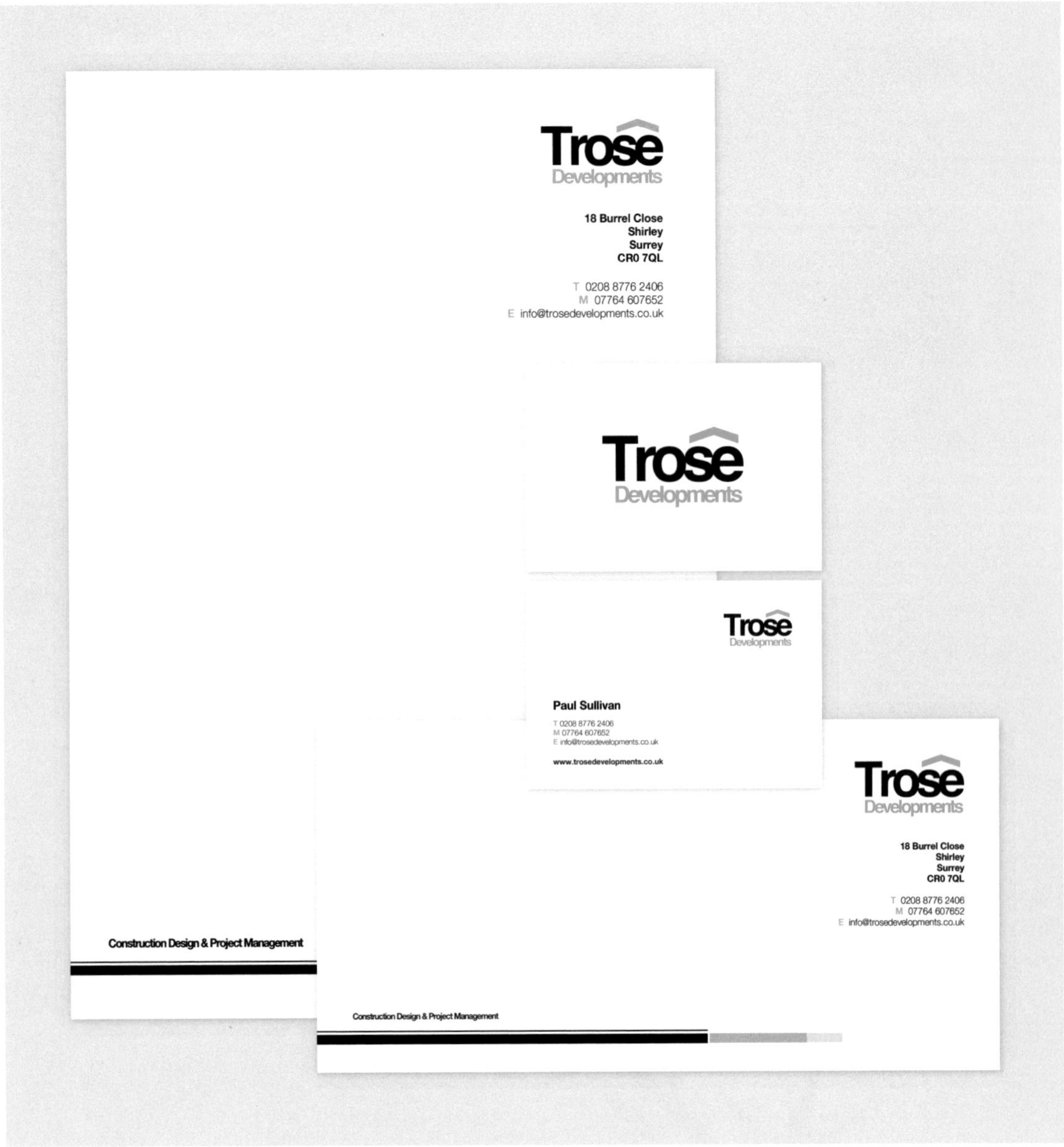

Client T Rose Developments
Year 2009
Design Emerge Studios

Client T'ika Flor De Vida
Year 2009
Design Machicao Design

Client	Taché-Levy Modern Art Gallery
Year	2007
Design	Sign*
Team	Astrid Verdeyen, Franck Sarfati

Client Tangram
Year 2007
Design Pentagram
Team Pentagram Design London

Client Taxi
Year 2010
Design Dogo

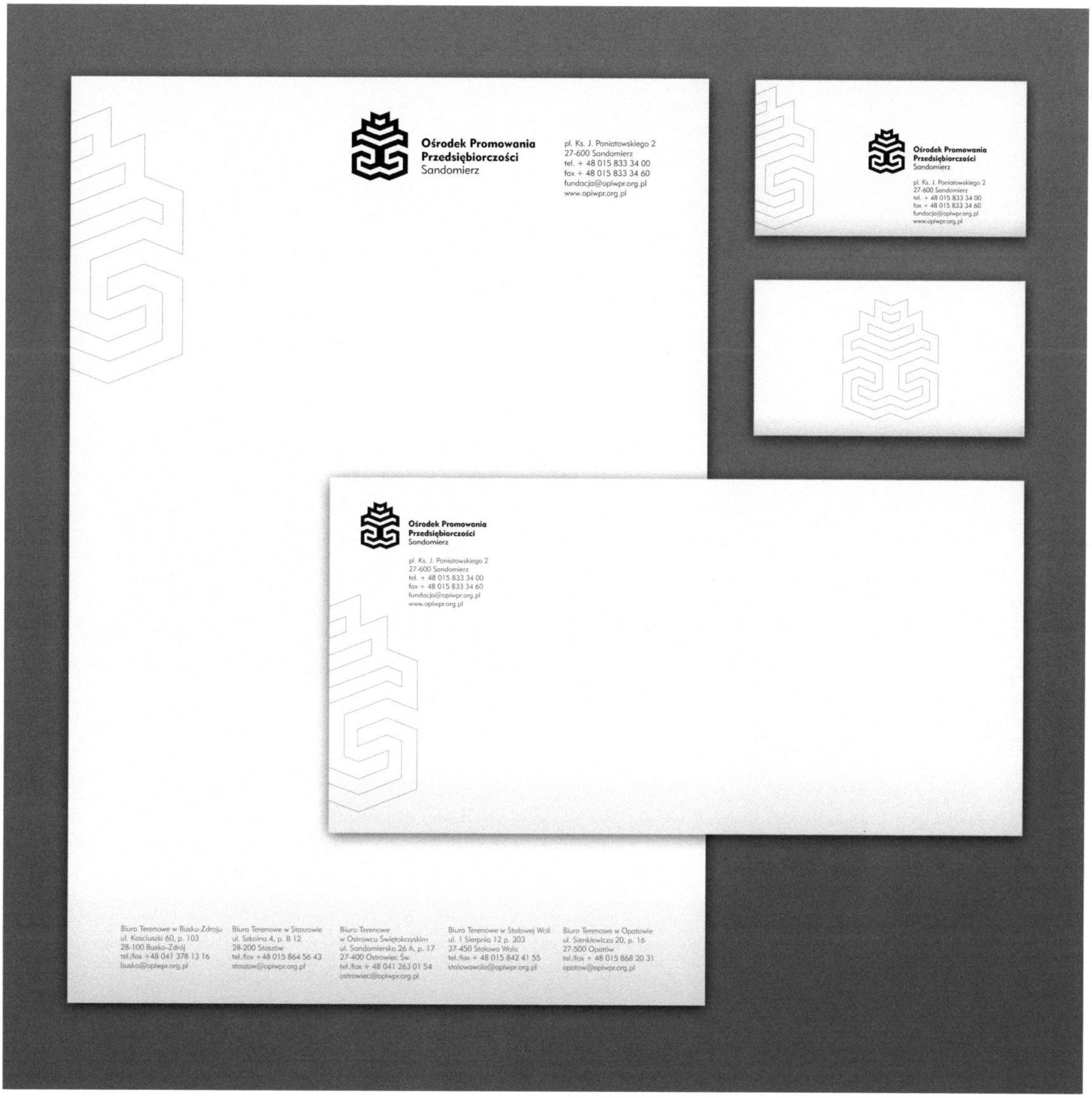

Client The Center for Business Promotion and Entrepreneur
Year 2008
Design Papajastudio

Tenbosch House/Sign*

Client Tenbosch House
Year 2010
Design Sign*
Team Astrid Verdeyen, Franck Sarfati

TENBOSCH HOUSE
"If you have a garden and a library, you have everything you need."
TENBOSCH HOUSE
Rue Washington 131 & 133
1050 Brussels, Belgium
T + 32 (0)2 888 90 90
info@tenboschhouse.com
WWW.TENBOSCHHOUSE.COM
TENBOSCH HOUSE
WWW.TENBOSCHHOUSE.COM

TENBOSCH HOUSE
NAME
ROOM
DATE
ROOM
DATE

The One Company/The One Company

Client The One Company
Year 2010
Design The One Company
Team Julie Hanson, Sarah Walsh, Andrew Lodge

one
One
The Nookin, 48 Leeds Road,
Oulton, Leeds LS26 8JY
0113 282 3600
hello@theonecompany.co.uk
www.theonecompany.co.uk
one
One
The Nookin, 48 Leeds Road,
Oulton, Leeds LS26 8JY
0113 282 3600
hello@theonecompany.co.uk
www.theonecompany.co.uk

The Vegetable Bar
7pm—3am
Freiburg Markthalle
Kaiser-Joseph-Strasse
79098 Freiburg
00 49 (0)761 7043 3155

Client	The Vegetable Bar
Year	2007
Design	Magpie Studio
Team	Creative Directors: David Azurdia, Ben Christie, Jamie Ellul; Designer: David Azurdia

Client The Walt Disney Family Foundation
Year 2007
Design Pentagram
Team Pentagram Design San Francisco

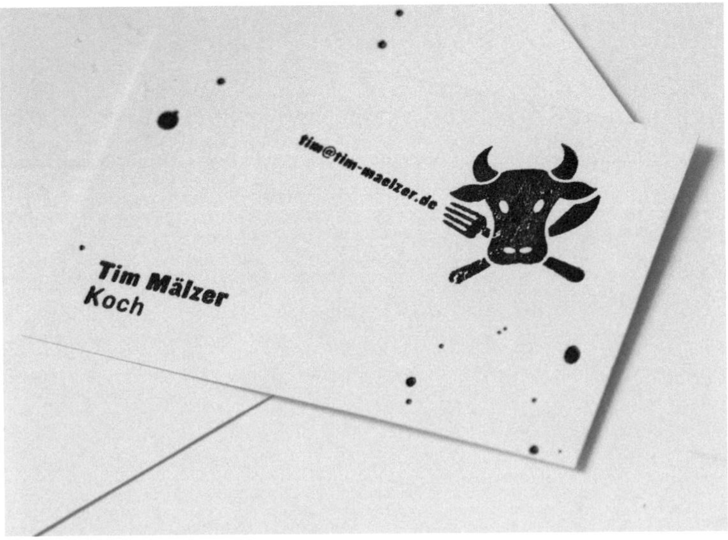

Client	Tim Mälzer
Year	2007
Design	weissraum.de(sign)°
Team	Bernd Brink, Lucas Buchholz

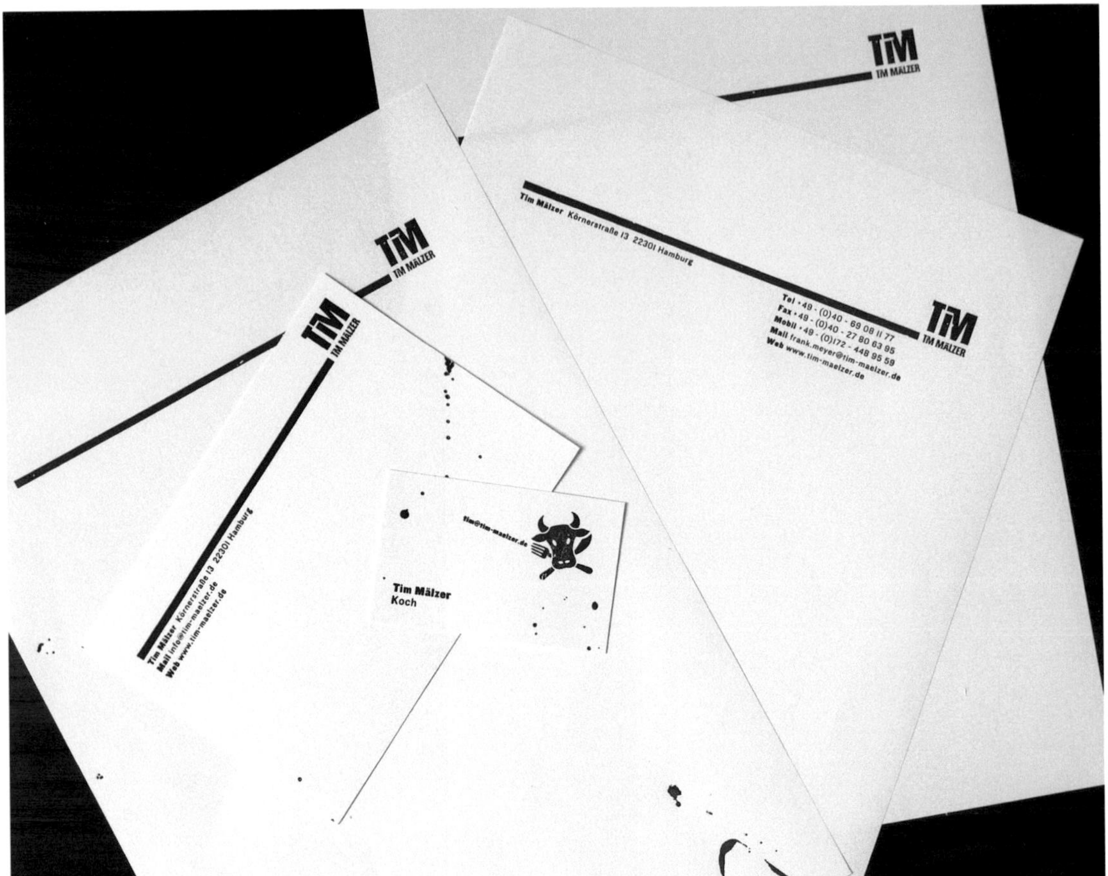

Client TLV
Year 2009
Design NNSS Visual Universes

Tornasol Films/Barfutura

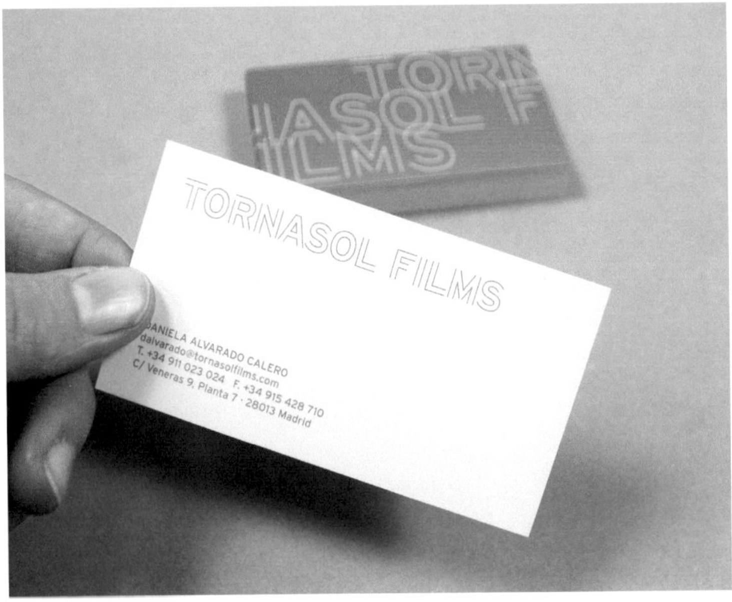

Client Tornasol Films
Year 2009
Design Barfutura

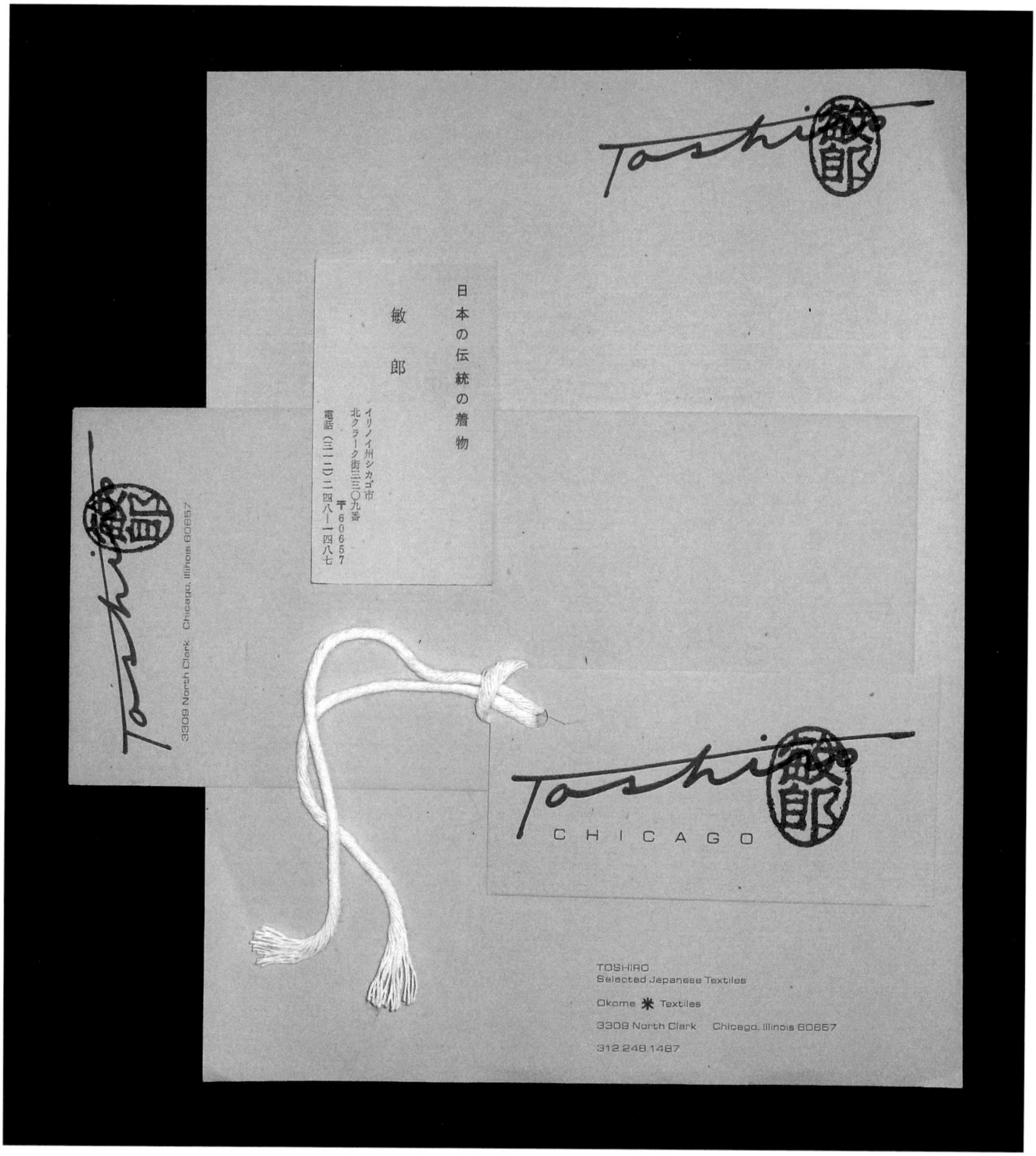

Client Toshiro
Year 2000
Design SX2

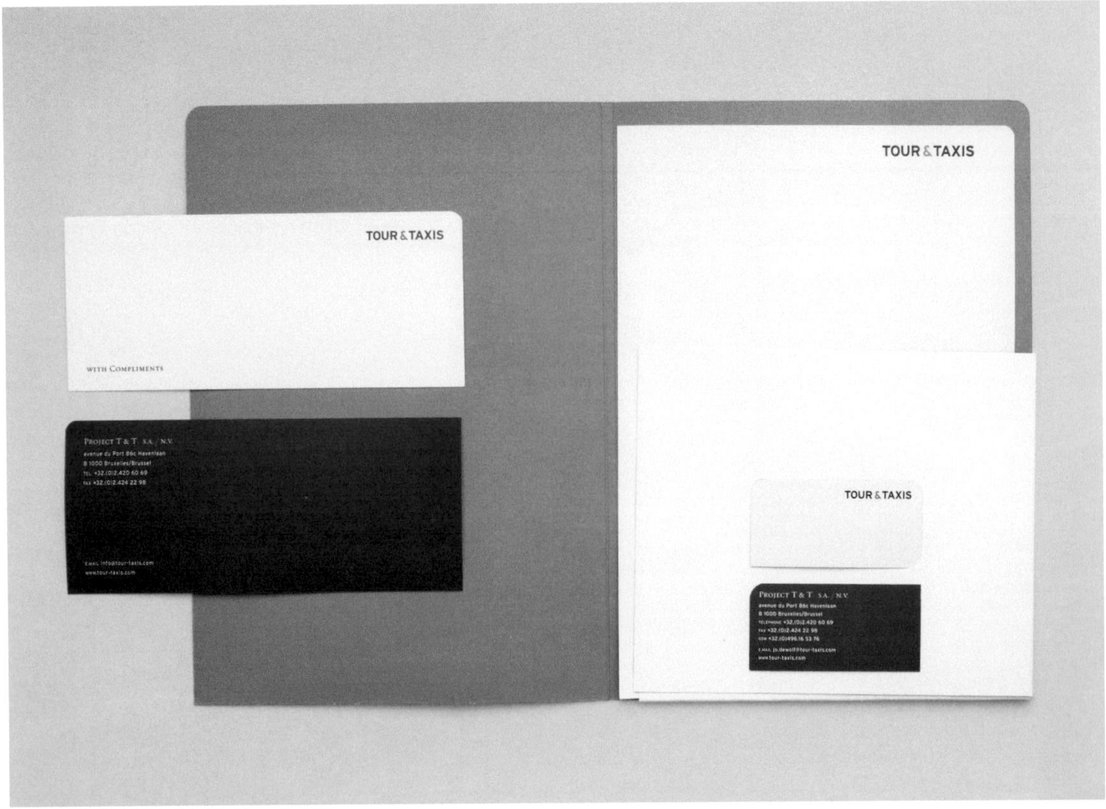

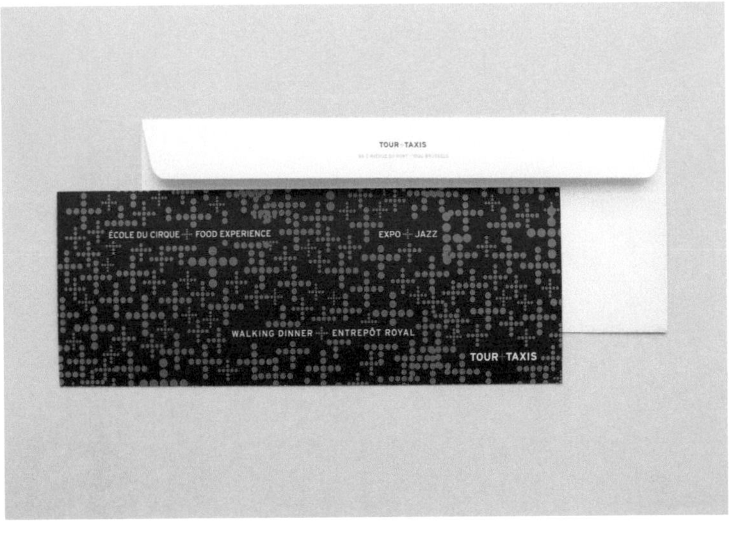

Client	Tour & Taxi
Year	2008
Design	Sign*
Team	Franck Sarfati

Tragon Corporation
350 Bridge Parkway
Redwood Shores, CA
94065-1061
TRAGON
Tragon Corporation
350 Bridge Parkway
Redwood Shores, CA
94065-1061
Tel 800.841.1177
Fax 650.365.3737
www.tragon.com
13 August 2008
Kit Hinrichs
Pentagram Design
387 Tehama Street
San Francisco, CA 94103
Dear Tragon Customers, Colleagues, and Vendors,
Over the past twelve months, Tragon Corporation has made a number of significant improvements to maintain and reinforce our leadership position in the field of sensory evaluation.
of San Francisco to create a completely new brand identity
and contemporary approach to strategic, innovative research.
five separate areas, each representing one of the five senses. The
our ability to look at products from all angles to find
each of our client's needs.
construction on Tragon's new headquarters in Redwood
Corporation, this state-of-the-art facility is evidence of
over the past year to provide our clients with the most
in the industry – including direct-data entry* and new Tragon
QDA® data analysis software.
We hope you're as excited about our bold new look and brand improvements as we are. As always, we welcome and value your feedback.
Sincerely yours,
Doug Vort
Chief Financial Officer
Tragon Corporation
Douglas Vort
President & CEO
Tragon Corporation
350 Bridge Parkway
Redwood Shores, CA 94065-1061
Tel 800.841.1177 Mobile 650.678.8951
Fax 650.365.3737 dvort@tragon.com
Tragon Corporation 350 Bridge Parkway Redwood Shores, CA 94065-1061

Client Tragon
Year 2007
Design Pentagram
Team Pentagram Design
San Francisco

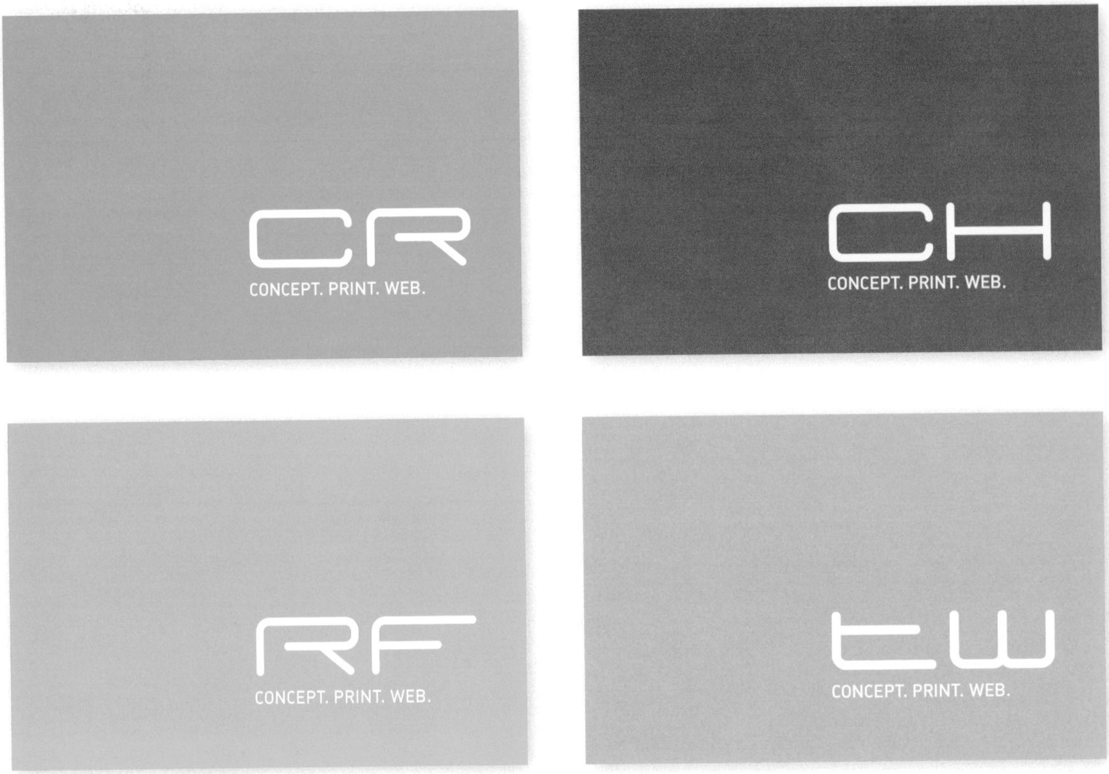

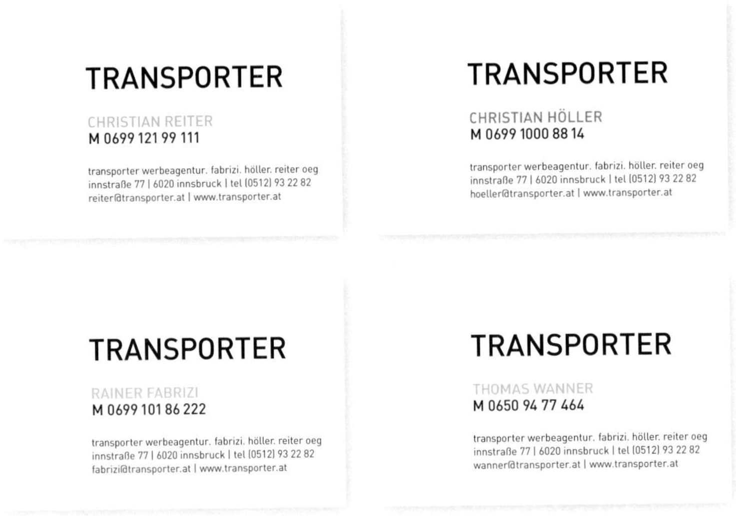
TRANSPORTER
CHRISTIAN REITER
M 0699 121 99 111
transporter werbeagentur. fabrizi. höller. reiter oeg
innstraße 77 | 6020 innsbruck | tel (0512) 93 22 82
reiter@transporter.at | www.transporter.at
TRANSPORTER
CHRISTIAN HÖLLER
M 0699 1000 88 14
transporter werbeagentur. fabrizi. höller. reiter oeg
innstraße 77 | 6020 innsbruck | tel (0512) 93 22 82
hoeller@transporter.at | www.transporter.at
TRANSPORTER
RAINER FABRIZI
M 0699 101 86 222
transporter werbeagentur. fabrizi. höller. reiter oeg
innstraße 77 | 6020 innsbruck | tel (0512) 93 22 82
fabrizi@transporter.at | www.transporter.at
TRANSPORTER
THOMAS WANNER
M 0650 94 77 464
transporter werbeagentur. fabrizi. höller. reiter oeg
innstraße 77 | 6020 innsbruck | tel (0512) 93 22 82
wanner@transporter.at | www.transporter.at

Client Transporter Visuelle Logistik
Year 2006
Design Transporter Visuelle Logistik

CR
CONCEPT. PRINT. WEB.
tw
CONCEPT. PRINT. WEB.

CONCEPT. PRINT. WEB.
CONCEPT. PRINT. WEB.
CR
CONCEPT. PRINT. WEB.
tw
CONCEPT. PRINT. WEB.

Client Truth Marketing
Year 2009
Design Socio Design
Team Nigel Bates

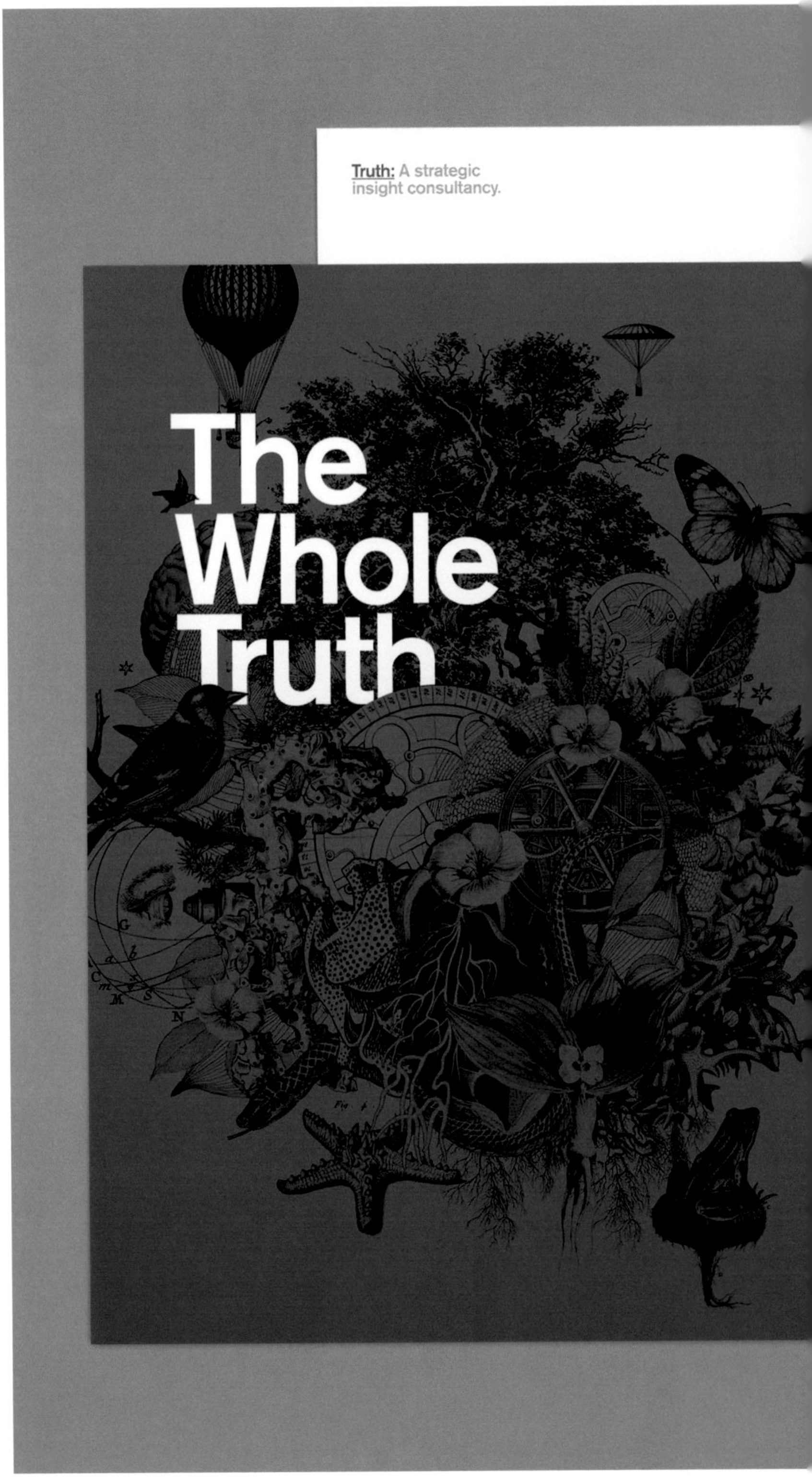

__Address:
24 Greville Street, Farringdon
London EC1N 8SS
__Contact Us:
Telephone:+44 (0)20 3008 4445
Facsimile: +44 (0)20 3008 4446
Email Address: info@truth.ms
Website: www.truth.ms
truth.
Registered Details:
Registration Number: 5217724
VAT Number: 843 7659 89
Truth: A strategic
insight consultancy.
__Address:
24 Greville Street, Farringdon
London EC1N 8SS
__Contact Us:
Telephone:+44 (0)20 3008 4445
Facsimile: +44 (0)20 3008 4446
Email Address: info@truth.ms
Website: www.truth.ms
truth.
With
Compliments
Truth: DVD/CD
Brand
Guidelines
Louise
McLaren
__Contact Us:
Telephone: +44 (0)20 3008 4445
Facsimile: +44 (0)20 3008 4446
Email Address: info@truth.ms
Website: www.truth.ms
__Address:
24 Greville Street
London EC1N 8SS
truth.

UNITED
EVERYTHING THAT MOVES YOU
EST. 1998
NIJVERHEIDSWEG 38-2 | 2031 CP | HAARLEM
THE NETHERLANDS | HQ@UNITEDRECORDINGS.COM
T: +31.(0)23.512.6900 | F: +31.(0)23.534.4505
WWW.UNITEDRECORDINGS.COM

Client United Recordings
Year 2007
Design DBXL

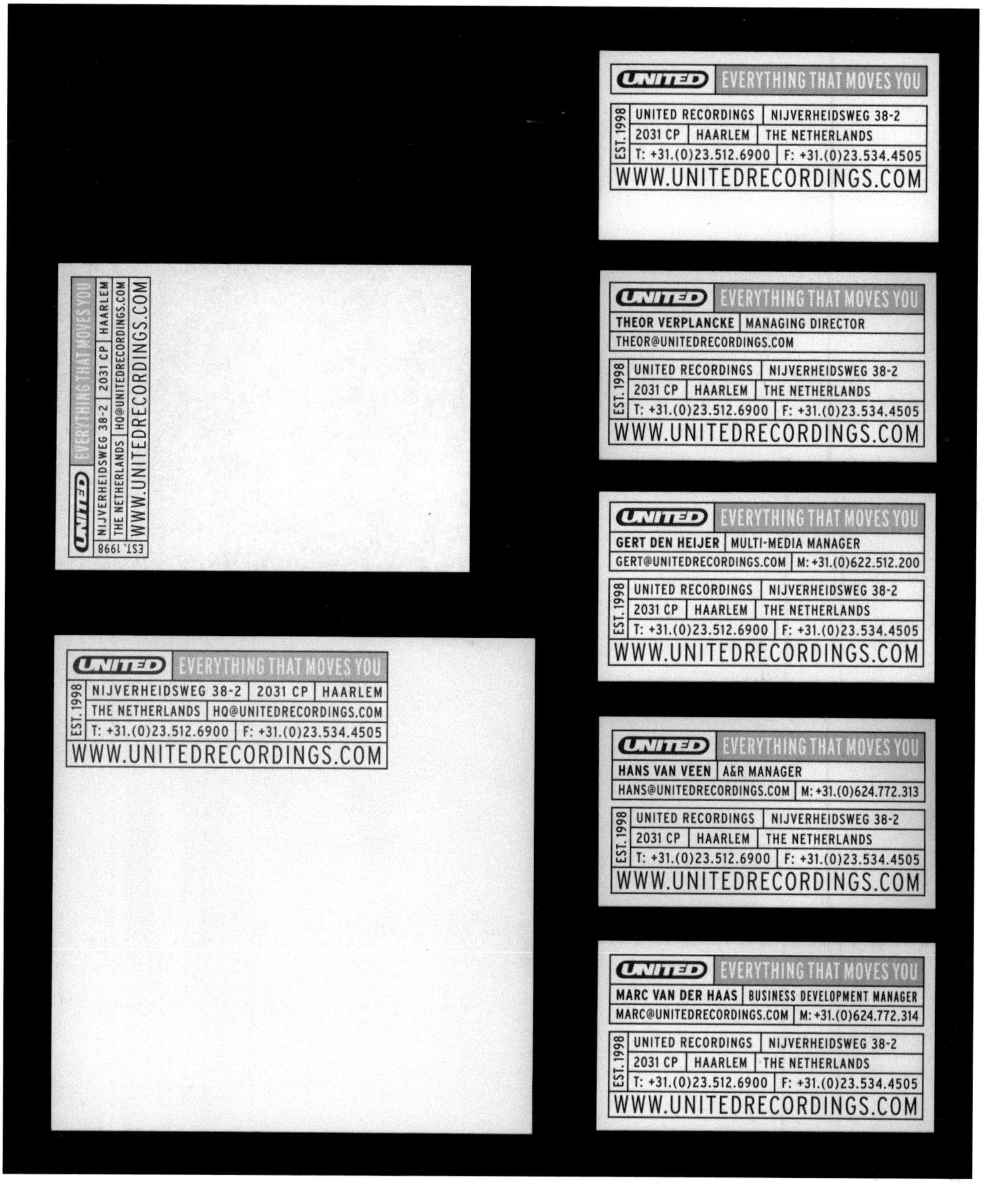
EVERYTHING THAT MOVES YOU
EST. 1998
UNITED RECORDINGS | NIJVERHEIDSWEG 38-2
2031 CP | HAARLEM | THE NETHERLANDS
T: +31.(0)23.512.6900 | F: +31.(0)23.534.4505
WWW.UNITEDRECORDINGS.COM
THEOR VERPLANCKE | MANAGING DIRECTOR
THEOR@UNITEDRECORDINGS.COM
GERT DEN HEIJER | MULTI-MEDIA MANAGER
GERT@UNITEDRECORDINGS.COM | M: +31.(0)622.512.200
HANS VAN VEEN | A&R MANAGER
HANS@UNITEDRECORDINGS.COM | M: +31.(0)624.772.313
MARC VAN DER HAAS | BUSINESS DEVELOPMENT MANAGER
MARC@UNITEDRECORDINGS.COM | M: +31.(0)624.772.314
NIJVERHEIDSWEG 38-2 | 2031 CP | HAARLEM
THE NETHERLANDS | HQ@UNITEDRECORDINGS.COM

Client Ve.Mar. Studio
Year 2008
Design Truly Design
Team Rems182

VE
MAR
ADVANCED SOLUTIONS
VE
MAR
ADVANCED SOLUTIONS
STUDIO VE.MAR. SRL
Corso Trapani, 73 - 10139 TORINO
Tel. 0113828294 - Fax 0113828301
www.studiovemar.it
CCIAA TORINO REA 1069951
P. IVA e C.F. 09656610012 - Cap. sociale: Euro 43.500

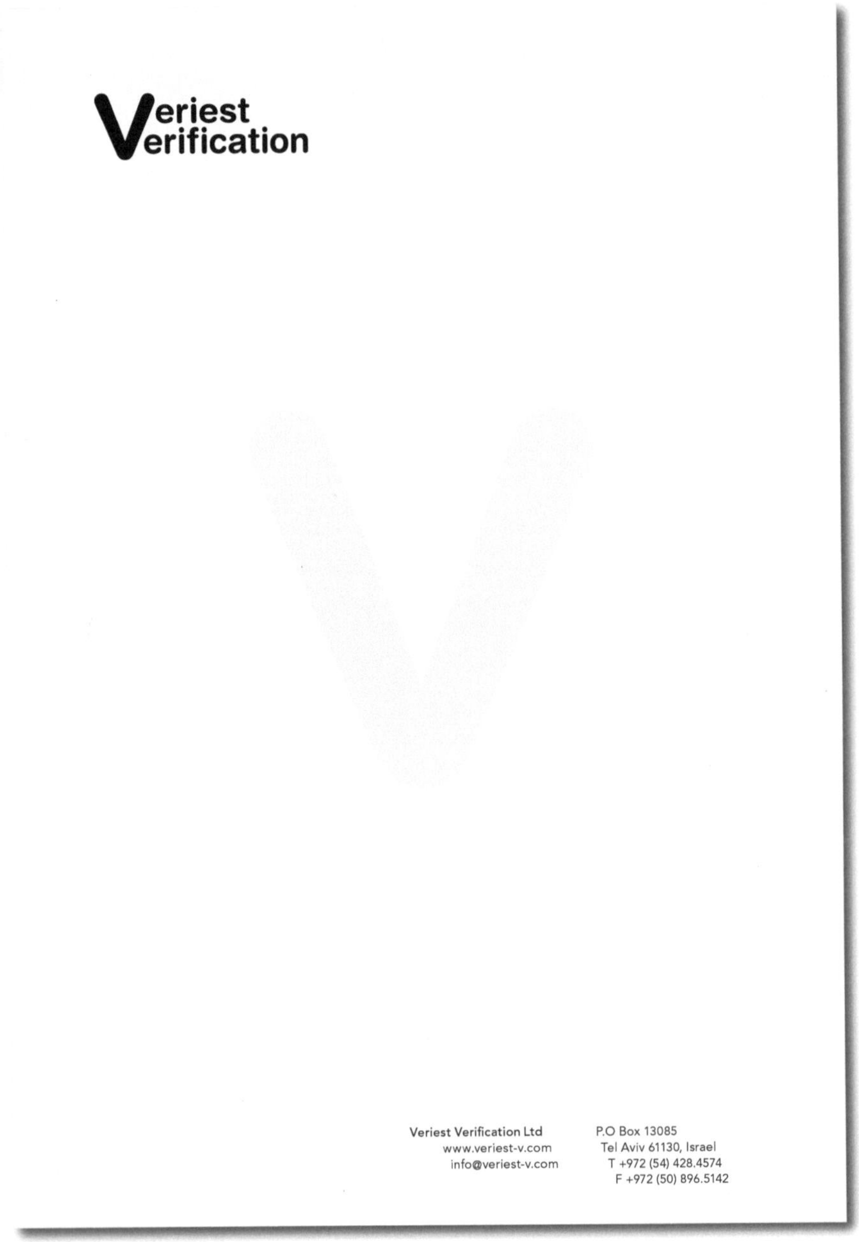
Veriest
Verification
Veriest Verification Ltd
www.veriest-v.com
info@veriest-v.com
P.O Box 13085
Tel Aviv 61130, Israel
T +972 (54) 428.4574
F +972 (50) 896.5142

Client Veriest
Year 2010
Design Dan Alexander & Co
Team Danny Goldberg

Veriest
Verification
Veriest Verification Ltd
www.veriest-v.com
info@veriest-v.com
P.O Box 13085
Tel Aviv 61130, Israel
T +972 (54) 428.4574
F +972 (50) 896.5142

Veriest
Venture
Noa Levy
Verification Engineer
Veriest Venture Ltd
ASIC design team
3 Hayozma St,
Kfar Saba, Israel
T +972 (9) 765.3962
F +972 (9) 766.6171
M+972 (54) 491.3288
Noa@veriest-v.com
www.veriest-v.com

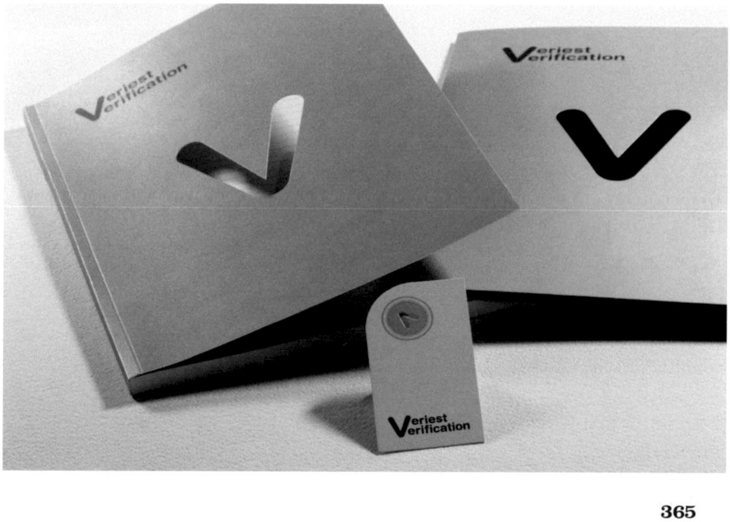
Veriest
Verification
Veriest
Verification
Veriest
Verification

A SHORT HISTORY
Vernon Park is Stockport's oldest park, opened in 1858. It was built by Stockport Corporation on land donated by Lord Vernon (George John Warren).
During the 1860's, the American Civil War decimated the English cotton trade and Stockport's unemployed mill workers were given low paid work helping to construct some of the park's features. They were so hungry that they gave it the nickname 'Pinch Belly Park'.
After decades of neglect, the park was restored to its former glory in 2000 with the help of a Heritage Lottery Fund grant. Its beautiful setting, looking across Goyt Valley, and a host of interesting heritage and horticultural features make it a perfect place to relax.
The Park is designated Grade II in the English Heritage Register of Historic Parks and Gardens as an important example of an early public park.
The original Stockport Museum building is in the park grounds, known as Vernon Museum.
VERNON PARK
VERNON PARK
VERNON PARK

Client Vernon Park
Year 2009
Design huvi

Client Vianet
Year 2010
Design Vianet
Team Marco Quintavalle

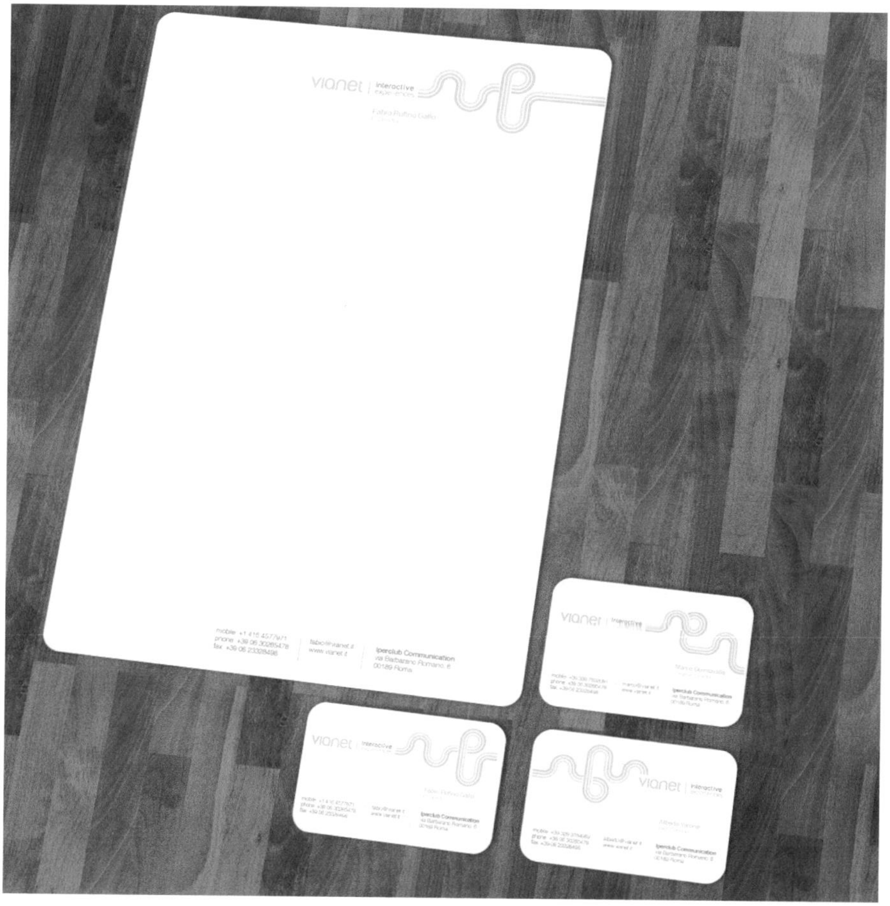

Client Victors
Year 2007
Design Kollor Design Agency

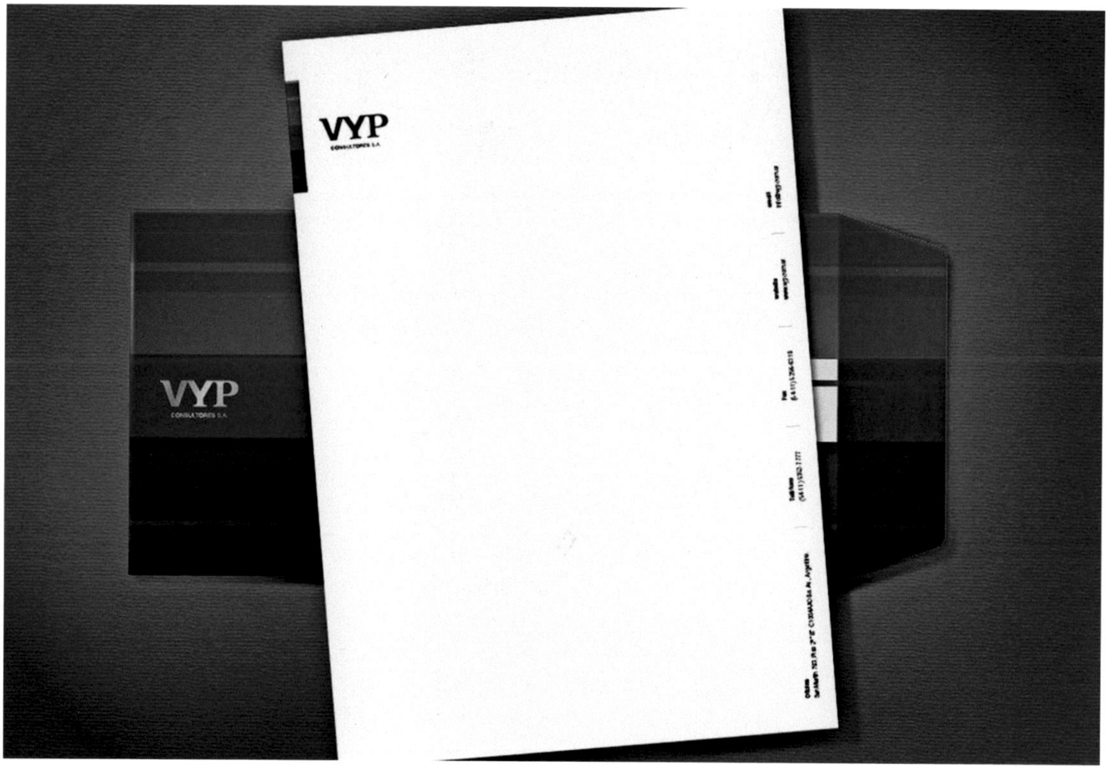

Client VyP
Year 2008
Design NNSS Visual Universes

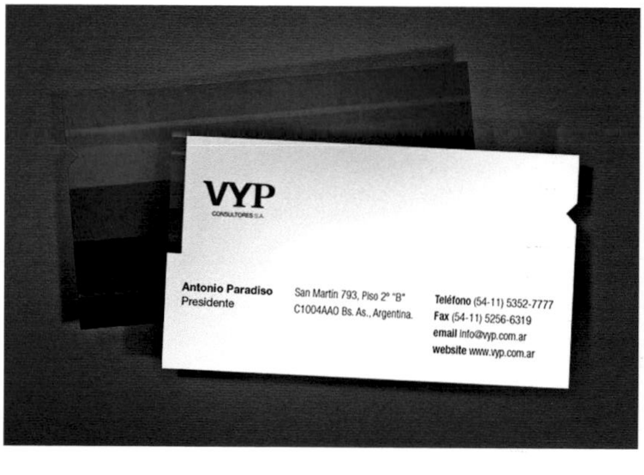

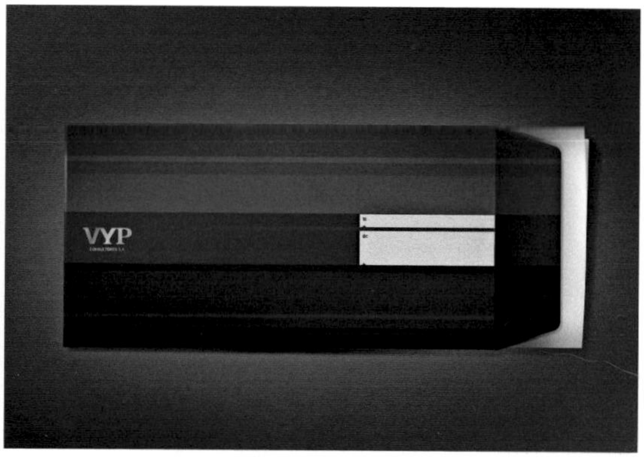

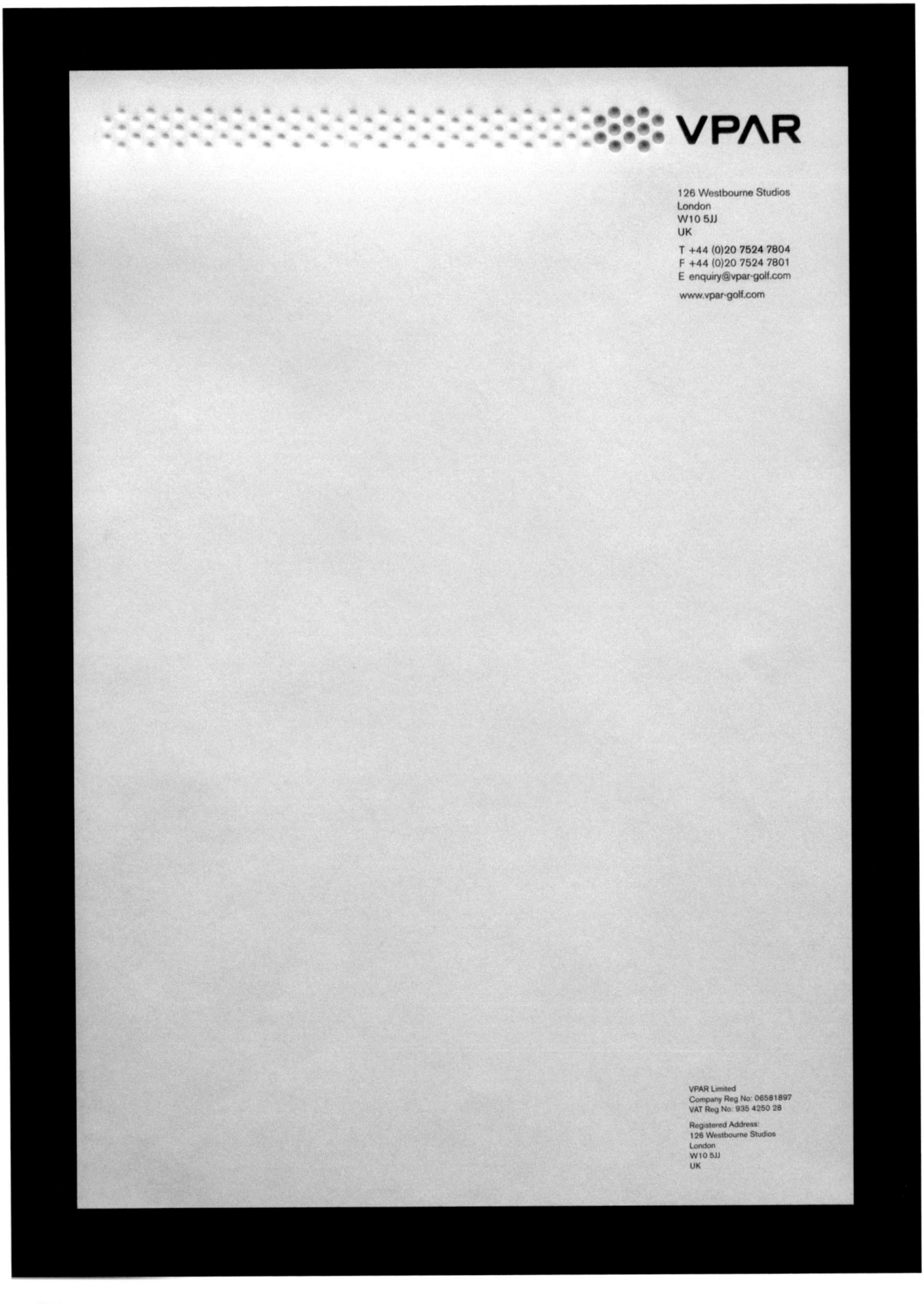
VPAR
126 Westbourne Studios
London
W10 5JJ
UK
T +44 (0)20 7524 7804
F +44 (0)20 7524 7801
E enquiry@vpar-golf.com
www.vpar-golf.com
VPAR Limited
Company Reg No: 06581897
VAT Reg No: 935 4250 28
Registered Address:
126 Westbourne Studios
London
W10 5JJ
UK

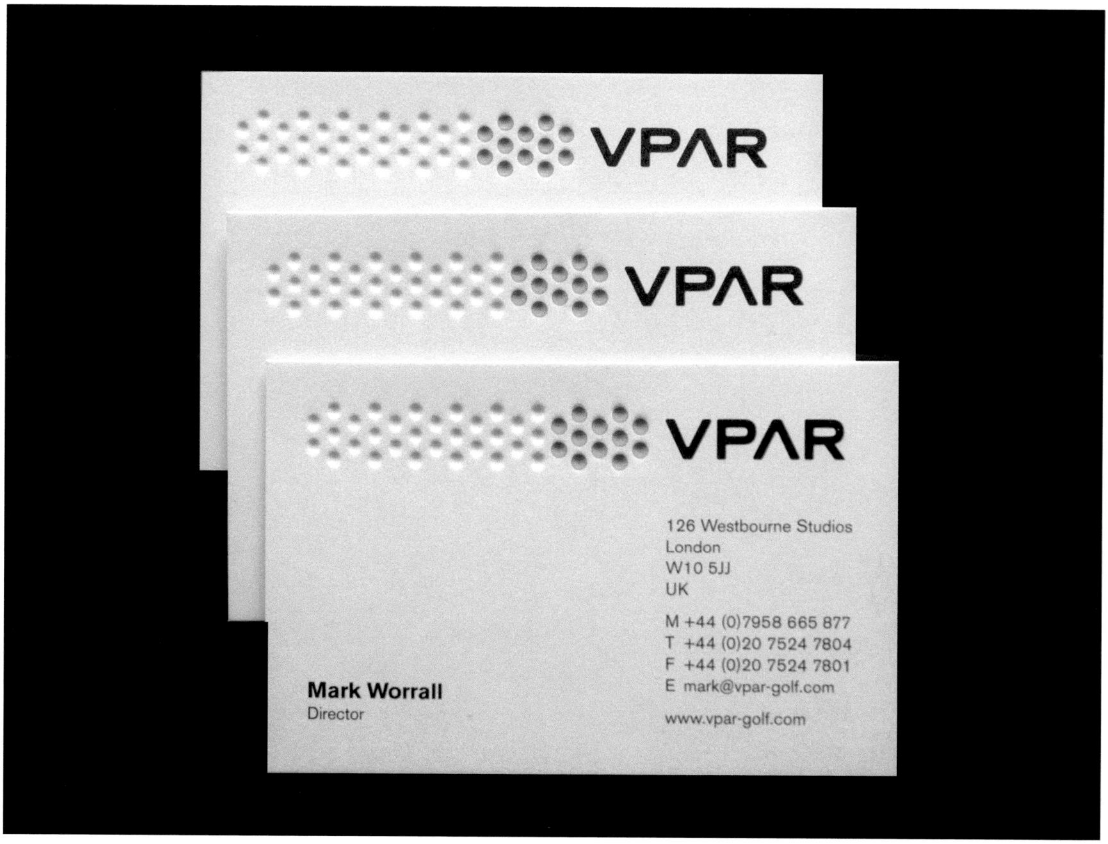

Client VPAR
Year 2009
Design SVIDesign

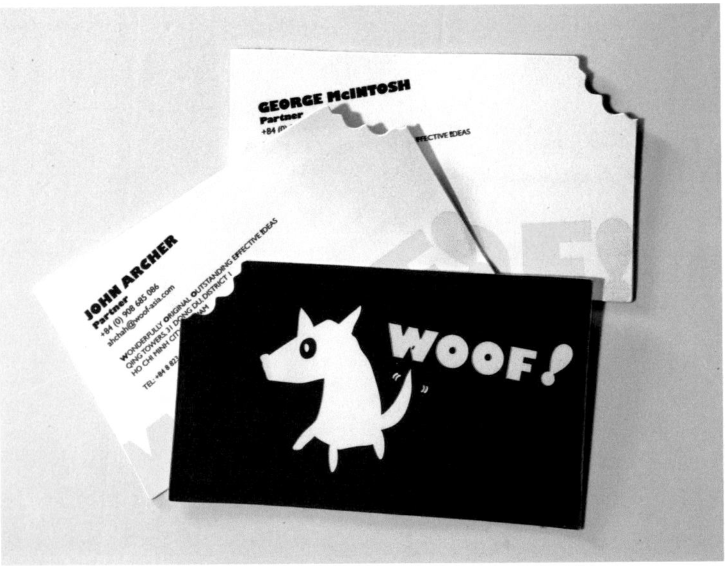

Client Woof
Year 2009
Design Design Positive
Team Scott Lambert, George McIntosh, John Archer

Client Xoco handmade chocolate
Year 2010
Design Zenteno Design Studio

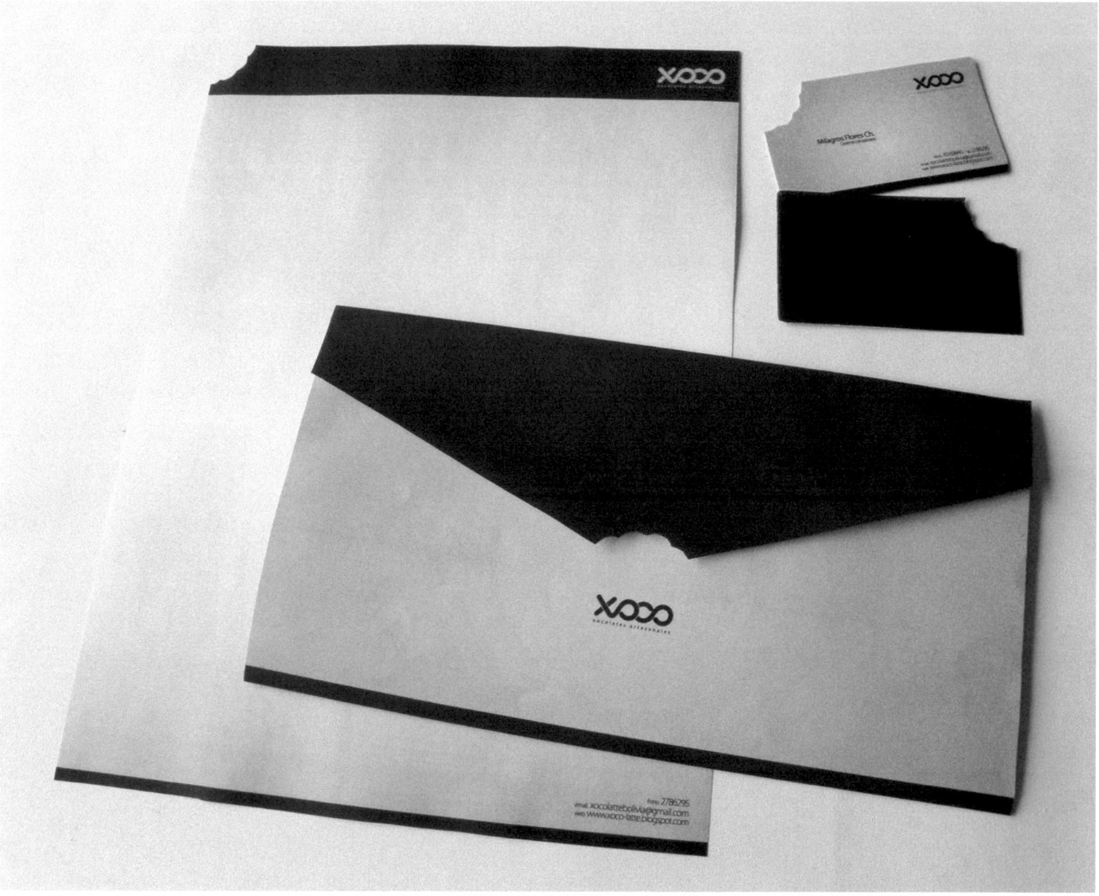

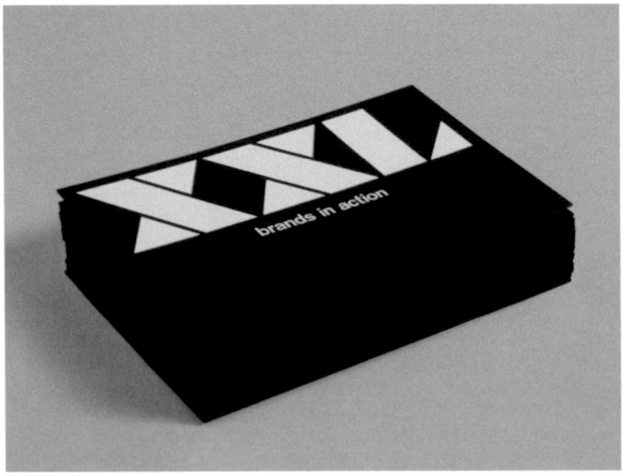

Client XXL
Year 2008
Design Base Design

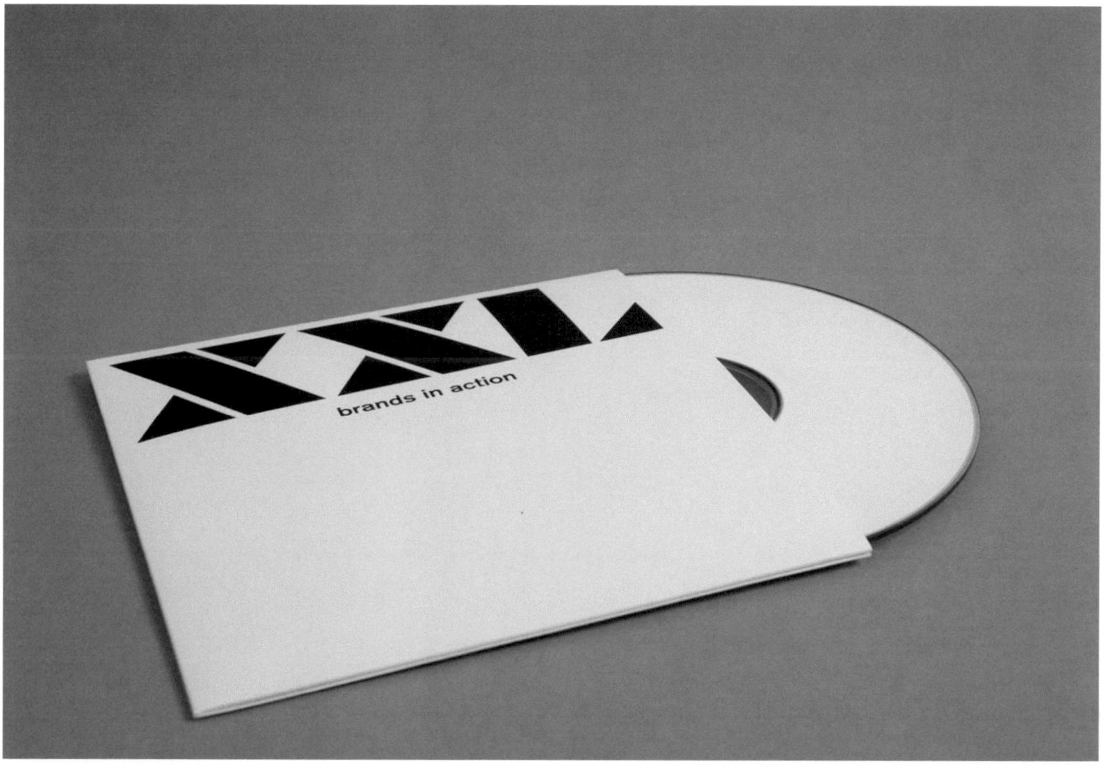
XXL
brands in action

XXL

Zentropy Partners/BLK/MRKT

Client Zentropy Partners
Year 1999
Design BLK/MRKT

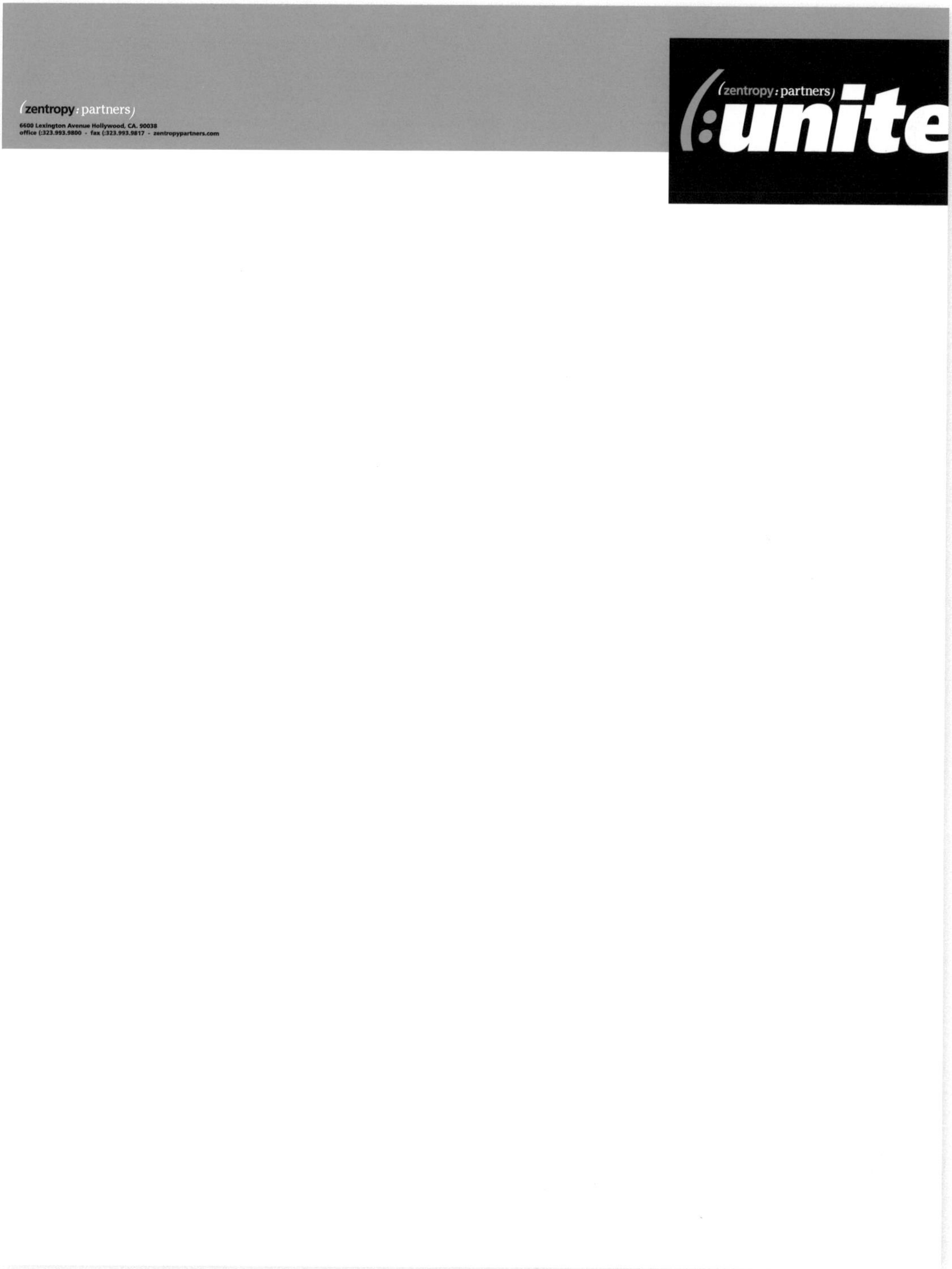
(zentropy:partners)
6600 Lexington Avenue Hollywood, CA. 90038
office (:323.993.9800 - fax (:323.993.9817 - zentropypartners.com
(zentropy:partners)
(:unite

Hola. Queremos decirte algo desde Zoom,
Carrer de sa Lluna 14 · 07650 · Santanyí · I. Balears.
Nuestro teléfono y fax es 971 64 54 68. Si quieres enviarnos
un email puedes hacerlo a info@zoommarketing.es
zoom
MARKET & SOCIAL RESEARCH
Att: John Doe Montevideo
Cooperativa de latón, S.A.
Ctra. De Barcelona Km. 35,1
28800 Alcalá de Henares - Madrid
Palma de Mallorca, a 27 de Ocubre de 2007
Asunto
Apreciado Sr. John Doe,
Lorem ipsum dolor sit amet, consetetur sadipscing elitr, sed diam nonumy eirmod tempor invidunt ut labore et dolore magna aliquyam erat, sed diam voluptua. At vero eos et accusam et justo duo dolores et ea rebum. Stet clita kasd gubergren, no sea takimata sanctus est Lorem ipsum dolor sit amet. Lorem ipsum dolor sit amet, consetetur sadipscing elitr, sed diam nonumy eirmod tempor invidunt ut labore et dolore magna aliquyam erat, sed diam voluptua.
At vero eos et accusam et justo duo dolores et ea rebum. Stet clita kasd gubergren, no sea takimata sanctus est Lorem ipsum dolor sit amet. Lorem ipsum dolor sit amet, consetetur sadipscing elitr, sed diam nonumy eirmod tempor invidunt ut labore et dolore magna aliquyam erat, sed diam voluptua. At vero eos et accusam et justo duo dolores et ea rebum. Stet clita kasd gubergren, no sea takimata sanctus est Lorem ipsum dolor sit amet.
Duis autem vel eum iriure dolor in hendrerit in vulputate velit esse molestie consequat, vel illum dolore eu feugiat nulla facilisis at vero eros et accumsan et iusto odio dignissim qui blandit praesent luptatum zzril delenit augue duis dolore te feugait nulla facilisi. Lorem ipsum dolor sit amet, consectetuer adipiscing elit, sed diam nonummy nibh euismod tincidunt ut laoreet dolore magna aliquam erat volutpat.
Ut wisi enim ad minim veniam, quis nostrud exerci tation ullamcorper suscipit lobortis nisl ut aliquip ex ea commodo consequat. Duis autem vel eum iriure dolor in hendrerit in vulputate velit esse molestie consequat, vel illum dolore eu feugiat nulla facilisis at vero eros et accumsan et iusto odio dignissim qui blandit praesent luptatum zzril delenit augue duis dolore te feugait nulla facilisi.
Reciba un cordial saludo,
Alejandra Araya
Direcora General
www.zoommarketing.es
zoom
MARKET & SOCIAL
Hola. Soy Biel Vidal Sitjes y
Carrer de Sa Lluna 14 ·
Nuestro teléfono y fax es
606 02 85 09 y si quieres
g.vidal@zoommarketing.es
Soy Director de Análisis de

Hola. Llego desde Zoom,
Carrer de Sa Lluna 14 · 07650 · Santanyí · I. Balears.
Nuestro teléfono y fax es 971 64 54 68. Si quieres enviarnos
un email puedes hacerlo a info@zoommarketing.es
zoom
MARKET & SOCIAL RESEARCH
www.zoommarketing.es
zoom
MARKET & SOCIAL RESEARCH
Proporcionamos la
información necesaria
para tomar las
decisiones adecuadas.

Client Zoom Market & Social Research
Year 2009
Design Jose Palma Visual Works

INDEX

Acknowledgements
Danksagungen
Remerciements

Travelling worldwide for research and to participate in conferences, I meet a lot of people personally, and many of them turn into working partners and eventually friends. A lot of this process still starts with a simple exchange of business cards. This book is not about a dying art. Rather, it celebrates the value of the things we can touch and feel, that we used to take for granted, and now we know more what they mean. To accomplish the research and produce this survey, I needed to go back to a lot of these people I had met, and also my colleagues at TASCHEN, starting with Daniel Siciliano Bretas, my all-time right hand, project manager, and editor. As always, his hard work and commitment, particularly in the design and layout of the book, has made all the difference. I have to thank him a lot. I also had the immense pleasure and honour to have the collaboration of Professor Jay Rutherford, from the Faculty of Art and Design of the Bauhaus University in Weimar, Germany. He has written a long essay for the beginning of the book, providing rich and historical information on how the subject evolved. His contribution was fundamental to the book.

I would also like to thank the design studios and branding agencies that submitted their incredible work, including those whose work was ultimately not included in the book. We look forward to working with all of you in the future! Thank you also to Jutta Hendricks, whose unstinting attention to detail has contributed immensely to the quality of this book and to others I have edited. Also a big thanks to Chris Allen, for proof-reading and checking; Jürgen Dubau, and all at Equipo de Edición for the translation. Finally, thank you to Stefan Klatte in production. It has been a pleasure to work with him once again. This team has been doing an amazing job!

I am sure that you will find many projects here to interest and inspire you.

Happy reading!

Julius Wiedemann

Imprint

Hohenzollernring 53, D-50672 Köln
www.taschen.com

To stay informed about upcoming TASCHEN titles, please request our magazine at www.taschen.com/magazine or write to TASCHEN, Hohenzollernring 53, D-50672 Cologne, Germany, contact@taschen.com, Fax: +49-221-254919. We will be happy to send you a free copy of our magazine which is filled with information about all of our books.

Design & Layout
Daniel Siciliano Bretas
Production
Stefan Klatte

Editor
Julius Wiedemann
Editorial Coordination
Daniel Siciliano Bretas
Collaboration
Jutta Hendricks

English Revision
Chris Allen
German Translation
Jürgen Dubau
French Translation
Valérie Lavoyer for Equipo de Edición

Pages 6, 11, 12: images taken from the collection of type specimens by Jan Tholenaar, Reinoud Tholenaar, and Saskia Ottenhoff-Tholenaar, reproduced with kind permission by the owners

Pages 14, 15: images taken from the collection of Adrian Wilson, reproduced with kind permission by the owner

Printed in China
ISBN: 978–3–8365–1897–0